Dominik Meier, Christian Blum
Power and its Logic

Political Science | Volume 64

This open access publication has been enabled by the support of POLLUX (Fachinformationsdienst Politikwissenschaft)

and a collaborative network of academic libraries for the promotion of the Open Access transformation in the Social Sciences and Humanities (transcript Open Library Politikwissenschaft 2019)

Bundesministerium der Verteidigung | Gottfried Wilhelm Leibniz Bibliothek –Niedersächsische Landesbibliothek | Harvard University | Kommunikations-, Informations-, Medienzentrum (KIM) der Universität Konstanz | Landesbibliothek Oldenburg | Max Planck Digital Library (MPDL) | Saarländische Universitäts- und Landesbibliothek | Sächsische Landesbibliothek Staats- und Universitätsbibliothek Dresden | Staats- und Universitätsbibliothek Bremen (POLLUX – Informationsdienst Politikwissenschaft) | Staats- und Universitätsbibliothek Carl von Ossietzky, Hamburg | Staatsbibliothek zu Berlin | Technische Informationsbibliothek Hannover | Thüringer Universitäts- und Landesbibliothek Jena (ThULB) | ULB Düsseldorf Universitäts- und Landesbibliothek Düsseldorf | Universitätsbibliothek Erfurt | Universitäts- und Landesbibliothek der Technischen Universität Darmstadt | Universitäts- und Landesbibliothek Münster | Universitäts- und Stadtbibliothek Köln | Universitätsbibliothek Bayreuth | Universitätsbibliothek Bielefeld | Universitätsbibliothek der Bauhaus-Universität Weimar | Universitätsbibliothek der FernUniversität Hagen | Universitätsbibliothek der Humboldt-Universität zu Berlin | Universitätsbibliothek der Justus-Liebig-Universität Gießen | Universitätsbibliothek der Ruhr-Universität Bochum | Universitätsbibliothek der Technischen Universität Braunschweig | Universitätsbibliothek der Universität Koblenz Landau | Universitätsbibliothek der Universität Potsdam | Universitätsbibliothek Duisburg-Essen | Universitätsbibliothek Erlangen-Nürnberg | Universitätsbibliothek Freiburg | Universitätsbibliothek Graz | Universitätsbibliothek J. C. Senckenberg an der Goethe-Universität Frankfurt | Universitätsbibliothek Kassel | Universitätsbibliothek Leipzig | Universitätsbibliothek der LMU München | Universitätsbibliothek Mainz | Universitätsbibliothek Marburg | Universitätsbibliothek Oldenburg | Universitätsbibliothek Osnabrück | Universitätsbibliothek Siegen | Universitätsbibliothek Vechta | Universitätsbibliothek Wien | Universitätsbibliothek Wuppertal | Zentral- und Hochschulbibliothek Luzern | Zentralbibliothek Zürich

This publication is compliant with the "Recommendations on quality standards for the open access provision of books", Nationaler Open Access Kontaktpunkt 2018 (https://pub.uni-bielefeld.de/record/2932189)

* * *

Dominik Meier, born in 1969, is the owner and Managing Director of Miller & Meier Consulting, a political strategy consultancy he co-founded in 1997. He is chairman of the German Association of Political Consultants (de'ge'pol), which was founded in 2002. Furthermore, he is Vice President of the Public Affairs Community of Europe (PACE) and a member of the Advisory Board of Transparency International Deutschland.
Christian Blum, born in 1980, is Head of Office and Network Coordinator of Miller & Meier Consulting. He is a lecturer at the German Academic Scholarship Foundation (Studienstiftung des Deutschen Volkes).

Dominik Meier, Christian Blum
Power and its Logic
Politics and how to master it

[transcript]

Bibliographic information published by the Deutsche Nationalbibliothek
The Deutsche Nationalbibliothek lists this publication in the Deutsche Nationalbibliografie; detailed bibliographic data are available in the Internet at http://dnb.d-nb.de

This work is licensed under the Creative Commons Attribution-NonCommercial-No-Derivatives 4.0 (BY-NC-ND) which means that the text may be used for non-commercial purposes, provided credit is given to the author. For details go to http://creativecommons.org/licenses/by-nc-nd/4.0/
To create an adaptation, translation, or derivative of the original work and for commercial use, further permission is required and can be obtained by contacting rights@transcript-verlag.de
Creative Commons license terms for re-use do not apply to any content (such as graphs, figures, photos, excerpts, etc.) not original to the Open Access publication and further permission may be required from the rights holder. The obligation to research and clear permission lies solely with the party re-using the material.

© 2019 transcript Verlag, Bielefeld

All rights reserved. No part of this book may be reprinted or reproduced or utilized in any form or by any electronic, mechanical, or other means, now known or hereafter invented, including photocopying and recording, or in any information storage or retrieval system, without permission in writing from the publisher.

Cover layout: Kordula Röckenhaus, Bielefeld
Printed by Majuskel Medienproduktion GmbH, Wetzlar
Proofread by Katharine M. Thomas, Karoline Tippelt-Wohl
Translated by Katharine M. Thomas, Michael A. Dudley
Layout and typeset by Karoline Tippelt-Wohl
Print-ISBN 978-3-8376-4497-5
PDF-ISBN 978-3-8394-4497-9
https://doi.org/10.14361/9783839444979

Table of Contents

Acknowledgements | 7

0   Introduction | 9
0.1   Preface | 9
0.2   Structure and Substance | 11
0.3   Methods | 14

1   The Nature of Power | 17
1.1   Definitional Approach | 17
1.2   Basic Principles of Power | 30
1.3   Humankind, Power and History – Follow-Up Questions | 47

2   The Concretions of Power | 59
2.1   Forms of Power | 59
2.2   Power and Symbolism | 69
2.3   Power Fields | 78
      2.3.1   Religion | 84
      2.3.2   The Economic Power Field | 91
      2.3.3   The Political Power Field | 109
2.4   The Common Good | 114
2.5   The Vectors of Political Power | 133
      2.5.1   Power Competence and Training | 136
      2.5.2   Power Knowledge and Strategy | 148
      2.5.3   Instruments of Power and Organization | 187
      2.5.4   Mastering the Power Vectors:
              Homo Consultandus and *Homo Consultans* | 208

3 The Practice of Power | 211
3.1. The Power Chess Model | 214
3.2 Empower Model | 219
    3.2.1   Political Logic | 219
    3.2.2   Poltical Language | 228
    3.2.3   Poltical Ethos | 234
    3.2.4   Tools and Techniques of Empowering | 239
3.3 Condensing | 244
    3.3.1   The Four-Phase Model | 244
    3.3.2   Tools and Techniques of Condensing | 265
3.4 Influencing | 269
3.5 Global Governmental Relations | 274
3.6 Concluding Remarks | 281

4 Literature | 285
4.1 Specialist Literature | 285
4.2 Additional Sources | 305

Acknowledgements

This book would not have been possible without the many years of inspirational exchange with Constanze Miller as well as with our friends, colleagues, clients, business partners and decision-makers from politics, business, civil society and academia. So many people contributed important input to Power and its Logic through discussions, lectures or publications that we are not able to mention them all by name. Nevertheless, special thanks are due to the staff at Miller & Meier Consulting and especially to Martin Alves for the illustrations and graphics. Since the publication of the original German edition, we have had ample opportunity to discuss our findings and, thus, improve upon the English translation. In this context, we have benefitted greatly from the suggestions and constructive criticism of Carsten Diercks, Gerd Kräh, Stéphane Beemelmans, Egon Flaig, Klemens Joos, Jakob Lempp, Peter Scholz, Dominique Reber, Erhard Weimann and Maria-Luise Schneider. Also, several insightful media reviews, most importantly by Thomas Sigmund and Isabell Trommer, have helped us refining our approach and methodology. Emily Faber, Peter Beyer, Ulrich Gamerdinger and Insaf Seeman have provided much-needed guidance for the book's presentation to the US audience. Finally, we wish to express our sincere gratitude to Katherine Thomas for revising and fundamentally improving upon a first translation of the manuscript and to Karoline Tippelt-Wohl for her invaluable support and meticulous work during the copy-editing process.

0. Introduction

0.1 PREFACE

Politics is about power and decision-making. This principle applies to all epochs, all systems and all cultures. There were and there are no power vacuums whatsoever. Moreover, regardless of whether we consciously enter the political arena or are involuntarily thrown into it, we all inevitably become participants in a zero-sum game for power. Accordingly, it is all the more important to understand and to master the rules of this game. This is true for all of us. We are all stakeholders of one kind or another – whether as official decision-makers, citizens, journalists, lobbyists or political consultants.

In recognition thereof, this book is aimed at providing readers with an honest, objective and comprehensive look at power and its logic. It is for the theorist and the practitioner alike. We welcome all interested readers, those lacking power and those wielding it. If the title has already attracted your attention, you are on the right trail. Our findings are based upon two decades of broad, in-depth experience in national and international political consultancy. Thereby, the focus of this book ranges from conceptual theories to concrete tools, all of which comprise the very foundation of our own proven Power Leadership Approach.

Such a perspective is urgently required. Particularly now, as democracies struggle and strive amidst the challenges posed by the digital age, a fresh but historically rooted approach is necessary. Given the prevalence of untrustworthy information, the importance of the ability – and the willingness – to distinguish political facts from political fictions, for example, cannot be overstated.

Democracies are based upon trust. They are, more specifically, dependent on the faith which members of society place in the processes, institutions and actors of the political realm on a daily basis. This faith must not and should not be blind. Just as transparency is to be expected of democratic institutions, it is also incumbent upon members of society to avail themselves of information and to comprehend the laws of power and politics.

Without an enlightened understanding in this regard, it is of no surprise that myths are amply cultivated. Utopian expectations and prejudices are rampantly spread and will erode, sooner or later, our democratic system. As confidence in democracies diminishes, the specter of apathy, anarchy and even autocracy will increasingly materialize.

In essence, this book constitutes an analytical demystification of power principles. At the same time, it is an inside view of the political cosmos and a reflection on the strategies with which its various protagonists compete for positions and advantages in the large zero-sum game. We trace how power is generated in everyday politics and the key role that consultants play here.

We initiate this examination of the fundamental logic of power by exploring three fundamental, interrelated questions which form a common thread throughout the book, providing our readers with ongoing orientation:

What is the nature of power?

What are its manifestations and fields?

How is it exercised and legitimized in political practice?

This *tour de force* through the thematic complex of power ranges from foundations to questions of specific power techniques, but is not an end in itself. Our book is based on firm convictions, backed up by daily experience. The practical mastery of power requires a profound grasp of its basic principles, modes of manifestation and conditions of legitimacy – and the theoretical understanding of power necessitates thorough familiarity with its application. Furthermore, to understand and master the phenomenon, the theory and the practice of power must be conceptualized in the context of each other.

In light of our aspiration to examine the issue of power in the context of an overall coherent design, this treatise is aimed at a broad audience, as alluded to above. In literary form, we intend to build upon the twenty years of intensive discussions which we have conducted with decision-makers from the fields of politics, economics, civil society and religion, as well as with the consulting industry and the academic community. Furthermore, we also wish to provide insights and suggestions for every citizen who has always wanted to know how power works.

In doing so, we deliberately refrain from moralizing our topic. *Power and its Logic* is first and foremost a descriptive analysis. It does not intend to patronize the readers in any manner. Quite to the contrary, it respects the sovereignty of their decision-making ability and their right to draw conclusions as they see fit with regard to their own political actions.

Corresponding to the three basic questions posed above, the book is divided into three systematically connected chapters: The Nature of Power – The Concretions of Power – The Practice of Power. Building on our analogy of the struggle for power as a zero-sum game, we could also speak of the opening game, the middle game and the final game of power. Despite this organic and contextual connection, each chapter can be read independently of the others. For example, we offer the hurried reader, who cannot wait to deal with the resources of the power consultant or the specific challenges of political strategy development and implementation, a leap into Chapter 3. Nevertheless, such a leap not only ignores the methodological foundations of power logic, but also the historical and sociological localization – and thus the functional genesis – of the political power consultant. In short, we encourage every reader to take the time to read *Power and its Logic* from beginning to end. Before we proceed *in medias res,* we wish to give a brief overview of the structure, content and method of the book to facilitate navigation through the thematic fields of power.

0.2 STRUCTURE AND SUBSTANCE

In Chapter 1, *The Nature of Power,* we encounter one of the most fundamental questions of the book: What is Power? For this definitional approach, we initiate dialogues with the most important political thinkers of human history: Aristotle, Confucius, Ibn Khaldun, Nicolo Machiavelli, Thomas Hobbes, Max Weber, Michel Foucault and many others. After a constructively critical examination of their theses and arguments, we opt for a pragmatic, application-oriented definition: power is doubled potentiality, more precisely, power is the potential assets of individuals and organizations to overcome the potential resistance of other actors.

By virtue of this characterization, power gains a probabilistic component, becoming the subject of strategy and scenario prognoses. In short, power becomes predictable. However, this definition by no means completes the analysis of the nature of power. Based on our definition, we determine whether power follows universal laws that are independent of time and place and are thus utilized in the present-day systems of the United States, Germany or China, as once in ancient Rome or in the medieval Abbasid Empire. The results of this analysis are summarized in a list of cross-cultural principles of power: power is present in all social fields and permeates all social relationships, it flourishes thanks to our open defenses and our natural pursuit of influence, it is morally neutral and receives shape and ethical valence only through the people.

Power is, as our interim conclusion maintains, an essential, irreducible component of our very existence. Accordingly, it is pointless to reflect upon how to erase it from the face of the earth. Instead, the far more pertinent question concerns how people exercise power in the various fields of society and, in particular, within the realm of politics. Indeed, the true challenge consists of using power legitimately, effectively and efficiently. Therefore, it is important to comprehend the manner in which power is substantiated throughout the various strata of the political community – both as an unconsciously effective structure that we are exposed to and as a conscious resource for the enforcement of individual interests.

In Chapter 2, *The Concretions of Power,* we focus on the manifestations, fields and resources of power. Based on Heinrich Popitz, the doyen of German power research, we classify four basic forms: action power, instrumental power, technical power and authoritative power. Each of these forms has its own characteristics and effects and requires specific skills on the part of the power holder. In addition, each manifests itself in the three major power fields of every society: religion, economics and politics. These fields are characterized not merely by their own symbols, practices and habitus, but also by their own power resources: indispensable means and skills to gain and exercise influence in each field.

However, religion, economics and politics are not only arenas of power struggle, they also compete with one other continuously for power. The field of politics has special status here insofar as it influences all aspects of social life through its institutional order and its collectively binding norms. Therefore, we focus on legitimacy and the resources of political power. The legitimacy question is inextricably linked to the guiding principle of the common good; political decisions and institutions derive their justification first and foremost by acting for the good of the community as a whole. The resource question leads us back to a triad that will accompany us throughout the book: power competence, knowledge of power and instruments of power. These resources of political power form a complex of interdependent conditions, which is why we call them the power vectors. Only actors who master all three vectors are able to survive in the struggle for political power.

Due to the immense importance of these three vectors of the theory and practice of political power, we dedicate the conclusion of Chapter 2 to their detailed discussion. Using the key concept of Aristotle's *téchne,* we define power competence as the practically intuitive mastery of political craft. Power competence – as we show on the basis of historical vignettes from antiquity to the present – is always handed down and practiced in political elites from childhood on. Power knowledge, on the other hand, comprises *epistémé*, that is knowledge of political strategy, narrative reasoning and administrative technique. Finally, under the heading of instruments of power, we discuss the technological and social tools that actors in the power struggle can and must use: weapons, communications, surveillance technology and mass media, as well as the military, police, intelligence services, administrations and informal networks.

The mastery and coordination of these three power vectors is a highly mentally and physically demanding task. Accordingly, it can hardly be tackled single-handedly. The political actor is thus a *homo consultandus*, a person in need of consultancy. In this respect, our diagnosis utilizes the term coined by Peter Sloterdijk, the contemporary German philosopher and cultural theorist. Sloterdijk's inspiring characterization recognizes, if you will, the advent of advocatory anthropology. At any rate, the *homo consultandus* must logically be supported by a *homo consultans*, more specifically, a political consultant, to assist in the exercise of power. This *homo consultans* already entered the historical world stage during antiquity, in the form of the Sophist. From this point on, the *homo consultans* has not strayed from the side of the powerful – whether as a medieval royal advisor or as a modern privy councilor. Thus, the central question presents itself: What are the functions, responsibilities, tools and techniques of this decisive protagonist in the representative democracy of our present age?

In Chapter 3, *The Practice of Power*, we answer this question. Moreover, we develop a curriculum for the political power consultant of the 21st century: Power Leadership. This approach, on the one hand, synthesizes the results and findings of our preceding discussion on power and its logic, and on the other hand, draws on the experience gathered in more than two decades of consulting.

This curriculum is both a practical guide for the budding consultant and a source of discussion and stimulation for the experienced power expert familiar with advisory tools. The power leadership approach describes the range of tasks and ethos of the *homo consultans* with regard to advising public officials and institutions as well as economic and civil society interest groups. In short: It lays the foundations for all applications of the political field.

The curriculum revolves – corresponding to the vectors of power – around three guiding principles: empower, condense and influence. Under the heading of empower, we describe techniques by which competencies may be imparted as well as their thematic priorities: political logic, political language and political ethos. This is the point at which the homo consultandus is trained for induction in the political arena, and is thus provided with an in-depth understanding of the rules of the zero-sum game of power. Accordingly, in this section, we discuss both the basic elements of individual coaching and training, and also consulting and positioning for organizations and institutions.

The second buzzword, condense, describes the procurement, filtering and prioritization of information as well as its classification and evaluation through analysis tools such as stakeholder mapping or topic identification. The aim of this informational counseling process, which we present using our tried-and-proven four-phase model, is to provide continuously updated and condensed knowledge of the political arena. This knowledge enables consultants and clients to share a common, accurate assessment of external opportunities and threats as well as of internal strengths and weaknesses, and it culminates in the strategy development process based on risk and scenario analysis.

Under the third and last keyword, influence, we discuss the task and methods of strategy implementation: team composition, project coordination, planning and organization of political formats and stakeholder dialogues, alliance formation, mobilization and campaigning. Political influencing, the concrete exercise of power in the field of politics through interaction with organizations and persons, is the actual litmus test for the empowering and condensing which precede it. Accordingly, we discuss the practical challenges that arise in this context – from political event management, to sensitive communication with clients and stakeholders, to strategy evaluation – challenges that all power consultants face continually in everyday political life.

The conclusion of the book is a reflection on the ever-growing relevance of globalization for the power consultant and the discipline of global governmental relations. We outline what it means to conceive and coordinate political strategies across national borders and what organizational requirements exist on the part of *homo consultans* and *homo consultandus*. The future of power consulting lies in the political, economic, technological and informational networking of the global power field. The most important challenge for homo consultans is to make this power field manageable by constantly optimizing tools and methods.

0.3 METHODS

The chapters on the logic of power, *The Nature of Power*, *The Concretions of Power* and *The Practice of Power*, are all linked to one another by a common methodology. Our analysis and presentation methods are based on the combination of five complementary elements: political theory and philosophy, anthropology, historiography, praxeology and practical experience. The selection is not eclectic. We deliberately chose this set of methods to render the full breadth of the phenomena of power comprehensible and explicable – from general definition and basic principles to the presentation of the power leadership curriculum.

Political theory and philosophy have the fundamental function of developing the definition of power and its conditions of legitimacy, especially with regard to the common good. To avoid Western-centric prejudice and to make the most of the intellectual achievements of human history, we seek dialogue with Western and non-Western writers of the past and present: from Lao Tzu to Jean-Jacques Rousseau, from Al-Mawardi to Ernst Fraenkel. In this way, we avoid a dogmatic commitment to doctrinal schools of thought and the paradigms associated with them. In the end, according to our methodological credo, every approach has to demonstrate whether it can open up the logic of power in theory and practice.

We refer to the discipline of cultural and sociological anthropology in order to explain the universals of power, that is, the factors that apply regardless of culture and epoch. Thus, referring to authors who dominate the discourse, such as Aristotle and Arnold Gehlen, we clarify which determinants characterize humans as *zoon politikon*, technicians and deficient beings, and what effects these anthropological constants have on the relationship between humankind and power. Of course, we assume that something like a general anthropology is indeed possible and meaningful. Without generalizable statements about the nature of humankind, no generalizable statements about the nature of power are possible; both aspects are necessarily linked.

Historiography has the key role of vividly demonstrating the phenomenon of power at the interface of universality and contingency. In our presentation, we refer to both historical and contemporary examples of specific techniques, laws, challenges and dilemmas of power – from ancient civilizations such as the Sumerians, Persians and Romans, through the medieval empires of Europe and Asia to the immediate present. On the one hand, these vignettes make it clear that the basic logic of power in every culture and every era of action is always the same and runs through the course of world history. On the other hand, they also illustrate that power always goes through a process of cultural-historical coding and contextualization, which is why its mastery requires both an understanding of the universals of power and the peculiarities of each context. This approach to our topic is not just illustrative. It also yields practical resources by benefiting from the experiences of previous generations and by using history as a textbook of power.

Finally, the method of praxeology comes into its own where power, as the object of analysis, becomes socially concrete and politics should be rendered tangible and experienceable in everyday life. With the term 'praxeology', we refer to a method borrowed from sociology and cultural studies, a method with which the powerful social structures and factual power relations of a community are developed from the convergence or divergence of political discourse and practice. In short, the praxeological perspective compares the statements and actions of political actors – individuals and organizations alike – and contextualizes the reproduction or discontinuation of political processes, rituals, institutions and symbols. Behind this method is the insight that power and domination exist only in and through their practical-discursive implementation in collective human action and therefore must be either repeatedly confirmed or modified and revised from one moment to the other. Through its organizational performance, praxeology creates orientation in the power field of politics and sharpens the eye for the essentials.

The foundation for all these methods of course must be experiential knowledge or familiarity with the struggle for power and influence gained from many years of consulting activity. Any theory – whether in philosophy, political science, sociology, theology or history – remains merely an abstract reflection if it is not supplemented by first-person, immediate experience with the logic of power. Therefore, this presentation feeds not least on decades of personal learning in the counseling of various people and organizations in the political power field, countless successes and failures in the co-shaping of democratic processes and a never-fading enthusiasm for the grand zero-sum power game.

1. The Nature of Power

1.1 DEFINITIONAL APPROACH

Power is multifarious. We encounter it generally and in political practice in many different forms. Power manifests itself in the martial pomp of a military parade, in the decision of a head of state on war and peace, in a parliamentary resolution or in the police checkpoint on the roadside. The structures of power penetrate social relationships – consciously perceived or unconscious. From the cradle to the grave, people are surrounded by these structures. Power is subtle and brutal, taciturn and eloquent. The striking heterogeneity of these social phenomena led Max Weber (1864 - 1920), in his posthumously published standard work *Economy and Society*, to classify the notion of power as "sociologically amorphous", i.e., shimmering and elusive[1]. There seems to be considerable doubt as to whether there is any singular definition of power. Indeed, it is questionable as to whether one specific generic concept, an umbrella term under which all power phenomena are convincingly subsumed, can be identified at all.[2] Although conscious of this challenge, it remains necessary to risk a definitional approach, although not in the sense of an incontrovertible designation. Instead, we are concerned with reaching a pragmatic working definition that is appropriate to our specific interest in this subject, both as an agent in political processes and as an observer of these processes.

We are not starting from zero here. For thousands of years, state theorists, philosophers, sociologists and historians have examined the concept of power and

---

1 Weber, Max ([1921] 1978). *Economy and Society: An Outline of Interpretive Sociology*, translated by Guenther Roth and Claus Wittich. Berkeley: University of California Press.; p. 53.
2 For example, the cultural scientist Lisa Zunshine draws the radical conclusion that power is absolutely indefinable, cf. Zunshine, Lisa (2008): *Strange Concepts and the Stories They Make Possible*, Baltimore: The John Hopkins University Press.; p. 50.

presented various, often contradictory, definitions and descriptions. The field can best be briefly outlined by means of two controversies, which at the same time provide orientation for our own definitional approach[3]. The first issue concerns the question of whether power is to be primarily understood as the capacity for goal-directed action, that is, as *power to*. Or is it instead to be regarded as the ability to control other persons, that is, as *power over*? The second issue is whether power is a resource that can be possessed by individual and collective actors, or whether it constitutes a social structure that directs or even completely determines the behavior of actors. Crucial for us is that both controversies are independent in terms of content. Resolving one of the disputes does not allow conclusions to be drawn as to the other. In order to approach a working definition, we outline both controversies below and discuss our positions in this context.

The notion of power as *power to* was anchored early in history. Already in *Metaphysics*, Aristotle develops his core concept of *dynamis*, which can be translated as a possibility, ability or agency, depending on the context.[4] Aristotle understands dynamis quite fundamentally as the ability of an organism – be it a human or an animal – to change itself or other things purposefully. Dynamic living beings are therefore those who have the potential to actively, and to a certain extent deliberately, influence their environment. We find this definition consistently through ancient times, as exemplified by the scholastics who translate the Greek dynamis into the Latin *potentia*. Excitingly, the 'potentia' concept prevails with almost no change of meaning throughout the Middle Ages.[5] Thomas Hobbes draws on this powerful definition of power in the early modern period, but narrows the power concept decisively. In his *Leviathan*, he puts forward the following new definition: "The power of a man [...] is his present means to obtain some future apparent good."[6]

---

3 Cf. Allen, Amy (2016): Feminist Perspectives on Power, in: Edward N. Zalta (ed.), *Stanford Encyclopedia of Philosophy*. [online] https://plato.stanford.edu/archives/fall 2016/entries/feminist-power/, retrieved on 21.12.2017.

4 Cf. Aristotle (2002): *Metaphysics*, translated by Joe Sachs (ed.), 2nd edition, Santa Fe: Green Lion.; For an in-depth analysis of the power principles see Saar, Martin (2010): Power and Critique. *Journal of Power*, 3 (1), pp. 7-20.

5 Cf. Geary, Patrick J. (2013): *Language and Power in the Early Middle Ages*, authored in the course of the Menahem Stern Jerusalem Lectures. Waltham: Brandeis University Press.

6 Such a pessimistic view is maintained by Hobbes, Thomas ([1651] 1997): *Leviathan. Or the Matter, Forme, and Power of a Common-Wealth Ecclesiasticall and Civill*, Michael Oakeshott (ed.), New York: Touchstone/Simon & Schuster.; p. 72.

Power, Hobbes says, is a specifically human category, and one which he now couples to the condition for realizing subjective interests.

To be sure, Hobbes remains faithful to the Aristotelian conception of origin inasmuch as he places the power of action at the center of his conception of power. The scope of power of a person or group of persons thus depends on the scope of their options for action to achieve their various goals. Hobbes's definition proves subsequently to be so influential for power theorists and practitioners in power politics that it finds its way into the present. An example of the aftereffect of this concept is the position of the philosopher Amy Allen, who sees power as the "ability to attain an end or a series of ends."[7] This ability, so notes Allen while concretizing the Hobbesian paradigm, does not have to be successful or force the realization of the desired purpose. An actor already has power if the execution of an action makes the intended effect likely to occur. Thus, Allen extends Hobbes concept with an explicitly probabilistic component. The power of an actor is determined not only by the extent of his or her options for action, but also by the likelihood that the corresponding acts will be successful in their implementation.

The genesis of the second competing notion of power as *power over*, according to which power is essentially a relationship of dominance between persons, is less easy to trace. For many social theorists Niccolò Machiavelli describes this conception for the first time explicitly in his power classic, *The Prince*[8]. However, it is indisputable that the most well-known of the definitions of this concept in modern times was put forth by Max Weber: "Power is the probability that one actor within a social relationship will be in a position to carry out his own will despite resistance, regardless of the basis upon which this probability rests."[9] It is worthwhile to dissect this compact definition into its components. First, as Weber points

---

7   Allen, Amy (1999): *The Power of Feminist Theory: Domination, Resistance, Solidarity,* Boulder, CO: Westview Press.; p. 126. See also Pitkin, Hanna F. (1972): *Wittgenstein and Justice.* Oxford: Oxford University Press.; Dowding, Keith M. (1996): *Power.* Minneapolis: University of Minnesota Press.

8   Cf. Machiavelli, Niccolo ([1513] 2000): *The Prince,* translated by Quentin Skinner and Russel Price (eds.), 12th edition, Cambridge: Cambridge University Press. For an in-depth discussion of Macchiavelli's significance with respect to the dominance model, see e.g. Karlberg, Michael (2005): Power of Discourse and the Discourse of Power: Pursuing Peace Through Discourse Intervention, *International Journal of Peace Studies,* 10 (1), pp. 1-23.; pp. 2-3. Critically, Holler, Manfred J. (2009): Niccolò Machiavelli on Power, *Rationality, Markets, and Morals,* 0 (1), pp. 335-354.

9   Weber ([1921]) 1978): p. 53. The number of Weberians among the power theoreticians of the present day is immense, among the more important ones, however, are: Barry,

out, the *power-over* concept implies a mutually dependent relationship between a ruler and a power-subject.[10] Whereas the Aristotelian definition of power, based on the mere capacity for successful and purposeful action, could be applied in a world in which only one human being were still alive, in such a scenario it would no longer be possible to speak of Weber's understanding of power. Power in the Weberian sense is irreducibly social, and it requires at least two persons.[11] Secondly, this power concept implies a potential resistance that is potentially overcome. In other words, power concretely presupposes a will that, if it opposes the will of those with power, can be overcome, should those with power so wish.[12] This, as Byung-Chul Han aptly states, does not necessarily imply that power must express itself in compulsion.[13] On the one hand, anyone who is subject to power can freely follow the wishes of the ruler without being compelled by coercive means. On the other hand, rulers can renounce the use of means of coercion and tolerate the power-subject's insubordination, without forfeiting their status as rulers. What is decisive, however, is that the amount of power an actor possesses is constitutively dependent on the extent to which he or she is capable of resisting others in the realization of his or her own interests. It does not matter if the resistance of others ever manifests itself or if the actor ever makes use of his or her ability. Finally, the third crucial component is that power is always associated with an opportunity to enforce interests. This aspect, which we have already encountered in discussion of the concept of *power to*, says nothing more than that the *power-over* concept has a probabilistic component. Having power over others is no guarantee that rulers can enforce their will. It simply means that if a ruler uses coercive means, there is a significant likelihood that these means will be successful in overcoming the resistance.

Brian (1989): *Democracy and Power*, Oxford: Clarendon Press and Mann, Michael (1986): *The Sources of Social Power: Volume I: The History of Power from the Beginning to A.D. 1760*, Cambridge: Cambridge University Press.

10 The Korean-born German author Byung-Chul Han succinctly characterizes this aspect by noting that power constantly exists in a tense, charged relationship between ego and alter. Cf. Han, Byung-Chul (2005): *Was ist Macht?*, Ditzingen: Reclam.

11 The obvious question, whether the converse is true, i.e. whether the social is irreducibly linked to the phenomenon of power, will be discussed in Chapter 2.2

12 Cf. Dahl, Robert (1957): The Concept of Power, *Behavioral Science*, 2, pp. 201-215.; pp. 202f.; and Dahl, Robert ([1968] 2002): Power, in: Mark Haugaard (ed.), *Power. A Reader*, Manchester: Manchester University Press, pp. 5-25.

13 Cf. Han (2005): p. 11.

This dualism of two power concepts is by no means a Western feature. It may also be found in other great cultural traditions. This is impressively demonstrated by the formative currents of classical Chinese ethics – Taoism and Confucianism.[14] Both schools of thought are concerned explicitly not with conceptual theoretical reflections, such as the Platonic dialogues, but offer practice-oriented guidelines for emperors and high civil servants.[15] Accordingly, we search in vain among them for an abstract definition of the concept of power. Nonetheless, we can find a very clear analysis of the ideal ruler personality. Both Lao Tzu, the founder of Taoism, and Confucius vehemently reject the quest for power – both power over and power to.[16] For example, Lao Tzu warns in his canonical collection of sayings, the Tao-Te-Ching (Dao de Jing in the Pinyin romanization) in Chapter 19: "Forget about knowledge and wisdom / and people will be a hundred times better off. [...] Throw away profit and greed / and there wont be any thieves. [...] Embrace simplicity / put others first."[17] The virtuous ruler should not, therefore, increase his capacity for action and strive for chances of success; he should rather withdraw from the active world. The keyword of Chinese philosophy here is wu wei, which translates to "doing nothing" or "abstaining from action."[18] Only by avoiding the fatal cycle of ever wishing, as it were, can the ruler set an example to his subjects and inspire them to loyalty and lawfulness. For similar reasons, the founders of Chinese ethics also reject the quest for control over other people. Thus, Confucius advises against ruling by decrees and punishments, arguing that the people affected inevitably become disaffected or even lose their conscience. Conversely, he notes that if one directs by essential power and observes morality in doing so, the people have a sense of right and wrong and achieve goodness.[19] Behind this is a simple consideration. Every attempt by political decision-makers to

---

14 Both currents have their origins in the fifth century BC. Their key texts are: Lao Tzu (2009): *Tao-Te-Ching*, translated by John H. McDonald (ed.), New York: Chartwell Books.; and Confucius (2005): *Lun Yu*, translated by Chichung Huang (ed.) as 'The Analects of Confucius (Lun yu)', New York: Oxford University Press.

15 An informative and humorous comparison of the theory-burdened Attic thinkers of antiquity and their Chinese counterparts is provided by Wong, David (2013): Chinese Ethics, in: Edward N. Zalta (ed.), *Stanford Encyclopedia of Philosophy*, [online] https://plato.stanford.edu/archives/fall2018/entries/ethics-chinese/, retr. on 21.12.2017.

16 Cf. Roetz, Heiner and Schleichert, Hubert (2009): *Klassische chinesische Philosophie. Eine Einführung*, Frankfurt a. M.: Klostermann.; p. 24.

17 Lao Tzu (2009): p. 47.

18 Ibid.: p. 20.

19 Cf. Confucius (2005): p. 69.

exercise power over others, and to force them against their will into doing something, provokes the development of countervailing power. This leads, so the thesis, towards violence and chaos. The alternative is a reserved and measured, but above all morally sound, style of government, a style that serves as a model for the population. In this context, Lao Tzus advice for the right state reads not just as a complement to the Confucian notion, but also as a prelude to the liberal political idea of a quiet and unobtrusive government whose people are honest, instead of a loud and obtrusive government whose people are deceitful and unreliable.[20]

Lao Tzu and Confucius are also well aware of the two concepts of power discussed, even if they forego a conceptual explication. We should not, however, in view of their critical attitude, jump to the conclusion that they intend to eliminate the phenomenon of power from the social world. That would be wrong. Power, is rather their provocative conclusion, can successfully and legitimately be exercised only when one does not try to seize and expand it, focusing instead on the cultivation of one's virtues, modesty and integrity. An insightful as well as poetic Confucian analogy insists that the good intentions of the ruling powers will be rewarded by the good behavior of the people being ruled. Confucius likens the virtues of rulers to the wind and that of ordinary people to the grass, noting: "When grass is visited by the wind, it must surely bend."[21] This statement may seem barely plausible, and has been repeatedly criticized as utopian by Confucius' successors.[22] Nonetheless, the notion addresses a central form of power, which we shall explore in more detail in Chapter 2.1. This is authoritative power, a form based on the human need for recognition and moral orientation.

This is not to say that, in addition to the Western tradition, only Chinese philosophy has made a significant contribution to the dichotomy of power to and power over.[23] The political thinkers of medieval Islam were as profoundly concerned with the nature of power, albeit some one thousand years later.[24] These

---

20 Lao Tzu (2009): p. 98.
21 Confucius (2005): p. 15.
22 Cf. Roetz & Schleichert (2009): pp. 38f.
23 However, Confucianism and Taoism have proven to be so influential within Asian cultural space that they have, for example, significantly shaped Japanese thinking about power since ancient times. For an overview, see Richey, Jeffrey L. (2015): *Daoism in Japan. Chinese traditions and their influence on Japanese religious culture,* Routledge Studies in Taoism, Oxon: Routledge.
24 A good overview is provided by Bowering, Gerhard (2015): Introduction, in: Gerhard Bowering (ed.), *Islamic Political Thought. An Introduction,* Princeton/Oxford: Princeton University Press, pp. 1-23.

thinkers include the historian Ibn Khaldun and the jurist Al-Mawardi, whose Al-Ahkam as-Sultaniyya (The Principles of Power) from the eleventh century remains one of the most important foundational texts of political Islam.[25] Representatives of this tradition, however, in contrast to those of the Chinese school of thought, do not offer their services to the ruling elite, but instead serve religious individual ethicists and state theorists. Two things are remarkable in this context. First, they incorporate almost without modification the Aristotelian concept of agency –dynamis – and translate it into a religious world picture in which man is accountable to God as an autonomous and independent being. The strong leaning towards Aristotelian thinking and the corresponding model of power is ultimately not surprising, considering that the Greek classics had been preserved and considered by Arab scholars since the eighth century – long before they (once again) found their way into the Western canon.[26] For the German Catholic theologian Bernhard Uhde, a keen examiner of this phenomenon, for example, the significance of said influence can be explained by the application of the Aristotelian principle of non-contradiction.[27] At any rate, Aristotelian logic and metaphysics are inextricably inscribed and taught in Islamic theology, and they thereby comprise a systematic framework. Moreover, the Islamic theorists take up the second conceptual understanding of power, the concept of domination, in a positive way and link it to a draft of the theocratic state. The most drastic position is found in Al Ahkam as-Sultaniyya: the rationality and the prudence of the people alone, according to Al-Mawardi, are not strong enough to unify them into a just and pious community; in addition, there are serious differences in terms of customs and mor-

---

25 Cf. Al-Mawardi, Abu al-Hasan (1996): *Al-Ahkam as-Sultaniyya. The Ordinances of Government*, translated by Wafaa H. Wahba (ed.), Reading: Garnet.; The English translation of 'sultaniyya' as 'of government' is actually relatively mild, almost euphemistic. The Arabic word 'sultan' means more than anything else 'power' as well as 'force' and 'strength'. See also Al-Baghdadi, Ahmad M. (1981): The political thought of Abu Al-Hassan Al-Mawardi, Thesis Presented for the Degree of Doctor of Philosophy, University of Edinburgh, [online] https://www.era.lib.ed.ac.uk/handle/1842/7414, retrieved on 21.12.2017.; In addition thereto see Ringgren, Helmer (1972): On the Islamic Theory of the State, *Scripta Instituti Donneriani Aboensis,* 6, pp. 103-108.

26 Cf. D'Ancona, Cristina (2013): Greek Sources in Arabic and Islamic Philosophy, in: Edward N. Zalta (ed.), *Stanford Encyclopedia of Philosophy,* [online] https://plato.stanford.edu/archives/win2017/entries/arabic-islamic-greek/, retrieved on 21.12.2017.

27 Cf. Uhde, Bernhard (2009): Religionen als Denkmöglichkeiten. Skizzen zur Logik der Weltreligionen, *Zeitschrift für Didiaktik der Philosophie und Ethik,* 1, pp. 7-16.; p. 8.

als. An absolutist theocrat, an imam, is therefore required, who can force the population to unity and virtue thanks to an unlimited plentitude of power.[28] The Imam receives his ministry through divine providence, and accordingly his authority is inviolable. Nevertheless, Al-Mawardi leaves a back door open. If the ruler is openly guilty of violating the commandments of God, the people have a right to resistance, that is, to the formation of counter-power.

This highly interesting and in the West surprisingly little explored topic could easily be pursued further. However, at this point, we wish to end our intercultural digression on the topic of power and return to the actual question at hand: the development of a useful working definition. Let us return, more specifically, to the fundamental dualism of the two power definitions. For our own definition, it is paramount to analyze the relationship between these two influential concepts of power and to ensure that they are practically manageable and applicable. Numerous power theorists have chosen the viewpoint that power to and power over are not competing definitional approaches. The interpersonal dominance model of power is only a special case of the more general action model of power.[29] Both approaches, it is argued, assume that actors have power only when and if they are capable of realizing their interests through purposeful action. The power-over concept therefore focuses only on the realization of interests against the potential resistance of other actors. Other theoreticians, such as Hannah Arendt, advocate clearly separating both definitions as power over others always involves overt or covert oppression and, unlike the power-to concept, is not normatively neutral, but morally evil.[30] This discussion does not need to be settled here. Only one of the power concepts discussed is suitable for a practical handbook on (political) power: the power-over concept.

The power-to concept, upon closer inspection, covers a far too expansive range of phenomena to make sense for our purpose. If power already exists, if an actor is able to realize a self-imposed goal through action, almost every single action is

---

28 Cf. Al-Baghdadi (1981).
29 Cf. Dowding (1996) and Pansardi, Pamela (2012): Power to and power over: two distinct concepts of power?, *Journal of Political Power*, 5 (1), pp. 73-89.
30 Arendt, Hannah (1969): *On Violence,* New York: Harcourt, Brace and World.; p.43. She strictly distinguishes among the concepts of power, strength, force, violence and authority, warning that confusing them with one another could result in a certain 'linguistic deafness' and 'blindness' as to reality. Lukes, Steven (1974): *Power. A Radical View,* London: MacMillan Press. The extent to which power over persons must always be a form of oppression, and whether it is correspondingly morally evil, will be discussed in Chapter 2.2.

an expression of that power. Reading a book to the last page, for example, would already be a case of this power-to concept. Such theoretical-philosophical reflections on the concept of power are less pertinent to our political discussion and, in terms of our colloquial conception of power, such conclusions are of no utility.[31] In addition, one quality criterion for definitions is their usefulness as classifications. Concepts, above all power concepts, serve to systematize and make manageable our world of experience through the demarcation and limitation of phenomena. And it is exactly this function that is not fulfilled by the power-to concept. It extends the term power to apply universally. Paraphrasing Hinrich Fink-Eitel, it leads to power ultimately meaning everything and therefore nothing.[32]

The power-over concept is much more precise, easier to describe and to implement. It also approximates a pre-theoretical understanding of terms for power practitioners. For example, if we say that the institutions of the European Union have lost power over their member states in the past few years, then we are simply describing the lessened likelihood that the Commission will pursue an independent policy against the resistance of national governments. What matters is that the power-over concept systematizes and unifies a large number of cases in which we speak of power (or lack of power) without at the same time – as with the rival model – subsuming cases that are intuitively understood as not having anything to do with power.

A second controversy regarding the systematization of different models of power is significant for the theory of power. This is a discussion between representatives of the commodity model and the structural model of power. The commodity model is based on Karl Marx's economic theory. The many adherents of this model – of whom few are convinced Marxists – come primarily from the economic and social sciences.[33] For them, power exists as a numerical resource to

---

31 For the assessment that the ability to connect to our pre-theoretical understanding of terms is also an important feature of definitions, see Sumner, Leonard W. (1996): *Welfare, Happiness and Ethics,* Oxford: Oxford University Press.; p. 10.
32 Fink-Eitel, Hinrich (1992): Dialektik der Macht, in: Emil Angehrn, Hinrich Fink-Eitel, Christian Iber, and Georg Lohmann (eds.), *Dialektischer Negativismus. Michael Theunissen zum 60. Geburtstag.* Frankfurt/M: Suhrkamp, pp. 35-56.; p. 36.
33 See also Korpi, Walter (1983): *The Democratic Class Struggle,* Boston: Routledge & Kegan.; Bourdieu, Pierre (1987): *Die feinen Unterschiede. Kritik der gesellschaftlichen Urteilskraft,* translated by Bernd Schwibs and Achim Russer, Frankfurt a.M.: Suhrkamp.; Conolly, William E. (1993): *The Terms of Political Discourse,* Princeton: Princeton University Press.; Ostheim, Tobias and Schmidt, Manfred G. (2007): Die Machtressourcentheorie, in: Manfred G. Schmidt (ed.), *Der Wohlfahrtsstaat: Eine*

realize interests and can be possessed, accumulated, distributed and again withdrawn by concrete actors.[34] So it is a good – 'a social good', as Amy Allen writes; a good which people or groups of people can possess in varying quantities and which they can autonomously command.[35] The power goods of actors can have many different natural, social, cultural or economic foundations. In a nutshell, the sociologist Walter Müller-Jentsch sums up power as a resource for organizations: "The entrepreneur has jobs, the worker has manpower – both have resources that the other needs to assert their non-trivial interests; both therefore have [...] power over the other actor."[36] In short, for these power interpreters, individual or collective actors have power insofar as they control means of production, insofar as they mobilize the members of a trade union, insofar as they have a substantial share of votes in a parliament, and so on. In all these cases, however, it is important that the decisive social good is power. Even if the power goods are constituted differently by actors, they can still be quantified and compared. These models are based on the momentous assumption that, given precise measurement and adequate information, power relations can be represented on a one-dimensional scale.[37] It seems likely that the unbroken popularity of the commodity model in the theory of power is linked strongly to this phenomenon of 'objective' measurability. In addition, it is characterized by its relevance to the everyday language of power discourse. We speak naturally of an 'unequal distribution' of power in societies or of a 'balance' of power between geopolitical actors. These statements are only descriptive if power, first, represents a type of distributable goods and, second, if the quantities of goods can at least ideally be scaled and judged to be equal.

Einführung in den historischen und internationalen Vergleich. Wiesbaden: VS Verlag, pp. 40-50.; and Müller-Jentsch, Walter (2014): Macht als Ressource von Organisationen, in: Monica Budowski and Michael Nollert (eds.), *Private Macht im Wohlfahrtsstaat: Akteure und Institutionen,* Zürich: Seismo, pp. 14-29.

34 Numerous formulations of this core thesis are found in the literature, but ironically, that of Iris M. Young, one of the most vehement critics of this model, is most succinctly phrased: "Conceptualizing power in distributive terms means [...] conceiving power as a kind of stuff possessed by individual agents in greater or lesser amounts." Young, Iris M. (1990): *Justice and the Politics of Difference,* Princeton: Princeton University Press.; p. 31.

35 Cf. Allen (2011): p. 4.

36 Müller-Jentsch (2014): pp. 14-29.

37 For an example of such a quantitative power index, see Stetter, Stephen (2004): Cross-Pillar Politics: Functional Unity and Institutional Fragmentation of EU Foreign Policies, *Journal of European Public Policy,* 11 (4), pp. 720-739.

It was the postmodern thinkers who challenged this model in recent decades.[38] For example, Michel Foucault clearly states in his monograph The History of Sexuality: The Will to Knowledge, "Power is not something that is acquired, seized, or shared, something that one holds on to or allows to slip away."[39] Likewise, Stuart Clegg suggests, "It [power] is not a thing [...] that people have in a proprietary sense. They 'possess' power only in so far as they are relationally constituted as doing so."[40] The radical change in the argument concerning the nature of power lies in the assumption that power is not a substance that individual or collective actors are able to possess. Rather, it is a social structure that can only be determined in many ways and that is formed by innumerable interpersonal relationships of mutual normalization, control and sanctioning, and which regulates, directs and in places even determines the behavior of individuals.[41] Foucault expresses this important counter-proposal with his usual rhetorical finesse, touching upon the pillars that connect these force relationships by linking themselves into systems, and recommending: "we should postulate rather that this multiplicity of force relations can be coded – in part but never totally – either in the form of 'war', or in the form of 'politics'; this would imply two different strategies (but the one always liable to switch into the other) for integrating these unbalanced, heterogeneous, unstable, and tense force relations."[42]

From this perspective, power suddenly appears as a social entity constituted by human behavior, yet independent and beyond the control of individuals – thus, an almost "superhuman reality."[43] For many practitioners of power, this picture at

---

38 Foucault, Michel ([1984] 1990): *The History of Sexuality: The Will to Knowledge, An Introduction*, Vol. I, translated by Robert Hurley (ed.), New York: Random House.; Clegg, Stuart (1989): *Frameworks of Power*, London: Sage Publications.; Young (1990); and Haugaard, Mark (2010): Power: A 'Family Resemblance' Concept, *European Journal of Cultural Studies*, 13 (4), pp. 419-438.
39 Foucault (1990): p. 94.
40 Clegg (1989): p. 207.
41 However, this conception of power actually goes back much further than postmodernism. As an early representative, the medieval state theorist Ibn Khaldun can be considered. Cf. Khaldun, Ibn (2011): *Die Muqaddima: Betrachtungen zur Weltgeschichte*, translated by Alma Giese, München: C.H. Beck. See also Gierer, Alfred (2001): Ibn Khaldun on Solidarity ("Asabiyah") – Modern Science on Cooperativeness and Empathy: a Comparison, *Philosophia Naturalis* 38 (1), pp. 91-104.
42 Foucault (1990): p. 93.
43 According to Han (2005): p. 96. Martin Saar (2010) sees it similarly and speaks in this context of a "transindividual relational entity". Cf. Saar (2010): p. 11.

first glance seems complex and far divorced from our political commonsense. The fact that it nevertheless has a high degree of effectiveness for political work can best be demonstrated by considering everyday actions. When we yawn, we put our hands to our mouths; if we see a woman with a stroller getting on the subway, we offer our help or at least make room; when we discuss with somebody, we usually let the other person speak. In all these cases, there is no powerful person or group of people forcing us to act or feel that way, nonetheless, our behavior is the object of direction and control. Here, in Foucault's words, "power relations permeate all levels of social existence and are therefore to be found operating at every site of social life – in the private spheres of the family and sexuality as much as in the public spheres of politics, the economy and the law."[44] These power networks, which form a complete social system of comprehensive control, unfold their effect through internalized norms. These encompass expected penalties for misconduct and positive incentives for compliance. People, as Foucault and other theorists concede, can selectively try to influence this system and make changes. All in all, nevertheless, it remains out of their control. These are, of course, extreme – barely manageable – challenges for policymakers: on the one hand, because the relevant actors with their wishes, goals and intentions for action have always been shaped and constituted by the super-personal system; on the other hand, because the system results from a vast plethora of innumerable cooperative and conflictive social relationships with no central direction, and is thus reconfigured daily. So, a definitive political entity does not exist. There are only "politics", that is, ensembles of political practices and discourses that constitute the space of the political, new and differently constituted in each case.

In this controversy, too, the question arises as to how both power concepts relate to each other and what significance this discussion has for our own definitional approach to the concept of power. With this discussion, we have arrived at the core of the power-theoretical discussion of modernity. Do we stick to the notion of autonomous subjects equipped with their own power? Or do we describe a system that places people and organizations in complex power grids?[45]

---

44 Foucault, Michel. (1980): *Power / Knowledge: Selected Interviews and Other Writings, 1972 – 1977,* translated by Colin Gordon, Leo Marshall, John Mepham and Kate Soper. Brighton: Harvester, p.119.

45 Exemplary for a critical assessment of the structural model is the statement of the political scientist Keith Dowding: "It is a mistake to think that because we are mapping the structure *of* power, that structures *have* power", Dowding (1996): p. 28, our accentuation.

Actually, there is no reason to take a side in this argument. Both approaches are valuable. A commodity model takes the strong pre-theoretical intuition that power can be deliberately used and accumulated by people and develops it into a well-crafted theory, allowing power asymmetries between actors to be analyzed and quantified. In turn, a structural model recognizes that social systems can develop a complex life of their own and direct their actions towards those who participate in them. At the same time, both approaches naturally also polarize. The commodity model puts an undue emphasis on the intentional exercise of power by concrete persons, ignoring the fact that these individuals, with their convictions and goals, are shaped by given social patterns. Translated into the language of the theory of power, this would mean not relying solely on a one-sided bottom-up perspective, which is fixed only on the concrete human as the object of analysis. In contrast, for the theory of power the structural model suffers by, to put it bluntly, degrading people as puppets of a ubiquitous social apparatus. This narrow top-down perspective, which looks only at structures but not at people, does not adequately reflect our day-to-day interpersonal reality. We are always finding ourselves in situations in which we – and not some anonymous power network – exercise power over others; be it a one-sided game of chess in which we dictate our opponents all the moves, or in a hierarchical employment relationship in which we specify an employee's activities.

The obvious conclusion for the current power theory discussion is to combine these two model approaches to integrate their analytical strengths and avoid their weaknesses. Power, we wish to state, occurs as a good or a means that people can use, and as a trans-individual social structure that controls human action. It is precisely this conflict between power as the attribute of concrete persons and power as the attribute of impersonal social systems that is a defining characteristic of modernity and an irreducible component of our discourses on power. This consideration, however, is by no means revolutionary or novel. Foucault rediscovered the human subject as the bearer of power and autonomous responsibility, and he addressed the above-mentioned antagonism of person and social structure.[46] Similar considerations can be found in the work of the political scientist Martin Saar, who advances towards an integrative design of both approaches from an opposite perspective.[47]

---

46   Foucault, Michel (1988): *The Care of the Self,* The History of Sexuality, Vol. 3, translated by Roberet Hurley (ed.), New York: Random House. See also Foucault, Michel ([1984] 1988): The History of Sexuality, Vol. 3: The Care of the Self, translated by Robert Hurley, New York: Vintage Books.

47   Cf. Saar (2010). See also Allen (2011).

Let's briefly summarize what has been said so far. In discussing the first controversy over the definition of power (power to versus power over), we have sided with those power theorists who understand power as a social phenomenon of domination, potentially overcoming potential resistance, for reasons of argumentative strategy. Power, as we have stated with Weber, is what you have when and only if you have the chance to assert your will against the possible reluctance of others. In discussing the second controversy (commodity model versus structural model), we choose neither of the models, but argue for a combination of both approaches. Power, we have stated, occurs as an attribute of concrete persons and also as an impersonal social structure. How do these two findings fit together for a modern theory of power? In our estimation, the commodity model and the structural model of power decisively complement the Weberian concept of dominance. According to this, power is to be understood as the means available to concrete persons for the potential control of other persons AND as the potential of a social structure to control the behavior of the persons participating in it. From our perspective, it is crucial that Weber's power-over conception leaves a gap in relation to the position of the 'power-bearer'. It simply leaves unresolved whether this position is filled by a concrete person or group of people or by an impersonal or super-personal social structure. And the discussion of the controversy between representatives of the commodity model and the structural model has clearly shown that it can be filled by both.

1.2 BASIC PRINCIPLES OF POWER

After having discussed pivotal questions in our definitional approach, notably which phenomena fall under the concept of power and which do not, we now wish to clarify which logic patterns these phenomena are subject to and which basic principles apply to them. There is already an implicit assumption associated with this question, namely that there actually are fundamental principles of power at all. However, we also go one step further. We believe that is possible to develop a list of power principles that are universal and globally consistent, that is, independent of time and place. In other words, the basic principles of power are the same everywhere and at all times. Before listing them in detail, let us first make our assumption of the universality and global consistency of the principles of power plausible.

Our argument is summarized as follows: (a) The nature of power depends on the nature of humankind; (b) the essence of humankind is universal and globally uniform; (c) therefore, the essence of power – and thus its principles – is universal and globally consistent. The first premise of this conclusion can easily be made plausible. Power, as we established in Chapter 1.1, is an irreducible social phenomenon that exists only in and through interacting relationships between people. Without people there is no power. Thus, the essence of power is inseparably connected with that of humankind. Accordingly, if there are no characteristics that are common to all people, no matter what time they come from and how they are socialized, then there are no universal principles of power. But if there are human characteristics that persist across all times and contexts, it suggests that the same applies to the logic of power.

That brings us to our second premise. The question of whether there is one kind of human nature has always been a bone of contention among historians, social scientists and philosophers. Until the late 1980s, the conception of critical theory and existentialism dominated the discourse to the extent that statements *about* humankind as such were deemed mere ideological constructs.[48] What a person is and what a person is not becomes, so the Marxist-inspired thesis, exclusively determined by changing economic conditions. Beyond that, there is no characteristic structure of human forms of action and life. This position has been contested in recent years, rightly so.

An important criticism comes from the realm of ethnology. The diversity of human life forms is immense, but nevertheless there are "features of culture, society, language, behavior, and mind that [...] are found among all peoples."[49] The list of these 'anthropological universals', which are determined by intercultural comparative research, is long. A well-documented example is the incest taboo, which applies without exception in all societies. Another universal is that of property, which, though in many variations, is a core element of the emergence of every human community. Such conspicuous universal structures can, so the thesis, exist only if there is an immutable essence of humankind. Otherwise they would be completely inexplicable.

Another criticism comes from philosophical anthropology in conjunction with biology. Here it is pointed out that the action, thinking, feeling, etc. of human beings is largely determined by their biological bodies and that this body has remained the same since the appearance of humankind about 300,000 years ago. A theoretician, who is currently experiencing a renaissance in this context, is the

---

48 Sartre, Jean-Paul ([1945] 2007): *Existentialism is a Humanism*, John Kulka (ed.), translated by Carol Macomber, New Haven: Yale University Press.
49 Cf. Brown, Donald E. (2004): Human Universals, Human Nature, Human Culture, *Daedalus,* 133 (4), pp. 47-54.

sociologist Arnold Gehlen.[50] Gehlen coined the basic concept of humans as 'deficient beings' with the explanation that, unlike animals, humans have not adapted to their natural environment. Humankind has no dense fur to offer protection from severe weather; no fangs or claws for defense against predators; and a far from good escape instinct. This deficit must be compensated for through cultural creations, from the simple construction of tools and houses to the creation of complex states.[51] Through the development of cultural techniques, bioethicist Jens Clausen adds, humans have not been able to overcome the threat of nature but have succeeded in reducing it.[52] All human social achievements – and thus also power relations – are ultimately only mechanisms for compensating for physical inadequacies. This circumstance, Gehlen concludes, is the essence of humankind. Insofar as this physical constitution is genetically determined, it is immutable and universal. Thus, human behavior, despite all superficial and cultural variance, always follows the same basic pattern.

To summarize again: if there is such a thing as a universal and globally consistent human nature, as we have said, it suggests that there are also universal and globally consistent logics of power – because the nature of power is inseparably linked to the nature of humankind. Since the findings of ethnology and biologically informed anthropology suggest that such a human nature exists, it follows that it is possible to compile a list of principles of power that apply everywhere and at any time. We will pursue this in the following. Our aim is not to derive an exhaustive listing from any higher principle or to prove rigorously each entry. Rather, our list is based on the reading of the scientific canon as a concept of power, on many years of political consulting experience, and not least on common sense.

(1) The Moral Neutrality of Power

Power has a bad reputation. And not only since the German rock group *Ton Steine Scherben* sang "No power for nobody!" in 1972, in keeping with the spirit of the 1968 student-fueled protest movement which had engulfed the world, encompass

---

50 Gehlen, Arnold ([1940] 1988): *Man, his Nature and Place in the World,* translated by Clare McMillan and Karl Pillemer (eds.), New York: Columbia University Press.
51 Cf. Heidegger, Martin (1953): *The Question Concerning Technology and Other Essays X,* translated and with an Introduction by William Lovitt, New York: Garland Publishing.
52 Cf. Clausen, Jens (2009): Man, Machine and in between, *Nature,* 457 (7233), pp. 1080-1081. See also Clausen, Jens (2006): Die Natur des Menschen: Geworden und gemacht. Anthropologische Überlegungen zum Enhancement, *Zeitschrift für medizinische Ethik,* 52, pp. 391-401.; p. 396.

ing the hippie subculture and the anarchistic 'Yippies' of the Youth International Party, among others. The 'modern' aversion towards power has somewhat older roots. "Now power is evil, whoever wields it" was the apodictical assertion of the cultural historian Jacob Burkhardt, made as early as the beginning of the twentieth century.[53] Indeed, Burkhardt equated the establishment of power to the commission of a crime. A similar view is held by Mikhail Bakunin, for whom power and oppression are synonymous.[54] Bernhard Taureck sums up this point of view, which is widespread not only among intellectuals, by asserting that one speaks of power as if it were a threat, as if it were "something evil."[55] There are three claims underlying this standpoint: acquiring power is always morally bad, exercising power is always morally bad and power is always intrinsically morally bad, whether it is used or not.

These three claims are wrong! Power in itself – that is our first principle – is neither good nor bad, but *morally neutral*. It acquires moral status only through its context. Its status thus depends on the specific question of who has how much power over whom in relation to what.

In other words, only this or that power can be morally good or bad, not power *sui generis*. What is the best way to prove our neutrality thesis? First of all, we should realize that there are only three logically possible answers to the question of the moral status of power itself. First, power in itself is always morally bad – that is the view of Burckhardt and Sartre. Second, power in itself is always morally good – which, to our knowledge, nobody has ever advocated. Third, power in itself is neither morally good nor bad – which is our thesis. There is no fourth possibility. Since nobody ever seriously supported the second thesis, we can focus on refuting the first thesis. This allows the correctness of the third thesis to be deduced.

A few examples suffice to refute the first thesis. Take the power of parents over their children. Unquestionably, parents, also loving and caring parents, have tremendous power over their offspring. This results from physical superiority, natural authority and children's need for assistance and guidance. Nevertheless, this power is – we can assume – usually used to the benefit of the children. The parents

---

53 Cf. Hinde, John R. (2000): *Jacob Burckhardt and the Crisis of Modernity*, Montreal: McGill-Queen's University Press.; p. 122. See also Burkhardt, Jacob (2000): Aesthetik der bildenden Kunst, Über das Studium der Geschichte, in Peter Ganz (ed.), *Jacob Burckhardt Werke. Kritische Gesamtausgabe Vol. 10*, Munich: C.H. Beck.; p. 419.
54 Cf. Newman, Saul (2004): The Place of Power in Political Discourse, *International Political Science Review*, 25 (2), pp. 139-157.
55 Taureck, Bernhard (1983): *Die Zukunft der Macht. Ein philosophisch-politischer Essay*, Würzburg: Königshausen & Neumann.; p. 11.

hold them against their will when they want to run across a busy road; they exercise their authority when children wish to play video games rather than learn algebra; they speak a word of power when it is time to go to bed – and so on. The responsibility for raising and educating offspring requires the possession of power in a straightforward manner. If parents, thinking in this context of Weber, were unable to assert their interests against the opposition of their child, they could not fulfill their educational task. That, by the way, summarizes the whole dilemma of anti-authoritarian education. A similar case is that of the physician, for example. Consider, more specifically, a psychiatrist who commits his suicidal patient to a closed unit. The power of the psychiatrist is not based on physical superiority or natural authority, but on legal norms and social conventions regarding the protection of a person deemed to be *non compos mentis*. Nonetheless, it has a similar function as in the case of adolescent education: the control of an underage or otherwise vulnerable person for his or her own benefit. We do not want to claim that all power that parents have over children and medical doctors have over patients is good. There are, unfortunately, tyrannical fathers and mothers, as well as incompetent physicians, in abundance. That notwithstanding, it is still good – or better said a social good – that parents and physicians are generally in power relationships with those under their protection. Power is therefore not a moral evil here, but a condition for the functioning of general welfare and care relationships. Thus, the thesis that power is always evil, 'no matter who exercises it', is already invalidated at this point.

However, the thesis of power as a universal evil is not only wrong in relation to social conditions in which those subjugated to power are underage or *non compos mentis*. It is also wrong with regard to relationships between responsible people. One uncontroversial example is about soccer. Here, the referees have power over the game, in so far as they can send players from the field, award free kicks, invoke penalties and order extra time – even against the will of thousands of fans and million-dollar professional clubs. Still, it would be absurd to scourge the impartial power as a moral evil. Rather, it is a necessary condition for the fair course of the game and for the observance of the rules, which are constitutive for the game. Again, we do not argue that the power of any individual referee is automatically and inherently good. That would be naive, notably in the face of fraud scandals that repeatedly shake the soccer world internationally. Rather, the power of arbitrators is generally a good thing.

Some readers may reproach us, asserting that our examples are banal and exclude the really exciting questions, such as whether political power is good or bad. We respond with two remarks. Firstly, in this chapter, we are not concerned with clarifying what the criteria of good or bad forms of power are.[56] We aim just to show that power in itself – understood as a generic term and not as concrete power in a specific context – is not a moral evil, but is morally neutral. And we do this through counterexamples in which the intuitive untenability of the thesis of the categorical wickedness of power becomes apparent. Secondly, our examples intentionally comprise everyday cases, as they are meant to show the omnipresence of the phenomenon of power in our daily lives and the unrealistic nature of the claim that power in all its facets is fundamentally evil.

(2) The Dialectical Relationship of Power to Freedom

Power and freedom, it seems, are antipodes. Where there is power, freedom must give way. And if we are truly free, then we are free only in so far as we are not subject to any power, because power always means the potential curtailment of our freedom of action.[57] Nevertheless, things are more complicated than this. The relationship between power and freedom is not a contrast, but rather – as our second principle – a *dialectical* relationship. That is, power and freedom condition *and* undermine each other. Their relation is one of objective and real contradiction.

To what extent do power and freedom condition each other? First of all, we can state that power presupposes freedom. We can only have power over entities that have autonomy and scope for action. We cannot *force or pressure* a stone or a tree – we can only work with or process such objects. In other words, the potential to subjugate a potentially reluctant will implies that an autonomous will exists first. Only when this potential for submission is realized and a free will is broken does power become force. But with that, it stops, as it were, to exist. This is most dramatically demonstrated by the example of the threat of deadly force. As long as we threaten to fatally shoot someone, we have power over them. We incentivize their free will to obey our orders by linking the alternative to obedience with the eradication of existence. Yet, as soon as we fulfill our threat, because those threatened refuse to voluntarily comply with our demands, our power over them expires.

---

56 We shall address this matter in Chapter 2.3.
57 This position is characteristic of the school of thought of political liberalism as represented by John Rawls, Ronald Dworkin and Claus Offe; cf. Rawls, John (1971): *A Theory of Justice*, Cambridge: Belknap Press of Harvard University Press.; and cf. Dworkin, Ronald (1977): *Taking Rights Seriously*, Cambridge: Harvard University Press. For a discussion of the relationship between freedom and power from a liberalistic perspective, see Carter, Ian (2008): How are Power and Unfreedom Related?, in: Cécile Laborde and John W. Maynor (eds.), *Republicanism and Political Theory*, Malden/Oxford: Blackwell Publishing.; pp. 59-82.

The mortally wounded, formerly threatened person is now completely divested of our power by death. That is why it is apt when Niklas Luhmann refers to the exercise of physical violence as an expression of the failure – and not of the success – of power.[58]

At the same time, however, freedom also requires power. This is what Wolfgang Sofsky and Rainer Paris point out, noting that power extends the freedom of one person against another by protecting them from external attacks and helping the individual to maintain his or her own independence.[59] The component of freedom consists in being free from the arbitrariness of others, from threats of violence, from dependencies, etc. The political theorist Isaiah Berlin calls this aspect of freedom a *negative freedom*.[60] Freedom, in this understanding, is a social space of non-intervention around the individual person within which they can act autonomously and unaffected by the wishes and goals of others. The spectrum of activities thus protected ranges from the most trivial everyday activities, such as the decision to drink coffee black and sugar-free, to essential cultural rituals such as the practice of religion. The larger this space of non-intervention, the greater the freedom of the person. The smaller it is, the less the freedom – to the point where it is degraded to the mere preserve of others and all opportunities for autonomous action are lost. What is the foundation of this space? The simple answer is: power. Only when a person has the chance to assert his or her goals and interests against others can he or she assert this space of non-intervention and be, in Isaiah Berlin's terms, *negatively free*. Of course, this power to assert one's freedom does not have to lie *directly* with the individual themselves, for example in the sense of a Hobbesian anarchy in which everyone tries to accumulate as much power (physical strength, weapons, allies, resources, etc.) as possible so as not to fall prey to the arbitrariness of others. In a state with a monopoly of force, individuals have power, above all indirectly, insofar as they are holders of state-guaranteed rights that provide them with a space of non-intervention and in whose defense they can call public security forces. Nevertheless, it remains to be noted, without power – be it direct or indirect – individuals have no guarantee of their freedom.

Power presupposes freedom – and freedom, in turn, presupposes power. Both are mutually conditioning. This sounds almost too good to be true. And, of course, that is indeed the case. As we emphasized at the beginning, both are not just mu

---

58 Luhman, Niklas (1987): *Beiträge zur funktionalen Differenzierung der Gesellschaft*, Soziologische Aufklärung Vol. 4, Opladen: Westdeutscher Verlag.; p. 119.
59 Sofsky, Wolfgang and Paris, Rainer (1994): *Figurationen sozialer Macht. Autorität – Stellvertretung – Koalition,* Frankfurt am Main: Suhrkamp.; p. 9.
60 Cf. Berlin, Isiah (1969): *Two Concepts of Liberty.* Oxford: Oxford University Press.

tually conditioning, they also undermine each other. This can be well illustrated by Berlin's model of the non-intervention space. The larger the space within which a person can act on account of his or her direct or indirect power, the smaller the remaining space of freedom for others. Somewhat exaggerated, it can be said that the power-reinforced freedom of one means the bondage of the other. To its extreme, this idea unfolds in a dictatorship in which exactly one person – namely, the dictator – enjoys maximum negative freedom and, in return, all other persons, apart from a small power elite around the ruler perhaps, enjoy only minimal freedom or none at all. Power, inasmuch as it means an opportunity to control people, is always a threat to and a limitation on others' ability to act. If I am subject to the power of another, theoretically I can still choose not to obey his or her orders and bear the devastating consequences – even to the death penalty. This is what Sartre means by his idea of *radical freedom*.[61] However, in fact, this idea of radical freedom has little to do with what we commonly understand by the term. Because if certain options for action are associated with such devastating consequences that a rational person would choose them only under very few, special conditions, then they are *practically* deleted from my range of decisions. It remains true: my freedom of action is limited by the power of my fellow human beings, and the greater their power in relation to me, the more limited are my options for action.

This paradox that power and freedom condition and undermine each other can only be demonstrated. It is not solvable, but belongs to our basic constitution as social beings. We are left with the practical task of constantly and rationally weighing up and balancing between the two factors. However, the question of how to do this is no longer part of our list of basic principles of power. It falls into the field of applied political philosophy.

(3) The Omnipresence of Power

Power is omnipresent. That sounds like a dystopia of total control in the spirit of George Orwell or an outrageous conspiracy theory. Nevertheless, this misunderstanding of our third principle can be clarified right at the beginning. We are not saying that humans are subject to someone's power in all that they do or that all their actions are the result of being influenced by others or a super-personal social system. Rather, as Foucault states, power is omnipresent "not because it has the privilege of consolidating everything under its invincible unity, but because it is produced from one moment to the next, at every point, or rather in every relation from one point to another. Power is everywhere; not because it embraces every

---

61 Cf. Sartre ([1945] 2007).

thing, but because it comes from everywhere."[62] In short, power does not include everything, but it can be found in every aspect of our social existence.[63]

Even this thesis seems hardly plausible, at first. It would seem that there are many areas in our lives where we interact as free and equal human beings and without ever exercising power over one another. Deep friendships come to mind, or love relationships. But this view is somewhat naive. It is related to the fact that we often do not perceive and thematize power in its banal, everyday appearances, but rather when it comes to the supposedly big issues: politics, economics, war. In fact, love relationships and partnerships are a good example of the emergence of power relations. Let's say our partner has taken it upon herself to invite her parents to our home. Her parents are nice people, but they have the nasty habit of constantly interfering in everything, giving advice without being asked and knowing better than you how to do something in the household. In short, they are not exactly ideal guests. Still, our partner is not interested in hearing about this from us, and after some back and forth, it starts to emerge – perhaps only in the subtext and not actually spoken – that she will sleep in the guest bed for the next few days if the visitors are not allowed to come. In this constellation, this is nothing less than a power relationship: our partner controls the resources – the withholding of closeness and tenderness – to enforce her will against our resistance.

Now, in and of itself, this example might not indicate much, except that love relationships are not a good candidate for a power-free social space. Nonetheless, it still may raise doubts as to whether there is such a thing as genuinely power-free spaces. So, let's try to generalize. In this respect, it helps to recall Weber's dictum that power refers to every chance to assert one's interests against the resistance of others, no matter what this opportunity is based on.[64] Two things matter here. First, there is no area of social existence in which people have no interests. Whether leisure, work, sexuality, friendship, sports, politics, science or art, with regard to each of these fields we have desires and goals that can clash with just as many but differently oriented wishes and goals of others. Given the presence of these interests, on the one hand, and the possibility of their frustration by conflicting interests, on the other hand, the practical necessity of power arises – that is, the chance to enforce one's interests against resistance, as it were. Secondly, that

---

62 Foucault ([1984] 1990): p. 93.
63 Popitz, Heinrich (1992): *Phänomene der Macht,* 2nd edition, Tübingen: Mohr Siebeck.; p. 15. See also Popitz, Heinrich (2017): *Phenomena of Power: Authority, Domination, and Violence,* Andreas Göttlich and Jochen Dreher (eds.), translated by Gianfranco Poggi, New York: Columbia University Press.; p. 6.
64 Cf. Weber ([1921] 1978).

same chance, as Weber aptly states, can be based on every means imaginable. Above, we have already mentioned the withholding of closeness and tenderness. Other everyday examples include: the bad conscience which we impose upon friends if they do not come to a party; the praise we can give or withhold from employees, depending on how they do their job; the tip that we can pay a waiter, or not, depending on whether we are satisfied with the service. The examples can be continued endlessly. Everything can be used as a means of establishing power resources. In short, because, firstly, there is a need to acquire power in all areas of life and, second, because everything can be used as a means of power, power must be manifested in all areas of life. People have a natural inclination to realize their interests (hence their interests), and consequently they have a natural inclination to seize the resources necessary for their realization.

To be clear, we are not cynics who believe that humans enforce all their interests through power, and we also do not believe that all social relationships are always and exclusively power relations.[65] Such an extreme position is just as implausible as the belief in genuinely power-free social spaces. People also realize their interests by modifying the colliding interests of others with good arguments and establishing a rational agreement. And they are inclined to give up their own goals and wishes with just as much regularity, if other people can give them good reasons for doing so. The realization of interests through power is only one component of our social relations. However, it is nonetheless ubiquitous, as the above reasoning has indicated.

(4) The Natural Aspiration of Humankind for the Expansion and Intensification of Power

Human beings tend to expand and intensify their power. That is our fourth basic principle. There may be exceptions to this general principle, but nevertheless striving for power is a general anthropological fact. There are three reasons for this. The German historian Friedrich Meinecke eloquently, if in somewhat archaic language, addresses the first reason: "The striving for power is an aboriginal human impulse, perhaps even an animal impulse, which blindly snatches at everything around until it comes up against some external barriers. And, in the case of men at least, the impulse is not restricted solely to what is necessary for life and health. Man takes a wholehearted pleasure in power itself and, through it, in himself and

---

65 Such a pessimistic view is maintained by Hobbes ([1651] 1997).

his heightened personality."[66] Thus, that which drives human beings to acquire, expand and fortify power is initially nothing other than the desire for power itself. Of course, Meinecke was not the first observer to gain this insight. It can already be found in the annals of Tacitus, who recognized the significance of power as a stimulant par excellence, as the very mainspring of the Roman Empire.[67] But it is not just that we regard power as intrinsically pleasurable, that is, as pleasurable independent of its relation to other pleasurable goods. Friedrich Nietzsche points out that people feel great displeasure in powerlessness and experience the lack of power as something intrinsically painful.[68] As we strive not only to increase our pleasure, but also to avoid suffering, we have a twofold motivational reason to accumulate power.

People, however, also seek power because it is useful, and not just for the direct enforcement of interests. Power means social status. For example, Weber states that the pursuit of power is often conditioned by the "social 'honor' it brings."[69] The powerful are admired, respected, loved, feared. They experience anticipatory obedience without ever having to use their power – and those who hope to benefit from their power seek their proximity.[70]

That power is indispensable in order to enforce one's interests against conflicting interests in all areas of life has already been emphasized in the discussion of the third basic principle. At this point, however, it is worth pointing out that from this perspective, maximizing power is the only instrumentally rational option. Hobbes, more than just about any other political theorist, has pointed to this fact with great clarity and ruthlessness. Humans, according to Hobbes, cannot help striving for more power, because they cannot secure their present power and fortify the means to attaining and maintaining a pleasant life without the acquisition

---

66 Meinecke, Friedrich ([1957] 1998): *Machiavellism: The Doctrine of Raison D'État and Its Place in Modern History,* translated by Douglas Scott, introduction by Werner Stark, New Brunswick, N.J. : Transaction Publishers.; p. 4.
67 Tacitus, Cornelius (1996): *The Annals of Imperial Rome,* translated by Michael Grant (ed.), London: Penguin.
68 See Nietzsche, Friedrich ([1844-1845] 1968): *The Will to Power,* translated by Walter Kaufmann and Reginald J. Hollingdale (eds.), New York: Vintage Books.
69 Weber ([1921] 1978): p. 386; see also p. 539.
70 According to Heinrich Popitz, this indeed represents a decisive characteristic of authoritative power. Cf. Popitz (1992): p. 29. Furthermore, Chapter 2.1 offers an in-depth assessment.

of additional power.[71] Behind this consideration is the idea that people, when they are content with a certain, limited amount of resources, run the risk of being supplanted by others. The constant threat to personal action spaces and standards of living sets in motion a race for power in which all actors seek to maximize their power resources. Now, let's point out that Hobbes limits this dictum to an anarchic state of nature and sees the race for power as preferably culminating with the establishment of a state. Nevertheless, such a restriction ignores the fact that even within a state community that guarantees us specific legal protection we can – and must – compete for power, ideally not with armed force but by virtue of economic, cultural and political means. Still, the competition for power, thus our sobering interim conclusion, is not actually over with the establishment of the state. No, not at all – the competition simply acquires rules governing – and ostensibly guaranteeing – its furtherance.

(5) The Basis of Power in the Vulnerability and the Neediness of Humankind

From an anthropological perspective, power has two universal roots: humankind's vulnerability and neediness. Popitz addresses the first root of power by stating that people can exercise power over others because they can hurt others.[72] As we have already emphasized in the discussion of Gehlen's anthropology, humans have no natural defense mechanisms, which renders them especially open to physical attacks. The possibilities for injury, and the imagination with which people have cultivated their development, are almost limitless. The human body can be hurt, tortured, mutilated and killed. The superior ability of one to injure another – whether through greater physical strength, agility, practice, weapons or cunning – gives rise to power over the other person. The credible threat of bodily injury allows the enforcement of one person's will against the other's resistance. If people were not defined by this characteristic vulnerability, they would be powerless in the truest sense of the word. They would not have to be afraid of experiencing

---

71 Concretely, Hobbes ([1651] 1997: p. 80) notes: "[...] in the first place, I put forth a general inclination of all mankind, a perpetual and restless desire of power after power, that ceaseth only in death. And the cause of this, is not always that a man hopes for a more intense delight, than he has already attained to; or that he cannot be content with a moderate power: but because he cannot assure the power and means to live well, which he hath present, without the acquisition of more".

72 Literally: "*Menschen können über andere Macht ausüben, weil sie andere verletzen können*". Popitz (1992): p. 25.

physical suffering or of their existence being wiped out, and they would not be forced to bow to the will of another.

The second root of power is that human beings are driven in their thoughts and actions by innumerable needs that others can use to exercise power against them. The spectrum ranges from basic needs for food and sleep to cultivated inclinations towards fine wines, expensive drugs or exquisite art. Common to all of these needs is that their fulfillment is conducive or even essential to the well-being of the person concerned, and that their frustration, depending on the intensity of the need, can result in grave suffering. The more needs a person has, the more diverse is the potential gain in pleasure, but also the dependence on others who can deny them. In short, people's neediness places them in the power of others. The Greek and Roman Stoics already became aware of the fatal connection between power and need in pre-Christian times. According to this school of thought, the key to bliss – the so-called *Eudaimonia* – lies in the virtue of modesty and detachment from one's own needs. Only if we give up our inclinations and focus on asceticism can we escape dependency on others and live an autonomous life. Meanwhile, contemporaries of the Stoics like the ethicist Epicurus pointed out the self-abasement and rejection of pleasure involved in such an approach to life. Epicurus doubted whether a self-sufficient but joyless life is worth living at all. Besides, there are certain basic needs that we just cannot shake off – like food. Thus, even the ascetic can still be threatened with the deprivation of means of subsistence and be forced to submit to the will of another. In conclusion, we can say that by minimizing our needs we can strive to assert our independence from the power of others – but each one of us remains, just by virtue of our basic human needs, subject to power.

(6) The Purposive Production of Power

Power relations are not a natural phenomenon such as, for example, the law of gravity. They are instead – according to our fifth principle – cultural artifacts, which arise through purposeful human action and can also be destroyed or changed again. The sociologist Henrich Popitz asserts that the belief that power arrangements are the products of human agency was already one of the cornerstones of the Greek *polis*.[73] There, for the first time in the history of civilization, the political order of human coexistence was regarded as being configurable, changeable – and was not understood as something God-given or inviolable.[74] Plato's *Politeia* is exemplary for this in that his objective here is to develop the

---

73 Popitz (1992): p. 12., with original accentuation: "*Glaube an die* Machbarkeit *von Machtordnungen*". See also Popitz (2017): p. 3.
74 Popitz (1992): p.12.

principles of a just social order and use them as a critical standard of assessment for existing conditions.[75] Only if one assumes that the distribution and organization of power is something that can be changed on the basis of rational insight, does it makes sense at all to advocate a better order of power. The political core concept of the reform and its more radical equivalent, the revolution, thus directly presuppose that power arrangements are 'made'.

At the same time, the purposive production of power results in the categorical obligation to justify it. If power relations between individuals are not God-given or ordained by nature but are configurable, they must, so Popitz, also be justified in the light of the reasonable interests of the persons concerned. This conviction, which has shaped our thinking about power since antiquity, finds its clearest expression in the classical contract theory of political philosophy. The argumentative starting point is that any social power relations are justified only if they are affirmed in a hypothetical decision scenario by a group of free and equal persons. First, because power is made by human beings, and secondly because it must serve the people's well-being. It thus follows that it must have its normative foundation in the (at least hypothetical) consent of these people. Since the heyday of contract theory in the seventeenth and eighteenth centuries, our faith in and enthusiasm for the limitless configurability of just orders of power have clearly diminished, in particular thanks to the great machinations and power experiments of utopian state systems such as realist socialism. Nevertheless, Popitz maintains that the certainty of being able to do things differently, to do things better, is not affected by this.[76] The scope of what is feasible may be more limited than the pioneers of political theory would presume. However, this does not change the fact that power is made and can be made differently and better.

(7) The Institutionalization of Power

Because power is purposively produced, it can not only be amassed by individuals or groups, but also institutionalized. This is our seventh basic principle. Power has, in other words, the potential for consolidation in the form of social structures – ranging from ritualized dependencies between individual rulers and their subordinates to the establishment of complex state power structures. According to Popitz, three institutionalization tendencies or lines of development can be identified: depersonalization, formalization and integration.

---

75 Plato (2006): *The Republic,* translated by R.E. Allen (ed.), New Haven: Yale University Press.
76 Popitz (1992): p. 15.

With the concept of *depersonalization,* Popitz understands power as being detached from a concrete person and transferred to an abstract social position. That is to say, an individual only holds power in this configuration if he or she has a certain position or office recognized by the members of the group. The individual's power ceases when he or she leaves the position or is forced to resign. Such offices and positions have – and this is of particular importance – no proper names registered to them, but by definition are open to the person who can fill them.

Formalization, on the other hand, refers to the detachment of power from the arbitrariness of an individual person or group in favor of a regulation of the use of that power. Formalized power relations are characterized by a dense network of standards of action and competence. These not only determine who has power over whom in relation to what, but also provide sanctions for those who use or extend their power beyond the established rules.

Finally, the *integration* of power refers to the situation whereby the exercising, distribution and accumulation of power become part of an overarching social order, thereby experiencing legitimate institutionalization and consolidation. It thus becomes an integral part of a political doctrine and a social model encompassing the most diverse areas of society.

For all three elements, the stronger they manifest themselves, the more institutionalized is power. And as the institutionalization of power increases, so does its reach, effectiveness, and constancy. Depersonalization, formalization and integration, as the sociologist Peter Imbusch notes, bring about an increase in stability and thus also a safeguarding of power which is consolidated in the institutionalization process and correspondingly difficult to undo.[77] In short, institutionalized power is not only characterized by being linked to a greater chance of successful enforcement and to a larger group of people than non-institutionalized power. It is also – once it has been established – very difficult to abolish.

How the degree of institutionalization of power can be exactly quantified or even just classified is a notoriously difficult question. Popitz proposes five levels that allow a general classification. The first stage is that of *sporadic power.* This is limited to an individual case, the repetition of which is not expected. Sporadic power manifests itself in a series of actions – often violent ones – that can be coordinated but are not aimed at establishing inter-temporal power relations. A striking historical example is provided by the raids of the unified Mongol tribes

---

77 Imbusch, Peter (2007): Macht: Dimensionen und Perspektiven eines Phänomens, in: Klaus-Dieter Altmeppen, Thomas Hanitzsch, and Carsten Schlüter (eds.), *Journalismustheorie: Next Generation. Soziologische Grundlegung und theoretische Innovation*, Wiesbaden: Springer, pp. 395-419.; p. 410.

under Genghis Khan in Eastern Europe in 1220.[78] The Mongol cavalry offered the European princes a show of power beyond compare, using tactical agility and superior bows and arrows to decimate the armies of knights and then murdering and plundering their way through the countryside. But Khan's hordes never expanded their power in Eastern Europe in the form of depersonalized and formalized social structures, preferring to return to Central Asia after their successful forays.

The second level of institutionalization is that of *normative power*. Compared to the first stage, it distinguishes itself by the fact that the ruler deliberately normalizes the behavior of the power-subjects, thus subjecting them to rules of action that are effective in the most diverse spheres of life, such as the economy, religion or sexuality. This allows the ruler to enforce behavioral regularities that persist even when those under power are not exposed to any acute threat of violence. Individual behavior becomes predictable. At this stage, deference has become normatively consolidated.[79] The advantage for the ruler is obvious. If there are codified and universally recognized rules of behavior, then the effort required to control behavior is much less than if the ruler always needs to issue new commands. The standardization of power therefore conforms to the requirements of efficiency. Paradigmatic for this stage of power institutionalization are the early stages of colonization by expanding states – be it the Roman Empire or the European nation states of modern times. They all share the goal of not only economically exploiting a conquered territory in the short term, like the armies of Genghis Khan, but of efficiently controlling it over the long term. For this purpose, normative power and the associated standards are indispensable.

The third and, according to Imbusch's assessment, most important stage is that of the *positioning of power*. It marks the transition from merely socially consolidated power to actual rule. Characteristic of this stage is the establishment of "supra-personal superiority."[80] Of relevance here are the aforementioned social positions – offices – with which concrete powers and competencies are linked but whose concrete owners are interchangeable. Positionalized power that is decoupled from the individual person allows rulers to determine successors and deputies, and thus to extend the continued existence of power beyond their deaths. The advantage of this level of institutionalization lies in its continuity and stability. Its historical roots are undoubtedly located in the institution of dynastic succession. In this case a person, as a member of a noble family, inherits the office of the

---

78 Cf. Marshall, Robert (1993): *Storm from the East. From Ghengis Khan to Khubilai Khan,* Berkeley: University of California Press.; pp. 90-117.
79 Popitz (1992): p. 44. Literally: *"[... Fügsamkeit normativ verfestigt]"*.
80 Popitz (2017): p. 95.

previous monarch, thus preserving the order of power. The seemingly paradoxical slogan "The king is dead, long live the king" expresses the basic principle of positionalized power like no other.

The fourth stage is characterized by the emergence of *positional structures of domination* or, less technically speaking, power apparatuses. At this stage, social positions are formed around the institution of the ruler; these in turn have independent powers of authority and control. On the one hand, this structure enables a form of division of labor in which the various public officials can specialize in specific fields of power, such as the military, economy, religion or politics.[81] This will further increase the efficiency gained through the normalization of power. On the other hand, it also ensures reciprocal control of the different social positions and, if necessary, the exchange of office-holders, if these prove to be incompetent. With *state rule,* the fifth and final stage of the institutionalization of power has been reached. Here a power apparatus – that is, a specialized structure of powerful social positions held by concrete persons – has succeeded in enforcing "monopoly claims on a demarcated territory, which extend to all three classical normative functions: legislation (legal norm), jurisdiction (monopolies over sanctions) and execution of norms (including the monopoly of violence)."[82] These central state functions do not have to be distinguished from one another in the form of a traditional, triplex separation of powers. They can also be gathered in the hands of a technocratic party elite or a clerical caste. Crucially however, the only significant difference between state rule and all other forms of institutionalized power is the unrivaled and successful claim to the performance of these functions by a power apparatus. This routinization of centralized territorial domination, as Popitz notes, creates considerable social constraints for the individual.[83] On the other hand, however, it also provides those ordering functions that are indispensable to our modern existence.

This concludes our listing of the principles of power. We have determined which logic the general phenomenon of power follows and which universal laws it is subject to or, in short, how power works. However, the question remains as to what consequences arise from these insights for us as human beings. We will now turn to this topic.

---

81 See Chapter 2.2 for more in-depth coverage of the power field.
82 Popitz (2017): p. 184.
83 Popitz (1992): p. 64.

1.3. HUMANKIND, POWER AND HISTORY – FOLLOW-UP QUESTIONS

At the beginning of the previous section, we stated that the nature of power necessarily depends on the nature of humankind. Power is an irreducible social phenomenon that exists only in and through interactive relationships between persons. Without people, there is no power. However, the converse is also true. Because humans are by nature social beings, they are constantly exposed to and must also deal with power. No one has so concisely encapsulated this insight as Aristotle with his *zoon politikon*, a political animal.[84] This designation signifies, firstly, that humankind instinctively aspires to fellowship and has been accordingly striving for organization into groups throughout world history. People share this characteristic, as Aristotle notices rather humorously, for instance, with bees. However, secondly and more crucially, the Aristotelian statement means that human beings cannot be thought of as detached from a cooperative community in which they are embedded. Our needs and goals, indeed our entire self-image, are constituted by communal ties. No matter what role and function we attribute to ourselves – whether father, manager, tennis player, environmental activist, model airplane maker or Catholic – we always assume a social context that gives meaning to our self-description. Any attempt to conceptually separate individuals from social ties in order to determine what they are 'in themselves' can only end in abstract and uninformative anthropology.[85]

---

[84] Mulgan, Richard (1974): Aristotle's Doctrine That Man Is a Political Animal, *Hermes*, 102 (3), pp. 438-445.; Papadis, Dimitris (2006): Is Man by Nature a Political and Good Animal, According to Aristotle?, *Phronimon*, 7 (1), pp. 21-33.; and Miller, Fred (2011): Aristotle's Political Theory, in: Edward N. Zalta (ed.), *Stanford Encyclopedia of Philosophy*, [online] https://plato.stanford.edu/archives/win2017/entries/aristotle-politics/, retrieved on 21.12.2017. Yu (2005) points out that this opinion is hardly restricted to Hellenistic or even Western schools of thought. Similar consideration, although differing in detail, may also be found in Confucianism. Cf. Yu, Jiyuan (2005): Confucius' Relational Self and Aristotle's Political Animal, *History of Philosophy Quarterly*, 22 (4), pp. 281-300.

[85] Accordingly, the economic and social scientific ideal of humankind as *homo oeconomicus*, i.e. as a socially unbound and instrumentally rational utility maximizer, is not only an ethically questionable but above all an extraordinarily weak explanation. See thereto Taylor, Charles (1989): *Sources of the Self: The Making of the Modern Identity*, Cambridge: Cambridge University Press.

Still, these social contexts and attachments, as we noted in the last section, are always permeated by power. Within the social field, power is ubiquitous. It manifests itself in friendships as well as in love relationships, in sports and in children's education. This leads to the following conclusion: (a) because humans are social beings, (b) and because the realm of the social is inextricably linked with power, (c) humankind is inescapably exposed to power. Of course, in the history of global civilization, people have never submitted to this fate without resistance. The most influential strategy of resistance can be found in Buddhism and Christian mysticism, as in the teachings of Meister Eckhart: the overcoming of (earthly) power through the dissolution of the self.[86] The radicalness of the idea cannot be overestimated. The individual can only shed the shackles of worldly existence and cease to be the object of others' power by overcoming his or her personal perspective on the natural and social environment through strict meditation, asceticism or hermitic retreat, it is argued. However, this is not a question of erasing the phenomenon of power, but of achieving a spiritual state of absolute emptiness and letting go, as it were, arriving in a domain in which power no longer matters because there is no longer a personal entity that is subject to it. Buddhism refers to this state as *Nirvana* or the *Pure Land*.[87]

At this point, we encounter an obvious intersection with the ancient life philosophy of the Stoics, as discussed in Chapter 1.2. Similar to Buddhism and some schools of Christian mysticism, the Stoics understand our earthly, spatio-temporal existence as a sphere of dependence, inadequacy, suffering, greed, and misguided needs that must be negated and overcome. The attraction of this way of thinking continues to this day, and we would hardly be inclined to speak pejoratively of or disparage it. Nevertheless, it is clear that a lifestyle of world renunciation is not a realistic option for everybody, not even for the majority of people. For most of us, our status as a *zoon politikon*, as a worldly and socially bound being, is not a burden, but an opportunity offering fulfillment. The consistent dissolution of the self does not seem to be a form of salvation, but instead an existential threat to all that is dear to us: familial and friendly ties, professional success, physical and mental

---

[86] Meister Eckhart (1260 - 1328) was a German theologian, Dominican philosopher and spiritual master who gained prominence during the Avignon Papacy and was ultimately tried as a suspected heretic. Cf. Hackett, Jeremiah M. (2013): *A Companion to Meister Eckhart,* Leiden: Brill.

[87] Regarding the Buddhistic concept of the Pure Land, see Bando, Shojun (1973): Jesus Christus und Amida. Zu Karl Barths Verständnis des Buddhismus vom Reinen Land, in: Yagi Seiichi and Ulrich Luz (eds.), *Gott in Japan: Anstöße zum Gespräch mit japanischen Philosophen, Theologen, Schriftstellern.* Munich: Kaiser, pp. 72-93.; p. 73.

enjoyment and, last but not least, the consciousness of ourselves as distinct persons with specific characters, our own biographies, likes, dislikes, values and persuasions. For those who are unwilling or unable to pay this price then, the problem of power remains. Since power is an inseparable part of our (worldly) existence, there is no point in worrying about how to get rid of it. Instead, we need to better understand how it manifests itself in concrete terms, how we deal with it, how we shape and legitimize it. Here, it is helpful to recall the discussion of the principles of power and to formulate questions from this position:

1. The phenomena of power are ubiquitous and diverse – but what are their specific shapes and forms, and how can the social fields in which they occur be classified?
2. Power must be justified – but how do we concretely legitimize it?
3. Power can be purposively produced – but how? What are the resources and techniques by which we gain, consolidate, multiply and exercise power, and how can they be used successfully?

With these questions, of course, we depart the sphere of general definition and enter into the domain of the concrete community with its historically contingent, religious, economic and political practices and habits. We turn our attention to the social concretions of power. This focus on power as a historically concrete, mutable phenomenon is indispensable because the relationship between humankind and power can only be experienced in the temporal-spatial dimension of historicity. In other words, every figuration of power is always the power of a concrete person or group in the historical context of their respective community. The talk of power *sui generis* is only an abstraction of this historically concrete form of our existence. In order to understand the phenomenon of power, we must therefore take into account the *existential challenges* that arise from the historicity of our existence. The discussion of these challenges introduces, as it were, the following chapter, Chapter 2, which is dedicated to the concretions of power.

The *first* existential challenge can be summarized in a simple slogan: *everything is changeable*. Every phenomenon in space and time is – within the parameters of logic, of the laws of nature and of the principles of power outlined in Chapter 1.2 – subject to continuous and sometimes dramatic transformation processes. Powerful states, such as the Roman Empire or the Achaemenid Empire, develop and disintegrate over a period of centuries; influential religions, such as Mithraism, suddenly fall into oblivion, while at the same time Christianity experiences a global ascent; seemingly incontestable forms of rule, such as the absolute monarchy, are swept away in revolutionary fury within a few days; technological innovations, such as the internet, turn understandings of communication and information on their heads within a generation. The changeability of the political, economic, religious, technological, and not least also of the natural world of humankind thus makes up the core of what we call history.

This insight is as old as occidental philosophy itself. It already resounds in the writings of the great pre-Socratic thinker Heraclitus, to whom the saying *panta rhei* (Greek: "all things flow") is attributed.[88] Heraclitus, however, does not mean that our natural and social environment is completely chaotic or so fluid that any orientation and planning becomes impossible. Indeed he insists, as the historian of philosophy Marcel van Ackeren notes, that change is by no means so disordered that everything is always and in all respects subject to change, a condition which would lead to nothing being identifiable.[89] Our existence is, consciously or unconsciously, rather in a field of tension of constants and variances. Consequently, the practical challenge for humankind is to predict *which aspects* of the natural and social environment change in *which way* and to decide what influence they themselves can and will have on these transformation processes. This *conditio humana* is a double-edged sword. On the one hand, it constitutes humankind as being capable of shaping their existence. On the other hand, it brings with it a constant uncertainty about the future, and thus the fear of loss for what has been achieved and the burden of assuming responsibility.[90]

In relation to the phenomenon of power, the changeability of our lifeworld first and foremost means that power may always be lost (but may also be gained). No ruler is inviolable, no state order is guaranteed perpetuity, no political alliance is set in stone forever, no power resource is inexhaustible. From this circumstance arises the necessity of a *strategic use* of power. Power actors must always align their actions with probabilistic goal-means-environment calculations that take into account the variability of their decision-making context; otherwise they run the risk of being outmaneuvered by other actors or being overwhelmed by changes in their environment (for discussion of the concept of strategy, see Chapters 2.5.2 and 3.3.1). In other words, those wanting to exercise power in a constantly changing environment face the challenge of predicting the behavior of their opponents

---

88 The pre-Socratic thinker Heraclitus is for Plato the "theorist of universal flux". Cf. Kahn, Charles H. (2008): *Art and Thought of Heraclitus,* Cambridge: Cambridge University Press.; p. 4.

89 van Ackeren, Marcel (2006): *Heraklit: Vielfalt und Einheit seiner Philosophie,* Bern: Peter Lang.; p. 107.

90 In more contemporary times, both aspects have been cultivated most notably in the philosophy of existentialism. See Sartre ([1945] 2007).

and allies as well as the development and effectiveness of their own means of power, in order to use these predictions to define their goals. Only through strategy does the changeability of the natural and social world become (at least partially) manageable. So anyone who does not plan the use of power and is only guided by instinct, will become the plaything of the Heraclitian concept *panta rhei*.

The very notion of strategic planning, however, also presupposes a concept of time as a manageable resource that can be used to one's advantage and that can be compartmentalized and measured in discrete units.[91] Once power actors conceive human history not as cyclical, i.e. as an eternal recurrence of the same states of affairs, but rather as linear and directed towards a future that is yet indeterminate, does strategy – understood as a probabilistic endeavor – fully come to its fruition. This is by no means trivial as historians such as Reinhart Koselleck and Hans Ulrich Gumbrecht have made abundantly clear:[92] In different cultures and eras, time has always been experienced and described differently, the relationship between past, present and future being sometimes conceived as one of cosmic continuity and sometimes as teleological connectedness or indeed characterized by caesuras and fractures. Historically speaking, then, the universal concept of one singular time that passes according to the same constant and universal laws for all peoples and cultures is relatively new and the outcome of global Western influence in the nineteenth century. Considering the fact that time is not an objective given as such, but culturally malleable, it is only natural that actors have also sought to utilize it directly as a power resource by introducing new calendars or changing the number of weekdays, e.g. during the French Revolution or Stalin's reign in the Soviet Union. Following Christopher Clark, we may label this specific power technique chrono politics.[93] In a way, chrono politics is a variant of technical power as described in section 2.1 in that it affects people's lives via technological means (such as metrical measurements and standardization) and forces them to adapt their habits or modes of production to new rhythms and tempos.

---

91 Cf. Clark, Christopher (2019): *Time and Power Visions of History in German Politics, from the Thirty Years' War to the Third Reich*, Princeton/Oxford: Princeton University Press.

92 Cf. Koselleck, Reinhart (2004): *Futures Past: On the Semantics of Historical Time. Series: Studies in Contemporary German Social Thought*, translated and with an introduction by Keith Tribe, New York: Columbia University Press.; and Gumbrecht, Hans Ulrich (2004): *Production of Presence: What Meaning Cannot Convey*, Stanford: Stanford University Press.

93 Cf. Clark (2019): p. 6.

The *second* challenge to humans in the context of their historical existence is: *everything has its price*. This does not mean, of course, that every act and every object may be monetized or that every person can be bought. We understand the term 'costs' rather in the widest possible sense – that is, as an acceptance of risks, losses and (negative) consequences. Accordingly, the principle states that all the merits and achievements of humankind are always linked to an (implicit) balancing of goods, considerable effort, a conscious sacrifice or renunciation.[94]

At first glance, this principle hardly seems tenable in its generality. Throughout human history, there have always been persons or groups to whom certain benefits and privileges have been conferred by birth or happy coincidence; benefits and privileges that others do not enjoy. Anyone born in the fifth century B.C. into the small group of the male citizens of Athens – and not into the much larger group of slaves and metics (resident foreigners without civil rights) – could make use of all the rights of Europe's first direct democracy. Those who belonged to the aristocracy in the Middle Ages or the modern era not only possessed exponentially more political and economic power than the rural population, but also enjoyed a higher life expectancy thanks to better medical care and a lower workload. A look at the present finally shows us a blatant discrepancy between the standards of living and the legal security of the industrialized and developing countries. Is not the absurdity of the principle 'everything has its price' revealed by these unearned – i.e. not acquired by achievement – privileges of whole nations?

However, a second, closer look shows a more nuanced picture, which also allows us to further sharpen the principle and its meaning. Let's start with the example of the medieval and modern European nobility. A central characteristic of this class is the understanding aptly outlined with the well-known dictum *"Noblesse oblige"* ("nobility obligates"). Behind this is the habitualized conviction that the aristocracy's supremacy is accompanied by exclusive obligations to the general public: exemplary behavior in all areas of life, a strict code of honor, charity towards the needy, constant readiness for military defense of the state and so on. The dictum *"Noblesse oblige"* thus means that the privileges of the peerage have a 'price', namely the fulfillment of exclusive social functions – connected with a specific life ideal. Now, it is clearly ludicrous to claim that in European history all members of the peerage fulfilled these requirements at all times. But such an admission misses the point: privileges, goods, resources, achievements,

---

[94] Cf. Flaig, Egon (2017): *Die Niederlage der politischen Vernunft. Wie wir die Errungenschaften der Aufklärung verspielen,* Springe: zu Klampen. Thereby, Flaig addresses the decline in political reason, arguing that man is squandering the achievements of the Enlightenment.

etc. do not exist in a vacuum, but are always and necessarily linked to specific social interactive relationships, anticipations, role models, and cost-benefit calculations. The one is never without the other.[95]

We can easily extend this conclusion that everything has its price, as understood above, to other areas: those who enjoy public attention and prestige must cultivate their reputation and accept that each of their actions and statements will be judged based on the proverbial gold scale; those who receive rich gifts from benefactors and friends are bound to gratitude and reciprocity; anyone seeking political, economic, artistic or scientific success must be willing to sacrifice other spheres of life, interests and, not infrequently, personal ties; and whoever strives for power in its various forms must learn to live with envy and adversaries. One might think that is only possible to break out of this paradigm through a lack of ambition, through a conscious unwillingness to will, as it were. Such a conclusion, however, would be deceptive. Even powerlessness costs something. Anyone who consciously renounces power as the potential for asserting their own interests against external resistance quickly becomes a plaything in the power of others. The attempted escape from the paradigm of "everything has its price" does not lead to freedom, but leads directly to the loss of autonomy.

Like the principle that everything is changeable, the principle that everything has its price is a *conditio humana,* a human condition. This has two practical consequences. Firstly, people at all times and in all cultural contexts face the task of identifying the price of the goods they have or seek. Secondly, they question whether they will pay the price and, if they do not want to, what alternatives to their current goals exist. Not only individuals have to face this problem. Especially in the context of political power, the cost issue is a continuous challenge for entire

---

[95] This insight is found in very different versions in all cultures. It culminates in a great, metaphysically far-reaching form in the principle of karma, which we know from the reincarnation religions of Hinduism and Buddhism. In a nutshell, this principle says that every one of our actions – that is, morally good as well as bad – is directly related to our own well-being. Every wrongdoing will be compensated in the mid-term (either in this life or in the next) by an evil suffered, every good action will result in a benefit. Thus, the principle of karma extends the principle of "everything has its price" to the ethical sphere by postulating a strict law of equivalency: everything we do has its ethical price and everything that comes back to us is well deserved. For a compact discussion of the karma principle and its moral-philosophical implications, see Kaufman, Whitley (2007): Karma, Rebirth, and the Problem of Evil: a Reply to Critics, *Philosophy East and West,* 57 (4), pp. 559-560.

states and their leadership elites. Of course, this question can only be repeatedly raised and clarified temporarily, but never finally settled.

The third challenge is: *not everything is achievable.* In Chapter 1.2, we have already emphasized that humankind is characterized by neediness, whereby actions are driven by natural inclinations (food, safety, closeness, etc.) and cultivated preferences (for exquisite wines, good books, expensive cars, new electronics, etc.). It is this characteristic, along with vulnerability, that exposes humankind to power. However, as the historian and political theorist Egon Flaig notes, there is another fundamental problem, that people's desires, however culturally oriented, tend to be insatiable.[96] The satisfaction of an inclination regularly initiates the formation of another inclination whose scope and fulfillment exceeds that of the previous one. On the other hand, this potentially infinite expansion of our range of needs is offset by a finite set of unevenly distributed resources. The result is that human needs remain continuously unfulfilled, frustrated. This *conditio humana* has – in general terms – two central effects: on the one hand, the unsatisfiability of their desires drives people to continuous innovation and stimulates inventiveness and entrepreneurship. Instead of accepting, e.g., a meager harvest that does not meet the nutritional needs of the community, grains are crossed in order to achieve higher yields in later years. Instead of accepting that the high production costs of a commodity make it attractive only to a small group of consumers, the manufacturing process is optimized so that new and less affluent buyers can be found. The history of humanity is a history of continuous increases in the efficiency and effectiveness of needs satisfaction against the background of finite resources. However, as Flaig recognizes, the principle of the unsatisfiability of all human desires is also a source of deprivation and disadvantage, of dissatisfaction and misfortune.[97] Even if we continuously optimize the process of satisfying needs through technology and cultural creation, we face a two-fold problem, first, that wishes grow along with improvements in this process and, second, that the all-round, fair – and ideally even global – satisfaction of all human needs is fundamentally utopian. The result of this is seen in continuous distribution struggles within and between communities, up to and including military conflicts. The key currency of these conflicts between individuals, classes and nations is, of course, power. The unfulfillability of desires cumulates in the struggle for influence.

However, this guiding theme, the phenomenon of power, represents a special case in this context. Unlike other objects of human inclination (knowledge, money, food, clothing, etc.), power is divisible but in its totality not enlargeable –

---

96 Cf. Flaig, Egon (2017): p. 46.
97 Ibid.: p. 47.

that is, it is a constant good. Accordingly, the pursuit of power is always associated with a zero-sum game. The power of one is the impotence of another. What I gain in power, someone else has lost. There is no cultural technique and no technology to optimize the satisfaction of the natural striving of humankind for power (discussed in Chapter 1.2) – at least not in the sense of an increase in the total.

The only thing which can be optimized is the ability of competing actors to succeed in this zero-sum game. As we discuss in Chapter 2, these techniques of power are highly specific to the social fields (religion, economics, politics, etc.) involved. At this point, however, we do not intend to anticipate, but only to summarize the conclusion. In a world of scarce, unequally distributed resources, the insatiable needs of humankind not only lead to the optimization of needs satisfaction but also to distributional struggles, and consequently to a struggle for power; and since power is a constant good, human efforts for optimization concentrate here on techniques and means in the struggle for power itself. The practical challenge is obvious: those who want to prevail or win in zero-sum games are forced to constantly evaluate and innovate their means of power. Standstill means defeat.

Finally, the fourth and final existential challenge that runs throughout the history of humankind is that *everything strives for meaning*. For some of our readers, this may appear to be an esoteric category overburdened with ponderous content and pathos. And indeed, associations with a philosophical and theological grand scheme, the meaning of life, are almost inevitable.[98] The principle which we have introduced, however, is not in danger of getting into these deep waters. It merely focuses on the central fact that we humans have always been asking ourselves and others why-questions, not only in search of explanations (Why do magnetic needles point north? Why do the stars in the sky change with the seasons? Why do people follow a herding instinct?), but also so-called normative why-questions (Why should we honor father and mother? Why should we exercise and keep fit? Why should we study the history of our community? Why should we pay taxes? Why should we have a democratic form of government?). The latter questions call for convincing reasoning and, unlike explanatory why-questions, this requires more than adequately addressing cause-and-effect relationships in our natural and social environment. We have to show what kind of justification there is for democracy or parental respect. If this cannot be found, the corresponding conventions, the norms and forms of order, are proved meaningless to us. And they lose their obligatory nature.

---

98 For a refreshingly unpretentious and well-written treatment of this topic, see Nagel, Thomas (1987): *What Does It All Mean?*, New York/Oxford: Oxford University Press.

The pursuit of meaning and justification, both in shaping our social order and in personal life projects and relationships, is an integral part of our anthropological constitution. It shapes the way we interact with each other, how we organize ourselves, and what demands we place on our communities. And accordingly, it also covers all areas of human life, from business and politics to sports, art and culture. Meaningfulness has an indisputable motivational force comparable to that of inclinations, positive and negative incentives, and authoritative attachments. If people regard a goal or a project as meaningful, they will seek, at least for the most part, to realize and defend it. If they classify it as meaningless, as barren of any justification and legitimacy, it will be virtually impossible to motivate them (without extrinsic incentives) for support and cooperation.

The demanding and searching for meaning has a consequence for the phenomenon of power, one which has already been implied in the discussion concerning the purposive production of power (see Chapter 1.2). The acceptance of power, be it the power of a head of government, football coaches, a church leader or a CEO, requires those subjugated to the power to recognize it as meaningful. Put simply, if power makes no sense, it lacks (intrinsic) motivational force. It has to rely on coercion. As we discuss in detail in Chapter 2.5.2 in our discussion of justification, however, such a constellation of power – especially in the area of political rule – is unstable. Power requires a justification. What is more, as we shall see, it needs a plausible understanding of the social world, based on shared history and common values and symbols.

The critical question of what gives meaning to our actions, our bonds and our communities has been answered in various ways through history. However, a central role has often – indeed, almost always – been played by religion, which is discussed as an independent field of power in Chapter 2.2.1. Religions provide sense by postulating a transcendent sphere beyond our natural senses which is populated by a deity or a pantheon, which is not only the source of moral values but which also embodies and defines a salvatory history of the world. By virtue of its capacity to satisfy the basic human need for meaning and at the same time to legitimize social forms of order and norms, religion is an almost unrivaled source of power. Therefore, it is not surprising that alternative paradigms providing human meaning, such as the Enlightenment or socialism, have always worked on religious models of reason and have even sometimes adopted religious logic systems and mindsets. Precisely because the pursuit of meaning is central to the justification of power, the struggles over it are among the most vehemently ideological battles in history. These give the following chapter a decisive, substantial foundation.

At this point, we wish to conclude our overview of the challenges and questions that shape the relationship between humankind, power and history. We now redeem the promises initially made and look at the concretions of power in order to clarify which forms it assumes, in which fields it occurs, what logic it follows there – and finally, how it is exercised and legitimized.

2. The Concretions of Power

How and where does power become concrete? With these two interrelated questions we delineate the basic forms of power, their most important social fields and conditions of legitimacy as well as their resources and instruments. After discussing the essence of power in the last chapter, this chapter focuses on the phenomenology of power. Since we not only classify and systematize the phenomena here, but also show how power is concretely legitimized and controlled, this section of the book is, so to speak, the hinge between the theory and the practice of power.

2.1 FORMS OF POWER

No other theoretician has systematized the heterogeneous field of forms and manifestations of power with such clarity as Popitz in his classic *Phenomena of Power*.[1] According to Popitz, every power phenomenon – irrespective of its historical and social context – can be classified in one of the following basic categories, with corresponding forms of action: the power of action, instrumental power, authoritative power and technical power.

The *power of action* refers to the ability of a person or group of people to perform actions that harm other people. Popitz regards this as the most direct form of power, and simultaneously the oldest as well, as it has been evident throughout the history of the exercising of human power.[2] The range of possibilities for injury, based on the characteristic vulnerability of humankind (see Chapter 1.2), is almost immeasurable. Accordingly, this form of power includes not only purely physical

---

1   Cf. Popitz (2017). For more in-depth coverage, see Poggi, Gianfranco (1988): Phänomene der Macht: Autorität-Herrschaft-Gewalt-Technik. Review, *Contemporary Sociology*, 17 (4), pp. 664-556.
2   Cf. Popitz (2017): p. 26.

injury, but also the infliction of social or economic harm. Those who exercise the power of action do not necessarily do so by beating, raping or shooting another person. It is also seen in the calling in of a loan from a debtor or the excluding of individuals from social life by ostracism. All of these subforms of the power of action can manifest in varying degrees. In the case of physical injury, the spectrum ranges from the infliction of pain to mutilation and killing. In the case of material damage, it extends from the mere reduction of resources to the complete withdrawal of means of subsistence – for example, through the destruction of arable land and systematic starvation. The severity of social harm begins with distancing and ignoring, and culminates in confinement and disempowerment.[3] However, the power of action is not just destructive. It also fulfills maintenance and productive functions. Anyone who wants to maintain a society and the corresponding system of rules of non-violent cooperation, will find that the power of action is indispensable. If the state executive bodies (police and military) have no power resources to do harm to opponents of the community (criminals, terrorists, hostile nations), then they can guarantee neither internal nor external security. On the other hand, the power of action has a productive effect when it is utilized to destroy established social orders and at the same time to create new ones. Paradigmatic for this are revolutions in which a social avant-garde, employing the combined use of physical, social and economic action power, destroys an old power apparatus and replaces it with a new regime.

The second form of power, *instrumental power,* is the ability to control the behavior of others through credible threats or promises. Successful threats control behavior because they cause others to fear that the threatening party is capable and willing to do something unfavorable to them. Successful promises have a behavioral effect, because the person doing the promising awakens the hope in others that he or she will act in a way beneficial for them.[4] In short, possessing instrumental power means having the power to dispose over other people's fear and

---

[3] Foucault prominently noted that the ostracization and confinement of ostensibly socially deviate persons as "mentally ill" is one of the most pervasive forms of the power of action. See Foucault, Michel (1995): *Discipline and Punish: The Birth of the Prison,* 2nd edition, translated by Alan Sheridan, New York: Random House.

[4] Basically, it would be more accurate to speak of a conditional promise. A conditional promise is distinguished from an unconditional promise by its if-then structure. By comparison: "I promise you that we will have ice cream on Sunday" (unconditional promise) versus "I promise you that we will have ice cream on Sunday, if you clean up your room today" (conditional promise).

hope.[5] Of course, it need not necessarily be founded on a basis of real power or be objectively justified – it is sufficient if the addressee is convinced that the action he or she desires or dreads will occur. Therefore, instrumental power can rely as much on a good bluff as on the real potential to harm or benefit the other. Crucially, however, a threat or promise often has a history: if a state has always lived up to its previous promises of military support to its alliance partners in exchange for regular levies, its allies have reason to believe that it will continue to do so in the future. If such announcements have so far turned out to be so much hot air, their addressees can safely assume that the trend will continue. Thus, instrumental power always depends on the threatening or promising party's balance sheet of past behavior.

According to Popitz, threats and promises have two common structural features. *Firstly,* the threatening or promising party divides all the options for action of the addressees into two classes: compliant behavior and non-compliant behavior. In this way, a situation is created where the choice is narrowed to two exclusive alternatives between which the addressees must decide. Only as long as the addressees have a free choice between two options – no matter how unattractive one of them may be – are they exposed to instrumental power.[6] *Secondly,* the threatening or promising party assumes a dual role, inasmuch as they are always both the issuer of a threat or a promise and the potential dispenser of a punishment or a reward, their own behavior is thus bound to the future behavior of the addressees. The threatening or promising party must react to the behavior of the addressees as announced otherwise credibility is lost and the basis of power forfeited, that is, the effectiveness of future threats and promises. In other words, the addressees of a threat or a promise can force issuers to show their true colors, as it were, forcing them from an active to a passive role. In this regard, we can take the example of the Greek economic crisis. It seemed that the European Union (EU) and the International Monetary Fund (IMF) had considerable instrumental power over Greece. They could compel the Greek state to embark upon a comprehensive economic and social reform program by promising to save it from bankruptcy by loan payments. The catch was that the EU and the IMF must indeed be ready to show their colors with respect to Greece's non-compliance and ultimately bankrupt the state, with all the negative implications for the European economy associated with

---

5   Popitz (1992): p. 79.

6   However, this talk of free choice must be viewed with some caution. If an option exists which results in the certain loss of one's life, it is difficult to reconcile this with our everyday understanding of free choice; see our discussion of the relationship between power and freedom in Chapter 1.2.

this. As it is dubious that the EU and IMF are willing to take this step, their instrumental power is less comprehensive than it initially appeared, and this inevitably gives the Greek state room to maneuver and gain concessions from its creditors.

Alongside these structural similarities of threats and promises there is, however, a significant difference. Popitz deems this to be a question of profitability.[7] Threats are obviously relatively cheap for the issuer or – less economically speaking – are not associated with any further effort, as long as they succeed. If the threatened party does what the threatening party wants, the latter does not have to make good the threat. The threatening party does not then have to expend any physical or economic resources. It only becomes expensive for the threatening party if the threatened resist, for example, because they believe that the threats are empty. The situation with promises is the complete opposite. Promises become expensive in case of success, because the addressee is rewarded for compliant behavior. On the other hand, such promises can be cheap, as it were, if the addressee acts non-compliantly. In this case, the promising party does not grant the reward. These differences can be well illustrated in tabular form:

Figure 1: Contrasting Profitability of Threats and Promises

		Behavior of the Addressee	
		compliant	noncompliant
Costs for the Issuer	expensive	promise	threat
	cheap	threat	promise

For this reason, threats and promises are used in very different ways. Threats are made when it is very likely that the threatened will comply with the wishes of those in power. It is no coincidence that all the norms governing our daily lives together (prohibition of theft, assault, insult, false statement, etc.) are linked to implicit threats, namely to the legal sanctions imposed on a failure to comply. Because the legislature rightly believes that the majority of the population is willing to comply with these standards, it is not necessary to secure their compliance by reward – such a measure would be downright absurd! However, promises are made when it is unlikely, or at least uncertain, that the addressee will submit to the wishes of those with power. They are not used in the area of the normal and

---

7   Popitz (1992): p. 92.

everyday, but only in exceptional situations. Anything else would be, as Popitz notes, a completely unprofitable power strategy.

These two principles of instrumental power – *"Threaten, if you can count on compliance!"* and *"Promise, if you have to expect non-compliance!"* – are universally valid. They result from the above-mentioned contrasting profitability of the two forms of instrumental power. However, the question of when precisely compliant or non-compliant action is to be expected can obviously not be given a universally applicable answer. It depends on the social, cultural, economic and political context in which the power strategies are applied. In the modern, generally stable democracies of the First World, whether Western or East Asian, it is sensible to forbid the possession of distinctly military weapons by threatening imprisonment. Indeed, this is an accepted standard in numerous jurisdictions characterized by the rule of law, such as the United Kingdom (UK), Australia, Japan, Germany, France, Italy and essentially the entire EU; this applies theoretically even in the USA, notwithstanding the constitutionally and inevitably emotionally charged debate as to the exact boundaries of the 2nd Amendment. Worldwide, at any rate, only a minuscule number of people living in a stable state would even think of hoarding fully automatic assault rifles, fragmentation grenades and anti-tank weapons in their homes. However, in an unstable state, shaken by unrest and ethnic conflict, the situation can be very different. Here, from a power-strategic point of view, it may be appropriate to reward militia members with amnesties or financial contributions for giving up their weapons and submitting to state authority. The possession of military weapons is not the exception in such states, but rather the rule. Accordingly, their surrender to the state is not to be expected.

The third form of power, *authoritative* power, is the ability to control other people through their need for recognition and guidance. People, according to Popitz, not only have a tendency to emulate moral, intellectual, social or spiritual models – they also want to receive praise from them. This need, which runs through all forms of human socialization, can be used by people who are recognized as authorities to influence both the external behavior and the attitudes and beliefs of others, and hence their overall worldview. Unlike instrumental power, for example, authoritative power does not function by setting positive and negative incentives in the context of the existing preferences of the addressees. Rather, it is based on the fact that those bound by authority freely bow to the wishes of the other, fixating the ruler as a role model.[8]

---

8   Cf. Popitz (1992): p. 26; p. 106. For a further analysis as to how Popitz comprehends the institutionalization of power in terms of expanding its scope, validity and effec-

The preeminent significance of authoritative power for the stable rule of order was discovered over two and a half thousand years ago by the masterminds of Chinese statesmanship, Confucius and Lao Tzu (see Chapter 1.1). Permanent rule, according to both theoreticians, is not based primarily on the ability to control the population with threats of violence or to lure them with promises. It is based, rather, on the exemplary moral character of the ruler and the respect that is shown to him. Confucius even goes so far as to say that the mere example of an honest emperor can sufficiently motivate the population to comply with the law. In this respect, he argues that a good ruler does not need to give orders, while noting as well that a bad, non-righteous ruler will not be obeyed despite a string of commands. When authoritative power is established in such a comprehensive form, according to Lao Tzu, a special form of autonomy arises. By bowing to the ruler's (anticipated) wishes, the subjects only follow their own will: "When great men rule, subjects know little of their existence. Rulers who are less great win the affection and praise of their subjects. A common ruler is feared by his subjects, and an unworthy ruler is despised. If a great man rules, the people barely know that he is there."[9] Thus, life and business can proceed, the people have a sense of freedom, an indeed subjective but nevertheless significant aspect in the relationship between the ruling and the ruled.

Those who have authoritative power have no need to resort to action power or instrumental power. The ruling person can trust that the authority-bound people will follow their wishes because they want to – not because they have to. To maintain this form of power, it is sufficient to proclaim recognition for compliant behavior and to disapprove of non-compliance. Similarly, Popitz, who is a connoisseur of pointed expressions, refers to this 'unarmed' force as the power of 'silent means'.[10] In addition thereto, the bearer of authoritative power does not have to

---

tiveness, see also Palumbo, Antonino and Scott, Alan (2018): *Remaking Market Society: A Critique of Social Theory and Political Economy in Political Times,* New York/London: Routledge.; p. 69.

9 Lao Tzu (2009): p. 39. Remarkably, exactly the same idea is found in Hegel's philosophy of law under the concept of "subjective freedom". Cf. Hegel, Georg W. F. ([1821] 2003): *Elements of the Philosophy of Right: Or Natural Law and Political Science in Outline,* Allen W. Wood (ed.), translated by H.B, Nisbet. 8th edition, Camebridge: Cambridge University Press.; p 22; p. 57. However, Hegel adds an "objective" component to this conception of freedom according to which a state system must guarantee essential fundamental rights and pursue a policy oriented towards the common good.

10 Popitz (2017): p. 45.

exercise consistent control over the subjects of power. Insofar as they increasingly internalize the ruler's wishes, values and rules of action and understand them as their own, they are, so to speak, keeping tabs on themselves and serving as their own strict judge.[11]

The fourth form of power is that of *technical power*. It refers to the ability to indirectly influence people by intervening in or modifying their natural and non-natural living conditions. The root of this form of power lies in the fact that human beings are by nature purposeful and intervene in their environment. The British philosopher John Locke pointed out the importance of this trait. According to Locke, human beings appropriate an alien nature by 'mixing' their labor power with it.[12] By successively implementing abstractly envisioned actions on a concrete object – for instance on a tree that requires felling or a stone that is to be hewn – the object is appropriated. The object thus becomes the formed expression of a goal, and if all the actions undertaken are successful then the makers recognize themselves in the object produced.[13] This specific type of action is termed technical action by Popitz. We would also speak today of creating facts on the ground.

---

11 Incidentally, this is indicative of an interesting relationship with respect to Sigmund Freud's concept of the superego. Cf. Freud, Sigmund ([1923] 1989): *The Ego and the Id. The Complete Psychological Works of Sigmund Freud,* James Strachey (ed.), introduced by Peter Gay, New York: W.W. Norton & Co. Similar to authoritative power, the superego is an ordinal instance internalized by the individual which increasingly replaces external rule-givers and enforcers, in the case of Freud, the parents.

12 Locke, John ([1689] 1988): *Two Treatises of Government,* Peter Laslett (ed.), Cambridge: Cambridge University Press.

13 Hegel and Marx have made this trait the foundation of their entire anthropology. Both are united by the conviction that humankind strives to abolish the contrast between themselves and the world, between subject and object, between inner and outer. This abolition is both theoretical and practical. Philosophy falls into the realm of the theoretical, above all epistemology, which aims to grasp and systematize the external world of spatio-temporal objects under concepts of human reason, and thus to overcome its foreignness and externality. Manufacturing work, in particular, falls into the realm of practicality. By transforming the natural world gradually into artifacts, i.e. artificial objects, through productive intervention, humankind creates living conditions that, without exception, bear their own "stamp." See also Quante, Michael (2010): After Hegel. The Realization of Philosophy Through Action, in: Dean Moyar (ed.), *Routledge Companion to 19th Century Philosophy,* London: Routledge, pp. 197-237.

The respective forms of action can be subdivided into three main types or modes: *modifying, producing* and *employing*.[14] The mode *modifying* signifies a mere altering of the existing environment – for example, when clearing a forest, damming a river or fencing a pasture. The mode *producing* marks the creation of a new object, an artifact. Such artifacts range in complexity from the straw hut to the nuclear power plant and in their variety of uses from the sledgehammer to the microscopic laser cutter. Finally, the mode *employing* marks the targeted use of artifacts, either for the purpose of engaging in the living and the inanimate environment or to produce other artifacts.

How can power be exercised with these different types of actions? For modifying action, let's take the example of two neighboring countries through which a river flows, supplying both territories with drinking water. If the political leaders of the country lying upstream decide to divert the river, they have a decisive impact on the neighboring country with just this one intervention in the natural environment. By depriving the neighboring country of drinking water, the upstream country can force the neighboring country into economic dependency and impose its own interests against the will of the other. Thus, the ability to modify the environment is what makes it possible to use natural resources as a lever.[15] Jean-Jacques Rousseau, born in the Swiss city-state of Geneva, rather dramatically described another instance of the power configuration of modifying: "The first person who, having enclosed a plot of land, took it into his head to say *this is mine* and found people simple enough to believe him was the true founder of civil society. What crimes, wars, murders, what miseries and horrors would the human race have been spared, had someone pulled up the stakes or filled in the ditch and cried out to his fellow men: "Do not listen to this imposter. You are lost if you forget that the fruits of the earth belong to all and the earth to no one!"[16] Whether you agree with this radical critique of the concept of landed property or not, it is clear

---

14 Popitz (1992): p. 160.
15 As expected, this power technique is a tried and tested means of influencing politics in dry areas. A longstanding bone of contention between Turkey and Iraq is e.g. the Turkish project for the construction of dams on the Euphrates and Tigris. The completion of this so-called "great Anatolian plan" would make the government in Baghdad dependent on Turkey's water policy in one fell swoop. To deepen this topic, see Khagram, Sanjeev (2009): *Dams and Development. Transnational Struggles for Water and Power*. Ithaca/London: Cornell University Press.
16 Rousseau, Jean Jacques ([1775] 1992). *Discourse on the Origin of Inequality*, translated by Donald A. Cress, Indianapolis/Cambridge: Hackett Publishing Company.; p.44

that Rousseau, one of the intellectual groundbreakers who paved the way for the French Revolution, clearly recognized the potential power offered by the control of land. Whoever controls the demarcation of land and territories decides on the mobility and space allowed to fellow human beings, they can grant right of passage and rights of use, allow people to enter or keep them out, etc.

The fact that the production and use of artifacts holds potential for power is easy to demonstrate. In this regard, we must not only think of the most obvious example of the production and use of superior weapons technology (cruise missiles, stealth jets, Gauss rifles, etc.). The power to produce and, if necessary, to monopolize a coveted product – be it a vaccine or software – is also a form of technical power. The power of Western industrialized nations over developing and emerging countries is largely based on superior technologies and the possibility of either withholding them or restricting their use. It is thus not surprising that the issue of technology transfer between geopolitical areas such as the European Union and China is prioritized by political decision-makers as a matter of power and, in case of doubt, purely economic considerations are subordinated to such power.

The extent of the technical power of an actor depends on three factors. The first factor, which is central to Popitz, is that of perfecting technical means.[17] The more effectively and efficiently someone masters the central modes of modifying, producing and employing in a particular field of application of power, the greater is his or her power. Accordingly, for example, the military-technical power of a nation is a function of its ability to produce and employ military technology. This is obvious and needs no further explanation. However, there are two other factors that Popitz does not address, which we regard as equally relevant. These are discussed in the disciplines of sociology, geography and ethnology under the keywords of 'vulnerability' and 'resilience'.[18] Vulnerability refers to people's exposure and susceptibility to risks, be these environmental hazards such as floods or droughts, or social risks such as impoverishment or crime. Resilience, on the other hand, refers to people's resistance to harm and their ability to adapt to changed, risky living conditions. We can illustrate these core concepts in the aforementioned example of a conflict pertaining to water, in which one state exercises technical power over another by diverting a river. Here, the vulnerability of the neighboring state is assessed by what alternative access to water it has, what reserves it has, how dependent its agricultural sector is on water and so forth. Its resilience depends, moreover, on how successful it is in saving water and dealing with peri

---

17 Popitz (1992): p. 179.
18 Gallopín, Gilberto C. (2006): Linkages Between Vulnerability, Resilience, and Adaptive Capacities, *Global Environmental Change,* 16 (3), pp. 293-303.

ods of drought by adjusting agricultural production, etc. Obviously, the influence that the upstream country can have on its neighboring state is much less if the lower state has alternative water sources and an adaptable agricultural sector. And this conclusion applies irrespective of whether or not the upstream state has effective and efficient means with which to divert the river in question.

We could cite any number of other examples, and inevitably, vulnerability and resilience have different meanings depending on the context. With regard to the health policy sector, for example, criteria such as mortality rates, supply of medicines, hygienic conditions, etc. are relevant; and with regard to the field of energy policy, aspects such as the availability of alternative energy sources, efficiency of existing means of production, energy consumption of the population, etc. are pertinent. At any rate, without going into more detail here, the following basic principles should be clear. The greater the vulnerability of an actor and the lower his or her resilience, the higher the likelihood that the exercise of technical power against him or her will succeed. The lower the vulnerability and the greater the resilience, the lower the probability of success. Thus, the impact and success of technical power depend not only on perfecting the resources of those holding power, but also on the vulnerability to risks of those potentially subject to power and their ability to deal with them.

Having outlined all four forms of power, we now examine their commonalities and interactions. First, it is obvious that both instrumental and authoritative power direct the behavior of those affected. Instrumental power works by setting out external incentives for action, which dock onto the pre-existing preferences of those subject to power. Authoritative power, on the other hand, has an effect on the inner life of actors and modifies their preferences in that a figure of authority provides them with or withdraws approval. Action power and technical power, in turn, have in common the fact that they affect the situation of those concerned. While the former has a direct effect on individuals as physically vulnerable organisms, social creatures or economic actors, the latter influences their surrounding natural and non-natural living conditions.

Second, all forms of power can be combined with and transformed into one other. Popitz himself gives a striking example of a diachronic variant, in noting that the "power of action can manifest itself in the conquest of foreign lands; the new possessions can become the sites of the instrumental power of exploitation, enduring oppression can be transfigured into authoritative power; and all these processes can find physical expression in walls and fortifications"[19], i.e. as tech-

---

19 Popitz (2017): p. 20.

nical power. Accordingly, in-depth analysis often reveals established constellations of power to be sediments of power transformations that developed from a simple act of violence. At the same time, different forms of power can complement and reinforce one other synchronously. Technical power, as soon as we enter the realm of inter-state conflict, is a crucial prerequisite for action power. Only those who have the technological and the economic capacity to produce military weapons on an industrial scale also have the potential to harm other state actors or to influence their actions by threatening military force. On the other hand, only those who have the power of action to protect their communities from external and internal adversaries can continue to perfect the technical resources required for superior technical power. These amalgamations suggest that all four forms of power are interdependent and enable one another, and thus are not separate forms, but are elements of a singular, internally differentiated power phenomenon.

By classifying the four forms of power, we have exposed the general structure of this phenomenon and developed a universal systemization for all eras, cultures and areas of society. What remains unresolved, however, is the crucial question of how these forms are made clear and communicable in interaction between persons and organizations, and how they are manifested in concrete terms in the various fields of society. We cannot avoid addressing this issue if we want to understand power as a historically concrete, mutable phenomenon (see Chapter 1.3). In the following sections, therefore, we will first shift our analytical focus to the relation of power and symbolism (Chapter 2.2), in order then to outline the central power fields of the community and their internal logics (Chapter 2.3).

2.2 POWER AND SYMBOLISM

Power and symbolism are closely linked to each other in our everyday language and public perception. When a politician chastises subordinates in front of an assembled press, we naturally speak of a 'demonstration of power'. A North Korean missile test or a Russian military parade is declared a 'display of power', and the glass palace of the European Central Bank in the German banking center of Frankfurt is described as a 'monument of power'. In his commendable monograph, Niklas Luhmann points out that this interconnection is not merely coincidental. Rather, in his eyes, it is an indispensable requisite for the formation of power.[20] The historian Norbert Elias quickly identifies the reason for this, claiming that people do not believe in power which is not made visible. They have to see it in order to

---

20 Luhmann, Niklas ([1975] 2003): *Macht,* Stuttgart: UTB.; p. 32.

believe it.[21] Power is, the argument goes, only potential to act, only an opportunity to further one's interests, and thus it is necessarily abstract. It is, metaphorically speaking, invisible. In order for it to be successfully exercized and expanded, it must be made visible through sensory symbols. This reasoning is plausible. However, it is useful to dig even deeper and to more precisely determine the multilayered, complex relationship between power and symbolism.

First, the concept of symbolism. What exactly a symbol is and in what relation it stands to what it symbolizes, is a persistent issue of contention among language theorists, linguists and epistemologists. In what follows, we derive orientation from the classical definition by Ernst Cassirer, who uses 'symbolic form' to refer to that energy of the mind through which a mental meaning or content is linked to a concrete sensory sign.[22] The generic term symbol thus designates all concrete objects and facts which can be grasped by our natural senses to which, by convention, a meaning is added that extends beyond the actual object and refers to an abstract, conceptual content. In addition to pictures (the anti-nuclear smiling sun, the imperial eagle, the dollar sign), these include gestures (finger wagging, Black Panther fist, Hitler salute), characters (Latin alphabet, hieroglyphs, operators of propositional, predicate and modal logic), sounds (warning sirens, fanfares, referee whistles), ceremonies (Christian communion, Labor Day demonstrations, yoga) and monuments (emperor statues, embassy buildings, triumphal arches). All symbols have in common that they do not provide their own interpretation, with the exception of certain warning colors, for which we humans have an evolutionarily developed sensitivity.[23] They require a community of interpreters and speakers who can decipher, communicate and pass them on. Accordingly, the significance of symbols is never permanent, but relative to the established, although mutable, community conventions; there are therefore repeated conflicts of interpreta

---

21 Elias, Norbert (1983): *Die höfische Gesellschaft. Untersuchung zur Soziologie des Königtums und der höfischen Aristokratie,* Frankfurt a.M.: Suhrkamp.; p. 179. In the original text: *"An die Macht, die zwar vorhanden ist, aber nicht sichtbar im Auftreten des Machthabers in Erscheinung tritt, glaubt das Volk nicht. Es muss sehen, um zu glauben."*

22 Cf. Cassirer, Ernst (1955): *The Philosophy of Symbolic Forms,* translated by Ralph Menheim, introduced by Charles W. Hendel, New Haven/London: Yale University Press. See also Cassirer, Ernst ([1910] 2010): *Substanzbegriff und Funktionsbegriff,* Werkausgabe Vol. 6, Hamburg: Felix Meiner.; p. 161.

23 Cf. Marples, Nicola M., Kelly, David J., and Thomas, Robert J. (2005): Perspective: The Evolution of Warning Colors is Not Paradoxical, *Evolution,* 59 (5), pp. 933-940.

tion over the significance of symbols, which are directly relevant to the analysis of power.

What connections exist concretely between power and symbolism? First of all, those who want to carry out a complex power action in cooperation with other persons over a longer period of time and a greater distance depend upon written communication – and thus on symbolic signs. This applies to a general who wants to implement a battle plan as well as to a taxation official developing a revenue plan or to a CEO who plans to take over a new business. Without recourse to symbolic signs through which instructions and goals can be communicated, the exercise of power remains temporally and spatially limited. In view of this, it is hardly surprising that the first expansive high culture in history, the Sumerians, were also the inventors of writing.[24]

Symbols, however, are not only a necessary *precondition* for the effective and efficient use of power. They themselves function in multiple ways as a *means of power*. First, domination, i.e. institutional power consolidated by supra-personal social positions (see Chapter 1.2), is reproduced and organized by means of continuous ritualization. Flaig points to this fact: "The function, the 'sense' and the character of an institution are not fixed once and for all. An institution exists only by being organized and staged over and over again. It exists *only in the execution of rituals*."[25] Flaig himself has here the ancient Roman people's assembly in view, whose meeting, decision-making and interaction with other institutions of the Roman Empire was highly ceremonial. But we can look at contemporary examples as well: election campaigns in representative democracies are *de facto* symbolic ritualizations of institutional power structures. They follow strict rules and conventions, are determined by clear sequences of events – from the publication of election programs to verbal exchanges in parliament to voting – and they include a clear allocation of the roles of the actors involved (the parties, the media, trade

---

24 Cf. Diakonoff, Igor. M. (1976): Ancient Writing and Ancient Written Language: Pitfalls and Peculiarities in the Study of Sumerian, *Assyriological Studies*, Vol. 20, Sumerological Studies in Honor of Thorkild Jakobsen, pp. 99–121. See also Volk, Konrad (ed.) (2015): *Erzählungen aus dem Land Sumer,* Wiesbaden: Harrassowitz Verlag.

25 Flaig, Egon (1998): War die römische Volksversammlung ein Entscheidungsorgan? Institution und soziale Praktik, in: Rainhard Blänker and Bernd Jussen (eds.), *Institution und Ereignis. Über historische Praktiken und Vorstellungen gesellschaftlichen Handelns.* Göttingen: Vandenhoeck & Ruprecht, pp. 49-73.; p. 71. For more in-depth analysis, we highly recommend the standard work: Veyne, Paul (1992): *Bread and Circuses: Historical Sociology and Political Pluralism.* Oswyn Murray (ed.), translated by Brian Pearce. London: Penguin.

unions and churches). Through their regular staging, they not only serve to reproduce the democratic regime, but also create a sense of expectation within the community. That this political-symbolic work requires a colossal and exhausting effort on the part of those with power, is obvious. Accordingly, Flaig points out that the execution of a power rite can never be completely controlled.[26] In every ritual situation, certain groups are able to intervene in the ritual process and to modify it. If they are heard by significant numbers of participants, then the political semiotics of the ritual will be shaken.[27] In other words, if the almost identical reproduction of previous rites serves to stabilize the balance of power, the disturbance or modification of the rite can be used to influence the status quo. Examples of symbolic attacks of this kind are found even in recent political history. Interestingly enough, several of them revolve around inaugural rituals in Western democracies. Among them are two memorable events in modern German political history. One is the apparent undermining of the parliamentary dress code in the German state of Hessen in 1985 at the swearing-in ceremony of the sneaker-wearing, Green Party politician Joschka Fischer, later Foreign Minister and Vice Chancellor; Fischer thus challenged the bourgeois establishment's sovereignty of interpretation over the political discourse. The second event was the omission of the phrase 'So help me God' by Gerhard Schröder in 1998, when he took office as German Chancellor, which symbolized a rejection of the close fusion of church and state.

No less prominent U.S. American examples come equally to mind. In 1977, as James Earl 'Jimmy' Carter was sworn into office as the 39th President in Washington, D.C., he broke with tradition and walked rather humbly along Pennsylvania Avenue with his wife, the First Lady Rosalynn, instead of relying on his chauffeur. And, of course, forty years later, as the 45th President was planning to take to the stage, there were some changes made. Donald Trump elected more pomposity for himself and Melania in 2017. Thus, he decided to replace the long-time announcer Charles Brotman (who had served as the inauguration parade announcer for every president since Dwight Eisenhower) with a supporter, displaying his disregard of the non-partisan informal agreement on a well-respected announcer and demonstrating his personal preferences, challenging established political norms and discourse.

Of course, such examples are abundant in other political spheres as well. It is fundamentally the case that the level of observance of the symbolism of power and its ritualization can generally be deemed to be indicative of whether a regime

---

26   Flaig (1998): p. 71.
27   Ibid.

is functioning smoothly. Wherever ceremonial productions are contested, power relations are in transition.

In addition to the staging and reproduction of relations of domination, symbolism also comes into play as a social means of communication for the subtle exercise of power. Status symbols such as company cars and airplanes, bodyguards, escort motorcycles and sumptuous reception rooms all make the otherwise invisible potential of power visible – as briefly mentioned earlier. They impressively convey a hierarchical order and at the same time provide orientation about responsibilities, competences, duties and dependencies within complex forms of social organization. Thus, as in the case of the ritualized staging of ruling orders, they ensure predictability, cognitive relief and stabilize the balance of power. At the same time, they make it possible to communicate the rise and fall of individuals within hierarchies in the simplest way. Nothing illustrates the growth in power of a department manager in a large corporation as forcefully as the move to a spacious office. And nothing makes the extent of military degradation clearer than the public tearing off of epaulettes and rank insignia by a superior, as was traditionally practiced in Western armies.

Furthermore, within territorial states, the symbolic representation of the ruler by means of statues, banners or television broadcasts makes it possible to bridge the spatial distance between the rulers and the power-subjects. The greater the distance between the ruler, as a physical person, and the ruled, the more important is the metaphorical visualization of the ruler in the everyday world of experience. Those who are constantly exposed to the admonishing gaze of the monarch, president or dictator are less inclined to disregard their laws. In this way, the symbolic representation of rulers contributes to the strengthening of their authoritative power (see Chapter 2.1). We are tempted to associate this form of power stabilization, above all, with totalitarian regimes, and indeed, the cult of personality has nurtured its most bizarre blossoms there. Nevertheless, this assessment falls short. Hans Georg Soeffner and Dirk Tänzer show in their worthwhile essay on figurative politics that politicians in modern democracies skillfully employ social media to maintain a symbolic presence in the lives of their constituents, easily equaling that achieved by autocratic rulers.[28]

In proceeding further, we encounter a fourth essential aspect: the symbolic staging of rulers can also be used for their retreat from the world of the ruled, thus

---

28 Cf. Soeffner, Hans Georg and Tänzer, Dirk (2007): Figurative Politik. Prolegomena zu einer Kultursoziologie politischen Handelns, in: Hans Georg Soeffner and Dirk Tänzer (eds.), *Figurative Politik. Zur Performanz der Macht in der modernen Gesellschaft*, Opladen: Leske und Budrich, pp. 17-33.

enhancing their mystification. In this way, the power gap between rulers and power-subjects is emphasized and consolidated. An early example of this strategy can be found in the history of Herodotus.[29] The Greek historian describes the reign of King Deiokes, who established the Median Empire in modern-day Iran in the eighth century B.C. Immediately after his coronation, Deiokes instituted a court ceremonial that created distance: with the exception of his closest confidants, no one was allowed to enter the throne room, state affairs were handled exclusively by messengers, Deiokes himself disappeared completely from public view. For this isolation, Herodotus has an obvious explanation: Deioke's subjects would regard and revere him as a creature of a different kind if they did not see him. The court ceremonial was thus used by the Median king for self-presentation as a superhuman and overly powerful person. The ruled had no opportunity to perceive him as a flesh-and-blood person – with ailments, signs of aging, physical inadequacies, etc. – and on the basis of these impressions to question his status as ruler. They had only a remote, faceless potentate upon which to project their own hopes, desires and ideals.

Beyond the self-staging of rulers, the relevance of symbolism to power strategy also comes into play in uniting and delimiting groups. In the language of social psychology, it serves to establish so-called *in-groups* and *out-groups*.[30] The dichotomy of 'us' and 'others', of 'inside' and 'outside', as the sociologist Johannes Scheu in reference to post-structuralist theorists points out, represents a most fundamental feature of the building of human communities in general. A visible and symbolically coded boundary distinguishing outsiders who are not part of the community is indispensable for the formation of the community itself. The French philosopher Jacques Derrida therefore uses the term "constitutive outside" to describe how communities define and sustain themselves by virtue of excluding and distinguishing themselves from those outside the community.[31] Examples of in-group formation through shared symbols can be cited *ad infinitum*: fans of baseball, basketball, football and ice hockey clothe themselves in their club colors, thus distinguishing themselves from supporters of other clubs; devout Muslim women cover their hair with a hijab and distance themselves from non-Muslims and less devout religious sisters; Neo-Nazis wear combat boots with white shoe-

---

29 Cf. Herodotus (1997): *Histories,* translated by Robin Waterfield (ed.), introduction and notes by Carolyn Dewald, Oxford: Oxford World Classics.
30 Cf. Tajfel, Henri (1981): *Human Groups and Social Categories,* Cambridge: Cambridge University Press.
31 Cf. Derrida, Jacques (2004): *Die Différance. Ausgewählte Texte,* Stuttgart: Reclam.

laces and thus identify themselves as radical opponents of democratic-liberal values. The corresponding symbols have been empirically proved to reinforce solidarity, empathy and cohesion among members – metaphorically, they are the glue that binds social groups together. In addition, the fact that standardized group symbolism offers an immense advantage for the exercise of action power (see Chapter 2.1) was already discovered by the military in antiquity. Exemplary is the introduction of combat uniforms by the Roman Empire. The iconic armor of the legionnaires not only created an esprit de corps that was unrivaled at the time, it also presented the Roman troops to their non-uniformed opponents (for example Germanic tribes) as a super-personal military entity that amounted to more than the sum of its individual members.

The flip side of this strategy is the symbolic exclusion and the concomitant subjugation and disempowerment of social out-groups. The Italian jurist and philosopher Giorgio Agamben has explored these topics in his sometimes dark, yet highly interesting work *Homo Sacer*.[32] Agamben based his analysis on an archaic figure of Roman antiquity – the *homo sacer* (Latin for 'holy man'), who is expelled from the community as the result of a grave offense and can be killed by all others without them being charged for a crime. This figure marks the prototype of social exclusion for Agamben. The *homo sacer* has lost all political and legal guarantees and all claims to procedural norms, and is thus reduced to mere biological existence, to naked life, as it were. Agamben goes so far as to deny the *homo sacer* status as a human person, as this status arises only through relationships of reciprocal recognition among community members – and precisely these are denied to the excluded. *Homines sacri,* we can complement Agamben, are predestined for symbolic labeling. An example thereof in poignant proportions is the marking of European Jews in the German Reich from 1935 to 1945 with the yellow Star of David. The star symbol not only marked the affected population as social outsiders and '*Volksschädlinge*',[33] it also enabled their efficient capture, deportation and elimination by the security authorities. To be sure, this specific combination of power and symbolism was not an original invention of the National Socialists. In addition to different clothing regulations, the labeling of ostracized and marginalized groups of people by branding or mutilation has always been an essential element of symbolic power strategies.

---

32 Cf. Agamben, Giorgio (1998): *Homo Sacer: Sovereign Power and Bare Life,* Werner Hamacher and David E. Wellbery (eds.), translated by Daniel Heller-Roazen, Meridian: Crossing Aesthetics, Stanford: Stanford University Press.

33 Literally: 'Vermine to the people'.

A sixth point concerns the control of communicative symbols. In her monograph *Literacy and Power*, Hilary Janks states: "[L]anguage, other symbolic forms, and discourse are powerful means of maintaining and reproducing relations of domination."[34] The plausibility of this thesis is impressively demonstrated by the case of literacy. Those who do not master the passive and active use of characters are excluded from many educational and career opportunities as well as many forms of social participation. The lack of access to written sources of information (books, newspapers, the internet) makes it almost impossible for those concerned to have an informed image of existing power structures in their communities. Consequently, power strategists have tried at all times to turn the use of written symbols into an arcane discipline reserved for only a few. The monopolization of writing by the Catholic Church during the European Middle Ages, for example, was partly responsible for its prominent position in the hierarchical order of the monarchical feudal state.[35] Thanks to this monopoly, it became an indispensable pillar of the monarchy and controlled national and international communication. But even in modern times there are examples of this use of symbols as a means of power. For example, forced illiteracy, as historians have documented, was one of the preferred methods of oppression by U.S. American slaveholders and the South African apartheid regime.[36]

Beyond literacy, however, there is another variation on how power can be exercised by controlling communicative symbols. The sociologist Paula-Irene Villa states that domination is assured by leaving the ruled with no symbolic forms other than those by which they are ruled.[37] This is based on the hardly refutable notion that there is a close connection between symbol and meaning, which determines the way in which people can communicate about existing power relations at all. In short, if rulers designate certain communicative symbols as taboo and others as

---

34   Janks, Hilary (2010): *Literacy and Power*, London/New York: Routledge.; p. 22.
35   Compare, among others: Urlacher, Brian R. (2016): *International Relations as Negotiations*, New York: Routledge.; p. 18; and Taylor, Mark C. (2007): *After God*, Chicago: University of Chicago Press.; p. 74.
36   Cf. Petesch, Donald A. (1989): *A Spy in the Enemy's Country. The Emergence of Modern Black Literature,* Iowa City: University of Iowa Press.; and Morar, Tulsi (2006): The South African's Educational System's Evolution to Curriculum 2005, in: Jayja Erneast and David Treagust (eds.), *Education Reform in Societies in Transition. International Perspectives,* Rotterdam: Sense Publishers, pp. 245-258.
37   Villa, Paula-Irene (2011): Symbolische Gewalt und ihr Scheitern. Eine Annäherung zwischen Butler und Bourdieu, *Österreichische Zeitschrift für Soziologie,* 36 (4), pp. 51-69.; p. 54.

universally binding norms, they can control social discourse or even completely silence (parts of) the population. A general example of this strategy is seen in the euphemistically labeled concept of 'cultural re-education', which bans ethnic fringe groups from using their own written language. In the long term, such measures mean that the descendants of the minority can only communicate in the written language of the rulers. They become – unwittingly and unwillingly – accomplices of their own oppression.

The founder of the modern Turkish state, Gazi Mustafa Kemal, alias Atatürk, implemented writing reforms as the heart of an overall social transformation project. In 1928, Atatürk ordered the abandonment of the Arabic script and initiated the exclusive usage of the Latin alphabet in Turkey; he also had countless Arabic loan words deleted from Turkish and replaced by neologisms. As the historian Anton J. Walter states, this was linked to the clear objective of separating the people at one stroke from their Arab-Mohammedan cultural basis and, instead, opening them up to the influence of European civilization and culture; Turkey should be disconnected from neighboring countries in the Near East and her foreign affairs instead linked with Western Europe.[38] The radical nature of this measure opens up a Pandora's Box, if one considers that the Arabic script is, according to Islamic interpretation, the writing of God, in that the angel Gabriel dictated the Koran to Mohammed. Atatürk, an enthusiastic secularist, thus cut off the Turkish people from the Islamic cultural and written tradition and at the same time minimized the influence of Muslim clerics on the shaping of politics. Now, almost 90 years later, it is still possible to note how durable the effect of this power strategy has been. With the rise of political Islam under the current Turkish President Recep Tayyip Erdogan, nevertheless, doubts also arise. Nevertheless, it is clear that Atatürk's reform contributed decisively to the fact that Turkey today occupies a strategically important position between East and West, the Orient and the Occident.

The last form of the articulation of power and symbolism that we wish to look at here concerns the culture of remembrance.[39] History is that what we make of it. *The* past *per se* does not exist, at least not in a robust, objective sense, there thus can only be different and potentially competing interpretations of the past. This

---

38   Cf. Walter, Anton J. (1960): Schriftentwicklung unter dem Einfluß von Diktatoren, *Mitteilungen des Instituts für Österreichische Geschichstforschung,* 68, pp. 337-361.; p. 340.

39   For standard works pertaining to the culture of remembrance, see Nora, Pierre (1996): *Realms of Memory: Rethinking the French Past,* Lawrence D. Kritzman (ed.), translated by Arthur Goldhammer, New York: Columbia University Press.

circumstance is highly relevant in terms of power strategy. Anyone who has the authority to interpret the past of a community or country can narrate it as a continuous success story, as a struggle against hostile powers or as a series of injustices and crimes.[40] As a result of the story told, the status quo of power politics can be preserved, the population can be mobilized for war or the groundwork can even be laid for a political and economic fresh start. The control of the culture of remembrance thus contributes "to the formation of a collective memory, which is of central importance for the identity of political communities" and which can be used to justify claims to power (see also our discussion of narrative justification in Chapter 2.5)[41].

2.3 POWER FIELDS

Power, as we initially stated, is not only multifarious, but also omnipresent. It manifests in a variety of forms, and it pervades all areas of life, no matter how far apart. In Chapter 2.1 we classified the basic forms of power and brought order into the diversity. In this section, we will now systematize the central social fields in which power occurs: religion, economics and politics. This triad does not exhaust the entire spectrum but represents, nevertheless, the main arenas.[42] Before looking at these three areas of power – with a focus on the field of politics – it is important to clarify what is meant by a power field.

---

40   Consider, for example, dialectical materialism, the ideology of the Soviet Union and its satellite states, according to which world history is comprehended as a mere series of class struggles. If one accepts this picture of history, one can claim, without major historical dislocations, the gladiator Spartacus as the forefather of the working-class movement, thus constructing a historical continuity of the socialist idea and tracing it back into antiquity.

41   Münkler, Herfried (2009): *Die Deutschen und ihre Mythen*, Berlin: Rowohlt. The historian Benedict Anderson recognized the importance of the targeted control of historical narrative for the creation of national identity; see Anderson, Benedict (1994): *Imagined Communities. Reflections on the Origins and Spread of Nationalism*, London / New York: Verso.

42   Cf. Poggi, Gianfranco (2001): *Forms of Power*, Cambridge: Polity Press.; pp. 18f.

The term is inextricably linked to the work of one of the most influential sociologists of the twentieth century: Pierre Bourdieu.[43] Bourdieu argues that as societies advance they increasingly organize themselves in a division of labor and differentiate into separate, systematically connected domains with their own functions. Among these areas, which Bourdieu calls both 'fields of power' and 'force fields', are not only the sectors of religion, economics and politics mentioned above, but also culture, science, the military and sport.[44] In this context, he characterizes a power field as a microcosm, a small, relatively autonomous social world within a larger social setting. Despite the functional differences between these microcosms, they share three constitutive traits: a class-specific habitus of the individuals involved, their own practices and hierarchies and a specific type of power resources for which the actors compete.

Ultimately, a habitus is nothing more than a set of socially learned rules of behavior, thinking, perception and evaluation schemes that we more or less unconsciously follow and which determine how we assess and interact with our world and our fellow human beings. Correspondingly, it functions as a social reflex: as soon as a person P with the habitus H gets into a situation of type S, he or she is very likely to display behavior B.[45] For Bourdieu, it is crucial that the habitus of different persons is inseparable from their class and from their social status within a field of power.[46] In this sense, a habitus constitutes a group characteristic. In the field of culture, it is part of the habitus of the educated middle class to cultivate an interest in the arts and music. This corresponds on the part of the precariat

---

43   Fundamental works in this respect: Bourdieu, Pierre (2002a): *Outline of a Theory of Practice,* Ernest Gellner, Jack Goody, Stephen Gudeman, Michael Herzfeld, and Jonathan Parry (eds.), translated by Richard Nice, , 16th edition, Cambridge: Cambridge University Press.; Bourdieu, Pierre (1987); Bourdieu, Pierre (1993): *Sozialer Sinn. Kritik der theoretischen Vernunft,* Frankfurt am Main: Suhrkamp.

44   Even Bourdieu has presented in his complete works no exhaustive exposition of all power fields. Accordingly, we will similarly refrain from trying to make a final listing here.

45   Bourdieu, Pierre (2002b): *Habitus. Habitus a Sense of Place,* Jean Hillier and Emma Rooksby (eds.), Aldershot: Ashgate.

46   Unlike Marxist theorists, Bourdieu does not make the concept of class dependent solely upon the position of a group of persons within the relations of production. For him, class is a multi-dimensional concept that also includes geographical, gender, ethnic and other principles of eligibility and exclusion. Cf. Bourdieu (1987): pp. 176f; pp. 182ff.

to an 'underdog' habitus, which is characterized not only by rejection of the prestige goods of high culture, but by a counterculture which includes its own aesthetic preferences and status symbols. The purview and spectrum of the various habitus types is immense. Thus, the field of socially learned dispositions encompasses not only aesthetic taste, but also decisions about what we eat (organic or cheap meat), how we dress (Barbour or bomber jackets), how we move (saunter along or stride out), which value orientation we have (progressive or conservative) etc. For Bourdieu, there is a simple reason for this. The different habitus forms are indispensable in easing the burden of human life, because they allow us to cope with all problems of a similar form that may emerge in new situations by virtue of a kind of practical generalization.[47] The habitual automation of action, perception, thinking and evaluation processes frees us from constantly having to weigh all options in every situation. Thus, it ensures a much-needed reduction in the complexity of our practical world.

However, the habituses of a power field not only reduce complexity in this way. They also bring forth field-specific practices and hierarchies. Basically, the term 'practice' refers to a coordinated sequence of actions that is performed collectively by several people and that is not a singular event with a fixed start and end point, but has continuity. For example, the winning touchdown by Zach Ertz at the Superbowl 2018 against the New England Patriots with barely two minutes remaining was 'only' a single event – whereas the regular training of the Philadelphia Eagles was literally a practice. The objective social world and its power fields exist for Bourdieu, and for many sociologists and historians inspired by him, only in and through practices; they consist of a system of interdependent sequences of actions that are constantly being reapplied and modified. Classic examples include production and monetary cycles, democratic elections and religious rites as well as administrative processes and legal procedures. Bourdieu maintains that these complex sequences of action could never be sustained, let alone coordinated, if the actors were not habitually disposed to doing so. In other words, only by incorporating the objective structures of the social environment in the form of unconscious patterns of behavior can the practices characteristic of a field be consistently reproduced. Conversely, the reproduction of class- and power-field-specific practices is also a precondition for the passing on of the habitus across the generations. After all, the habitus is not taught or rehearsed abstractly, but is acquired while growing up within the existing structures of the social world. Accordingly, it is not even a question of what was there first – habitus or practice. Both elements of the field of power, being mutually dependent, are equally original.

---

47   Bourdieu (1993): p. 172.

Figure 2: Mutually Constituent Relationship of Habitus and Practices

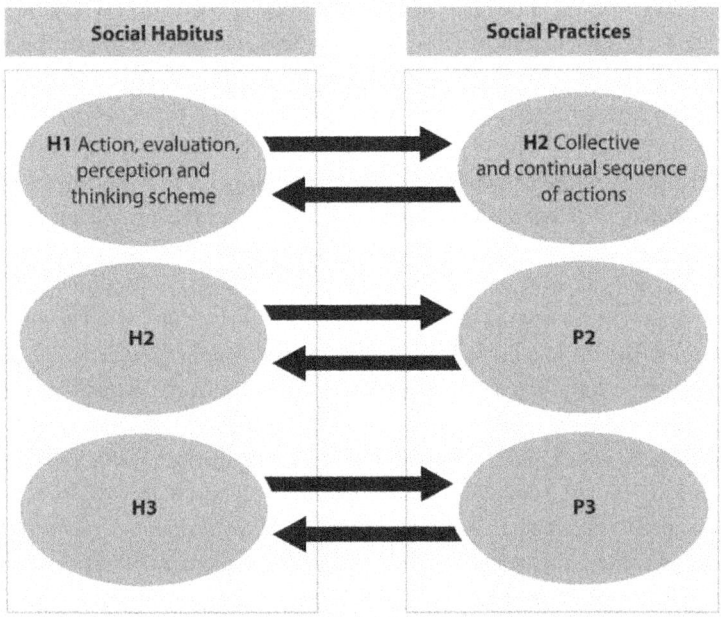

A crucial point, however, is that all practices involve *specific and hierarchically ordered* positions that are occupied by the actors involved and are linked to different levels of power. In some fields, such as the military, economics or religion, these positional hierarchies are often highly formalized. They can be divided, firstly, into dichotomous pairs – Commander/Command Recipient, Employer/Worker, Priest/Layman, Master/Student – and, secondly, into complex orders of jurisdiction and competence (e.g. organizational charts, command structures of the army, diocesan hierarchies). Even less formalized fields such as culture are characterized by hierarchical positions and by the social inequalities that accompany them. One practice that Bourdieu addresses in more detail concerns the relationship between artists and patrons, which he characterizes, with a dash of polemics, as a hidden exploitative relationship.[48]

The hierarchical positions within the practices, which together comprise the respective power fields, are each based on the different dispositions of the *specific power resources* of a certain field.[49] Instead of resources, Bourdieu often prefers

---

48 Cf. Bourdieu (1987): pp. 497f.
49 For our introductory discussion on the conception of power as a quantifiable and distributable resource, see Chapter 1.1.

to speak of the 'capital' of a field, but without explicitly relating it to the notion of economic capital. In this respect, he sees the differences which constitute the main classes of living conditions as subsisting in the aggregate of capital, with this being the sum of all effectively usable resources and power potentials.[50] Simply put, the more power resources actors have at their disposal, the better their positioning within the practices of the field. However, the questions as to what *constitutes* a power resource and what the power of an actor actually *is based on*, will encounter fundamentally different answers from field to field. An analogy aids understanding here: power fields can be compared with card games that have different goals and in which different trumps apply. In the political arena, for Bourdieu, the goal of the game is to control the state and legitimately enforce the vision and division of the social world. And the most important trumps – or power resources – include prestige, networking, free time and education.[51] In the field of scientific research on the other hand, the decisive power resources are publications, successful third-party financial grants, and citation ratios. Here too, the better actors are in accumulating and utilizing these resources, the more influential is their positioning and their chance to assert their interests within the scientific field of power. In this context, Bourdieu emphatically points out that the distribution of power resources within a field is by no means static – even if the deterministic aspects of his habitus model could give rise to this conjecture – but instead, is continuously contested.[52] Thus, social fields are for Bourdieu areas of struggle in which the power resources of the social actors are constantly in disposition.[53]

---

50   Cf. Bourdieu (1987): p. 196.
51   In their careers, young researchers repeatedly find that teaching experience is a largely irrelevant resource in the field of science. Holding good seminars and having an excellent relationship with the student body are not enough, for example, to win a trophy in this power game. The same tends to apply to medial presence. The PhD in German Studies, Richard D. Precht, may be celebrated in the feature pages for his popular philosophy books, but he is nevertheless not taken particularly seriously in university philosophy and scholarly communities.
52   For example, Bourdieu, Pierre (2005): The Political Field, the Social Science Field, and Journalistic Field, in: R. Benson and E. Neveu (eds.), *Bourdieu and the Journalistic Field*, Cambridge: UK: Polity Press, pp. 29-47.; "A field is a field of forces and a field of struggles in which the stake is the power to transform the field of forces". Ibid.: p. 44.
53   For an in-depth discussion in this regard, see Hillebrandt, Frank (1999): Die Habitus-Feld-Theorie als Beitrag zur Mikro-Makro-Problematik in der Soziologie – aus der

Obviously, for a successful power strategy in a particular field, it is not only necessary to know the positions of the respective actors and to know which habitus determines their actions. Above all, it is essential to know the relevant power resources – or, in the language of the card game, to know which color is the trumps. Anyone who tranfers power resources from a field such as economics, without further ado, to another field, such as art, can quickly be shipwrecked. Every power field follows its own logic – that is what Bourdieu means when he writes of a "relatively autonomous social world" – and, accordingly, the resources of power in question cannot easily be interconverted and substituted for one other.

This complex of problems docks onto a key issue that has been extensively explored not only by Bourdieu but also by the Italian sociologist Gianfranco Poggi: the relationship *between* the realms of power.[54] Both Poggi and Bourdieu argue that power struggles do not take place only within individual fields. The different fields also compete with each other for supremacy. Poggi, referring to Bourdieu's card game analogy, calls this conflict the "struggle over 'trump-ness'" that is, the struggle over which color is trumps.[55] In concrete terms, each power field strives to make its type of power resources the fundamental principle of the social world to anchor and marginalize other forms of power resources. If we accept this premise, then we can elegantly explain and systematize the most important ideological conflicts of our time as "struggle [s] over, trump-ness". Thus, Soviet-style communism can be understood as an attempt to establish the absolute primacy of the political field above all other fields, notably above the field of economics. The central control of economic processes by a technocratic elite, the abolition of market mechanisms in the allocation of consumer goods and services and the nationalization of the means of production – all these are efforts to negate the autonomy of the economic sphere.[56] The antagonist in this struggle for supremacy

---

Sicht des Feldbegriffs, Working Papers zur Modellierung sozialer Organisationsformen in der Sozionik, [online] https://www.tuhh.de/tbg/Deutsch/Projekte/Soziо nik2/WP2.pdf, retrieved on 21.12.2017.; p. 16.

54 Cf. Poggi (2001): pp. 21-15; and Bourdieu (2001): p. 52.
55 Cf. Poggi (2001). p. 24. Notwithstanding the obvious similarity between "trumping" in a card game and "Trumpism" in the political power concept, any resemblance in this context is purely coincidental.
56 Cf. Rigby, T. H. (1978): Stalinism and the Mono-Organisational Society, in: Robert Tucker (ed.), *Stalinism: Essays in Sociological Interpretation,* New York: Norton, pp. 53-76. Incidentally, the extreme hostility to religion of Soviet Communism is directly apparent in this context. The systematic suppression of religious practices and habitus

of the power fields is, of course, liberalism following John Locke or its more radical form, libertarianism.[57] Its basic premise is the absolute primacy of the market over all other social fields and the degradation of the system of political institutions to a mere 'night watchman state'. Anyone looking for ideologies that insist upon the categorical primacy of the religious sphere over all other power fields must only look as far as Iran or Saudi Arabia, or the remaining territories of the terrorist organization of the Islamic State.

Now that we have analyzed the core concept of the power field and its crucial components, let's take a closer look at what we consider to be the most important fields: religion, economics, and politics.

2.3.1 Religion

According to Poggi, religion is simultaneously the oldest and the original power field of human history: "[t]he primordial form of prescribed collective conduct has ritual everywhere, while the primordial form of collectively entertained belief has always been myth."[58] In short, any form of power was originally legitimized and institutionalized by religious cult; all chiefs were originally priests; all forms of rule originally theocracies. What distinguishes the social realm of religion from other realms has always been a matter of controversy among theological scholars. Wolfgang Eßbach, for instance, casts considerable doubts on the possibility and plausibility of a universal definition, given the diversity of belief systems, religious scriptures and experiences.[59] We, however, do not seek to analyze religion as such – i.e. from the comprehensive external perspectives of sociology, historiography, philosophy etc. or from the internal perspective of the believers and. Thus, we also make now claim of adequately capturing the essence of what it means to have faith in a divine entity or to experience its presence. Rather, we shall focus exclusively on religion as a field of power and on religious leaders and institutions as power-seeking actors, who are caught in a permanent struggle with other power fields. Considering this limited area of inquiry, we turn to the classic and pertinent definition of Émile Durkheim, the founder of French sociology: "A

---

    in the territory of the Soviet Union and its satellite states is an expression of the attempt to destroy the competing power field of religion in the long term.

57 Cf. Locke, John ([1689] 1988). The most impressive defense of the radical-libertarian understanding of the state is still Nozick, Robert (1974): *Anarchy, State, Utopia,* New York: Basic Books.

58 Poggi (2001): p. 64.

59 See Eßbach, Wolfgang (2014): *Religionssoziologie I*, Paderborn: Wilhelm Fink.

religion is a unified system of beliefs and practices relative to sacred things, that is to say, things set apart and forbidden – beliefs and practices which unite into a single moral community called a Church, all those who adhere to them."[60] Why this field emerged so early in the historical process of differentiation into functionally independent areas of society is unequivocally clear. Indeed, like no other system of habitus and practices, it takes account of the human need for ethical orientation, meaningfulness, a coherent image of the world and self, and it yields an answer to the problem of mortality.[61] Religions (predominantly) posit a transcendent realm, beyond our natural senses, populated by a deity or a pantheon, which is the source of moral norms and ultimate authority in rewarding right conduct and punishing offenses.[62] In this way, religions do not just yield an answer to the question concerning the binding nature of collective principles of action, they also create the expectation of salvation and fear of hell.

Given that the transcendent, which exceeds our natural senses, is at the center of religious conceptions,[63] religious dogmas (whether monotheistic, polytheistic,

---

60 Durkheim, Émile ([1912] 1915): *The Elementary Forms of the Religious Life*, translated by Joseph Ward Swain, London: George Allen & Unwin.; p. 47.

61 Ultimately, this is already in the well-known passage from the Gospel of Matthew "One does not live by bread alone" in a nutshell, cf. Luz, Ulrich (2002): *Das Evangelium nach Matthäus*, Neukirchen-Vluyn: Benziger/Neukirchener. Behind this is the notion that a genuinely spiritual need is part of human nature, a need which can not be satisfied on the purely material level of goods.

62 From a power-strategic perspective, the transcendence of the divine captivates through the (empirical) unfalsifiability. As religion decouples its object from the realm of the sensible, it immunizes itself against other fields of power and corresponding ideologies. In dealing with the field of science, religion can always point out that the supersensible experience of the divine escapes (natural) scientific explanatory access and therefore does not fall within its domain. Against this background, it is again not surprising that many theoreticians, who are firmly anchored in the field of science, have made (empirical) falsifiability the conditio sine qua non of a plausible hypothesis; for a brief overview see Popper, Karl R. (1989): Falsifizierbarkeit, zwei Bedeutungen, in: Helmut Seiffert and Gerard Radnitzky (eds.), *Handlexikon zur Wissenschaftstheorie,* München: Ehrenwirth, pp. 82-85.

63 Here, however, a conditional restriction to monotheistic and modern understanding of religion is appropriate, since, for example, the gods of the Greek world of belief were not wholly absorbed in transcendence, but were physically involved in earthly events. An ancient Hellene would probably have thought it possible to meet the god Apollo or the dryads in an olive grove.

pantheistic, etc.) can always only be the object of faith, not of knowledge. This central insight is encapsulated by the theologian Karl Rahner who argues that actual transcendence is to a certain extent always behind human beings at the unavailable origin of their lives and knowledge. And this actual transcendence is never overtaken by metaphysical reflection and can be considered as pure and objectively unmediated, at most (if at all) experienced in mysticism.[64] It therefore follows that Rahner characterizes the attitude of the faith as a venture in which one allows oneself to be captured.[65] The attitude of humankind to the transcendent – the question of faith or unbelief – can ultimately not be pursued by argument. The most astute scholar can produce numerous ontological proofs of God, but will still be unable to convert a convinced atheist. Conversely, the attempt to shake devout Christians, Muslims or Buddhists in their convictions by producing evolutionary or cognitive scientific objections is equally pointless. In this sense, the religious attitude is structurally similar to other emotional attitudes such as love, dislike, enthusiasm, etc. We can give a friend a thousand good reasons that a common acquaintance is *the* woman for him, but all those reasons cannot force our friend to fall in love with her.[66] Love is – just like faith – not rationally decided, it is rather something that somehow overcomes us.

The non-knowability and incomprehensibility of the transcendent is not just a trick with which religions avoid scrutiny. According to Rahner, the explanation lies rather in the matter itself. Because the Divine conditions the possibility of all human action, thinking and cognition, it cannot itself be grasped by human cognition. Metaphorically speaking, the final standard cannot be re-measured. The limit that gives everything its 'definition' cannot, in turn, be determined by an even more remote border.[67] Readers who are of a more scientific bent and find this formulation too mystical may well find an analogy helpful – the principle of inductive inference.[68] In short, inductive inference involves inferring a general rule following observation of a finite number of uniform cases. For example: all previously observed organic creatures rely on water for survival, so all other (not yet observed) organic creatures are dependent on water for survival. This method is a

---

64 Rahner, Karl (1984): *Grundkurs des Glaubens. Einführung in den Begriff des Christentums,* Freiburg: Herder.; pp. 45f.
65 Ibid.: p. 63; p. 69.
66 Ibid.: p. 72.
67 Ibid.: p. 72.
68 Cf. Vickers, John (2014): The Problem of Induction, in: Edward N. Zalta (ed.), *The Stanford Encyclopedia of Philosophy,* [online] https://plato.stanford.edu/archives/spr2019/entries/induction-problem/, retrieved on 21.12.2017.

core principle of empirical research. If you gave it up you could put aside most disciplines of the natural and social sciences. But what reasons do we actually have for applying this method? The obvious answer is, because it has previously provided considerable success and insight. But this justification is completely untenable: it applies the principle of inductive inference to itself, thus already presupposing its plausibility. The obvious conclusion seems to be that the principle itself is not justifiable – it is rather a precondition for the possibility of substantiation and justification. The theological argumentation sees an analogous situation with the transcendent: because it is always (implicitly) presupposed in every reflection on our human existence and environment, it must be categorically discarded as a possible object of human cognition. More generally speaking, there are pre-reflexive, that is neither derivable nor finally recognizable, conditions of our relations with ourselves and the world, and according to religious conviction, these include the transcendent or divine.[69]

Of course, this circumstance has never prevented the academic disciplines of religions, the theologies (the logics of the divine), from setting up dogmas of the transcendent – such as the Trinity of the Christian God, the idea of universal and compensatory justice through karma in Hinduism, or the uniqueness of God in Islam. However, these dogmas do not have the status of knowledge, but only of "possibilities of thinking"[70]. Thus, the religious scholar Bernhard Uhde: "The possibility of thinking of the contents of religion does not mean that their contents are necessary for thinking – but necessary under the premise of their principles which, for their part, appear to be hypotheses according to secular knowledge"[71]. The concrete formulation of religious meaning is based on very different, fundamental hypotheses as to how the divine is to be thought of. If one accepts these same hypotheses, then the further religious dogmas, practices and habitus follow with *logical* necessity. This point is immensely important to the analysis of power. Since every religious field has an inherent logic, every religious field can be logically analyzed. In other words, by rationally describing and systematizing religions, theology also lays the foundation for making religious habits and practices comprehensible and tangible from the perspective of power logic.

---

69 We ourselves do not refer to the plausibility of the corresponding thesis. Our starting point is to argue neither for nor against the transcendental, but only to make the underlying thought models vivid and comprehensible. For further details, see Rahner (1984): pp. 54-96.
70 Cf. Uhde (2009): p. 7.
71 Ibid.: p. 8.

Anyone who can gain the authority to interpret the realm of the religious, canonize it in the form of binding rituals and narratives, and thereby position themselves as mediators between the transcendental and the earthly, gains considerable potential to assert their interests. Thus, Poggi comments: "When meaning, norms, and aesthetic and ritual practices are monopolized by a distinctive group, it may possess considerable [...] power"[72]. This group can be classified as clergy for simplicity, its followers as the laity. The power of the clergy over the laity is thus based on three pillars or, to remain within our taxonomy, on three forms of resources: first, the need of the laity for meaning and moral orientation; secondly, the hope of the laity for the reward of good deeds in the hereafter and salvation by the deity; third, the fear of the laity of the punishment of offenses and damnation. The attentive reader will not fail to notice that to dispose of the "fear and hope of others" – paraphrasing Popitz – is the attribute of instrumental power (see Chapter 2.1). Accordingly, in the sphere of power of the religious, instrumental power manifests itself in such a way that the higher-ranking actors, the clerics or priests, guide the laity through promises of salvation and threats of damnation. The peculiarity of the religious field is that priests are not forced to bluff in their promises and threats because their expertise, as already mentioned, is aimed at the transcendent. Whether the deity (or the numerous gods of a pantheon) will actually reward behavior conforming to instructions in the hereafter cannot be proven false for obvious reasons; and of course the same applies to punishments of non-conformity through the agony of hell. Poggi compares this power strategy somewhat cynically with a protection racket.[73] The extortioner convinces potential protégés that they are endangered in various ways (e.g. as a result of original sin, we all share in the alienation of Adam and Eve from God); in the second step, the extortioner then offers protection against these dangers – although for a consideration – (e.g. if you accept Christianity, accept the holy sacraments, and pay the tithe, you will be reconciled with God). The flip side of this power-strategic specificity is that the success of the promises and threats depends on the laity actually believing the religious narrative of the clergy – as these can be neither verified nor falsified. So the great strength of religious power is also its Achilles heel: "religious power rests on the hold on people's minds of engaging, compelling ideas. When this hold is loosed, religious power largely dissolves."[74]

---

72 Poggi (2001): pp. 60f. See also Mann, Michael (1986): pp. 22ff.
73 Cf. Poggi (2001): p. 68.
74 Hence Weber's sober definition of a prophet as purely a personal charisma bearer who, by virtue of his mission, proclaims a religious doctrine or a divine command. Cf. Weber: ([1921] 1978): p. 250.

Of course, this does not mean that instrumental power is the only form of power in the religious field. Religious habits and practices can be realized or supported by all forms of power. Of particular importance is undoubtedly authoritative power, that is, the ability to control other persons through their need for recognition and direction. For example, Weber emphasizes that the success of religious visionaries and prophets, such as Moses, Jesus, Zarathustra, Buddha and Muhammad, was inextricably linked to their charisma.[75] Only those who have the ability to position themselves as spiritual and moral models and to deem their virtues as worthy of imitation can establish a faith community and inspire their followers with a religious narrative. The authoritative power of the founders of a religion is sustained beyond their death insofar as their lives and activities are internalized by the faithful and handed down through generations. To be considered in this regard, for example, is the Ahadith, the collection of the sayings of Muhammad, which comprises not only aphorisms but also everyday remarks of the founder of the Islamic religion. This represents the central source of Muslim jurisprudence and moral-spiritual orientation in addition to the Qur'an.[76] In general, we can say that many, if not all, faiths are traceable back to a charismatic founder whose personality is at the heart of the religious narrative. Preserving authoritative power is a key element of religious power strategies. Only if the priesthood succeeds in presenting itself as legitimate heirs of the founders and as keepers of their heritage they can hope to inherit the charisma and authoritative power of the founders.

As mentioned above, religion is the first and original social power field. Accordingly, it is predestined to compete with other power fields and to vie with them for supremacy over the entire social sphere. Examples of how religious habits and practices penetrate or anchor themselves in other fields can be cited *ad infinitum*. We confine ourselves here to two rather striking cases: without exaggeration, the religious legitimization of political power can be regarded as one of the defining characteristics of the Middle Ages. For centuries, the notion – strange to modern ears – that a government does not derive its authority from the protection of fundamental liberal rights or democratic will, but from the grace of God, was been the paradigm of European politics. By way of illustration, we can turn to the proverbial "Walk to Canossa" undertaken by the Salian King Henry IV in 1076-1077 in an attempt to persuade Pope Gregory VII to lift his excommunica

---

75   Hence Weber's sober definition of a prophet as purely a personal charisma bearer who, by virtue of his mission, proclaims a religious doctrine or a divine command. Cf. Weber: ([1921] 1978): p. 250.

76   Cf. Burton, John (1994): *An Introduction to the Hadith,* Edinburgh: Edinburgh University Press.

tion. This is not the place to address the intricacies of the so-called Investiture Controversy between emperor and pope on the relationship between temporal and spiritual power. Suffice to say that the decisive move in the power struggle between the two was the pope's expulsion of the young king of the Holy Roman Empire from the church, depriving the king of all political legitimacy and plunging the empire into serious turmoil. The king had no choice but to make a pilgrimage over the Alps to Bologna in the dead of winter, humbly wearing a penitential hair shirt and asking for forgiveness from the head of the church at Canossa Castle.

An example of the intervention of the religious into the power field of the economy, which continues to be relevant to this day, is the prohibition of Riba ('usury') in Islam.[77] According to the prevailing orthodoxy of Islamic law, Muslims are strictly forbidden to raise or pay interest, Riba is one of the six major or deadly sins of Islam and is also outlawed by the sayings of Muhammad. The fact that this ban strongly restricts possible business models in the banking sector is obvious. The religious proscription of profit that does not stem from direct trade in goods or services but from trade in financial capital, is – as emphasized by Bourdieu and Poggi – an obvious attempt to limit the autonomy of the economic sphere. In the struggle over 'trumpness' between the power fields, the Riba ban is an attack on the societal relevance of economic power resources. Therefore, it is hardly surprising that there have always been attempts in the Islamic cultural area to soften or distort the economically devastating effects of this regulation by creatively reinterpreting the sacral texts. One method, for example, was to let financial transactions be settled by 'infidels', e.g. Jews or Christians. The fact that the ban on Riba is still upheld is seen in the rapid rise in demand for Islamic financial products in the last decade, as shown in a study by *The Economist*. In 2014, around \$2 trillion of capital assets worldwide were rated as 'sharia-compliant'[78].

---

77 For an overview of this topic, see El-Gamal, Mahmoud A. (2006): *Islamic Finance: Law, Economics, and Practice,* Cambridge: Cambridge University Press. See also Ashrati, Mustafa (2008): *Islamic Banking. Wertvorstellungen, Finanzprodukte, Potenziale,* Frankfurt am Main: Frankfurt School Verlag.

78 The Economist (2014): Islamic finance: Big interest, no interest, in: Economist from 13th Sepmtember 2014, [online] http://www.economist.com/news/finance-and-economics/21617014-market-islamic-financial-products-growing-fast-big-interest-no-interest, retrieved on 21.12.2017.

2.3.2 The Economic Power Field

Now, let us turn to the second power field, the economy. Drawing initially on the definition prevalent in economic sciences, the economic sphere is viewed as a social system for the production, distribution, consumption and exchange of goods and services.[79] Apart from early hunter-gatherer cultures and the socialist-communist alternatives of the nineteenth and twentieth centuries, the universal organizational principle of the economic sphere is the market. According to Poggi: "[It] consists in a large set of independent though interdependent units (firms, households, single producers or consumers) which 'traffic' with one another in a formally peaceable manner [...]; that is, they exchange their respective outputs for money at mutually agreed prices; they also compete with one another, each seeking to make its output more valuable to prospective exchange partners than those of other units."[80] By participating in monetary exchanges, market participants generate an open-ended network. Its condition depends – ideally – only on what the actors contribute to the exchange, distribution, production and consumption processes. However, there is already a significant qualification to be made here: the peaceable and voluntary nature of the interaction relations mentioned by Poggi can only be guaranteed by an external and empowered agency – the state.[81] Only if a system of institutions exists that guarantees the property rights, contracts and fundamental rights of the individual, if necessary by force, are the transaction mechanisms central to the market economy even possible. Consequently, the political power field is from the outset inscribed in the economic field.

As the historian and power theorist Michael Mann states, the function of the economic power field or the reason for its emergence as part of the societal process of differentiation is obvious: it serves the "satisfaction of subsistence needs through the social organization of the extraction, transformation, distribution and consumption of the objects of nature"[82]. While religion satisfies humankind's intangible need for spiritual orientation and meaningfulness, the economy satisfies material needs, from basic items such as food, shelter and medical care to likings

---

79 Cf. Mann, Michael (1986): p. 25.
80 Poggi (2001): p. 124.
81 Even most libertarians admit as much. Cf. Hayek, Friedrich A. (1939): *Freedom and the Economic System*, Chicago: Chicago University Press.; and Nozick (1974). Criticism nevertheless is offered by Rapaczynski, Andrzej (1996): The Roles of the State and the Market in Establishing Property Rights, *The Journal of Economic Perspectives*, 10 (2), pp. 87-103.
82 Mann (1986): p. 24.

developed through civilization such as tobacco, alcohol or sweets. The neediness of humans is, as we have demonstrated in detail in Chapter 1.2, among the main roots and most fundamental principles of power. The overall societal power position of the economic sphere in relation to other social spheres is thus clear: it results from the fact that the labor-sharing practices of producing and distributing goods and services are indispensable for satisfying needs. Alone, an individual would never be able to produce even a fraction of the required goods and services.

Nevertheless, a number of economists from the famous Viennese school, especially Eugen Böhm von Bawerk, denied that power plays a role within the economic field.[83] They suggest that the transaction mechanisms of the market (i.e.: who buys what from whom at what price and who works for whom at what cost) are determined only by the relationship between supply and demand – and not by factors of power. The state ensures this by guaranteeing the peaceableness and voluntariness of economic practices. This position was early contested, for instance in the influential essay *The Domination Effect and Modern Economic Theory* by the French economist François Perroux.[84] Perroux formulates his counter-thesis as follows: "Economic life is something different from a network of exchange. It is, rather, a network of forces. The economy is guided not only by the search for gain but also by that for power. The two motives are seen to be intermingled in the policy of a firm or of a national economy."[85] Power, according to Perroux, is an irreducible component of economic life; indeed, power is the foremost purpose of economic life. It expresses itself in this sphere in the form of the eponymous 'domination effect'. "Between two economic units, A and B, the domination effect is present when, in a definite field, unit A exercises on unit B an irreversible or partially irreversible influence. [...] For example, a business firm in many cases influences decisions concerning price and quantity made by another firm, client or competitor, the inverse not being true."[86] If power manifests itself in one actor being able to influence the decisions of another in terms of price and product design, production form, contract, type and duration of employment rela

---

83 Cf. Böhm von Bawerk, Eugen (1914): Macht oder ökonomisches Gesetz?, *Zeitschrift für Volkswirtschaft, Sozialpolitik und Verwaltung,* 23, pp. 205-271.

84 Perroux, François (1950): The Domination Effect and Modern Economic Theory, *Social Research,* 17 (2), pp. 188-206. For a more in-depth analysis, see Sandretto, René (2009): François Perroux, a precursor of the current analyses of power, *The Journal of World Economic Review,* 5 (1), pp. 57-68. For a similar approach, see Blau, Robert (1965): *Exchange and Power in Social Life,* New York: Wiley.

85 Perroux (1950): p. 188.

86 Ibid.

tionships, etc., without the second actor being able to counter this, then the question arises: What is the basis of economic power? Moreover, what are the power resources of this field?

The answer to this question fills libraries. Ultimately, nevertheless, four basic types of power resources can be identified: capital, qualifications, ownership of raw materials and land, and finally data.[87] Since more than 200 years, the generic term of capital has been firmly anchored in economic literature.[88] For a better overview, we can categorize it into three areas. Real capital or capital stock refers to nothing other than the control by a private or state-owned enterprise of the means of production by which goods (cars, medicines, sugar, computers, etc.) can be produced and services (healthcare, school lessons, manicures, political consultation, etc.) can be provided. Therefore, the category of real capital includes items as diverse as factories, machinery, office buildings, coffee machines, taxis, tattoo machines, notepads, pens, etc. In contrast thereto, financial capital refers to the financial resources of a company that are used to expand, renew, and preserve real capital. The third and most recently identified aspect is that of human capital, which represents the performance potential and productivity of the workforce.

Differences in capital between the players in the economic sphere are significant in determining differences in power. Highly capitalized companies can afford to pay higher wages and lure the best workers from their competitors. They can increase production volumes and flood the market with products, force competitors into price wars, drive market trends through innovation – and so on. In short, they can dominate the market decisions of other players. Amidst all of this, however, we should not overlook one thing: there are very few players, namely companies, in this sphere that have capital at all in the sense introduced above. Most protagonists participate in the market only as sellers of their labor. The result is a further power gap, which Marx was not the first to draw attention to, but rather a theoretician who has little to do with socialist thought. In his classic *The Wealth of Nations,* Adam Smith writes: "Many workmen could not subsist a week, few could subsist a month, and scarce any a year without employment. In the long run the workman may be as necessary to his master as the master is to him; but the necessity is not so immediate."[89] Even though firms and employees are structur

---

87 Poggi (2001): pp. 127-135; and Scott, John (2001): *Power*, Cambridge: Polity Press.; p. 73.
88 Cf. Krugman, Paul and Wells, Robin (2015): *Economics*, 4th edition, New York: Worth Publishers.; pp. 252f.
89 Cf. Smith, Adam ([1776] 2012): *An Inquiry into the Nature and Causes of the Wealth of Nations,* London: W. Strathan.; p. 76.

ally dependent on each other – the firms need the labor power, the workers the wages – their power relations are asymmetrical.[90] Poggi, a friend of concise aphorisms, puts it this way: "It is capital that hires labor, not vice versa."[91]

In the power struggle between companies and employees, however, a second power resource is central: qualifications. While unskilled workers have little choice about which employment they pursue, and above all under what conditions (wages, holidays, workplace design, training, etc.), the situation for qualified workers is completely different. Here it is worthwhile to cite in more detail from the excellent essay *Power, Property, and the Distribution of Income* by the economist Erich Preiser: "[P]ower presupposes that the economic agent has the possibility of stipulating conditions, that he may accept or refuse offers, that he can evade pressure; such a possibility presupposes in its turn [...] qualifications higher than average, i.e. some specifically rare skill."[92] If actors possess an ability that is in high demand by firms but is very rare (for example, programming and IT skills, engineering know-how), they can reverse the balance of power and in turn dictate terms of employment. The same is true of individuals with skills which are rare in the population overall and which they master exceptionally well (e.g. star pianists or major league baseball allstars).

The third power resource of the economic field that we wish to touch upon is the ownership of resources and territory. The power-strategic relevance of both factors is immediately obvious. Actors who are the sole (or one of a few) suppliers of a resource that is difficult to substitute (diamonds, uranium, rare earth elements, oil, etc.) can, first, as monopolists or oligopolists, drastically increase prices without losing customers.[93] Second, they can force market participants to enter into or break off economic ties with other players, under threat of depriving them of the resource in question. And thirdly, they can hinder the development of alternatives or, indeed, bring them to a standstill by lowering prices. In short, the supplier, in the sense of Perroux, is able to dominate the behavior of other economic actors without them possessing the possibility of developing countervailing power. The remarkable aspect in this context is that a lack of capital in the sense introduced above can be compensated for strategically by control over raw materials. An impressive example is the rise of the oil-rich Gulf monarchies, most notably Saudi

---

90   Preiser, Erich (1971): Power, Property, and the Distribution of Income, in: Kurt W. Rothschild (ed.), *Power in Economics,* Harmondsworth: Penguin, pp. 119-140.
91   Poggi (2001): p. 127.
92   Preiser (1971): p. 136.
93   For an in-depth discussion of the monopoly and oligopoly nomenclature, see Krugman & Wells (2015): pp. 387-444; cf. also Scott (2001): p. 73.

Arabia, since the early 1940s. Although in the mid-twentieth century these states lacked significant capital (real, financial or human capital), by exploiting their oil resources they quickly became influential regional powers with global corporate holdings, rapidly offsetting their capital backlog.

The same applies to the possession of economically and/or politically significant territories. Actors controlling a strait important to international maritime trade or the territory of an oil pipeline can mobilize immense instrumental power in the economic sphere. The downside: a concentration of such power resources motivates the development of economic and political countervailing power. An example is the still-smoldering gas dispute between Russia and Ukraine.[94] Until the 2010s, Russia transported most of its natural gas exports via Ukrainian pipelines to Europe. This transit route was practically the only option for the Russian corporate entity Gazprom. The result of this dependency was that the Ukrainian side was able to obtain gas from Russia far below market price. In 2005, Russian President Vladimir Putin ended that practice. The prices were re-fixed and sharply increased. This decision triggered a rapidly escalating exchange of blows. The leadership in Kiev refused to accept the new prices; Gazprom stopped supplying gas to Ukrainian buyers; Ukraine diverted exports intended for European customers (including Germany, France, Austria, Hungary) for its own use. The drop in supplies to Europe and the rapidly developing political pressure forced both sides to the negotiating table. However, agreements reached in the short term were always characterized by a short half-life. It was only in autumn 2014 that a compromise could be reached. Ukraine's decision to give up its blockade was decisively influenced by Moscow's decision to construct the alternative Nord Stream route through the Baltic Sea, allowing gas to be directly exported to Europe. This project abruptly enabled Moscow to bypass Ukraine and, if not to completely devaluate, at least to weaken its territorial power resources. It is obvious that the parallel mobilization of political-military action power against Ukraine (including the occupation of the Crimea and the battle for Donetsk) effectively supplemented this economic strategy. Thus, the gas dispute also provides a compelling example of how an actor skilled in power strategizing, the Putin government, can successfully combine power resources from different fields.

---

[94] For more information, see Stulberg, Adam N. (2015): Out of Gas? Russia, Ukraine, Europe, and the Changing Geopolitics of Gas, *Problems of Post-Communism*, 62 (2), pp. 112-130.

Another example of the importance of territories as power resources, which we will briefly discuss here, is the Suez Canal.[95] This artificial waterway in northeastern Egypt connects the Mediterranean with the Red Sea and, since its opening in 1869, has been under Ottoman, then British and finally Egyptian control. The Canal allows ocean-going vessels crossing between the North Atlantic and the Indian Ocean to avoid the passage around the notorious Cape of Good Hope at the southern tip of Africa. Conservative estimates suggest that this results in a time saving of over 40%. Several dozen container ships pass through the roughly 190-kilometer-long passage every day. The power potential is obvious: whoever controls the Suez Canal dominates the mechanisms of international maritime trade.[96] They can dictate prices, lock out competitors, privilege allies, etc. However, the international status of the Suez Canal was established between the original builders, the Ottoman Empire, and the large and significant European powers early on. Since the Treaty of Constantinople in 1888, this has been a neutral zone with free passage for all commercial and military ships; the options for political instrumentalization are correspondingly limited. However, the strategic importance of the Suez Canal is shown by the fact that this neutrality has been repeatedly called into question in the last 100 years: in 1916 by the Central Powers in the First World War; in 1941 by the Axis Powers in World War II; in 1956 by the Egyptian government under head of state Gamal Abdel Nasser; and finally in 1967 in the Six-Day War between Egypt and Israel. Each time, the actors tried to assert a sole claim to power over and use of the Suez Canal – and each time, after bloody clashes, the status quo was restored. The Constantinople Agreement is still valid today, and its enforcement is the responsibility of the Egyptian government. The fact that the Egyptian government continues to be supported by the West despite innumerable human rights violations owes something to its role as the guardian of this neutrality. For large shipping companies there is no greater nightmare scenario than the sea passage being controlled by Islamist fundamentalists. As a result of this risk, the present military regime of Fatah al-Sisi controls crucial power capital.

Data constitute the fourth and final power resource of the economic field. In a way, they comprise a special case. Without question, accumulating, storing, monopolizing, analyzing and evaluating data has always been a component of power.

---

95 A historical overview is offered by Karabell, Zachary (2003): *Parting the Desert. The Creation of the Suez Canal*, New York/Toronto: Knopf.
96 Only the Panama Canal, which connects the Atlantic Ocean with the Pacific at the Isthmus of Panama, is of similar maritime and thus geopolitical significance. Cf. Major, John (1993). *Prize Possession: The United States and the Panama Canal, 1903–1979*, Cambridge: Cambridge University Press.

However, it is only the technological, economic and social developments of recent decades, which we refer to as the interdependent phenomena of digitization, globalization and acceleration that have made data probably the most important power resource of our days. For the first time in human history, there are computers and software-based algorithms that can collect and correlate large amounts of data worldwide, allowing unprecedented forms of information retrieval and information exchange. The effects are dramatic: in the age of 'big data', we experience nothing less than the blending of professional and private spheres (for example, on social networks like Facebook or Weibo) and the flow of individual contexts into multiple horizons of experience. The metaphor of the net, which stands alongside the term 'World Wide Web', is apt in two ways. Since the onset of the digital revolution, we have been connected to countless people and organizations in all imaginable areas of life, and we can communicate and collaborate across continents in fractions of a second.[97] But at the same time, this digitized existence is inescapable, a retreat into a self-sufficient life is, once and for all, history.

What does all this have to do with power? Let us look first at the importance of data power from an *organizational and economic* point of view, and then take a closer look at its *political* relevance.

The superior ability of organizations – whether corporations or NGOs – to collect, read and correlate the data of (potential) customers and supporters is a dramatic competitive advantage over competitors. If an organization knows its 'followers' – which websites do they visit and for how long? What sports do they prefer? Which products do they buy? What religious, sexual and aesthetic preferences do they have? – the organization is better able to develop *tailor-made products and services*. Indeed, the former CEO of Tableau Software, Christian Chabot, described data as the "oil of the twenty-first century." In the competition for data power, actors who can position themselves as intermediaries or enablers between end-users and other (digital) service providers have an advantage. Platforms and portals are thus increasingly becoming one of the key players in the market. This strategy has been perfected by, for example, the Chinese company WeChat. Its smartphone app, which dominates Asia, not only has chat capabilities, but also acts as a payment software, game portal and search engine. WeChat provides a universal platform through which the company can not only access user data, but is also able to establish a power relationship with other companies because it con

---

[97] By means of illustration, according to a survey by Internet World Stats in June 2016, the number of internet users worldwide amounted to 3,675,824,813 people, [online] http://www.internetworldstats.com/stats.htm, retrieved 21.12.2017.

trols user access to the service providers and can thus determine the conditions of economic cooperation.

Access to and use of data not only plays a core role in the design of innovative products and services, it is also critical in *predicting market trends and positioning organizations*. The keyword here is currently 'Predictive Analytics'. From data obtained through social networks, the so-called Internet of Things (IOT) and countless sensors in machines, algorithms can derive forecasts with extremely high probabilities predicting the development of oil prices, the rise and fall of stock prices and government bonds, and even pregnancies.[98] When venture capitalists invest in Airbnb, it's not just about the business model of the booking platform. Rather, the company's comprehensive data on rental costs, housing and demand-supply ratios allow a better prediction of real estate price development in large cities than any other database. In short, anyone who can read Airbnb's data has an extremely powerful tool for predicting market trends.

The third aspect of economic data power concerns the market segment of *horizontal and vertical search engines*. While horizontal search engines such as Google, Bing or Yahoo allow cross-subject searches, vertical search engines such as Yelp or TripAdvisor are topic-, location- or subject-specific. They specialize in restaurants, travel destinations or news. For both divisions, however, a common principle applies: the more processed and structured the data that the search engine has available, the more precise is its search performance and the linking of the data – and the greater the information gain for the searchers. At the same time, this results in a self-reinforcing effect: with each individual new request, the algorithm of the search engine improves, thus extending the competitive advantage.

Last but not least, data form part of economic power mechanisms as commodities. As mentioned above, they are indispensable for the development of products and services as well as for customer loyalty, market positioning and other core elements of organizational economic development. That is why many players in

---

98 Some years ago, the US supermarket chain Target demonstrated the quality of its prognoses by sending coupons for diapers and other baby products to a teenager in Minnesota. The consumption behavior of the young woman had indicated a pregnancy. The targeting was spot on. The particularly peculiar point about the story was that the girl had at this point not even entrusted her own parents with the news of her pregnancy, cf. Hill, Kashmir (2012): How Target Figured Out A Teen Girl Was Pregnant Before Her Father Did, in: Forbes Magazin from 16th February 2012, [online] https://www.forbes.com/sites/kashmirhill/2012/02/16/how-target-figured-out-a-teen-girl-was-pregnant-before-her-father-did/#418017cd6668, retrieved on 21.12.2017.

the economic sphere have specialized in collecting, processing, presenting and reselling data. Data, to put it in the language of economics, are a "monetarily measurable factor of production" and, accordingly, a predestined commodity[99]. Representatives of this business are not just data management corporations like Arvato or Doubleclick, but also campaign platforms such as change.org.[100] This platform markets itself as a non-profit citizen movement, on whose homepage people can place petitions for free. *De facto,* however, there is much to suggest that change.org stores data from petition signatories, condenses the data into profiles and then releases them – for fundraising purposes, for example.

The immense economic importance of data in the twenty-first century entails a global shift in the *focus of value creation*. In the pre-digital age, value creation was generated first and foremost from material products, i.e. from 'hardware', but we are currently experiencing a shift to 'software'. Because digitization covers the entire manufacturing realm (from the kitchen appliance manufacturer offering machines with access to web-based cookbooks to the vehicle manufacturer who develops autonomouscars), the processing of and sovereignty over data is becoming the core issue of a connected economy. All this should not, however, distract from one crucial condition: data alone are not knowledge but mere disaggregated par

---

[99] Ibid.: p. 275. In the US, the current market value of specific categories of data (from addresses to social security numbers to information on bankruptcies suffered) can even be determined online with a so-called "data calculator", cf. Swipe Toolkit, Data Calculator, [online] http://archive.turbulence.org/Works/swipe/calculator.html, most recently retrieved on 21.12.2017.

[100] Change.org received the 2016 BigBrotherAward for its negative handling of user data from the association Digitalcourage e.V., c.f. Bakir, Daniel (2016): Big Brother Awards 2016: Change.org - eine Weltverbesserer-Plattform als gierige Datenkrake, in: Stern from 22th 2016, [online] http://www.stern.de/wirtschaft/news/big-brother-awards--change-org-als-datenkrake-ausgezeichnet-6807950.html, retr on 21.12.2017. The allegations are supported by a report by Tilo Weichert (the former, well-respected data protection officer of the North German State of Schleswig-Holstein and internet activist), which alleges that change.org, contrary to its self-portrayal, is abusing user data and, moreover, disregarding EU data protection law, cf. Netzwerk Datenschutzexpertise (2015): Datenschutzrechtliche Bewertung des Internet-Beteiligungsportals Change.org von Dr. Thilo Weichert, [online] http://www.netzwerk-datenschutzexpertise.de/dokument/datenschutzrechtliche-bewertung-des-internet-beteiligungsportals-changeorg, retrieved on 21.12.2017. See also Casano, Olivia (2016): Why You Should Think Twice Before Signing a Change.org Petition, [online] http://www.konbini.com/en/lifestyle/change-org-data-mining/, retrieved on 06.02.2018.

ticulars about people, machines, transactions, etc. In order to develop and evaluate strategically relevant information from such particulars, sophisticated big-data software and, increasingly, artificial intelligence are needed. These developments are only in their infancy. The economic sphere is facing deep, far-reaching revolutions in the wake of future technological innovation.[101]

The data power of the economic sphere has always been intensively and critically pursued by *politics* – on the one hand as a risk in the "struggle over 'trumpness'", on the other hand as a condition for enabling and potentiating one's own ability to act both internally and externally. After all, just as wars cannot be waged without an armaments industry, the state cannot control people without the control of communications media (ranging from printing through telegraphy and telephony to e-mail traffic). Data power was and is always highly relevant for political actors such as ministries, tax authorities, parties, military or intelligence services. The digital revolution has only contributed to perfecting this resource. Four areas are central in the context of politics: first, surveillance; second, cyber warfare; third, communication and influencing; and fourth, forecasting and simulation.

Even before the revelations of the former US National Security Agency (NSA) employee and whistleblower Edward Snowden it was already well-known that big data had also revolutionized the intelligence service, and their significance has since increased exponentially.[102] Spies were, until the 1980s, limited to planting 'bugs' and listening in on individual telephone lines, whereas now, in the digital age, they enjoy the prospect of *data surveillance,* i.e. *dataveillance,* mass data monitoring.[103] The foundation of this monitoring process is the storage of globally available digitized data (IP addresses, e-mails, search queries, credit card debits, tweets, etc.) gathered, for example, through the tapping of the thousands of submarine data cables that transport countless pentabytes of information around the globe every day. This gigantic raw mass is examined by automated arithmetic operations on key concepts, patterns and connections, ordered, linked with cross-references and classified. The analysis is crucial: it allows intelligence agencies to

---

101 For a recommendable overview, see Schwab, Klaus (2017): *The Fourth Industrial Revolution.* Köln: World Economic Forum.

102 Cf. Lyon, David (2016): Snowden, everyday practices and digital futures, in: Tugba Basaran, Didier Bigo, Emmanuel-Pierre Guittet, and R. B. J. Walker (eds.), *International Political Sociology, Transversal lines.* London/New York: Routledge, pp. 254-271.

103 Insiders speak of a "collect it all approach", cf. Hu, Margaret (2014): Small Data Surveillance vs. Big Data Cybersurveillance. *Pepperdine Law Review,* 42 (4), pp. 773-844.

identify terrorists, to create movement patterns, to assess the risk of events, to profile foreign politicians and, last but not least, to acquire economically sensitive information from other nations (keyword: industrial espionage). Pioneering this battle for public data power are the NSA and the British Government Communications Headquarters (GCHQ). With their respective surveillance programs *Tempora* and *Prisms,* both intelligence agencies can analyze data from up to two billion people in a single day.

While dataveillance's sole aim is to obtain information, the aim of *cyber warfare* is to directly or indirectly harm opposing states and non-state actors, e.g. terrorist groups or paramilitary organizations.[104] The distinction is not always easy to make, as military analyst Martin C. Libicki points out. Nevertheless, he proposes the following definition: "*cyberattack* [...] is the deliberate disruption or corruption by one state of a system of interest to another state. [...] CNE (spying) is not an attack (as disruption and corruption are)."[105] The military and economic powers of political actors increasingly depend on computer networks, and because these networks can be infiltrated from external sources Libicki suggests that cyberattacks represent an exponentially increasing security risk. States, according to the military logic, must therefore continuously expand both their ability to defend against cyberattacks and their attack capacity – for the purpose of deterrence.

Basically, two distinct forms of cyberattacks can be identified: first, direct damage to hardware or software by hacker attacks and malware; second, indirect damage to the opponent through the targeted placement of false information and propaganda. There have been countless examples of the first form of cyberattack in the recent past. In 2007, the Estonian government decided, in the face of massive Russian protest, to relocate a Soviet military monument from the center of Tallinn to the outskirts of the city. A few weeks later, Estonia's major government websites were flooded with queries and shut down by thousands of computers *de facto* remotely controlled by virus attacks. The government had no choice but to temporarily cut the country completely off from the global data network and fundamentally revise its security infrastructure. The Kremlin never officially took responsibility for the attack, but blocked all further investigations. Only three years later, a serious incident occurred in the Iranian uranium enrichment plant of Natanz: the entire control system of the highly sensitive centrifuges – *Siemens* products from Germany – went haywire, as it were, and the turbines were irreparably damaged. The prestige project of the then President Mahmoud Ahmadinejad was

---

104 A truly informative introduction to this topic area is offered by Libicki, Martin C. (2009): *Cyberdeterrence and Cyberwar*, Santa Monica: Rand.
105 Ibid.: p. 23.

shut down shortly before its planned culmination. It quickly became clear that behind the malfunction was a so-called cyberworm named 'Stuxnet', which had been developed and introduced by US military forces together with Israel[106]. It would hardly be exaggerated from today's perspective to suggest that the Stuxnet attack was what made possible the so-called "EU +3 Atomic Energy Agreement" of 2015 to ensure exclusively civilian nuclear energy use by Tehran.[107]

The indirect form of cyber attacks is now inextricably linked to the terms 'social bot' and 'fake news'. Social bots are uniquely programmed and then largely "autonomously acting programs on the Internet [that] disguise their true identity and pretend to the user that they are real people"[108]. This masquerade is maintained by software robots using specially created Facebook profiles, Twitter and Reddit accounts or other social media accounts. Through these profiles, massive amounts of political opinions or fake news are placed in social networks and the comment columns of media pages. Once fed by a basic vocabulary of keywords by their programmers, the bots can independently regenerate the information themselves, adapt it to current events, or even communicate to human users in real-time chats.[109] Scientific surveys such as the study *When Social Bots Attack,* as conducted by the University of Graz, impressively demonstrate how quickly people

---

106 For technical details as to the Stuxnet sabotage see Farwell, James P. and Rohozinski, Rafal (2011): Stuxnet and the Future of Cyber War, *Survival,* 53 (1), pp. 23-40. For the political background, see Sanger, David A. (2012): *Confront and Conceal: Obama's Secret Wars and Surprising Use of American Power,* New York: Crown Publishers.

107 See additionally: European External Action Service (2015): Joint Comprehensive Plan of Action, [online] http://www.eeas.europa.eu/statementseeas/docs/iran_agree ment/iran_joint-comprehensive-plan-of-action_en.pdf, retrieved on 21.12.2017.

108 Hegelich, Simon (2016): Invasion der Meinungsroboter, *Analysen und Argumente,* 221, pp. 1-9.; A good overview of the current state of research is offered by Woolley, James C. (2016): Automating Power: Social Bots Interfere in Global Politics. *First Monday,* 21 (4), [online] http://firstmonday.org/ojs/index.php/fm/article/view/ 6161/5300, retrieved on 21.12.2017.

109 Incidentally, as is so often the case, the sex and erotic industry was at the forefront of this technological development. Already in the early 2000s, for example, the 'chat and cheat' portal Ashley Madison utilized so-called 'chat bots', which posed as real women and successfully pulled money out of the pockets of male online visitors.

fall prey to artificial profiles.[110] The law of large numbers plays a decisive role here: Simon Hegelich, an expert in political data science, claims that with deployment software for just $500, it is possible to control 10,000 Twitter accounts.[111] The propagandistic power potential is obvious: "Bots manipulate the trends in social media, and these trends are incorporated into political and economic decision-making processes."[112] On the one hand, politicians can be misled as to the mood among the population. One example is the immense accumulation of pro-Russian posts in German social media during the Crimean annexation in 2014, which were in sharp contrast to actual survey findings and were probably launched by Kremlin-loyal programmers. On the other hand, groups can be mobilized or stirred up against each other. In 2015, for example, a botnet of the Ukrainian paramilitary network Pravyj Sector (Right Sector) spread the false news that Russia-led separatists were targeting Kiev with missiles.[113] However, the problem of influencing trends not only affects human media consumers. Even software-based algorithms that comb through social networks for policy analysis can fall for social bots and forward deficient management reports to decision-makers. Therefore, this power and technology field is characterized by a continuous innovation competition between analysts and manipulators.

The importance of big data for *influencing democratic competition* is the third focus of political data power. A crucial component here is the efficient combination of data-driven dialog communication and *psychometrics*. Psychometrics is a scientific method for measuring the psyche of a person and typing according to personality dimensions (needs, fears, hopes, social behavior, etc.). Until the advent of the internet age, this was a tedious and time-consuming discipline, coupled with interviews, detailed questionnaires and the entire toolbox of empirical social science. Since the digital revolution, people increasingly communicate via digital media. In this way, information about them is permanently recorded in the internet

---

110 Cf. Wagner, Claudia, Mitter, Silvia, Körner, Christian, and Strohmaier, Markus (2012): When social bots attack, Modeling susceptibility of users in online social networks, Proceedings of the WWW'12 Workshop on Making Sense of Microposts, pp. 41-18.
111 Cf. Hegelich (2016): p. 3.
112 Ibid.
113 Cf. Hegelich, Simon and Janetzko, Dietmar (2016): *Are social Bots on Twitter Political Actors? Empirical Evidence from a Ukrainian Social Botnet*, Proceedings of the 10th International AAAI Conference on Web and Social Media, [online] https://www.aaai.org/ocs/index.php/ICWSM/ICWSM16/paper/view/13015/12793, retrieved on 21.12.2017.

– it only needs to be analyzed. In the political arena, data mining and data targeting have been part of everyday business for over a decade. Campaigning without detailed knowledge of the target groups and their main topics is no longer possible today. The pioneers here are the USA, where an extremely liberal and rather unrestricted data protection law gives the campaign strategist far greater room for maneuver in the use of data power than in Germany, for example. In election campaigns, experts can now exactly determine voting preferences down to the street name and house number. Using a modest number of online activities (blog and magazine subscriptions, discount campaigns, club memberships, etc.) it is possible to derive the political attitude of a person and their probable voting decision – even if the actual activities have nothing to do with politics.

The relevance for democracies is obvious: in "grassroots campaigning," for example, campaigns address targeted citizens in order to transport content to multipliers who then disseminate or multiply the political messages and make their voice and face available to the campaign. In this way, "protest events, civil initiatives, support associations and citizens' lobbies can emerge", which function as political "pressure groups."[114] In addition, methods based on big data allow political parties to divide all voters into supporters, opponents and undecideds. And above all, they allow targeted communication and motivation through tailor-made dialogue communication on preferred homepages, in social networks and through e-mail messages that are oriented to the preferences of the individual. In short: through the combination of psychometrics and data-driven communication, exactly that aspect of the party program is brought to the notice of the target group most receptive to it. Two major events of 2016 are paradigmatic for the triumph of data-driven political influencing: Brexit and the election of Donald Trump as US President. Both the EU opponents under Nigel Farage and the Republican candidate relied heavily and successfully in their election campaigns on the digital component of their dialogue strategies. This success, which most commentators had not predicted, also shows that the classic media – television, newspapers and radio – have lost their exclusive political gatekeeping function. The opinion battlefields of the future lie in digital space. Of course, the aforementioned targeted identification, communication and motivation has potential not only for democratic actors but can also, obviously, serve dictatorships and autocracies, allowing them to optimize their psychological indoctrination.

---

114 Speth, Rudolf (2010): Grassroots Campaigning, in: Olaf Hoffjann and Roland Stahl (eds.), *Handbuch Verbandskommunikation,* Wiesbaden: VS Verlag, pp. 317-332.; p. 317.

The fourth and final aspect of political data power – the topic of *prognosis* – almost sounds like science fiction. In his 1956 short story *The Minority Report*, writer Philip Dick creates a world in which a group of mutants can predict crimes. The security authorities in Dick's narrative draw a pragmatic, if ethically dubious, advantage from this prophetic gift: they arrest the persons in question before said suspects even become perpetrators. For Dick's contemporaries such considerations were entertaining, but above all unrealistic. Today things are different. Under the heading "Predictive Policing" the algorithm-based evaluation of crime statistics and case data (for example, place of crime: villa quarter, type: theft of hi-fi system, number of perpetrators: four, etc.) are summarized. This can be used to determine the probability with which a certain kind of crime is committed when, where and by whom. An impressive example is provided by the *Crime Reduction Utilizing Statistical History (CRUSH)* software developed by IBM.[115] In 2005, the IT Group, together with the Memphis Police Department, designed the program that uses the local police database to identify future crime trends, calculating and identifying hot spots where perpetrators will strike at certain periods. From then on, squad cars patrolled exactly those areas within the predicted time periods. Within a few years, the crime rate in Memphis fell by more than 30%. At the same time, the Police Department was able to reduce active personnel and use its human resources more efficiently.

Obviously, however, the power of forecasting based on big data is not limited to the area of crime prevention. A recently developed offshoot of *Blue CRUSH*, appropriately christened *CRASH (Crash Reduction Analyzing Statistical History)* by its inventors, can use traffic data to calculate accident probabilities and predict traffic jams. In health policy, comparable algorithms from medical statistics and medical records can identify specific health risks, depending on the population and age group. The list could be continued *ad nauseam*. From a power theory perspective, these prognostic instruments are excellent control tools for state institutions. At a stroke they make the developments and patterns of behavior of populations in all imaginable fields of action comprehensible and therefore more controllable. Foucault, the great theoretician of universal control (see Chapter 1.2), could not have imagined it better. At the same time, however, the question is raised as to whether everything that is feasible is morally acceptable or reasonable.

We can only address this genuinely ethical and power-strategic problem very briefly; it is not the focus of this book and, besides, we are only at the starting

---

115 Cf. Figg, Erinn (2014): The legacy of Blue CRUSH, in: High Ground News from 19th March 2014, [online] http://www.highgroundnews.com/features/BlueCrush 031214.aspx, retrieved on 21.12.2017.

point of the relevant technological changes.[116] Ultimately, in the context of data power, these issues revolve around one key point, no matter whether we are talking about economic or political issues: whom does data actually belong to, and what rights can the "owner" of the data legitimately claim against others? The extreme opinions can be quickly outlined. According to the libertarian position, no one can assert a sole right of disposition. The data that a person creates by sharing a newspaper article on social networks, booking a trip to the Maldives, or measuring their heartbeat with an internet-enabled device belong to everybeody – and therefore to nobody. By contrast, the radical counter-position focuses on individual rights and views the individual as the sole decision-making authority about what happens to their data, who is allowed to exploit these data and for what. It quickly becomes clear that both positions are ideals, are not practicable and are thus unjustifiable. The first approach makes short work of the idea of privacy and disregards the legal-moral element of our liberal constitutional state. The second approach, in turn, implies the paralyzing of the politico-economic capacity to act. It *de facto* declares every single individual sovereign and thus leads the idea of political community to an absurd extreme.

Decisions about the use of data power reflect, in particular, the political balance of power in societies – it is thus a contested field, which is located between the two extremes. The ethics of data are, so our concise conclusion, thus a political issue. They must be created, implemented and constantly re-examined and reformed in a process of negotiation and decision-making in the light of technological innovations and cultural paradigm shifts. It is important to differentiate between the public and the economic sector: state institutions are assigned a protective task towards the general public (see Section 2.5.3 on instruments of power), which does not apply to companies. Because, for example, police and intelligence agencies have the exclusive function of effectively warding off attacks on the population by terrorists, criminals and other enemies of the community, their data power and the corresponding legal restrictions and requirements must also take these tasks into account.

At this juncture, we wish to conclude our discussion of economic power resources and the focus on data and address the relation of the economic sphere to the other fields. We have already highlighted its significant position. Without a system for the production and distribution of goods and services, the other fields and their practices could not be sustained. The experiences of the twentieth century – above all the failure of Soviet Communism – also suggest that the economic

---

116 Compare, however, e.g. Richards, Neill M. and King, Jonathan H. (2014): Big Data Ethics, *Wake Forest Law Review,* pp. 394-422.

power field can only develop its full productivity with the guarantee of a degree of autonomy and the safeguarding of the market mechanism. Due to this special status, it is predestined to intervene in other fields in the "struggle over 'trumpness'" and to enforce the primacy of its power logic. We do not have to go so far as to accept a simple "money-rules-the-world-scheme." Nor do we have to follow Marx and see politics and religion as only the causally irrelevant "superstructure" of an economic "substructure."[117] Such authoritative views underestimate the defensibility of religious and political fields against economic strategies of appropriation. Nonetheless, such strategies do shape the social world.

A historical example of the advance of the economic logic of power into the sphere of religion is – of course – the trade in indulgences.[118] The original idea of indulgences, which has existed since late antiquity, is hardly offensive. It signifies "a remission of the temporal punishments of sins granted by the church outside of the sacrament of penance and valid before God";[119] allowing not the forgiveness of sins themselves, but a renunciation of their punishment in the hereafter through good deeds, prayers, pilgrimages, alms, etc. This practice was only vehemently criticized when the Renaissance popes came up with the idea of trading the divine renunciation of punishment as a commodity in order to fill the coffers of the Roman Curia. All of a sudden, solvent patricians, mercenaries and noblemen could buy their salvation and continue to sin without worry, because the church would grant them an indulgence in return for money. The problem was, as the great historian of religion, Nikolaus Paulus, states, "that the indulgence, which was supposed to be primarily a spiritual instrument of pastoral care, was used primarily as a source of income":[120] From a power-strategic point of view, this circumstance is

---

117 Poggi (2001): pp. 58f.; attempts to salvage Marx's theory. According to his interpretation, the author of Capital assumes a systematic equality between the three central power fields – religion, economics, politics. However, this interpretation does not withstand an examination of the original sources and a more detailed secondary reading. For Marx, all the laws of the social world are derived from the laws of the economic sphere; political, religious, cultural and other phenomena arise only from more fundamental economic processes.
118 For an overview of the classics on this topic, see Paulus, Nikolaus ([1922] 2000): *Geschichte des Ablasses im Mittelalter. Vom Ursprunge bis zur Mitte des 14. Jahrhunderts*, Darmstadt: Wissenschaftliche Buchgesellschaft.; and Paulus, Nikolaus ([1923] 2000): *Geschichte des Ablasses am Ausgang des Mittelalters,* Darmstadt: Wissenschaftliche Buchgesellschaft.
119 Paulus ([1922] 2000): p. 1.
120 Ibid.; p. 379.

as dramatic as it is interesting. By trading with indulgences, the central power resource of the economic field suddenly became a crucial power resource within the religious field. Whereas previously actors had to submit to genuinely religious rules and the commandments of the clergy and sincerely (or at least plausibly) repent of transgressions, they could now apply the logic of the market one-to-one to religious practice. Against this background, the fury of the Reformation, which was ignited by these events, and the great success of the ecclesiastical revolutionaries around Martin Luther, are hardly surprising. What was at stake here was ultimately nothing more – and nothing less – than the autonomy of the Christian religion as an independent power field.

The intervention of the economic sphere in the power field of politics is a standard topic of political debate. Nevertheless, we would do well here to make a clear distinction, which is often ignored in everyday politics: a distinction between the assertion of economic interests in the political decision-making process on the one hand and the attempt to export the power logic of the economy into politics, on the other. The former is, in our opinion, a legitimate aspect of political decision-making (see Chapter 2.4)[121]; the latter is an attack on the autonomy of the political power field. We can speak of such an attack, for instance, when people try to buy political decisions and/or offices. Of course, the keyword here is corruption. At this point we do not want to conduct a detailed debate on the concept of corruption. For us it is only relevant that in the course of corruption political decisions are treated like commercial services and political offices like commodities. In the same way as in the above case, this is an attempt to anchor the principles of the market and its central power resources in a non-economic field, thereby marginalizing the power logic and resources of that field. This phenomenon is devastating not only for politics and its core tasks, but ultimately for the economic sphere itself. This can be seen in the global corruption index, which has been collected since 1995 by *Transparency International.*[122] Mismanagement, inefficiency and social misery are so closely correlated with corruption that one cannot believe it a coincidence.

---

121 In his seminal work on interest representation at the EU level, Klemens Joos accurately observes that lobbying links the systems of politics and the economy by overcoming barriers to communication through its mediation activity. Ideally, then, lobbying acts as a translation mechanism between the two sides. Joos, Klemens (2016): *Convincing Political Stakeholders: Successful lobbying through process competence in the complex decision-making system of the European Union,* Weinheim: Wiley.

122 See www.transparency.org.

2.3.3 The Political Power Field

Let us then turn to the last great power field, politics. What distinguishes the political and what differentiates it from other spheres of society is a notoriously difficult question.[123] Instead of becoming entangled in lengthy conceptual struggles, we use the following definition: the basic principle of the political is the authorization and enforcement of collectively binding norms of action. What is at stake in politics – at its core – is the organization of social coexistence through community rules that can be enforced if necessary with the power of action, that is, violence. Whether these rules are determined in the form of the Civil Code and the Criminal Code, in the form of the Babylonian legal code Hamurabi from the eighteenth century BC or through orally communicated taboos is unimportant at this stage. Equally irrelevant is the separation of authoritative political powers into legislative, executive and judicial branches. The decisive factor is that we can speak of a political power field if and only if the governing, enforcing and supervising authority is (to a certain extent) institutionalized and accepted in its authority (see Chapter 1.2). There must be, in the words of Carl Schmitt and Byung-Chul Han, a sovereign.[124] Otherwise we are not dealing with politics, but with the opposite: anarchy.[125]

In view of this sketch of the political field, it is obvious how the phenomenon of power manifests itself or what it means to possess political power. Having political power means, in our opinion, being able to influence: first, the content and scope of common rules; second, the enforcement of the rules and the sanctioning of violations; third, procedures for the authorization of new rules and the revision

---

123 However, it is clear that we cannot progress with generic phrases like "Everything is political!". If we accept Bourdieu's and Poggi's assumption that there are a multitude of (relatively) autonomous power fields competing with each other, then these fields must also be clearly demarcated.

124 Cf. Schmitt, Carl (1934): *Politische Theologie. Vier Kapitel zur Lehre von der Souveränität*, Berlin: Duncker & Humblot.; see also Han (2005): pp. 91ff.

125 Here, we understand anarchy as a state of randomness. If the nature of the political is inextricably linked to the enactment and enforcement of norms of action, then anarchy must necessarily be the opposite of the political. This position is certainly not undisputed. For an overview of the debate, see Franks, Benjamin and Wilson, Matthew (eds.) (2010): *Anarchism and Moral Philosophy*, Basingstoke: Palgrave.; an interesting perspective from the standpoint of economics is offered by Skaperdas, Stergios (2008): Anarchy, in: Donald A. Wittman and Barry R. Weingast (eds.), *The Oxford Handbook of Political Economy*, pp. 881-898.

or abolition of existing rules. In short, political power is power over the form and content of collectively binding decisions. Those with this power decide (or participate in decisions concerning) what the tax rates are for whom, whether homosexual and heterosexual partnerships are legally equal, what powers the security authorities possess, the requirements necessary for the approval of medications, etc. The more intense and extensive the influence of actors in this sphere of decision-making is, the broader their control over the political field and the better their positioning within the hierarchical practices of that field.

Aristotle already used this core finding as the very starting point of his typology of political systems.[126] For him, all forms of political communities can be systematized on the basis of two questions. First, how many people have political power – one, several or all? Second, do they use this power for good or for bad? This results, in turn, in a division into six basic forms:

Figure 3. Typology of Political Systems According to Aristotle[127]

		Ethical Status of Power	
		good	bad
Number of Rulers	One	Monarchy	Tyrannis
	Several	Aristocraty	Oligarchy
	All	Isonomy	Democracy

The question of whether this typology is precise enough to convincingly classify the various forms of political organization or to account for the diversity of political power distributions and relationships does not need to be addressed in more depth. From today's perspective, considerable doubts remain. In addition, the simple division into good and bad forms of rule seems extraordinarily simplified. However, a completely different point is decisive: even the Attic forefather of state

---

126   Aristotle (2017): *The Politics*, translated by Sir Ernest Barker, Oxford: Oxford University Press.
127   In fact, Aristotle originally uses the term 'democratia' to refer to a form of political decadence. Of course, this early influence did not affect the long-term success of the term. Here is not the place to discuss in depth Aristotle's understanding of democracy.

and constitutional doctrine clearly recognized that the question of who possesses political power in a community (and to what extent) is crucial in the assessment and classification of state forms of organization.

Before we address the difficult problem of what political power is based on and with which resources it can be acquired and extended, we should focus on the function of the political power field, analogously to the fields of religion and economics discussed above. The significance of the religious sphere, as we have said, results from the satisfaction of immaterial needs; that of the economy from the satisfaction of material needs. Both have their origin in the neediness of humankind and are thus inseparably connected with the basic principles of power. But what about the political? Things are not so simple here. There are two competing explanatory approaches – let's call them, for matters of simplicity, *Hobbes's account* and *Rousseau's account*[128].

Hobbes's account goes like this: human beings are by nature purposive-rational egotists who, in order to satisfy their needs, are willing to take advantage of others and enforce their interests against the will of others. Therefore, in order to maximize need satisfaction, human beings strive for power. Since all humans share this disposition, they necessarily enter into a violent rivalry for power. And since they are similarly endowed with physical and mental assets, there is no foreseeable end to the conflict. This competition is ultimately to the all-round disadvantage of the participants, because it not only consumes resources, but also condemns people to an existence in constant fear of death. It can only be contained by one decisive step: the establishment of an institution with political power that can set collectively binding rules of action (prohibition of robbery, assault, murder, etc.) and draconically punish non-compliance with these rules thanks to a monopoly on the use of force. The purpose of the political sphere is to prevent human violence and ensure peaceful coexistence. It is first and foremost about the pre

---

128 Of course, our narratives go back to the two great classics of modern state theory: Hobbes' Leviathan ([1651] 2008) and Rousseau's *Du Contrat Social*, cf. Rousseau, Jean Jacques ([1762] 2012): *Of the Social Contract and Other Political Writing*, translated by Quintin Hoare, London/New York: Penguin. Both approaches, by Hobbes and by Rousseau respectively, to the foundation and justification of political power are, to a certain extent, indeed extremes, but in our estimation they nevertheless comprise informative extremes. Among those belonging to the camp of Hobbes are Locke ([1689] 1988), Nozick (1974) and Poggi (2001). In Rousseau's camp, we encounter Hegel ([1821] 2003), Rawls (1971) and Luhmann ([1975] 2003), but also Confucius (2005) and Lao Tzu (2009).

vention of the well-known war of all against all; the function of political power is a negative or preventive one. To demand more from it would be presumptuous.

Rousseau's account, on the other hand, is different. Human beings are naturally dependent on – and also inclined – to cooperate with others. Individuals alone would perish. However, when they bundle their skills with others and develop common goals, they can not only ensure their own survival, but also promote the happiness and well-being of all. The key question, nevertheless, is how to achieve this synergy of individual competences and how to act effectively and efficiently in joint action. The logical answer is the establishment of a political institution that sets binding rules of action for all persons. These rules allow individuals to shape their collaborative relationship so that they can realize their shared goals with the greatest chance of success. They create security of expectations and lower transaction costs; by virtue of sanctions for breaches of the rules they provide incentives for all individuals not to obstruct the pursuit of community interests. The purpose of the political sphere is to facilitate interpersonal cooperation and the achievement of shared goals. It is first and foremost concerned with the promotion of the common good. Above all, the function of political power is a positive or constructive one. To demand less from it would mean discarding its potential.[129]

If you are at least somewhat familiar with the classics of political theory, you will have noticed that we have left out central elements of Hobbes's and Rousseau's positions. We have not gone into the defense of the absolutist monarchy in the *Leviathan* or the utopian, radical-democratic approach of *Contrat Social*. This is not negligence. Our point is simply to demonstrate that political power can be justified in two completely different ways: either solely by controlling interpersonal violence or by promoting the common good.

Obviously, both approaches correspond to very different ideas concerning the institutional configuration of political power and the relationship of politics to the other power fields. A follower of Hobbes's account, for whom the function of political power is exhausted in ensuring peaceful coexistence, will usually opt for a minimal state. In such a system, e.g. social, educational and cultural policies play at best a subordinate role, and the intervention of the political in other fields, such

---

129 At this point, we would like to briefly prevent a possible misinterpretation. Of course, political power in Rousseau's story also has the function of controlling interpersonal violence. Supporters of Rousseau's position acknowledge that the ability and motivation of human beings to harm others is an elemental problem of socialization. In the end, however, this protective and preventive function is in the end nothing other than the precondition for the actual goal of political power, namely the promotion of the common good.

as economics and religion, is minimized. In contrast, a follower of Rousseau's narrative, which places the realization of the common good at the focus of political power, must advocate a more interventionist model of the political sphere. In this way, greater tensions automatically arise with other power fields seeking autonomy.

Of course, both positions are idealizations, but they are to this day the opposite poles of a persistent conflict over the function and limits of political power. Overall, however, Rousseau's approach has largely asserted itself. The socio-cultural and economic complexity of our society and its differentiation into the most diverse and competing spheres of power have meant that modernity has to think along the lines of the concept of the common good. The decoupling of political rule from this idea would lead to a dramatic deficit in legitimacy and thus provoke the collapse of the system. Beyond these historical and power-theoretical considerations, however, it would be conceptually and normatively unsatisfactory. Commitment to the common good is a core element of our modern, democratic constitutional state.

Nevertheless, this clarifies neither what is behind the term "common good" nor how it relates to democracy. Consequently, it is necessary to analyze the concept of the common good and to elucidate the legitimacy of political power, especially with regard to the democratic constitutional state. This analysis also allows us to answer a question that we deliberately deferred until now; namely, what the specific power resources of the political field are. We touched upon a preliminary answer at the beginning of this section with reference to Bourdieu's main assets in the political power struggle: prestige, networking, free time and education. Still, this ad hoc collection, with all due respect to Bourdieu, is based neither on a functional analysis of the political field nor on a thorough clarification of its legitimacy. Both are indispensable to gaining a clear picture of which capabilities, means and goods are at all eligible as resources of political power. In other words, addressing the resource question first requires an answer to the questions of function and legitimacy.

Thus, the direction of argumentation is clear. In what follows, we discuss the legitimization relationship between political power and the common good (Section 2.4). Building upon this, we then discuss (Chapter 2.5) the power resources, techniques and instruments that are relevant for this political field. The culminating point of our investigations in Chapter 2 is thus the politically legitimate, efficient and effective use of political power.

2.4 THE COMMON GOOD

Political power is only legitimate if it serves the common good. This approach to justifying domination runs through the political thinking of world history – regardless of whether we consider Western cultures, China, India or the Orient.[130] Without exaggeration, we can speak of a global guiding notion that has always been violently controversial (see Chapter 2.3), but that has determined the political discourse since the times of Ancient Greece. The welfare of the community is often in a conflictual, at times even dilemmatic relationship to the self-interest of individual community members.[131] The extent to which individual interests and the common good can diverge is shown not only in military conflicts in which the death of soldiers (or civilians) is deliberately risked in order to preserve the safety of the general public. The conflict also becomes virulent in everyday disputes, e.g. when rail tracks are built through residential areas, when landfill sites are established, in the taxation of income classes, and in the regulation of harmful consumer goods, etc. The management of these conflicts is one of the most important and, above all, most difficult tasks of policymaking. Despite these sometimes tragic problem constellations, which it is often not possible to settle satisfactorily, the common good is given high priority in today's political discourse. According to a survey by the political scientist Jürg Steiner, around one-third of all speeches in plenary debates in Germany, Switzerland, the United Kingdom and the US are related to the common good.[132] Slogans related to the common good are equally

---

130 For an intercultural perspective, see, among others, Zaman, Muhammad Q. (2006): The Ulama of Contemporary Islam and their Conceptions of the Common Good, in: Armando Salvatore and Dale F. Eickelman (eds.), *Public Islam and the Common Good*, Boston/Leiden: Brill, pp. 129–155.; Hiriyanna, Mysore ([1949] 2005): *The Essentials of Indian Philosophy*, New Delhi: Shri Jainendra Press.; pp. 53-56; and Zhang, Ellen (2010): Community, the Common Good, and Public Healthcare, Confucianism and its Relevance to Contemporary China, *Public Health Ethics*, 3 (3), pp 259-266.

131 Cf. Blum, Christian (2010): Dilemmas Between the General and Particular Will – a Hegelian Analysis, in: Ignacia Falgueras, Juan A. García, and Juan J. Padidal (eds.), *Yo y tiempo: la antropología filosófica de G.W.F. Hegel*, Malaga: Contrastes, pp. 231-239.

132 Cf. Steiner, Jürg (2012): *The Foundations of Deliberative Democracy. Empirical Research and Normative Implications*, Cambridge: Cambridge University Press.; p. 96. Steiner uses equivalent terminology with respect to the concepts of public good and shared benefits.

popular with trade unions, NGOs, associations and churches.[133] Steiner's conclusion is clear: in political conflict situations, it is the "social norm to express arguments in terms of the common good."[134] And, he hastens to add that this norm applies not only to democracies, but also to dictatorships, autocracies, oligarchies and other systems that violate the principle of popular sovereignty.

Of course, all of this does not mean that political actors really always have the interest of the public in mind when citing the common good. As Steiner aptly states, "[P]oliticians and ordinary citizens may not always be truthful when they argue using the common good to justify their position. They may use common good-arguments in a strategic way to defend their self-interests.[135] And there is another problem: even more than is the case with the key concept of power, the definition of the common good is highly controversial. Political decision-makers use the concept in all possible policy fields (security, social, cultural, environmental, transport, etc.) and often use it to justify contrary goals and concerns. With so much contentual arbitrariness in political discourse, it is not surprising that sociologists like Walter Hesselbach have dismissed the common good as a mere 'empty formula.'[136] Polemically put, the "common good" is what politicians refer to when they cannot think of substantial arguments but want to give their concerns a sense of impartiality and moral integrity. A third problem arises in the context of political ethics: since the twentieth century and the rise of modern totalitarian ideologies, the common good is suspected of actually being a profoundly anti-liberal, collectivist and anti-democratic idea.[137] The principle of legitimacy of the common good, so the critique, implies reference to a higher moral value which stands above the (allegedly) limited interests of individual citizens and in whose

---

133 For an overview as to the determinations made in the name of the common good, see Blum, Christian (2015): *Die Bestimmung des Gemeinwohls*, Berlin: De Gruyter.; pp. 7ff. It is noteworthy that recourse to the common good is completely independent of classical right-left political divisions. The common good is appealed to by environmentalists, right-wing populists and even Antifa.

134 Steiner (2012): p. 95.

135 Ibid.: pp. 92f.

136 Cf. Hesselbach, Walter (1971): *Public Trade Union and Cooperative Enterprises in Germany*, London: Frank Cass.; p. 111.

137 Cf. among others, Schumpeter, Joseph A. ([1942] 2003): *Capitalism, Socialism and Democracy*, London: Routledge.; and Berlin, Isaiah (1969): *Four Essays on Liberty*, Oxford University Press.; and Mouffe, Chantal (1993): *The Return of the Political*, London/New York: Verso.

realization democratic procedures are only a hindrance. It virtually compels embracing rule by experts or leaders gifted with special 'providence.'

We would do well not to brush this criticism aside. On the other hand, it would be just as dangerous to simply shelve the common good as a legitimizing condition of political power. Two questions arise in this context. First, how can the common good be determined? And second, what is the relationship of the common good to modern, constitutional democracy? These issues should be addressed with the above-mentioned points of criticism in mind: a plausible concept of the common good must be both coherent in content (i.e., not merely an empty formula) and compatible with democratic popular sovereignty (not totalitarian). In order to better focus on the subject, we venture a short tour de force through the current politics, jurisprudence and philosophical public interest debates. Here, three schools of thought compete with one another: proceduralism, substantivism and integrative theory.

Proceduralism is the dominant paradigm of political science. It dates back to the legal theoretician Glendon Schubert and the democracy researcher Ernst Fraenkel, yielding the following definition:[138]

> *Definition:* The common good consists in the output of a political system whose procedures (1) give all individuals the same opportunity to assert their interests in the political decision-making process and (2) implement the asserted interests fairly, effectively and efficiently through policy decisions.

Due to the predominance of proceduralism, innumerable formulations of this core thesis can be found of which the best known is that by Fraenkel. According to Fraenkel, the common good is "the resultant of the parallelogram of divergent economic, social and conceptual forces" of a political system,[139] in which "the rules of the game of political competition are handled with fairness [and] the rules of law governing the political decision-making process are followed without

---

138 Schubert, Glendon (1960): *The Public Interest: a Critique of the Theory of a Political Concept*, Glencoe: Free Press of Glencoe.; and Fraenkel, Ernst (1991): *Deutschland und die westlichen Demokratien*, Frankfurt am Main: Suhrkamp. Fraenkel's book is among the best German political theory works ever published. See also Mackie, Gerry (2003): *Democracy Defended*, Cambridge: Cambridge University Press.; Benhabib, Seyla (1996): Toward a deliberative model of democratic legitimacy, in: Seyla Benhabib (ed.), *Democracy and difference: Contesting the boundaries of the political*, Princeton: Princeton University Press, pp. 67-94.

139 Fraenkel (1991): p. 273.

fail."[140] This idea is hard to overestimate in its radicalism. It states nothing more than that the consistent application of democratic procedural rules (one vote per person, the majority principle, separation of powers, etc.) and the preservation of corresponding rights (freedom of expression and freedom of conscience, freedom of association, etc.) guarantee the realization of the common good. To use the words of Amy Gutman and Dennis Thomson: "Once the right procedures are in place, whatever emerges from them is right."[141] This common good automatism applies regardless of which specific interests are fed into the political system. The theory thus claims to suffice without any substantive concretion of the common good in the form, for instance, of a list of goods or of values. The only thing which matters is that the system meets the formal quality requirements of procedural theories. We can visualize this understanding of the system in a simple input-output model, as known from sociology. The input is provided by the interests of the citizens, which are fed into the political decision-making process by various political channels. These are received by the system's institutions and implemented in the form of policy decisions (health laws, environmental regulations, tax reforms, budgetary decisions, etc.), which together make up the system's output.

Figure 4: Basic Model of the Procedural Concept of the Common Good

Interests		Input	Political Decisions - Procedural Rules (fair, efficient, effective) - Basic Rights (universal) - Decision-makers (competent, law-abiding)	Output	Political Decisions	
I1	➡				➡	P1
I2	➡				➡	P2	Common Good
I3	➡				➡	P3
I4	➡					

How is this common good concept to be regarded? At first glance, the procedural core idea (common good is that which is always produced by a fair, efficient and effective system as the policy output) might appear to be somewhat far-fetched. However, it suddenly becomes more plausible if we apply two principles. The *first principle* can best be described as the 'principle of sovereignty' or "the principle of democratic interpretation."[142] It means that the members of a community have

---

140   Ibid.: p. 275.
141   Gutman, Amy and Thompson, Dennis (2004): *Why Deliberative Democracy?*, Princeton/Oxford: Princeton University Press.; p. 24.
142   Cf. Furniss, Richard and Snyder, Edgar (1955): *An Introduction to American Foreign Policy*, New York: Rinehart.; p. 5.

the authority to interpret what is to be considered as the good of their community. In other words, the common good is not 'out there' waiting to be discovered, but the citizens themselves are the autonomous creators of their collective welfare. This principle takes the *de facto* interests of citizens as seriously as possible by regarding them and not the judgments of experts or a technocratic elite as the constitutive basis of the common good. If we attribute the right to define the common good to the people of the state, the question automatically arises as to how this interpretative sovereignty should be implemented, because unfortunately (or fortunately) we do not always and everywhere agree on what constitutes the good of the community. Profound dissent and conflicts of interest are constantly on the agenda. This is where the second principle comes into play, the "procedural principle."[143] It states that the members of a community exercise their right to define the common good through fair, efficient and effective democratic processes that give every citizen the same opportunity to influence the final policy, the output. Why democratic procedures, and why the insistence on fairness, efficiency and effectiveness? Here, the democratic theorist Tom Christiano has by far the most impressive and convincing explanation: "This equality proceeds from the importance of interests as well as the separateness of persons. No one's good is more important than anyone else's. No one's interests matter more than anyone else's."[144] Because every single citizen or human being is of equal worth, the interests of every citizen must be equally weighted. This moral principle is unquestionable for Christiano. It ultimately results in the right to democratic participation that is equally shared by all persons. On this basis, the requirement of efficiency and effectiveness is quickly explained: it is not enough that the procedures of the political system give all persons equal opportunities to assert their interests in the course of political decision-making. They must also implement these interests in a goal-oriented and successful manner, and be characterized by an appropriate relationship between ends and means in situations of material and temporal scarcity of resources.

Let's summarize: supporters of the proceduralist approach to the common good argue, firstly, that the common good is constituted by the *de facto* interests, wishes, concerns, values and beliefs of citizens; and second, that citizens can assert these interests on an equal footing and through democratic participation. If we apply both principles – that is, the principle of interpretive sovereignty and the procedural principle – the procedural core idea emerges: the output of a fair, effi

---

143 Cf. Blum (2015): p. 55.
144 Cf. Christiano, Thomas (2004): The Authority of Democracy, *The Journal of Political Philosophy*, 12 (3), pp. 266–290.; p. 269.

cient and effective system represents the common good because it is constituted by the democratically asserted interests of the citizens.

However, there are numerous serious objections to this theory of the common good.[145] Here we focus on only two points of criticism. These are the *inadequacy objection* and the *error objection*.

The inadequacy objection concerns Fraenkel's most explicit and demanding condition that the common good consists in the outcome of a system in which "the rules of the game of political competition are handled with fairness [and] the rules of law governing the political decision-making process are followed without fail." Only if all the norms related to the democratic consideration of interests and decision-making are always fully and strictly adhered to can politics realize the common good. The problem is that this requirement is unviable in reality and in day-to-day politics. We do not mean to say that our Western democracies are hopelessly corrupt, or that they only serve the interests of a small, influential elite. That would be a fanciful reproach. But still, we have to agree with the political scientist Claus Offe "'normal,' i.e. actual political processes are constituted in such a way that they never bring about the *uniform* consideration of values and interests."[146] There are many reasons for this, such as human error, lack of time and resources, manipulation, errors in institutional design and so on. The consequence is dramatic. Real political systems can never realize the common good firstly, because they are inadequate in terms of the formal requirements of proceduralism, and secondly, because proceduralism defines the common good exclusively as the output of adequate systems. Of course, if you follow this line of argument then the common good is relegated to the heaven of "regulative ideas", to use an expression by Immanuel Kant. It would then be one of those principles which we like to use for orientation but which we can never implement in the here and now, such as world peace or the friendship of all peoples. This conclusion, however, is profoundly implausible, because democracies that work well (if not perfectly) do actually serve the common good – not always, but certainly at least occasionally.

While the inadequacy objection focuses on political procedures, the error objection is concerned with the input side of the proceduralist model. It suggests that the citizens of a state can be wrong about what serves their common good and that therefore the fair, efficient and effective realization of their interests is not neces

---

145 For a more detailed overview, see Blum (2015): pp. 88-98.
146 Offe, Claus (2001): Wessen Wohl ist das Gemeinwohl?, in: Lutz Wingert and Klaus Günther (eds.), *Die Öffentlichkeit der Vernunft und die Vernunft der Öffentlichkeit. Festschrift für Jürgen Habermas,* Frankfurt am Main: Suhrkamp, pp. 459-488.; p. 486.

sarily worthwhile. The great ethicist James Griffin bluntly sums it up: "[N]otoriously, we mistake our own interests. It is depressingly common that even when some of our strongest and most central desires are fulfilled, we are no better, even worse, off."[147] The reasons for this are manifold: misinformation, lack of information, wrong conclusions drawn from correct information, etc. All of these factors are devastating, and this applies in particular to the hopelessly complex field of politics (e.g. for the highly technical field of fiscal policy or health policy). The Austrian political economist Joseph A. Schumpeter may be accused of having had an extremely pessimistic view of humankind, but the verdict from his classic work on capitalism, socialism, and democracy still contains a spark of truth: "Thus the typical citizen drops down to a lower level of mental performance as soon as he enters the political field. [...] He becomes a primitive again. His thinking becomes associative and affective."[148] Accordingly, the problem is that political interests may be misguided because of a variety of errors; the system input, which according to proceduralist reading should be constitutive for the common good, can be deficient. In computer science, this is called a "garbage-in, garbage-out" problem: if what we feed into the system is already faulty, then what comes out in the end cannot possibly be correct.

Thus proceduralism reveals two profound problems: the principle of interpretive sovereignty (the common good is always constituted by the *de facto* desires, interests and judgments of the citizens) falls prey to the error objection. The procedural principle (the citizens assert their interests through adequate, equitable procedures of political decision-making) falls prey to the inadequacy objection.

Consider, in the face of this sober interim conclusion, substantivist competition theory. From the logical perspective of systematic argumentation, substantivism reads like an answer to the deficits of proceduralism. In fact, it is older, well over a thousand years. Substantivism goes back to the works of Aristotle and Thomas Aquinas.[149] Among its modern-day representatives are political scientists John Dryzek, David Estlund and Ian O'Flynn, in addition to constitutional law

---

147 Griffin, James (1986): *Well-Being, its Meaning, Measurement, and Moral Importance,* Oxford/New York: Oxford University Press.; pp. 10f.
148 Schumpeter [1942] 2003: p. 263. Even Rousseau, otherwise a great philanthropist and certainly one of the most important optimists in the history of political philosophy, has a similar view; he expresses himself in a more friendly manner, claiming that the people are "never corrupted, but frequently misguided". Cf. Rousseau ([1762] 2012): p. 30.
149 Cf. Aristotle (2017).

scholar Ernst Forsthoff.[150] His common-sense conception can be summarized as follows:

Definition: The common good consists of a universal list of objectively valuable goods that (1) are relevant to the community as a whole, (2) exist independently of citizens' preferences, judgments, and political decisions, and (3) can potentially be identified through cognitive effort.

Substantivists readily admit that there can be deep-rooted controversies and disagreements about the common good in societies.[151] However – and this point is crucial – these differences are ultimately only due to citizens' cognitive inadequacies. If we were all rational and well informed, we could spell out the common good in the form of a list of universal goods.[152] According to Dryzek, we can at least approximate this list by taking into account so-called "state imperatives" – functions that every community must fulfill to survive and evolve. For Dryzek, these include internal and external security, economic growth and the conservation of ecological resources. Estlund, on the other hand, opts to pursue the common good *ex negativo,* namely by virtue of a list of 'primary bads' such as war, famine, political and economic collapse, epidemics and genocide.[153] According to Estlund, governments promote the common good by preventing or controlling these basic evils; however, he admits that this criterion is, at best, a crude indicator.

Regardless of whether Dryzek or Estlund's specific considerations are plausible, substantivism as such has an astounding force of justification. The argument against proceduralism speaks *for* substantivism. The logic is this: if citizens and policymakers can be wrong about which policy serves the common good and which does not, then there must be something they can be wrong about: a list of goods independent of people's beliefs and preferences. Otherwise, we would have

---

150 Cf. Forsthoff, Ernst (1984): *Der Staat der Industriegesellschaft. Dargestellt am Beispiel der Bundesrepublik Deutschland*, Munich: C.H. Beck.; Dryzek, John (2000): *Deliberative Democracy and Beyond: Liberals, Critics, Contestation*, Oxford/New York: Oxford University Press.; Estlund, David (2008*): Democratic Authority: a Philosophical Framework*, Princeton: Princeton University Press.; and O'Flynn, Ian (2010): Deliberating About the Public Interest, *Res Publica,* 16, pp. 299-315.

151 Cf. O'Flynn (2010): p. 304.

152 In the realm of individual ethics, such approaches are also logically called objective lists. Cf. Crisp, Roger (2013): Well-Being, in: Edward N. Zalta (ed.), *Stanford Encyclopedia of Philosophy,* [online] http://plato.stanford.edu/entries/well-being/, retrieved on 21.12.2017.

153 Cf. Estlund (2008): p. 161.

to accept that there is no collectively authorized policy – no matter what lack of information or irrational emotion it may be based upon – that could ever be harmful to the public good. This would clearly be an absurd concession.

Once we have accepted this substantivist logic, politics suddenly appears in a very different light. Here the main function of political decision-making is to generate as many true beliefs about the common good as possible and avoid as many mistakes as possible. This sounds like a deeply elitist or anti-democratic understanding of politics, because under these conditions it seems almost imperative to involve only experts in politics and to exclude others as completely as possible from decision-making processes. Indeed, this accusation was and is repeatedly raised against substantivism.[154] Substantivists, however, counter this objection with a time-honored riposte known since Aristotle's days as the "argument of the wisdom of the crowd." Aristotle argues as follows: "There is this to be said for the many: each of them by himself may not be of a good quality; but when they all come together it is possible that they may surpass – collectively and as a body, although not individually – the quality of the few best [with whom Aristotle refers to, among others, political experts; comment by authors D.M. & C.B.], in much the same way that feasts to which many contribute may excel those provided at one person's expense."[155] The Attic philosopher justifies this assumption as follows: "For when there are many, each has his share of goodness and practical wisdom; and, when all meet together, the people may thus become something like a single person, who, as he has many feet, many hands, and many senses, may also have many qualities of character and intelligence [...] some appreciate one part, some another, and all together appreciate all."[156] Translated into our modern, technical language, this means that the advantage of democracies is that through participatory politics they ensure a synergy of the cognitive competences of all citizens and therefore are more reliable in terms of serving the common good than elitist systems.[157] In short, even if we attribute to political systems the very function of correctly determining the common good, as substantivism does, we are not

---

154 The locus classicus of this criticism is Arendt, Hannah (1961): *Between Past and Future,* New York: Penguin.
155 Aristotle (2017): p. 108.
156 Ibid.
157 The modern version of this Aristotelian argument is the jury theorem of the mathematician and enlightener Marie Jean de Condorcet in his *Essai sur l'application de l'analyse à la probabilité des decisions rendues à la pluralité des voix,* Cf. Condorcet, Marie J. (2011): *Ausgewählte Schriften zu Wahlen und Abstimmungen,* translated by Joachim Behnke, Carolin Stange and Reinhard Zintl (eds.), Tübingen: Mohr Siebeck.

committed to the rule of the common-good experts; the most appropriate system is always democracy, even under the substantivist concept of common good.

Figure 5: Basic Model of the Substantivist Concept of the Common Good

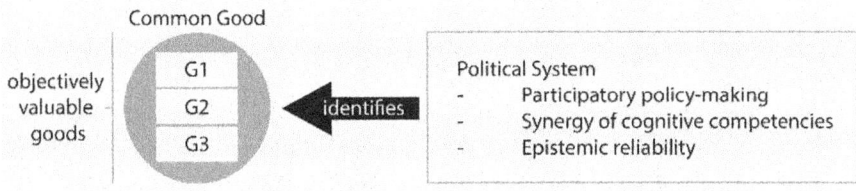

The substantivist model of the common good seems at first glance to be superior to proceduralism. At second glance, however, appropriate doubts arise. There are numerous objections. Here we focus on two: the self-defeatingness objection and the paternalism objection.[158]

The self-defeatingness objection is based on two steps. First, we must consider that the Aristotelian "argument of the wisdom of many" is by no means self-evident or even trivially true – indeed, it is controversial. The economist Bryan Kaplan, for instance, argues that democracies have notoriously bad balance sheets concerning the common good, because the election decisions of the vast majority of citizens are irrational.[159] This argument needs to be substantiated or defended. However, the process of doing so is not very attractive to substantivists, as it involves completely spelling out the objective list constituting the common good and then testing the competing hypotheses by comparison (which system is better: democracy or expertocracy?). The problem is that once we have established a list that can compare the common-interest accounts of both systems (optimistically

---

One can say without exaggeration that this subject has fed entire generations of political scientists and philosophers. The most astute contemporary representatives are unquestionably List, Christian and Goodin, Robert (2001): Epistemic Democracy: Generalizing the Condorcet Jury Theorem, *Journal of Political Philosophy*, 9 (3), pp. 277-306.

158 Cf. Blum, Christian (2014): Why the Epistemic Justification of Deliberative Democracy Fails, in: Andre S. Campos and José G. André (eds.), *Challenges to Democratic Participation: Antipolitics, Deliberative Democracy, and Pluralism*, Lanham: Lexington Books, pp. 47-65.

159 Cf. Caplan, Bryan (2007): *The Myth of the Rational Voter: Why Democracies Choose Bad Policies*, Princeton: Princeton University Press.

assuming that this objective pursuit is possible at all), democratic decision-making in fact becomes superfluous. Citizens no longer have to be involved in politics because it is more time- and cost-saving to directly implement the objective list. The argument defeats itself. However, ultimately there is a very simple consideration: citizens have an *intrinsic* right to be involved in determining the common good. And this right cannot be represented with a purely efficiency-based argument (such as: we get the best outcome if, and only if, we involve all citizens in politics).

Compared to the self-defeatingness objection, the paternalism objection is very straightforward. It says that substantivism fails to take seriously the desires, beliefs and values of members of the community and patronizes people.[160] The belief that the common welfare is an objective good and independent of factual policy decisions denies that the interests of the citizens are in any sense constitutive of their common good. The radicalism of this position is enormous: according to a substantivist interpretation, it is fundamentally possible that political decisions serve the common good, even if they are categorically and vehemently rejected by the population in the long term. This is, however, hardly convincing. Each of us knows from personal experience that our subjective interests are crucial to our welfare. We only have to think about how painful the frustration of key wishes and goals in life is and how badly this affects our well-being. This does not mean that the common good is constituted *solely* by the actual political preferences of citizens, such as proceduralism argues. Nonetheless, it seems esoteric to suggest that they should not matter at all. However, this is exactly what substantivists represent, and their theory is correspondingly implausible.

As a result of this unsatisfactory and theory-driven stalemate between proceduralists and substantivists, various authors have recently arrived at an obvious conclusion: if both positions insufficiently consider elementary principles of political logic and power-strategic principles, a new direction must be taken towards determining the common good. It is important to combine the merits of both positions without having to suffer their disadvantages. The corresponding attempt is the *integrative approach*.[161] In the following, we discuss a variant of this approach in more detail.

---

160 An excellent overview of the antipaternalistic tradition of argumentation is available, for example Dorsey, Dale (2012): Subjectivism without Desire, *Philosophical Review*, 121 (3), pp. 407-442.

161 Representatives of this general theory are, among others, Anderheiden, Michael (2006): *Gemeinwohl in Republik und Union*, Tübingen: Mohr Siebeck.; Bohlken, Eike

This account is based on two complementary premises. Firstly, "what constitutes the well-being of a concrete community is always and necessarily contested."[162] The substantivist notion that all citizens would agree on one and the same understanding of the common good, if only they were well-informed, objective and rational, is – the argument goes – remote from reality. In fact, our societies are characterized by deep and stable disagreements over what is best for the community.[163] And the remarkable thing is that, as a rule, the opposing positions in such disagreements are also rationally well founded. There is not just *one* solution for central political issues such as: What distinguishes a just social policy? What help do we owe to refugees? Is national sovereignty more important than European integration? Rather, there is a spectrum of equal, but highly controversial solutions whose plausibility is inseparably linked to personal values and attitudes.[164]

For this reason, it is also misleading to speak of the people's interpretive sovereignty over the common good, as the proceduralists do. There is no body of people in the sense of homogeneous actors with a single will. Instead of this Rousseauian fiction, numerous competing formations of interest exist in political competition, leading to conflicting interpretations of the common good. And because this competition is characterized by caesura (elections, votes, referendums, etc.), but is never ended, the struggle over the common good is never over.

Taking these core elements of political reality seriously has decisive consequences: the common good, as it results from the social struggles concerning its interpretation, is not only one of many possible concepts of common good – but it is always *preliminary* and *provisional.* It is always subject to temporality and the possibility of later revision.

According to the second premise, these struggles for interpretation require a clear regulatory framework within which to be carried out. This has a formal and an informal component. The former includes the principle of democracy, which

---

(2011): *Die Verantwortung der Eliten: Eine Theorie der Gemeinwohlpflichten*, Frankfurt/New York: Campus.; Hartmann, Bernd J. (2012): Self-Interest and the Common Good in Elections and Referenda, *German Law Journal*, 13 (3), pp. 259-286.; Blum (2015); Meier, Dominik (2017a): Das Gemeinwohl: Ein Blick aus der politischen Praktik, *INDES Zeitschrift für Politik und Gesellschaft,* 4, pp. 153-159. Of course, there are immense differences between these authors. Therefore, the position presented here only claims to be a variant of the integrative approach.

162 Meier, Dominik (2017a): p. 158.
163 Cf. Vavova, Katia (2014): Moral Disagreement and Moral Skepticism, *Philosophical Perspectives*, 28 (1), pp. 302-333.
164 Cf. Stocker, Michael (1992): *Plural and Conflicting Values,* Oxford: Clarendon Press.

assures all citizens equal participation in political decision-making, and the principle of the liberal constitutional state, which gives all citizens the same fundamental freedoms and rights. Democracy and the rule of law thus lay down the formal rules of the game. They are there to ensure that the struggles for interpretation are fair and that no group of interests distorts the result of decision-making in their favor or establishes a monopoly on the common good.

However, the implementation of these rules of the game alone is, in and of itself, no guarantee of fair competition. The political scientist Böckenförde has urgently pointed out this problem: "The liberal, secularized state lives on conditions that it cannot guarantee. That is the great venture that is made for freedom's sake. On the one hand, a free state can only exist if the freedom it grants to its citizens is regulated from within, from the moral substance of the individual and the homogeneity of society. On the other hand, no attempt can be made to safeguard these internal regulatory forces on the part of the state, that is, by means of compulsion and authoritarian command, without the state giving up its freedom."[165] This quotation has been incorporated into the Doctrine of Law as a "Böckenförde dictum," and its main message is clear. Precisely because the democratic constitutional state grants its citizens the freedom to conduct an open-ended fight about the nature of the common good, it can also be restricted or abolished by them in the name of the (supposed) common good. If the state enforced its constitutional values with force against the sovereignty of the people, it would be nothing more than a dictatorship. It would have led itself to absurdity. According to Böckenförde, this paradox can only be contained by a deeply rooted democratic culture within the population. Beyond all other considerations as to the content and organization of the common good, a basic political consensus is required that recognizes, firstly, that it is legitimate to argue about the common good, and second, that the result of this competition is always provisional.

This consensus, as Böckenförde asserts, can indeed neither be guaranteed nor enforced. That is, nevertheless, no reason for the fatalism that sometimes resonates with the great constitutional lawyer. Political culture is not a matter of chance, but one of training. In his monograph addressing the "majority decision," Flaig details how, in Athens and Rome, respect for collective decision-making was practiced through community rites from infancy.[166] Democratic education and the teaching

---

165 Böckenförde, Ernst-Wolfgang (1967): Die Entstehung des Staates als Vorgang der Säkularisation. Säkularisation und Utopie, Ebracher Studien, Ernst Forsthoff zum 65. Geburtstag, Stuttgart / Berlin / Cologne / Mainz, pp. 75-94.; p. 93.

166 Cf. Flaig, Egon (2013): *Die Mehrheitsentscheidung: Entstehung und kulturelle Dynamik,* Paderborn: Ferdinand Schöningh.

of basic political values such as freedom, justice and tolerance are, not without reason, a solid part of the school curricula of the constitutional state. It is obvious that this institutionalized training must be flanked by cooperative civil society organizations such as churches, sports clubs, neighborhood associations, etc., if it is to be successful.[167] And even so, the basic political consensus remains fragile. This is shown not only by the success of the totalitarian ideologies of the twentieth century, but also by the more recent growth of right-wing populist movements. Regarding the latter, the entry of the Alternative for Germany (AfD) party into German Parliament in the 2017 national elections is a strong indicator. This party campaigned purely on anti-immigrant sentiment. It follows that communicating, maintaining and upholding respect for openness and the ability to revise political decision-making are all core tasks of the democratic state.

The second component of the regulatory framework is outside the formal legal rules of the game. For the sake of simplicity, we can call them *interpretative horizons* of the common good. This collective term covers all the patterns of perception, evaluation and behavior of the competing interest groups that determine their respective understandings of the common good. These thus correspond to the habitus of the social classes and groups that are relevant to the common good (see Chapter 2.3). While these social, cultural and economic contexts are not codified, they are nonetheless extremely powerful. First, they determine the extent to which and concerning what political content actors can come together in the struggle for the common good. Second, they determine which areas are non-negotiable. The interpretive horizons are just as varied as the formations of social interests. They refer to, for example, the patriotic idea of a homeland, the Christian conviction of the sanctity of life, the American ideal of the "pursuit of happiness" and the social democratic principle of distributive justice. And they come into effect in shared rites such as national holidays, parades, military parades, Lent, sports competitions, bullfights or the Rhenish Carnival. All these values, rituals, conventions and symbols have one thing in common: they are constitutive of how we – as genuinely social beings – understand community and the common good.

In a certain sense, these interpretive horizons are even more elementary than the formal rules of the game of interpretation. We cannot abstract from them, because they have always been part of our biographical narrative, of our self-image

---

167 Thus, e.g., Robert D. Putnam shows in his influential book Making Democracy Work that democratic culture is inextricably linked to horizontal networks and mutual trust within civil society (so-called social capital); cf. Putnam, Robert D. (1993): *Making Democracy Work: Civic Traditions in Modern Italy*, Princeton: Princeton University Press.

and worldview. Separating individuals from their various habitus quite simply removes their individuality – that is, that which constitutes them (see Chapter 1.3). The consequence for the issue of the common good can be summarized as follows: "The struggle over the common good is never *simply* a struggle over the common good, but is always a struggle over a common good of a *concrete* community,"[168] with a specific constellation of social habitus and corresponding practices, symbols, values and rituals.

As already mentioned, both components – the formal political norms and the non-codified interpretive horizons – mark the boundaries of struggles over the common good. To use a metaphor from mathematics, together they form the *common good integral*. This integral is a *practical heuristic* to demonstrate the interpretive struggle over the common good and make it tangible. To understand the formal legal aspects and their practical functioning, a combination of political expertise and many years of experience with the logic and dynamics of power in the political field are indispensable. The interpretive horizons of the common good can in turn be deduced using the method of political praxeology, which analyzes the divergence and convergence of discourse and practice (see Introduction).[169] Applied to the question of interpretative horizons, we can substantiate the praxeological program with three central questions. First, *where are discrepancies between the statements of political actors and their actual behavior?* Second, *where is the reproduction of political rites disturbed, subtly reinterpreted or charged with another meaning?* And third, *where is a political symbol provided with new content and connotation?*

Such contradictions (and parallels) must be documented, registered in serial records, and compared. If this is possible, then the interpretive horizons of the common good can be precisely described and analyzed. However, this process, like the struggle over the common good, is never complete. Since the different interpretive horizons reflect the internal power relations of the actors (who has when how much influence over the habitus, values and symbols of a group of interests?), they are contested and changeable. For this reason, political praxeology cannot be finalized. It remains a continuous task and challenge.

---

168 Meier (2017a): p. 158.
169 See Giddens, Anthony (1984): *The Constitution of Society. Outline of the Theory of Structuration,* Berkeley: University of California Press. However, while both masters of sociology influenced the term "political praxeology" they rarely used it themselves. It is found, for instance, prominently in Bracher, Karl-Dietrich (1991): *Betrachtungen zum Problem der Macht,* Opladen: Westdeutscher Verlag.; p. 25.

Let's summarize briefly. The variant of the integrative approach presented here is based on the insight that the common good is the subject of continuous social struggles for the power of interpretation, for which there is no one, permanent solution. It is therefore also misleading to speak of *the* common good; rather, we are dealing with *a* common good, as it emerges – a posteriori and provisionally – from the competition between interest formations. This competition must be carried out within a fair, democratic regulatory framework and in the context of concrete, socio-cultural interpretive horizons. The latter, we conclude, can be described and analyzed by political praxeology.

The great advantage of this position is its pragmatic political realism. *First,* it takes the political differences in a society seriously, by declaring the common good an intrinsically contentious term whose meaning can and must constantly be challenged in the competition of ideas, interests and values. *Second,* it takes the fundamental differences between different communities seriously by recognizing the different societal habitus of citizens as constitutive for their understanding of the common good. The meaning of community, justice and a good life cannot be understood in isolation from the concrete ways of thinking, perceiving, evaluating and acting of the citizens. And these differ from community to community.

From this concept of common good we can develop three necessary and jointly sufficient *legitimacy conditions* for political power and one central derogation:

(1) Adherence to Democratic Fairness and the Rule of Law

Political power is only legitimate if it is authorized by a fair, democratic decision-making process in which every citizen has the same opportunities for participation, and if it upholds the requirements of the liberal constitutional state. Because there can never be only one permanent solution to the struggle for interpretive sovereignty over the common good, and because there are stable, justified disagreements about the substance and organization of the common good in our societies, each person must have the same opportunity to incorporate their interests, values, and beliefs into decision-making. Boundaries are set here only by ensuring the equal fundamental freedoms and rights of all persons.[170] Any decision-making procedure that deviates from this risks individual interest groups distorting or monopolizing the result of struggles for interpretive sovereignty in their own favor.

---

170 These include, e.g., freedom of opinion and conscience, freedom of religion and assembly, inviolability of the person, right to a fair, public trial and protection against arbitrary arrest; see Rawls (1971): p. 81.

(2) Maintaining the Basic Political Consensus

Secondly, political power is legitimate only if it upholds the basic political consensus that, first, it is always permissible to argue about the common good, and second, that the outcome of this competition is always provisional. This condition of legitimacy is derived from Böckenförde and does not refer to the formal, legal rules of the game of political power like the first condition, but rather to the democratic culture and the "internal regulatory forces" of the community. These, unlike the formal, legal rules of the game, cannot be enforced with state authority. They must be produced, reproduced and transmitted in civil society and in the various interest groups themselves. Nevertheless, they are indispensable for ensuring that the struggle over the common good is a continuous, fair competition. Therefore, political power is illegitimate if it attacks this basic consensus.

(3) Recognition of the Interpretative Horizons of the Various Interest Formations

Third, political power is only legitimate if it recognizes the specific interpretative horizons of competing interest groups. The interpretive horizons of the interest groups, their thinking, perception, evaluation and action schemata, are constitutive of how their members understand community, the common good, and themselves as social beings. They form the uncoded conditions determining the extent to which and with reference to what content people come together in the struggle over the common good. Recognition does not mean uncritical acceptance in this context. Rather, it means that the exercise of political power over the (different) values, beliefs, and lifestyles of the citizen must be justifiable.[171] It must be based on rational reasons and arguments that are understood, if not necessarily shared, by those subject to power. The question of what renders an argument rational is highly controversial in political theory and philosophy.[172] However, three criteria are unanimously accepted as a minimum. Firstly, arguments must not be knowingly based on misinformation or mislead addressees by omitting relevant facts. Secondly, to use the expression of the philosopher Harry G. Frankfurt, they must not be "bullshit."[173] In his influential monograph *On Bullshit,* Frankfurt distin

---

171 Cf. Habermas, Jürgen (1984): *Theory of Communicative Action*, Vol. 1, translated by A. McCarthy, Boston: Beacon Press.

172 An excellent overview is offered by Alvarez, Maria (2016): Reasons for Action: Justification, Motivation, Explanation. in: Edward N. Zalta (ed.), *Stanford Encyclopedia of Philosophy*, [online] https://plato.stanford.edu/entries/reasons-just-vs-expl/, retrieved on 21.12.2017.

173 Cf. Frankfurt, Harry G. (2005): *On Bullshit,* Princeton: Princeton University Press.

guishes between the act of lying and that of 'bullshitting'. While liars purposely say untruths, a bullshitter cleverly uses rhetorical phrases and slogans that are meaningless; he is completely indifferent to the truth value of his own statements. Above all, such nonsense sentences aim to fool listeners or readers with knowledge or originality, or to impress them with a flood of incoherent expressions. In this sense, they are as manipulative as lies. Finally, the third criterion of rationality states that the arguments must be checked by those presenting them in good faith and to the best of their ability for objective plausibility and logical consistency, and that they must also be verifiable by the addressees. In other words, the argumentative underpinning of the exercise of political power is always linked to a duty of due diligence and self-criticism on the part of those with power, and to the possibility of falsification.

The core idea of the third condition of legitimacy is thus that the exercise of political power is embedded in a practice of the reciprocal giving and receiving of reasons that display sensitivity to the interpretive horizons of competing interest formations. In concrete terms, this means that we are obliged to justify our actions even and especially to political opponents, recognizing their position as representing a legitimate social attitude. However, this condition has a limit: if the values and beliefs of an interest group contradict the three legitimacy conditions mentioned above – and are thus, e.g. anti-constitutional, racist, misogynist or anti-democratic – then the political opponent becomes an enemy.[174] Enemies of the democratic constitutional state and its liberal values are not entitled to recognition by political power. Indeed, they must rather be combated with all the means of the rule of law. That is the principle of defensive democracy.

We would do well to recognize enmity as a fundamental fact of the political realm. If you cannot accept this, or do not want to accept the challenges of military intervention and confrontation, you are gambling away the future of the democratic constitutional state. At the same time, the principle of enmity has a central dialectical function for the community. On the one hand, the enemy radically ques

---

174 The distinction between opponents and enemies is, in our opinion, central to the legitimacy conditions of political power. Opponents are actors with whom we do not share the interpretive horizons of the common good (or at least not all the interpretive horizons), but with whom we are connected in mutual recognition (in the sense discussed above) and in common acceptance of the democratic constitutional state. Enemies, on the other hand, are actors with whom we not only have no common interpretative horizons, but who also disregard or even actively combat the democratic rule of law and recognition. On the concept of the enemy in political theory and legal theory, see Schmitt, Carl ([1932] 1991): *Der Begriff des Politischen,* Berlin: Duncker & Humblot.

tions our own political identity – our values, our territory, our way of life; on the other hand, these things are only constituted as our own identity, distinguishing features and criteria for demarcation by this radical questioning.[175] Ultimately, democracy only becomes democracy through the challenge posed by dictatorship and tyranny and in its struggle with them. Only along this path will its citizens become aware of their particularity and their worthiness of protection – and acquire the insight that, if necessary, this way of life must also be defended even if the struggle requires great sacrifices.

(4) Derogation: Permitted Restrictions on Legitimacy Conditions

The three conditions of legitimacy, we believe, have a high normative value. Together, they legitimize political power. However, that does not mean that they apply categorically and without exception. The democratic constitutional state can be confronted with exceptional situations that make it necessary to restrict participatory policymaking and the validity of corresponding fundamental rights. Obvious examples are: wars, coup attempts, devastating terrorist attacks and natural and technical disasters (such as nuclear meltdowns, pandemics, floods etc.). All these events have in common the fact that they can represent an acute threat to the existence of the community and can only be contained by swift and effective state action. However, the latter is often only possible if the ongoing struggle for the common good (which is time-consuming and resource-consuming) is suspended in the political decision-making process, allowing political power to focus completely on averting the threat. This exception is linked with a clear limitation: it applies if and only if the community and its value system are existentially threatened. And it immediately ceases when the threat is averted.

This concludes our discussion of the concept of the common good and the three legitimacy conditions. In the next, final section, we will examine the resources of political power and clarify in detail what power in the political field depends on, and how it is acquired and exercised.

---

[175] The community-constitutive function of the principle of enmity is detailed in Schmitt, Carl ([1963] 1992): *Theorie des Partisanen. Zwischenbemerkung zum Begriff des Politischen,* Berlin: Duncker & Humblot.; pp. 87f. "An enemy is not something that has to be removed for some reason or destroyed because of its lack of value. The enemy is on my spiritual level. For this reason I have to struggle with him to gain my own measure, my own form". (Our emphasis.)

2.5 THE VECTORS OF POLITICAL POWER

What is the foundation of political power? More precisely, what is the capacity of actors to assert their interests in the political field of power against the potential opposition of others? This question has implicitly engaged political practitioners and theorists since the beginning of human history. However, it has been explicitly addressed for the first time relatively recently, by one of the most influential and controversial thinkers of modern times: Machiavelli.[176] The Italian political theorist, who gained considerable knowledge of political power not only in the academic sphere, but above all in his career as chancellor in Florence, distinguishes between the *internal* and *external* resources of actors: instinct and political wisdom on the one hand – networks and reputation on the other. Only through the clever combination of these factors can a ruler, as Thomas Schlöderle writes in his reprise of Machiavellian argumentation, be established "as a specialist in politics, as a craftsman of power."[177]

We do not intend to re-narrate Machiavelli's system, but it serves as a guiding principle of our own analysis. According to our initial thesis, there are three types of political power resources: *power competence, power knowledge* and *instruments of power*. Power competence and power knowledge form the subjective, internal side of power capacity. These are the resources that are inseparably linked to the actor and that he or she has acquired through education, training and empowerment. We describe power instruments as the objective, external side of power capacity. These include the power tools that actors have at their disposal. This triad is characterized by the fact that no resource type can be substituted by another, no one alone is sufficient for political power. A knowledgeable actor has as little influence without political tools and practical competence as one who has instruments but no experience or knowledge to use them effectively and efficiently. Only when combined do the three resources form the foundation of political power. To underline this interdependence, we speak of power vectors. In the language of philosophical logic, one could say that all three resources are necessary and together are sufficient for political power.

---

176 A great overview of Machiavelli's opinions as to the resources of power is offered by Schölderle, Thomas (2002): *Das Prinzip der Macht,* Berlin/Cambridge: Galda + Wilch.; pp. 70-120.

177 Ibid.: p. 94.

Figure 6: The Interdependence of the Three Power Vectors

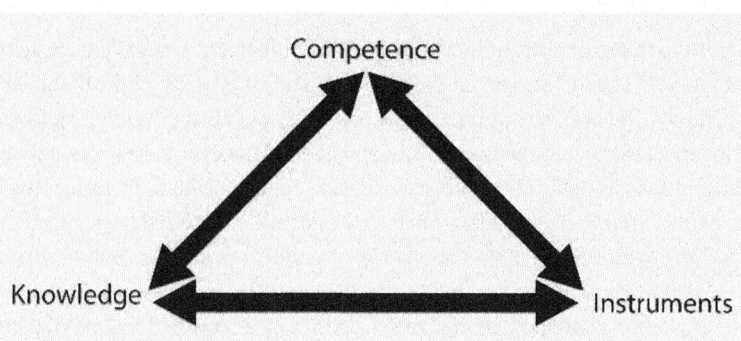

In a *first step* we conceptualize the basic categories – competence, knowledge and instruments – in order to distinguish them from one another. In a *second step* they are then substantiated with regard to the sphere of institutionalized political power, i.e. rule as understood by Popitz (see Chapter 1.2). This stepped approach allows the development of a precise system and prevents conceptual misunderstandings.

The terminological pair of competence and knowledge is basically a linguistic fallback position. In Greek antiquity, more than two thousand years ago, classic thinkers, above all Plato and Aristotle, developed a much more elegant taxonomy: téchne and epistémé.[178] *Téchne,* translated by us as *competence,* is the practical mastery of an activity, a craft, an art. Anyone who has, for example, played a good deal of soccer, knows intuitively what to do to pass their opponents, shoot flanks and push the ball into the net. The practice of playing soccer is something which they have embodied, in flesh and blood. As soon as they step onto the field, they have noted their opponents' positioning, identified points of attack, spotted weaknesses in the defense – and they act accordingly.

This does not mean that such athletes have even a trace of strong, theoretical expertise on how successful soccer playing works. There are countless examples of this. When asked how he managed a difficult 1-0 in a German Soccer Bundesliga match against numerous defenders in 2015, the young star Leroy Sané had a classic response ready: "I didn't think and just concentrated on putting the ball

---

178 Cf. Parry, Richard (2014): Episteme and Techne, in: Edward N. Zalta (ed.), *Stanford Encyclopedia of Philosophy,* [online] https://plato.stanford.edu/entries/episteme-techne/, retrieved on 21.12.2017.; and Fantl, Jeremy (2012): Knowledge How, in: Edward N. Zalta (ed.), *Stanford Encyclopedia of Philosophy*, [online] https://plato.stanford.edu/entries/knowledge-how/, retrieved on 21.12.2017.

inside the net."[179] The same approach applies to a baseball home run. As the baseball player David Ortiz said: "I'm not thinking home run, I just want to put a good swing on the ball. When you go looking for home runs, you get off of your swing. So you don't think of homers when you go up to the plate." Such cases sound banal, but they contain an important insight: someone who competently executes a complicated practice (playing football, painting, making music, etc.) is not automatically able to elucidate the right techniques and strategies to a layperson.

These are questions that belong rather to the *epistémé*. *Epistémé* is commonly translated as *knowledge*, but essentially the term is even more precise. It describes factual knowledge about persons, facts, processes, strategies and laws. Knowledge understood in this way is not practical know-how, but the reflected and communicable understanding of a specific subject area. Those who have a trained *epistémé* of playing soccer, for example, have in-depth knowledge of factors that are decisive for victory and defeat (weather, home or away game, physical fitness, motivation, etc.), know the advantages and disadvantages of specific training methods and know when and against which teams play should be offensive rather than defensive. At this point, it should be clear that an excellent sporting *epistémé* does not at all imply a good *téchne*. An outstanding game analyst and theoretical expert can be completely hopeless on the pitch.

Epistémé and *téchne*, knowledge and competence, are thus two categorically different assets. The philosopher Jeremy Fantl puts it in a nutshell: "Knowledge-how and knowledge-that are distinct kinds; to know how to do something is not just to know the right facts about how to do it, and to exercise knowledge-how you need not first implicitly or explicitly consider a fact about how to do it."[180] We also acquire both assets different ways: *téchne* we obtain by practical action, i.e. by the continuous practicing of series of actions, by socialization and training; *epistémé*, on the other hand, is in the broadest sense book knowledge, which we gain through theoretical or scientific effort.

Pragmatically minded readers might note here that there is a clear hierarchy between the two assets: what counts first and foremost is practical competence. If you have the right instincts or good training and thus master difficult practices from the bottom, you do not have to worry about the theoretical substructure – it is not decisive for success and failure anyway. Exemplary for this attitude is the famous sentence by the German actor Siegfried Lowitz: "Critics are like eunuchs:

---

179 Bild (2015): Schalke feiert Torheld Sané, in: Bild from 27th September 2015, [online] http://www.bild.de/sport/fussball/leroy-sane/schalke-feiert-torheld-sane-42697996.bild.html, retrieved on 26.01.2018.
180 Fantl (2012): p. 1.

they know how it's done, but they can't do it." In other words, it is crucial that you *can do it*, and not that you *know how*. Despite all the witty insight of Lowitz, however, doubts are appropriate. Complex power fields such as politics are characterized by a highly differentiated mix of actors, procedural rules, processes, interests and issues. This cannot be mastered solely by practical competence in the above-mentioned sense. If you do not know which decision-makers have the say in legislation, which legal barriers constrain the room for maneuver of an institution and how the interpretative horizons of competing interest groups are composed, you will not get far even with political instinct and a well-schooled feel for power. In short, competence and knowledge are complementary and non-substitutable assets.

In comparison to the conceptual pair of knowledge and competence, the meaning of the key concept of the instruments is quickly explained. This encompasses all the material and immaterial resources of actors that are indispensable for the realization of their goals but do not directly belong to the actors themselves. For a craftsman or a soldier, for instance, these instruments include concrete material objects like hammers and measuring sticks, or weapons and armor, in the case of knowledge workers they are above all networks, sources of information, contacts and the social relationships they share with other persons. Instruments are therefore the objective complement to the subjective assets of the actors. Their quality and scope determine how successfully we can practically apply our competence and knowledge.

Thus the power-strategic foundations are laid to concretely determine and use the vectors in the field of the political. What we have at hand with the triad of competence, knowledge and instruments is no less than a universal system of order and explanation of the inherent logic of political power.

2.5.1 Power Competence and Training

From this starting point, let us first take a look at the vector of power competence. Our approach takes a historiographical-praxeological form (see Introduction), investigating in which historical phases prototypical, outstanding forms of power competence existed and what lessons are to be drawn from these models. This method not only offers a vivid and applied understanding of our subject matter. It also highlights important practical resources by benefiting from the experiences of previous generations.

The most impressive example of lived and traditional authority is the Roman Republic, which flourished from the fourth to the first century BC. The unique feature of Republican Rome is that over the centuries it was dominated by less than two dozen senatorial families whose tradition, education and self-image were focused on a single purpose: to rule. Patrician families such as the Julia, Tullia, Claudia or Sestia not only stood at the top of the social pyramid of the republic for generations. They also exercised their power with the Roman public by having themselves elected to political offices and by having the people vote on their bills. The extraordinary complexity and competitive pressure of this mixed system of aristocracy and democracy can hardly be overestimated. Accordingly, political competition was, as the historian Johannes Keller writes, "the elixir of life" for the senate nobles.[181] At the same time they acted in court as defenders and prosecutors, and they led the Roman legions on conquest campaigns. The members of the senatorial class were – in a word – all-rounders of political power.

The question as to how a small group of politician families managed to remain at the top of an aristocratic-republican state for generations, not only making Rome the undisputed leading power of antiquity, but also maintaining internal stability, has long occupied historians. In his very readable book, *Den Vätern folgen ("Following the Fathers")* the historian Peter Scholz offers an answer that leads to the core of our research subject: through clearly regulated, functionally sequential levels of socialization all (male) family members were from early childhood taught a specifically senatorial style of thinking and acting through experience, skills and beliefs that together created an independent habitus.[182] And, Scholz adds a few pages later, the dominant position of a few families lay in the fact that they, over several generations, understood the assumption of power as a traditional task of the family and passed on the associated ethos and commitment to the common good to the next generation.[183] The secret of the success of the republican elite was, in short, that it understood politics as both an ethical obligation to the Roman public and as a matter of training.

It is noteworthy, however, that this practice of growing into a ruling role took place in a high-ranking, literate culture, but was not supported by book-reading and theoretical instruction. The skepticism with which the Roman elite viewed the Greek sense of epistémé is paradoxically expressed by one of its more eloquent

---

181 Keller, Johannes (2004): Römische Interessengeschichte. Eine Studie zu Interessenvertretung, Interessenkonflikten und Konfliktlösung in der römischen Republik des 2. Jahrhunderts v. Chr., Inaugural-Dissertation zur Erlangung des Grades eines Doktors der Philosophie, [online] https://edoc.ub.uni-muenchen.de/5172/1/keller_johannes.pdf, retrieved on 21.12.2017.; p. 48.

182 Scholz, Peter (2011): *Den Vätern folgen. Sozialisation und Erziehung der republikanischen Senatsaristokratie,* Berlin: Verlag Antike.; p. 13.

183 Ibid.; p. 31.

authors particularly well. Thus, Cicero writes in his treatise *De re publica*: "Think of me rather as one of the toga-wearing people, who has been given a liberal education thanks to his father's kindly concern, and who has been fired from boyhood with a love of learning, but who has, nevertheless, been trained by experience and family sayings much more than by books.""[184] Our understanding of this great rhetor is that ruling is not something that we learn to understand on the basis of abstract principles and information, but through lived practice. Politics has to become 'second nature', literally running through our veins. For Cicero and for the Roman elite, the key to political power was first and foremost practical competence – *téchne*.[185]

How was this power of authority acquired and passed on? At this point, the title of Scholz's monograph (*Den Vätern folgen*) can be ungrudgingly praised for its brilliance: the offspring of the Roman patricians acquired their power competence by "following the fathers" – both metaphorically and in the immediate sense. *Firstly,* all members of the senatorial aristocracy understood themselves only as small links in a long family chain, whose ancestors – *the maiores* – were not only the object of cult worship, but also functioned as constant role models for political action. In order to achieve a lifestyle fitting to one's rank, it was enough to practice remembrance of the important personalities of the family, the *domesticae laudis exempla*. Values and norms for one's own actions were gained from the family's past.[186] This culture of remembrance was cultivated by ritualized retelling of the heroic deeds of famous rulers in front of the portrait gallery of the ancestral home. Each narrative revolved around the cardinal virtues of the senatorial aristocracy, which at the same time formed the central elements of their power competence: self-discipline, rhetorical brilliance, soldierly courage, competitive strength,

---

184 Cicero, Marcus Tullius (1998): *The Republic. The Laws*, translated by Niall Rudd, Oxford/New York: Oxford University Press.; p. 18, our emphasis.
185 Of course, we should not go too far: it would be absurd to say that Roman culture ignored power knowledge (in the sense of epistémé) as a factor of power. But it is remarkable how much emphasis the senatorial families put on educating their sons to be political practitioners who could make decisions in a completely habitual way; cf. also Schlinkert, Dirk (1996): *Ordo Senatoris und Nobilitas. Die Konstitution des Senatsadels in der Spätantike*, Stuttgart: Franz Steiner Verlag.
186 Schlinkert, Dirk (1996): pp. 140f. Remarkably, this kind of ancestral cult is found to be of great importance in the teaching of power competence not only in the Roman Republic, but also in ancient China; see the volume by Scheidel, Walter (ed.) (2015): *State Power in Ancient China & Rome,* Oxford/New York: Oxford University Press.

awareness of tradition and official dignity. Emulating them was the guiding principle of the *vita honesta* – the venerable life of every Roman patrician.

Secondly, however, this emulation focused not only on legendary ancestors who had moved to the hereafter, but also on the fathers of this day: the reigning *patres familias* of the patrician dynasties. From the ages of seven to sixteen, the senatorial offspring accompanied their fathers at every turn. The patrician sons were present when the family board received its adherents, the so-called *clientes*, and gave them legal counsel, political advice or financial support. They accompanied their fathers to the theater, to the forum, to banquets with influential friends, to the baths and even on campaigns. In this way, enriched by practical advice, anecdotes, instructions and minor assignments, they became acquainted with the entire political cosmos of the Roman Republic. Throughout these years of learning, the fathers' educational task was not to pass on abstract values and principles to the younger generation as isolated individual virtues, but to give them an awareness of the role they were to fill in the future, thus 'implanting' them with an ethos and specific patterns of rule.[187] Nowadays, this sort of passing on of power competence would probably be called 'on-the-job training.'

At the age of sixteen, the official political apprenticeship, the *tirocinium fori*, formally began. In this phase, the young patrician was entrusted to a senior, possibly an influential relative, in the office of a *quaestor, censor* or even *consul*. Under his supervision, the youth entered day-to-day business. Among his duties was, among other things: the writing and joint rehearsals of speeches before the people and senate, the search for legal norms and precedents for legal proceedings, the drafting of bills, the preparation of election campaigns, continuous reporting on public political sentiment, and organizing local festivals to mobilize followers.[188] In all these activities friendships were formed, relationships cultivated, networks developed and, above all, one thing was learned: the competent exercising, protection and accumulation of political power in a system characterized by labor-intensive competition for political influence and distinguished offices. Parallel to this civilian political training was a probation in the mentor's military staff, the *tirocinium militiae*. Whenever the mentor took to the field against hostile states or barbarian tribes, he took his protégé with him, and not just to assist in administrative or strategic tasks. It was a matter of course that young patricians should prove

---

187 Scholz (2011): p. 96.
188 An impressive insight into the election campaigns of the Roman Republic and its extremely modern techniques and tactics is offered by Cicero, Quintus Tullius (2009): *Commentariolum petitionis*, translated by Günter Laser (ed.), Darmstadt: Wissenschaftliche Buchgesellschaft.

themselves in close combat against the enemies of Rome, command troops and, if necessary, give their lives for the Republic; a politician without scars on his chest was viewed suspiciously in the Senate.

Behind this practice stood the firm conviction, shared by all strata of Roman society, that power competence required probation in both political and military leadership. Anyone who was seen by the fathers and the electorate to fail in one of these leadership tasks was, without sentiment, excluded from a further career in public office – the *cursus honorum*.[189] Nepotism was largely alien to the Roman Republic. This rigorous training produced a highly specialized type of human being whose entire existence was tailored to a singular function. Scholz who, despite all scholarly detachment, cannot deny his great and contagious enthusiasm for the Roman patricians suggests that the "essential task [...] of the senatorial aristocracy consisted – sociologically speaking – in their political activities of coping with crises on behalf of the general public. [...] They constantly had to incorporate new unforeseeable difficulties and events in their political action, it was difficult for them to repeatedly resort to proven measures or routines when settling conflicts, they were often rather forced to venture something new and risky – and this seems to have become second nature to them."[190]

It is worthwhile to pause for a moment and reflect on what has been said. Critical readers might argue that so far we have not given any definition of power competence, but have analyzed only a specific historical phase of its evolution and tradition. This objection is understandable. But it misses the point by assuming that an abstract definition is even possible. As we initially stated, competence or *téchne* is not encyclopedic factual knowledge, but the habitualized mastery of a craft or an art. Power competence thus exists when the principles and mechanisms of political power have become second nature to actors, when – as Scholz aptly writes – they can dispel or settle conflicts over influence without resorting to "proven measures or routines." Precisely because power competence is not merely an operational routine, but also the creative and experiential ability to successfully dare "new and risky things" in the sphere of political power, no schematic guidance or general definition can be given here. Instead, we can only outline the sociocultural framework under which power competence is acquired and passed on. Here, the Roman Republic is not just a prototype; because it so purposefully (and biasedly) focused on this power vector, it represents a world historical zenith of the *téchne* of the political.

---

189 For an analysis of the career path in ancient Rome, see Veyne (1992): pp. 339f.
190 Scholz (2011): p. 24.

Of course, this *téchne* is not irretrievably lost with the decline of the Roman Empire in late antiquity. It would be more appropriate to say that it overwinters and reconstitutes itself in various configurations adapted to various socio-cultural contexts – without, however, ever losing its basic logic.[191] Accordingly, the later traditions of power in the Western world can be interpreted as contextualizations of the Roman model. In her pertinent historiography of the dynastic succession in the Empire of the Merovingians and Carolingians, Brigitte Kasten provides a medieval echo of the senatorial-patriarchal tradition: "The 'good' son and successor was basically the one in which the father lived on."[192]

In addition to this basic attitude, according to which power competence is essentially acquired through practical mimetic imitation of the paternal model, there are also parallels in the successive transfer of political responsibility. Numerous European rulers involved their descendants in ruling as soon as possible, on the one hand handing them their own territories during their lifetimes and, on the other, giving them command of independent military campaigns. These stages of development and tradition were sometimes even named analogously to the Roman model. Of course, they did not even approximate the orderly, ritualized form we know from the Roman Empire.

The deliberate adoption of Roman customs and practices, which was promoted mainly by spiritual advisers to the royal family, also contrasted with the "extraordinarily dangerous existence" in the medieval-courtly sphere of control.[193] These changed parameters of power competence had tangible practical consequences. While lack of a power instinct or a slow perceptive faculty often led to the loss of office and dignities in the Roman Republic, in the Middle Ages they could often mean the loss of life and limb. With a keen sense of excitement and drama, Kasten characterizes the monarchical power-cosmos as an environment in which power-hungry uncles tried to prevent their nephews from becoming kings with poison

---

191 The obvious question of which historical conditions ensured this transmission of power competence has no one answer. But the Catholic Church seems to have provided a decisive, epoch-spanning link between antiquity, the Middle Ages and the modern age; see. Cf. Pecknold, Chad C. (2010): *Christianity and Politics: A Brief Guide to the History,* Eugene: Cascade Books.

192 Literally in the famous letter from the royal advisor Alcuin to Charlemagne: "The father lives on in the son, [...] if dignity and noble wisdom exist in his successor", see Kasten, Brigitte (1997): *Königssöhne und Königsherrschaft. Untersuchungen zur Teilhabe am Reich in der Merowinger- und Karolingerzeit,* Hannover: Hahnsche Buchhandlung.; p. 7.

193 Kasten (1997): p. 33.

and daggers, newly wedded royal women strove to place their own children on the throne, and nobles from opposing camps planned to topple the royal family. Correspondingly, power competence was often demonstrated less in polished rhetoric or excellent networking, but rather in the cold-bloodedness of choosing the right time to draw a blade on a relative. In the Middle Ages, the creative ability to dare the "new and risky" praised by Scholz often took the form of the effective use of action power (see Chapter 2.1).

These conditions continue, as the great power pragmatist Machiavelli impressively described, even into European modern times. Nonetheless, in the transition between the Middle Ages and the Renaissance, there was also a decisive innovation in the development of power competence compared to Roman antiquity: the playful mediation of strategic thinking through chess.[194] Thanks to deeper trade relations with the Islamic world, the 'Game of Kings', with its historical roots in India, gradually became part of the courtly culture of Europe. Already in the twelfth century, young nobles were systematically introduced to the art of opening gambits and mating moves; the influential polymath and royal personal physician Petrus Alphonsi even ranked the mastery of chess as one of the seven basic skills that makes a good knight.[195] The reasons are obvious: like no other game, chess trains strategic and tactical thinking, creative solutions, stress resistance and the ability to empathize with opponents in order to identify their strengths, weaknesses and goals; it ultimately embodies all the relevant elements of the political competition for power (see also Chapter 3.1). The study of the game prepared the young nobility not only for the dangerous microcosm of the court, but also for their tasks as political decision-makers and generals. Since that time, chess has not only been preserved as a training tool and a power tradition, but at the same time has enjoyed a global spread spanning all social and cultural spaces. It is without doubt one of the most important legacies of the medieval culture of power competence.

Before we speak of the further development of the Roman ideal of power competence in our present time, let us dare to take a detailed look beyond the horizon of Western culture – to pre-modern Japan.[196] This digression is not only important

---

194 Cf. Vale, Malcom (2001): *The Princely Court,* Oxford/New York: Oxford University Press.; pp 170-179; for a historical overview, see also Eales, Richard (2002): *Chess: the History of a Game,* London: Hardinge Simpole.

195 Cf. Vale (2001): p. 171.

196 We consciously speak of 'pre-modern' Japan, because the classical occidental periodization of antiquity, the Middle Ages and modern times cannot be plausibly applied to Asia. Instead of a series of fundamental upheavals, historical continuity plays a much greater role in the Japanese cultural space. This only came to an end in 1853,

as a means to avoid a Western bias. It also illustrates that while the vector of power competence obeys, as it were, universal logics, it inevitably undergoes highly specific cultural adaptation processes. The period from the twelve to the nineteenth centuries was often marked by internal conflicts, external threats and dynastic changes along the Japanese archipelago, encompassing Honshu, Hokkaido, Shukiko and Kyushu. However, at the same time, it was characterized by a singular historical constant: the undisputed political and cultural dominance of the *bushi* warrior elite – better known to us as the samurai.[197] Jeffrey P. Mass, one of the most important Western authorities on Japanese history, describes the structure of the political order as "warrior government".[198] Marius Jansen adds in his pertinent volume *Warrior Rule in Japan* from 2008: "Japan was ruled by warriors for the better part of a millennium. From the twelfth to the nineteenth century its political history was dominated by the struggle of competing leagues of fighting men."[199]

The supremacy of the samurai in pre-modern Japan was reflected in the strictly hierarchically ordered and impermeable social structure. At its head were the members of the warrior nobility, led by the *shōgun,* whose title can be translated as commander-in-chief or generalissimo. They were followed in rank by the peasants and artisans as productive layers of society. The lowest rank was occupied by the merchants, who according to Confucian doctrine made dirty money deals. Outside of this hierarchy lay the imperial house of the *tennō*, which at best assumed a representative role. Samurai Japan was first and foremost a military regime.

At this point, we would do well to put aside romanticizing Western glasses and not restrict the *bushi* to the role of sword masters or even Japanese 'knights'. As the social historian Wolfgang Schwentker demonstrates, they were much more than that. In the Shogunat, they carried out the tasks of police forces, tax collectors, administrators and the masters of ceremonies of the Shinto state religion. In short, the samurai occupied all the nodes of political power for more than 600 years; they were also the only members of the community who were even allowed to have a

---

when the infamous 'black ships' of the US Navy ended the country's self-imposed isolation and its partition from the West under threat of force; for more details on this topic, see Walworth, Arthur (1946): *Black Ships Off Japan: The Story of Commodore Perry's Expedition,* New York: Knopf.

197 A recommendable introduction to this topic is provided by Schwentker, Wolfgang (2008): *Die Samurai,* Munich: C.H. Beck.

198 Cf. Mass, Jeffrey P. (1975): *Warrior Government in Early Mediaeval Japan: Study of the Kamakura Bakufu, Shugo and Jito,* New Haven/London: Yale University Press.

199 Jansen, Marius (ed.) (2008): *Warrior Rule in Japan,* Cambridge: Cambridge University Press.; p. vii.

family name and carry arms. Through this combination of functions and privileges, they embodied the idea of the Japanese state for all the lower levels of society. This understanding is codified in the *Shido* script of the famous seventeenth-century philosopher and military strategist Yamaga Soko: "The samurai leave business to the farmers, artisans and merchants and confine themselves to living the way. If anyone emanating from one of the three castes of the people is guilty of a moral violation, then the samurai punish him and thus uphold the moral principles of the land."[200] The samurai were thus not only warriors, but also cultivated educators and ethical points of reference.

The exceptionally long and successful maintenance of this monopoly of power in all relevant power spheres is due to a specific form of authority, the principles of which Schwentker concisely summarizes: "To rule and serve – both tasks coincided in the ideal samurai."[201] The competitive element that distinguished the Roman Republic had no place in the understanding of the Japanese warrior nobility. Here the habitus was not based on the impulse to make a name in the political arena or on the battlefield, but on the core virtues of loyalty and conformity. Thanks to their conscious renouncing of individual happiness and an unconditional willingness to serve the lord, the samurai were predestined to be a ruling class.[202] They formed a highly cooperative power formation that was capable of concerted action – be this the implementation of administrative standards or a punitive military expedition.

Their concept of loyalty and the associated asceticism have their roots in Zen Buddhism, and similar elements are found in Chinese political philosophy (see Chapter 1.1). It is worth noting, however, the thouroughness with which the principles of Zen are incorporated in the *bushidō*, the code of conduct of the samurai. The *junshi*, in which the samurai followed their lord into death if there was no chance of victory on the battlefield, constitutes the most radical expression of the loyalty of a vassal to his master.[203] But beyond ritual suicide, unconditional solidarity with one's own power elite, while putting aside all of one's own interests, formed the core element of the power logic of the samurai. The reference to Zen Buddhism is, however, highly relevant for us for another reason. In *Zen and the Way of the Sword: Arming the Samurai Psyche,* the theologian Winston L. King points out that the Japanese reception of this religious-philosophical trend is par

---

200 Cited after Brockers, Wolfgang (2014): *Karate – Essays,* Norderstedt: BOD.; p. 119.
201 Schwentker (2008): p. 92, as translated.
202 Ibid.: p. 93.
203 Ibid.: p. 80.

ticularly characterized by its prioritizing of intuition over reflective reason.[204] Instead of problematizing the human relationship to the natural and social world or accumulating knowledge about this relationship, the disciples of Zen aspired to being at one with the cosmos. Only those who had achieved this unity through the abandonment of self-directed thinking and through overcoming the antagonism between subject and object could, according to the conviction of the samurai, rule selflessly and justly, and could succeed on the battlefield without a moment's thought. At first glance, this anti-intellectual impetus could be interpreted as the unequivocal primacy of the *téchne* over the *epistémé*.[205] Upon somewhat closer inspection, however, a differentiated picture of Zen emerges: the dissolution of the boundaries between the two vectors, a merging into one another that escapes the strict dichotomy. In other words, through the overriding role of intuition – which the samurai sharpened through meditation and asceticism – *epistémé* becomes associated with or reflected in *téchne*. This also explains why reading books or studying theoretical content was very important for the life of the warrior nobility, especially from the sixteenth century. The *epistémé* did not play a priority role in their self-conception, but it nevertheless played an asssociated role.

The central virtues of the samurai and the associated habitual dispositions ("rule and serve") were handed down from generation to generation within the warrior nobility. For Schwentker, the close relationship between the master and the student, which has an outstanding significance in both Zen Buddhism and Confucianism, is in the foreground.[206] From the age of three, the warrior nobles were introduced to fighting techniques and tactics, first in the family home and a little later under the aegis of an older samurai, who always taught only one student. Military probation was practical – whether in defense against Mongol invasions or in the suppression of peasant uprisings. At the same time, however, there was also instruction in literature and statecraft, theology and philosophy. Underlying this curriculum was the understanding that "in addition to a mastery of warcraft, high literacy skills were fundamentally part of the competences of the warrior class."[207]

---

204 Cf. King, Winston L. (1993): *Zen and the Way of the Sword: Arming the Samurai Psyche,* New York: Oxford University Press.; pp. 188f.
205 As to the anti-intellectualism of Zen, see Perez, Louis G. (1998): *The History of Japan,* Westport/London: Greenwood Press.; p. 34.
206 Cf. Schwentker (2008): p. 46.
207 Thus "there's nothing more disgraceful than being illiterate", comments Niehaus on the literacy of the warrior nobles in early modern Japan, see Niehaus, Andreas (2013):

This resource-rich and time-consuming training depended on one condition: the 'productive' estates of society, the farmers and craftspeople, had to be willing to co-finance the education of the elite through taxes. In the long run, this could only succeed if the *bushi* daily demonstrated their goals of integrity, erudition and military clout by virtue of practical action.

Privileged access to a highly specialized, practice-oriented training system from earliest childhood proves to be a leitmotif of power competence, which we already encountered in republican Rome, albeit under quite different cultural precedents. What the senatorial families and the *bushi* had in common was not a specific canon of values, but rather a highly efficient technique by which to pass on and monopolize political power, combined with their unconditional identification with the community and their practice of living as role models. The reproduction of power through practice can be considered in this context as a central formula of power competence. Undoubtedly, the *téchne* of the power of the samurai deserves a monograph in its own right, but we end here our digression into pre-modern Japan and return to our original narrative: the continuation and transformation of the Roman model of power competence through history.

Perhaps the most significant modernization of the Roman ideal of political power competence is found in the USA, from the seventeenth century to the present day. In his genealogical standard work, *America's Political Dynasties,* Stephen Hess identified a central common feature: the dynastic impulse.[208] The US, one of the most competitive political systems in the world, is ruled by an electoral

---

"So gibt es nichts schändlicheres als illiterat zu sein" – zur Literalität der Kriegerklasse im frühmodernen Japan, in: Gesine Boesken and Uta Schaffers (eds.), *Lektüren 'bilden': Lesen – Bildung – Vermittlung,* Münster: Lit Verlag, pp. 199-216.

208 Cf. Hess, Stephen (2016): *America's Political Dynasties: From Adams to Clinton,* Washington: Brookings Institution Press.; p. 2. Of course, this does not mean that successful political dynasties are a unique feature of the US – John H. Fiva and Daniel Smith point out in detail that the dynastic tradition of political power is common in countries such as Germany, Ireland, Canada and Norway. Cf. Fiva, John H. and Smith, Daniel M. (2016): Political Dynasties and the Incumbency Advantage in Party-Centered Environment, *CESifo Working Paper Series,* 5757, pp. 1-46. Nevertheless, the US is the country in which the principle of modern electoral aristocracy has been perfected, see also Dal Bó, Ernesto, Dal Bó, Pedro and Snyder, Jason (2009): Political Dynasties, *Review of Economic Studies,* 76 (1), pp. 115-142.

aristocracy, which columnist Stewart Alsop once called "the people's dukes."[209] The numbers speak for themselves: "Forty-four American families have had at least four members of the same name elected to the federal office, and in seventy-five families three members of the same name held national office."[210] Politician families such as the Kennedy, Bush and Clinton clans, as well as past dynasties like the Roosevelts and Adams, have passed on and will continue to pass on positions in the House of Representatives and the Senate and even the Presidency to their children – with the express approval of the electorate.

The explanation for this extraordinary continuity is now familiar to us: the teaching of power competence from childhood by embedding it in a highly specialized and elitist learning environment. Anyone born into a US-American political family takes part in festive parades for the Fourth of July from their earliest childhood, accompanies their parents to fundraising events and rattles hundreds of doors with them, mobilizing the electorate. As they get older, the offspring make speeches at election campaigns, conduct debates in the halls of prestigious universities to promote their fathers or mothers – and in the medium term themselves. This socialization not only ensures an unprecedented understanding of political symbolism and the importance of shared rites (see Chapter 2.1). It also favors the development of empathy for the needs of voters and the unconditional ability to network. Last but not least, it allows these individuals to move confidently in a variety of social and cultural contexts. It opens, metaphorically speaking, the horizon beyond its own sociotope.

In the absence of an analytical study on the socialization of the US political elite we resort to a vignette. In his account of the consolidation of power in the Clinton dynasty, Hess comes to the political education of Bill and Hillary Clinton's daughter Chelsea; and it is worthwhile citing the chronicler extensively: "[B]eing politically special, virtually from birth, creates a range of experiences that can turn the exceptional into the ordinary. When do you know which of your classmates are true friends and which are the ones who just want to hang out at the governor's mansion? What gifts are appropriate and which are over the top? Is there public behavior that children without famous parents do not have to learn but for those like Chelsea is best learned young?"[211] These lessons in the know-how of power strategy, which the Clintons' daughter acquired, so to speak, in

---

209 Miller, Zeke (2013): Political Dynasties Return, in: Time from 5th March 2013, [online] http://content.time.com/time/subscriber/article/0,33009,2148168-3,00.html, retrieved on 21.12.2017.
210 Hess (2016): p. 3.
211 Ibid.: p. 590.

passing, were supplemented by rigorous but playful training in political communication. Hilary Clinton reminisces in her autobiography *Living History*: "Bill and I tried to prepare Chelsea for what she might hear about her father or, for that matter, about her mother. We sat around our dinner table in the Governor's Mansion role-playing with her, pretending we were in debates where one of us acted like a political opponent who criticized Bill for not being a good governor."[212] It goes without saying that being introduced to the craft of power by two distinguished and exceptional politicians represents an extreme competitive advantage over competitors who have not profited from such training. In short, those who acquire power competence through a combination of talent and practical experience, have an excellent chance of passing it on to their families. Of course, the Clinton vignette is not an isolated case; it stands prototypically for dozens or hundreds of political biographies. For the research team around the economist Ernesto Dal Bó, who have worked intensively on the topic of dynastic rule in democracies, these findings can be summarized in a simple slogan: "Thus, in politics, power begets power."[213]

2.5.2 Power Knowledge and Strategy

With this, we conclude our discussion of power competence and turn to the second power vector, that of knowledge. We owe the term to the sociologist Max Scheler, who introduced the *terminus technicus* in his monograph *Die Wissensformen und die Gesellschaft,* literally "Forms of Knowledge and Society."[214] Scheler distinguishes power knowledge (also translated as "practical knowledge" and "knowledge that produces effects") from cultural knowledge (or erudition) and salvation knowledge. While cultural knowledge aims to form and cultivate the individual personality, and salvation knowledge to create sense and a coherent world view (see also Chapter 2.3), power knowledge is directed towards the practical mastery of animate and inanimate nature as well as of fellow human beings. In the period after Scheler, the term underwent a normative narrowing and has unfortunately been reduced to the monopolization of political information by an elite operating in a supposedly clandestine fashion. We, on the other hand, want to take the term as literally as possible in the following discussion – that is, as a

---

212 Clinton, Hilary (2003): *Living History,* New York: Simon & Schuster.; p. 97.
213 Dal Bó, Dal Bó & Snyder (2009): p. 1.
214 Cf. Scheler, Max (1980): *Problems of a Sociology of Knowledge,* translated by Manfred S. Frings, London: Routledge.

collective term for all that knowledge or *epistémés* that is indispensable for the exercise of political power.[215]

That knowledge is an important source of power is, of course, not actually an insight of Scheler's. Three hundred years earlier, Francis Bacon made the crucial connection between knowledge and power explicit in his scientific essay *Novum Organum Scientiarum:* "human knowledge and human power come together in one."[216] The scientist and philosopher Bacon focuses on human knowledge of (inanimate) nature and how to control it. But Bacon's dictum can easily be applied to the social world, especially the sphere of political rule: superior knowledge of the universal principles of power (Chapter 1.2), their forms (Chapter 2.1), conditions of legitimation (2.4.) and the mechanisms, strategies, tactics and issues of the political sphere signifies a clear competitive advantage in the war of interpretation over the common good. This knowledge is the knowledge of power.

Power knowledge, understood in this way, is divided into three forms of knowledge: *justification knowledge, leadership knowledge* and *administrative knowledge.* The first form of knowledge legitimizes the exercise of power through the continuous justification, defense and further development of a common political narrative. The second form is the formal knowledge of decision-makers about how political goals can be enforced against the opposition of competing interest formations, and how power devices – the positional fabric of rule after Popitz – can be controlled efficiently and effectively. The third type is bureaucratic expert knowledge and refers to concrete procedures and specific policies.

All three forms of knowledge forge an interdependent complex. Justification knowledge provides a structure of justification for why the common good is best enforced in this particular, concrete political system and why citizens should campaign for this order – but it must necessarily be complemented by leadership and administrative knowledge if it is to be permanently successful. In turn, leadership knowledge can only be translated into political power if, on the normative level, it corresponds to a plausible narrative and, on the implementation side, to an adequate understanding of topics and processes, i.e. when the administration recognizes the often superior leadership skills of decision-makers. But the decision-makers must also have learned to obtain and utilize knowledge from the bureaucracy. Administrative knowledge can only be exercised as political influence if decision-makers are in a position to select it expertly and to use it strategically. Otherwise, to put it rather bluntly, it gets stuck on the way up.

---

215 For further information pertaining to this approach, cf. Hamilton, Peter (2015): *Knowledge and Social Structure,* London/New York: Routledge.

216 Bacon, Francis ([1620] 1902): *Novum Organonon,* New York: P.F. Collier.; p. 11.

In addition to this interdependence, all three forms of power knowledge are united in that they share an essential feature: they must be actively present, i.e. it must be possible for actors to retrieve or access them at any time. There is one obvious reason for this: power operates under conditions of scarcity of time and material. Delays, coordination problems, queries and research not only cost money – they cost power.

Subsequent to this outline of the three knowledge formats (justification – leadership – administrative) and their mutual relationships and similarities, we want to discuss these formats individually, starting with the concept of justification. Its indispensability stems from the fact that power is subject to a continuous, explicit and implicit need for legitimacy and constantly strives for validation, i.e. for normative justification. This principle applies to all forms of governance – regardless of whether we are dealing with the Stalinist regime of North Korea, the Chinese one-party state, the autocratic presidential system of Russia or the German representative democracy. The reason for this lies in a universal power principle, which we already discussed in Chapter 1.2: the purposive production of power. Because power relations are not nomologically necessary, that is, not determined by the laws of nature, but can be altered by humans, they are subject to the permanent reservation of being changed. Justification knowledge provides, in short, the answer to why power relations could be different but should not be. Those with justification knowledge can give normative answers to the following questions: Why do I rule (and not another)? Why does the political system have this (and not that) constitution? Why do I use this (and not that) policy? Why should citizens choose me (and not another candidate)? And so on. Power systems whose decision-makers can give no or only unsatisfactory answers to these questions are permanently unstable. Only justification knowledge has the motivational power to bind the members of a community in the long term to its established order (see our discussion of the normative justification and the pursuit of meaning in Chapter 1.3).

However – and this point is crucial – justification knowledge is not expert academic knowledge of political philosophy. It is not important to strictly and rationally deduce the legitimacy of the current political order using abstract, ethical and logical principles. Justification knowledge is rather knowledge of how to develop and interpret an all-encompassing *political narrative*.[217] Of course, such a

---

217 Cf. Mayer, Frederick W. (2014): *Narrative Politics: Stories and Collective Action,* Oxford: Oxford University Press. The importance of a narrative for the legitimacy of power is not only a recurrent theme of political theory, but also a mantra of campaign leaders and campaign strategists. Thus, e.g. Stan Greenberg, a policy guru of the US Democrats, follows the slogan: "A narrative is the key everything"; similarly, James

narrative is not an arbitrary fable, short-term fashion or legend with a political foundation. It is rather a communal understanding of the social world and the localization of the community in this world, based on a shared history, shared values and shared symbols – "a shared means of making sense of the world [...] grounded in assumptions, judgments, contentions, dispositions and capabilities."[218] This principle is pertinently expressed in the philosopher Alasdair MacIntyre's essay *Is Patriotism a Virtue?*[219] According to MacIntyre, successful political narratives describe communities as intrinsically valuable, multi-generational projects whose identities are fixed by "special features, merits, and achievements, which in turn are reflected in distinctive political, cultural and religious norms and practices."[220]

There are three factors that should be emphasized in this context. *Firstly,* this narrative permeates *all levels of political action* and affects (directly or indirectly) all members of the community. It creates a synchronous and diachronic unity in the multiplicity of political institutions and activities by locating them in the context of the overarching history and idea of the state. A particularly powerful example of such a narrative, its interpenetration and the way it provides unity, is that of the French *grande nation,* the guardian of the republican values of freedom, equality, and fraternity. This idea, dating back to the year of the revolution, 1789, has since become the one fixture of French history, in relation to which all other events and political decisions are ordered. Thus, the idea not only allows Napoleon's military expansion to be described as the triumphant advance of modern liberalism, and to place the secularism of post-revolutionary France on an Enlightenment foundation; it also makes it possible to view Vichy's collaboration regime as the mere 'slip-up' of an indomitable, freedom-loving people. At the same time, this idea of the state legitimates the Fifth Republic and is enshrined as a guiding principle in the constitution. The triad of freedom, equality and fraternity can be found on the facade of every French town hall, on flags, coins and stamps. Accordingly, the slogan and narrative it embodies is the normative foundation for France's political elites, on which they can and must build their agenda – preserving and evolving the narrative. It is therefore only logical that the motto is used by the right-wing *Front National,* France's Socialists and the *En Marche* movement

---

Carville: "We could elect somebody from the Hollywood Hills if they had a narrative to tell people about what the country is and where they see it", cited according to Polletta, Francesca (2011): Storytelling in Politics, *Contexts,* 7 (4), pp. 26-31.

218 Dryzek (2000): p. 18.
219 Cf. MacIntyre, Alasdair (1984): *Is Patriotism a Virtue?*, Kansas: University of Kansas Press.
220 MacIntyre (1984): p. 85.

of President Emanuel Macron, elected in May 2017. The controversy between the power actors is thus not based on whether the three fundamental values of the *grande nation* are the guiding principles of the French narrative, but on what they mean for the political present-day of the citizens, through which policies they can best be realized and which actors can offer the most plausible interpretation of the great national narrative.[221] Anyone who knows how to seize upon this narrative (or a comparable narrative in other states) is thus capable of comprehensibly and accessibly ordering every political event in a normative framework and thus of presenting a holistic justification of political rule.

Secondly, the *project character* of the community, described by MacIntyre, comes to fruition in the political narrative and creates a sense of belonging among members – including identification with previous generations and long-dead ancestors.[222] The shared narrative is not just an account of the genesis, telos and development of the community; it is an interactive story in which every member is called to participate. In this way, it takes account of the human need to be part of a larger whole whose meaning outlives individual existence. This explains the immense motivational power of the great political narratives and the importance of justification as a guarantor of political stability. The question of concrete participation and commitment is obviously dependent on the nature of the narrative, its dramaturgy and its design. The spectrum ranges from mere compliance with the law and authority by ordinary citizens to the unconditional sacrifice of the patriot for his or her country.

The political narrative of the German people differs significantly from other national narratives in Europe. Because of its historical breaks and the ominous

---

221 The situation with, for example, the guiding principles of the US narrative: the 'American dream' and 'manifest destiny,' is quite similar. These principles are understood as a postulate of free personal development and advancement in a community characterized by a historical sense of mission and pioneering spirit. Again, the point of contention between the power actors is exclusively how these principles are to be interpreted politically and what their practical implications are for policymaking. While democratic liberals, for example, classify social redistribution as a condition of self-fulfillment, libertarian republicans see this as improper state intervention in the autonomy of the individual; see Hochschild, Jennifer L. (1996): *Facing up to the American Dream. Race, Class, and the Soul of the Nation*, Princeton: Princeton University Press.

222 At this point it is appropriate to remember the ancestor cult of the Roman patricians (see Chapter 2.5.1): the recourse to the maiores as ancestors of an unbroken tradition of republican power practice creates a frame of reference from which the following generations can draw legitimacy.

shadow of Nazi crimes against humanity, this contemporary narrative is dominated, above all, by the critical examination of one's own past (see our remarks on power, symbolism and coping with the past in Chapter 2.1). According to the post-National Socialist narrative, the slogan: "Never again!" is the motivation for citizens to commit to a system. This suggests that the political order in Germany owes its legitimacy first and foremost to the prevention of new crimes against humanity committed under the banner of racism and nationalism. It should, however, be questioned whether this justification scheme, which feeds solely on the conscious breaking with the criminal past, is sufficient for a positive sense of being, for solidarity and civic engagement. Without complementary reference to the tradition of the German nation of culture, the great thinkers of the Enlightenment, such as Kant and Leibniz, and the literary genius of Goethe and Schiller, such a narrative can neither unfold the motivational power of other national narratives nor can it fulfill its unifying function. It follows that the current strengthening of right-wing populist tendencies in the Federal Republic of Germany has its roots – at least to a certain extent – in the unresolved lack of positive content in the German national narrative.

Finally, *the third point* is that the narrative has to be *constantly justified, defended, cultivated, further developed and symbolically (or even religiously) charged by all those involved.* Opponents and enemies of the ruling actors constantly challenge it by telling their own narrative or interpretation, and cast doubt on the rationale of their counterparts. A look into the recent past brings to mind the propaganda skirmishes of the Cold War, in which not only economic systems, intelligence services and the military, but above all the great political narrators and meaning-makers fought for domination of the globe. These confrontations also had a significant Manichean trait, creating a simple good-bad scheme from the issues behind the narrative – Capitalism or planned economy? Democracy or communism? Competition or socialist performance principle? A similarly simplistic confrontational image of macro-narratives is now offered by the repeatedly cited clash of Occident and Orient, Christianity and Islam, used by extremists on both sides to cast doubt on the legitimacy of moderate, non-confrontational powers.

The constant questioning of the legitimacy of power by counter-narratives renders the substantiation of political narratives one of the most important leadership tasks in the political sphere of influence. Therefore, let us take a look at the sources from which any political narrative feeds. In doing so, four fundamentals can be identified, which determine each other to differing degrees. The *first source* comprises *political experience in a maximum of three generations.* The shared experience and remembrance horizon of these generational cohorts is staked out by key events or circumstances that have either been directly experienced or made present through the oral transmission of eyewitnesses. We deliberately want to broadly define the term "political experience": it not only refers to formal political processes, but also to symbolically relevant events. With reference to the German present, it includes, for instance, not only the 'economic miracle' of the 1950s and 1960s, the fall of the Berlin Wall in November 1989 and the refugee crisis of 2015, but also the soccer "Miracle of Bern" of 1954 and the flight of the (East German) cosmonaut Sigmund Jähn in 1978. All of these happenings – insofar as they are continually present to the members of the community and play an outstanding discursive role – are central resources for the narrative. Power actors can and must refer to them if they want to anchor their narratives in the political everyday discourse and in the practical reality of the citizens. Narratives that use motifs solely from the distant past run the risk of appearing antiquated and out of date; they lose their binding effect because they do not give the impression of having anything to do with our present day.

On the other hand, political narrative that fails to remember history cannot guarantee the continuity and narrative cohesion that are central to great narratives. This leads us to the *second source*, the *collective memory and the culture of remembrance* of the entire political community. Even if there are overlaps with the direct experience horizon of the generational cohorts already mentioned, the focus of the collective memory is on the past of the community which has not been directly experienced by its living members. The majority of the history of political communities is rendered present to their members only through literature, art and architecture, and to a lesser extent, through photography, sound recordings and film. Nevertheless, the 'remembrance' of these events – not understood as the mental recalling of one's own subjective experiences, but as an exegesis of interpretive testimonies of the past (see Chapter 2.1) – is decisive. It allows, in MacIntyre's words, the community to be conceived as a project uniting generations and centuries, whose essence and value is not exhausted in the present or simply in the sum of its living members. Collective memory is kept alive by the continual interpretation of past testimonies, and it is this that makes talk of cultural traditions, of moral obligations to the ancestors, of historical guilt and historical achievement possible. However, as the cultural scientist Aleida Assmann notes, the past that is thus interpreted is neither a mere backdrop on which to project present (power) interests nor an autonomous sphere detached from the present: "The past is a mirror in which we perceive ourselves beyond the moment and in which we repeatedly put together what we call the self. This mirror can heroize and throw back one's image in double size, but it can also highlight negative and shameful features. Although the past does not have an autonomous ontological status and relies on our devotion to it, it is much more than a dependent variable of our needs and inclinations. It exceeds individual and collective access; it can neither be monopolized nor conclusively evaluated."[223]

This circumstance – the fact that the past cannot be monopolized and needs to be continuously reassessed and questioned – does not detract from the immense power potential of collective memory. The explosive power of historical memory is clear from the example of the Battle of Amselfeld on the plains of Kosovo, the national-historical myth of the Serbs. On June 28, 1389, the army of the Ottoman Sultan Murat I, advancing on the Balkans near Pristina, met the Orthodox Christian defenders of the Serbian Prince Lazar. After a long battle, during which both commanders lost their lives, the armies wiped each other out. This military stalemate did not change the fact that the Ottomans were able to subjugate the Balkans in the following years. These are the barren facts. Then, still in the fourteenth century, the legend began. The fallen Serbian fighters were transformed into blackbirds after the battle – in testimony of their sacrificial deaths in defense of Christianity. This is the birth of the political narrative of Serbia as a community that stood up as the defender of the Occident against the Orient, a defender characterized by the will to fight against overpowering enemies. The stage of this great narrative has remained Kosovo ever since, the declared 'heartland' of the Serbian people. This narrative was taken up over 600 years later by the President of the Yugoslav Republic of Serbia, Slobodan Milošević, on the one hand to underpin the special status of Serbia as an independent nation oppressed by Tito's League of States and, on the other hand, to establish a claim to power over Kosovo. Milošević's strategy proved extremely successful in the medium term. The nationalist narrative and its real political implications were enthusiastically received by his compatriots. They set the starting signal for the dissolution of Yugoslavia and Serbia's reach for supremacy in Southeastern Europe. The long-term consequences are well known: the military escalation between the republics finally ended with NATO forcing the capitulation of Serbia and Kosovo's independence. It would be wrong to put the myth of the Amselfeld at the beginning of the chain of causes of the Yugoslav war; such a reading is inappropriate for this multi-causal conflict situation. Nonetheless, the episode makes it clear how collective memory can be an effective and destructive catalyst if it is put to clever political use.

Moving beyond immediate experience and political experiences passed on through collective memory, *the third source* is the analysis of academic and scientific evidence to justify the narrative. This includes, on the one hand, the great historical investigations by authors of the type of Theodor Mommsen, Oswald

---

223 Assmann, Aleida (2007): *Geschichte im Gedächtnis. Von der individuellen Erfahrung zur öffentlichen Inszenierung*, Munich: C.H. Beck.; p. 10. (Our translation)

Spengler and Ernest Gellner, who use historical methods to trace the genesis and development of communities; and on the other hand, the outstanding work on state theory that has found its expression in constitutions, legal systems and value systems. In order to avoid too great a focus on historiography in our discussion of justification knowledge and political narratives, we will now focus on the latter. Anyone who has been led to believe that the theory of the state and political philosophy is a purely academic endeavor without no impact on real politics and the great national narratives of history, is recommended to take a walk in the Paris Pantheon. There, in the crypt, in the company of literary greats such as Voltaire and Victor Hugo, lies the resting place of Rousseau – and if you look closely, you can notice a stylized hand clenching a lit torch, apparently slowly pushing aside the coffin lid. The imagery of this symbolic staging is unmistakable: in the memory of France, the Swiss philosopher, always sickly during his lifetime, is as vital as ever, ready to pave the way for future generations or to rekindle the fire of the revolution. Without Rousseau's *Contrat Social,* the French Revolution as the birth of the narrative of the *grande nation* is just as unthinkable as, for example, the American narrative without the *Federalist Papers* by Alexander Hamilton, John Jay and James Madison.[224] Both can be considered the intellectual founding documents of the internal and external understandings of the French and American nations. Where Rousseau campaigned for republican unity, general will and absolute popular rule, the US founding fathers argued for federalism, representative democracy and the separation of powers. Both argumentative directions have not only shaped, indeed dominated, the intellectual debates of their communities, but also their institutional organizations. They are the state-theoretical touchstones which the political elites of the present are still dealing with.

Anyone who is in search of a comparable intellectual foundation for the German narrative, superimposed by fractions and controversies as it is, will most likely find what they are looking for in Hegel's philosophy of law.[225] Whatever the controversies about his historical significance, the Stuttgart thinker can be classified as the Prussian political philosopher par excellence. His political writings

---

[224] See Rousseau ([1762] 2012) and Madison, James, Hamilton, Alexander, and Jay, John (2002): *The Federalist Papers*, Richard Beeman (ed.), New York: Penguin. Of course, the influence of these political thinkers was by no means limited to France or the USA alone. As Sylvain Fort notes, Rousseau's oeuvre was intensely and controversially received by the German Enlightenment experts as early as the eighteenth century; see Fort, Sylvain (2002): *Les Lumières francaises en Allemagne. Le cas Schiller,* Paris: Presses Universitaires de France.

[225] Cf. Hegel ([1821] 2003).

all revolve around the core idea of not only reconciling the principle of free will with the necessity of political order, but of inextricably intertwining the two. This cumulates in the monarchical administrative and corporate state as the final realization of the historical telos of the German people. Noteworthy is Hegel's antirevolutionary slant, which seeks not to change existing relations in favor of an ideal long-term goal, but rather calls for the recognition of the given order. The human pursuit of perfection, a reading of Hegel can suggest, cannot in any case be achieved in the power field of the political: the necessity for compromise is too great, the competition between interest groups is too intense, and external world history is too unpredictable. Rather, perfection can be more readily redeemed in the internal sphere, in art, religion, and finally in philosophy. Admittedly, this astonishingly pragmatic way of thinking, which after Hegel was intensively received by hundreds of thousands of lawyers, administrators, politicians and academics, has not remained unchallenged in Germany. We can certainly read the subsequent writings of German state theorists, above all the Marxists and the Frankfurt School, as vehement attempts at refutation. This very circumstance, nevertheless, tends to underpin the status of the Hegelian work as the intellectual core document of the German political narrative, with which the following generations have continuously wrestled.

We wish to leave discussion of the scientific and academic source and turn to the fourth and final source: the *religious-sacral element*. It is evident that religions play a key role in the foundation of political narratives in all – or almost all – communities. As Böckenförde states in his essay on political theory and political theology, they have held this function, unrivaled among humankind, for thousands of years.[226] There are three central reasons for this. First, viewed from a historical point of view, constitutional thinking originated within the realm of religion,[227] as the most striking concepts of the modern age (and indeed the pre-modern era) are indeed secularized theological concepts.[228] In other words, given that the contemplation of legitimacy has always been historically mixed with religious and in particular theological thinking, sacral schemata form a far from negligible, if not always considered, essence of justification knowledge. This does not mean that all

---

226 As to this reciprocal relationship, see Böckenförde, Wolfgang (1983): Politische Theorie und politische Theologie. Bemerkungen zu ihrem wechselseitigen Verhältnis, in: Jacob Taubes (ed.), *Der Fürst dieser Welt. Carl Schmitt und die Folgen*, Religionstheorie und politische Theorie Vol. 1, Munich: Wilhelm Fink Verlag, pp. 16-25; p. 16.
227 Ibid.: p. 18.
228 Schmitt (1934): p. 49.

narrative justifications of political power are always explicitly or implicitly referenced to the assumption of a deity, but it does signify that their concepts and above all logic forms always possess a sacral pedigree.

Second, as stated in our discussion of the religious field of power (see Chapter 2.3), religions offer a coherent worldview and self-image as well as ethical orientation for rulers and the ruled alike.[229] Presupposing belief in an otherworldly, sacral order, there is evidently no better justification for a secular, profane order than the simple slogan: "Deus vult" – "God wills it." Throughout the course of history the notion of God's will being embodied in political systems is repeatedly seen in the logics supporting the founding of the systems of rule: from the Assyrian Priest-Kings to the Chinese God Emperors to the European, absolutist monarchs by God's grace to the self-proclaimed Caliph of the terrorist Islamic State, Abu Bakr al-Baghdadi. Of course, not every religion-based, political narrative culminates in theocratic rule. Even democratically authorized rulers resort to the use of religious motifs when legitimizing their power and creating a narrative frame of meaning – be it by citing the God-given exceptionalism of their nation and its missionary consciousness, like the neo-conservative government under US President George W. Bush, or by declaring common Christian values to be the link between European nations, like former French President Nicolas Sarkozy. Shared beliefs thus create as strong a cohesion and a sense of us among people as having a shared history, and these accordingly flank the historical sources of the political narrative with norms and meanings that go beyond history.

Third, we should not forget that religions – like political narratives – have the character of great, continuing stories. As a rule, they are not static, but eschatological. They tell a history of salvation and of the world with a clearly defined starting point (the creation) and end point (the last judgment).[230] The founding of the Muslim *umma,* the political community of the faithful under the Prophet Mo

---

229 Appropriately recognized by Böckenförde (1983: p. 19) in relation to the Christian faith when he states that Christian religion is not only the worship of God in the form of a cult, but also extends its lessons into almost all walks of life and interprets the surrounding reality of human life. This inevitably leads to statements / doctrines that concern the orders of political coexistence, their status, tasks and areas of competence as well as their legitimacy.

230 Remarkably, eschatological elements are found not only in the Mosaic-Monotheistic religions (Judaism, Christianity, Islam), but, e.g., also in Buddhism, Hinduism, Zoroastrianism and in the Old Slavic religion; for an overview see Walls, Jerry L. (ed.) (2008), *The Oxford Handbook of Eschatology*, Oxford/New York: Oxford University Press.

hamed, stood under the auspices of the imminent judgment of the world by which the pious would be rewarded and the sinners punished. Corresponding motifs and political prophecies can already be found in ancient Egypt in the second millennium BC. Localizing communities on a historical timeline that can be interpreted theologically as well as strategically makes it possible to place all political events – wars with other states, internal unrest, but also economic, scientific and cultural successes – in a religious context of explanation. In this way, state crises can be interpreted as divine tests to be passed, military conflicts as predetermined defensive struggles against heathens and apostates, and the continuity of a dynastic rule or political elite can be explained as the fulfillment of a great divine plan.

Critical readers might argue that not all major political narratives encompass this sacred, eschatological component – and in fact, we have already referenced the atheistic-secular narrative of the *grande nation* several times.[231] However, this component (or at least its logic and motifs) could indeed be much more widespread than may at first appear. This can be seen in the political narratives of socialist-communist states in the twentieth century: the ideological core of this narrative, Marxism-Leninism, with its prediction (or prophecy) of a classless society at the end of a historical struggle between workers and capitalists, has all the features of a classic salvation story. This is not surprising, considering that Marx's understanding of history as a teleological process that must go through a necessary series of historical epochs, is directly inspired by Hegel. And again, he stood firmly on the ground of Christianity.

All sources of the political narrative and at the same time the most important foundations of justification knowledge have been identified. The obvious question of how individual actors can make concrete use of these sources in order to legitimize their position of power in a specific community has, of course, not yet been answered. However, as this is so contextually specific and can only be addressed against the background of the narrative resources of the respective communities, no universal answer can be given here. In addition thereto, as mentioned repeatedly, this point also plays into the sphere of political leadership and strategy issues

---

231 The French revolutionaries, however, did not want to abandon religion completely: parallel to the enforced dechristianization, Robespierre introduced a Culte de l'Être suprême ("Cult of the Supreme Being"), centering on worship of the allegory of reason. However, this attempt to create a liturgical hybrid of enlightenment pathos and quasi-sacral staging failed due to the lack of interest among the population and was quickly shelved after the end of Jacobin rule; see Culoma, Michael (2010): *La religion civile de Rousseau à Robespierre*, Paris: L'Harmattan.

and cannot be discussed separately from them; which leads us now to the second great form of power knowledge: *leadership*.

The first and most obvious key aspect associated with the core concept of leadership is that of *political strategy*.[232] The notion of strategy is a definitional 'perennial.' Its definition is as controversial among experts as those of power, the political and the common good. Nevertheless, we can approach the concept of strategy by delimiting it from the related concept of *tactics*. Both tactics and strategies are mental constructs or instructions that players consciously utilize to achieve their goals in competitive situations – be it in chess, on the battlefield, in marketing or in the political arena. The difference is that tactics are always oriented to the situation or to the current time. They determine how actors behave and respond when faced with a specific situation (such as a battle behind enemy lines or a heated political debate with critical discussion partners). Strategy is always cross-situational. It does not guide the behavior of actors in a concrete action context, but it can, for example, determine *what situations the actors create, which opponents they seek disputes with and which not, and which allies they attempt to win in order to realize their goals efficiently and effectively*. The occurrence of unforeseen events that conflict with the interests of an actor is a sign of strategic failure, but not an indication of wrong tactics. We can make this distinction even clearer by means of a military example. Whether the decision of the Central Powers during the First World War to counterattack the Entente at the twelfth Isonzo Battle in October 1917 was correct, is a question of tactics.[233] Whether their decision to build the Isonzo Front at all and thus to risk a war of position against Italy was expedient, is a question of strategy.[234] The first question concerns the achievement of a local, situational goal: winning a battle. The second question, on the other

---

[232] Cf. Raschke, Joachim and Tils, Ralf (2008): Politische Strategie, *Forschungsjournal NSB*, 21 (1), pp. 11-24.; and Raschke, Joachim and Tils, Ralf (2011): *Politik braucht Strategie – Taktik hat sie genug*, Frankfurt am Main/New York: Campus.

[233] The answer is yes. The counterattack of the Austrian and German armies led to the collapse of the Italian defenders. However, this did not change anything in the course of the war or the looming defeat of the Central Powers.

[234] The answer is no. The total of twelve Isonzo battles on the territory of today's Slovenia are a dramatic testimony to the strategic failure of the top military commanders. Not only did they tie up considerable troop contingents without achieving any significant territorial gains, they also cost countless lives and led to increasing war fatigue.

hand, is about achieving a global, cross-situational goal: winning the First World War.[235]

Based on this distinction and drawing on the work of Joachim Raschke and Ralf Tils, strategies can all be summarized as "success-oriented constructs based on cross-situational, goal-means-environment calculations."[236] This definition applies universally, regardless of whether we are in the field of sports, economics, warfare or politics. However, what constitutes a successful political strategy and what components it comprises is another matter. Raschke and Tils have already laid important foundations for this topic[237] which we take as a starting point and develop into an independent system enriched by practical and theoretical insights. According to our core thesis, a successful political strategy has four components: *strategy foundations, strategy capability, strategy development* and *strategic steering*.

Figure 7: Components of Successful Political Strategy

---

235 The decision as to whether a specific construct of action must be classified as tactics or strategy is, of course, not always easy. However, this has nothing to do with the vagueness of our concepts, but with the different connotations and usage contexts. Specifically, it is about whether we grasp a decision framework as a singular situation or as a cross-situational sequence of events and act accordingly. This is not primarily a theoretical but rather a genuinely practical question, because the standard to be applied is ultimately always success and failure. For a more in-depth discussion, see also Strachen, Hew (2005): The Lost Meaning of Strategy, *Survival*, 47 (3), pp. 33-54.
236 Raschke & Tils (2008): p. 12.
237 Ibid. as well as Raschke, Joachim and Tils, Ralf (2007): *Politische Strategie. Eine Grundlegung*, Wiesbaden: VS Verlag.

The *foundations* of political strategy are found in the appropriation of a specialized view of the social world that Foucault aptly calls 'governmentality' – a neologism that combines the terms 'govern' and 'mentality.'[238] Those who master governmentality have, on the one hand, systematically absorbed the phenomenon of power in its various principles, forms, fields and conditions of legitimacy (see Chapters 1.2 to 2.4) – whether through political experience, theoretical reflection or, ideally, by virtue of a combination of both. On the other hand, they have developed a powerful political scheme of orientation. The latter, as can be elucidated with Raschke & Tils, is an "empirically based model that has been further developed and systematized from the starting point of the orientation parameters of strategic players."[239] As the expression 'model' suggests, this orientation scheme is not an exact illustration of political reality, but rather an abstraction. It brings together the central parameters of the political: time horizons of policy decisions and processes, policies, topics, organizations, persons, symbols and the public.[240]

Through the combination of power penetration and the orientation scheme, strategic actors can rasterize social reality, isolate the important from the unimportant and gain an overview of the decision-making environment. At this point, we wish to prevent a possible misunderstanding: governmentality is not a cognitive *déformation professionnelle,* because of which actors would perceive their environment, other persons, institutions and topics only in the context of success-oriented purpose-means relations. Instead, it is a specific mindset that everyone can acquire and use purposefully by virtue of cultivating political skills and areas of knowledge – Foucault also speaks of the "techniques of the self."[241] The strategic systematization and orientation of governmentality is best illustrated by the following comparison. If a botanical layperson roams a forest with a PhD forest scientist, the former sees one thing above all: many trees; the latter sees not only spruce, pine and ash, but also ecological problems, management potentials and landscape developments. The sensory data are the same for both persons, but the conclusions drawn from this data differ dramatically. Analogously, the political-strategic layperson perceives the political power field primarily as a confusing mingling of politicians, parties and talk shows. However, those with sophisticated

---

238 Cf. Lemke, Thomas (2001): The birth of bio-politics: Michael Foucault's lectures at the College de France on neo-liberal governmentality, *Economy and Society*, 30 (2), pp. 190-207.
239 Ibid.: p. 15.
240 Raschke & Tils (2007): p. 162.
241 Cf. Foucault, Michel (1984 [1990]): *The Use of Pleasure*, The History of Sexuality, Vol. 2, translated by Robert Hurley (ed.), New York: Random House.; p. 11.

governmentality at their disposal see a differentiated multilevel system, constituted by formal and informal relationships between decision-makers, stakeholders, institutions and issues, whose function revolves around the legitimation, allocation and exercise of power. The skilled eye recognizes the powers of competing and allied actors, identifies opportunities and risks. Indeed, it is this view that makes successful strategy development and implementation possible.

The second component is that of strategy *capability*. It describes the ability of the power actor to implement strategic decisions effectively and efficiently – under real conditions of political competition in which other protagonists pursue conflicting political strategies. This faculty is based on seven factors or, as we will say below, strategic powers. As a rule of thumb, we can state that the greater the strategical powers of the actor, the greater his or her strategic ability and thus chances of successfully implementing a strategy.

The deciding factor here is, first of all, the degree of *organizational capability*, i.e. the ability to set clear strategic goals and to make corresponding decisions. On the one hand, this presupposes the institutional establishment of a hierarchy of decisions in which internal powers, management tasks, responsibilities and control functions are defined and linked with specific roles or offices. On the other hand, it requires the preliminary clarification of the political direction or, as Raschke and Tils aptly summarize, the establishment of a corridor that defines the content of the interest formation – through topics, positions and symbols.[242] This creates a common understanding of the politics and internal coherence. The relevance of these interrelated aspects is immediately evident: without political leadership, a strategic actor is unable to act; without a clear political direction, he is aimless.

While organizational capability represents an actor's intrinsic strategic potency, the second factor, *mobilization capability,* refers to the actor's relationship to his or her strategic environment. Political mobilization is a form of communication and action that enables organizations of the political power field, such as parties, associations, companies, NGOs, trade unions and churches, for example, to activate a variegated group of people (voters, members, customers, believers, patients, etc.) in order to assert their respective strategic interests. It thus functions as a social catalyst in which the mobilized make their voices and faces available to the organization and become active in working for the organization's goals.[243] A key instrument of political mobilization is the campaign. Given that very different actors each with their own policy goals initiate campaigns, and the instru

---

242 Raschke & Tils (2008): p. 18.
243 Speth, Rudolf (2013): Verbände und Grassroots-Campaigning, in: Rudolf Speth (ed.), *Grassroots-Campaigning*, Wiesbaden: VS Verlag, pp. 43-59.; p. 43.

ment is used in both advertising and in political communication, it is necessary to specify the function of a campaign very accurately. Campaigns are aimed at the (re)election of a president or chancellor, the boycott of products or companies, the adoption or withdrawal of laws and regulations, the support or rejection of infrastructure projects, etc. Ulrike Röttger offers a now classic definition providing good orientation. Campaigns are "dramaturgically designed, thematically limited, time-limited communicative strategies for producing public attention [...], they draw on a set of different communicative tools and techniques – promotional means, marketing-specific instruments and classic PR measures. Attracting attention is the minimum goal of campaigns of all kinds. The aim is moreover to generate confidence in the credibility of the organization and approval of one's own intentions or follow-up actions."[244] This dense description makes clear that convincing campaigns or the ability to mobilize involves not only a plausible and captivating political discourse – with a starting point, climax and end point and continuous tension – but also a set of methods, fed by the media and journalism. These instruments are flanked by a resource that we described and discussed in Chapter 2.3: data power. Since successful campaigning is today unthinkable without detailed knowledge of the respective target group and their interests, political mobilization stands and falls not least with the effective use of instruments such as data mining and data targeting. Algorithm-based data analysis not only enables precise target group preferences to be determined, but also allows the development of a tailor-made approach and motivation: on the one hand through targeted dialogue communication on platforms, in social networks and via e-mails, but on the other hand through classical analogue instruments such as personalized letters or visits. The strategic potency of mobilization capability is thus based on a combination of dramaturgical wit, communicative skills, technological know-how and tightly conducted campaign management. The significance of the latter for success can hardly be overestimated. This is particularly clear in the United States, where the management of election campaigns has an almost military organizational structure. The great art perfected by US campaigners is to develop a fully organized top-down campaign that citizens nonetheless perceive as a motivating grassroots movement.

The third factor of strategic potency, *network capability,* also refers to the relationship between the power player and the environment. However, this is specifically about the ability to forge alliances with other organizations and interest

---

244 Röttger, Ulrike (2009): Campaigns (f)or a better world?, in: Ulrike Röttger (ed.), *PR-Kampagnen. Über die Inszenierung von Öffentlichkeit*, 4th revised and expanded edition, Wiesbaden: VS Verlag, pp. 9-26.; p. 9.

formations to increase the reach of the actor's own concerns or to achieve greater credibility. Political networks of this type can only be established if there is a sufficient intersection between the potential allies. For example, alliances between environmental organizations such as the National Wildlife Federation (NWF), NatureServe and the Worldwide Fund for Nature (WWF) are much easier forsed than between the automotive industry and the Alliance for Biking and Walking.

Not only shared themes and goals but also common habitus and practices and shared interpretative horizons of the common good (see Chapter 2.4) are decisive for the formation of effective, permanent alliances.[245] One example is the development of the relationship between the Catholic Church and the trade unions from the late nineteenth to the twenty-first century. At the time of the 'working-class Pope' Leo XII, who in 1891 wrote the most influential political encyclical of recent history with *Rerum Novarum,* the Catholic Church and the organized workforce agreed surprisingly often on core political questions.[246] Leo's partisanship on issues such as equal pay and employee protection met with great approval from labor leaders; and they in turn left no doubt about their support for the Pope's theological and moral program. However, as the unions turned to atheistic socialism and the Catholic Church withdrew from 'wordly affairs', this alliance eroded rapidly. This circumstance seems all the more remarkable when one considers that core issues of Catholic social teaching, such as solidarity with underprivileged sections of society or the principle of subsidiarity, are still highly compatible with trade union discourse. It makes clear, however, that thematic convergence is not sufficient for alliance formation if a consensus as to (at least) the basic values becomes impossible among the different power actors.

Political alliances – between parties, companies, NGOs, churches or other organizations – are highly effective tools of political strategy. Nonetheless, their formation must actually be oriented towards or correspond to the strategic goal. Two dimensions of evaluation are crucial for this: quality and quantity. When it comes to achieving a highly focused goal that attracts little public attention with a small, specialized circle of decision-makers and stakeholders – such as the amendment to a pharmaceuticals directive – then an alliance with a few, highly competent partners is preferable. Here the exchange of information, the pooling of expertise and professional reputation are in the foreground. The situation is different with a

---

245 Cf. also Beamish, Thomas D. and Luebbers, Amy J. (2009): Alliance-Building Across Social Movements: Bridging Difference in a Peace and Justice Coalition, *Social Problems*, 56 (4), pp. 647-676.

246 Cf. Leo XIII. (1891): Circular issued by our Most Holy Father Leo XIII, by Divine Providence Pope, on the Labor Question. Rerum Novarum, Munich: Herder.

broad strategic goal in that it not only involves numerous power fields and interest groups, but also holds immense public mobilization potential – such as the conclusion of the Transatlantic Trade and Investment Partnership (TTIP) between the EU and the US. The deal failed significantly because supporters had not established a broad alliance that integrated various organizations and layers of society, underscoring public interest in the cause. Instead, the impression of a shielded, exclusive and elitist clique of political decision-makers whose rulings were contrary to (alleged) popular will became established in the various sectors of the European public. Conversely, the TTIP opponents were able to forge an EU-wide coalition of globalization opponents, environmentalists and animal rights activists, but also right-wing *and* left-wing populists, and kick off a protest wave of enormous proportions with simple slogans such as "TTIP kills" or "Tango vs. TTIP."[247] The sheer number of voices and the emotionalization of the subject made recourse to content-related expertise and to the reputation of experts practically useless; the credibility trap was inescapable.

The cases discussed make two things evident. First, despite all differences, the potencies of mobilization and network capabilities are often closely intertwined in practice; second, the public factor in alliance formation is always a strategic risk or opportunity that requires consideration and evaluation. To be sure, the cases mentioned here – the amendment of a single directive on the one hand and the conclusion of a free trade agreement on the other – are in some ways extreme examples of political and strategic goals. In most cases, actually, neither quantity nor quality alone can be seen as being crucial to the formation of a goal-oriented network, but rather a balance between the two dimensions. Therefore, we can state that the potency of network capability is based not only on the ability to create nodes or intersections (in terms of themes, practices, habitus), but also on judgment that allows the envisaged alliance to be balanced in terms of quality and quantity.

Nevertheless, the best alliance is strategically ineffective if its members are unable to communicate key messages credibly and with a lasting effect to the addressees. This challenge leads us to the fourth strategic potency: *mediation capability*. This is the ability to convey those concerns, interests and opinions that are relevant for the strategic achievement of goals to other persons and institutions. We would do well to take the word 'mediating' literally: it does not just involve

---

247 For a good overview, see Bauer, Matthias (2016): The Political Power of Evoking Fear: The Shining Example of Germany's Anti-TTIP Campaign Movement, *European View*, 15 (2), pp. 193–212.

making a message intelligible, i.e. its translation into the language of the addressee, but also involves being convincing. Anyone who successfully conveys a request, for example, creates a rational and empathetic connection in dialogue – he or she is recognized as a trustworthy communication partner worth listening to. There are two key factors here that at first glance seem to conflict: truthfulness and rhetorical finesse.

Being truthful does not mean that our statements must be beyond doubt and always true. Such a requirement is far too sophisticated from an epistemological point of view because it presupposes an infinite cascade of meta-knowledge and imposes unrealistically high standards of self-examination on those communicating a message. Rather, truthfulness means that statements and practical actions coincide, that is, that discourse and practice are consistent. Power actors in whom discourse and practice in no way agree are perceived by their addressees either as erratic or as bigoted. They are implausible. And even if their arguments are convincing, they will generally be opposed.[248]

How devastating this divergence between saying and doing can be for the achievement of strategic goals can be seen, for example, in the failed 'Remain' campaign by ex-British Prime Minister David Cameron aiming to ensure the continued membership of Great Britain in the EU.[249] Cameron's political ascent was not only due to acrimonious agitation against Brussels institutions and migrant workers from neighboring EU countries, but also to his announcement that the British were to vote on leaving the European Union. When the referendum was scheduled, the prime minister nevertheless advocated that the country remain in the EU – with the well-known result. The crux is that a politician who has done everything to stir up aversion against the EU among his constituents cannot credibly promote staying in it. Such mediation is not truthful and can therefore hardly promise success. The election campaign of US presidential candidate Hilary Clinton offers a similar picture. The Democratic politician, who had maintained strong relationships with the US financial sector for decades, and raised more than $ 20

---

248   At this point there is a close connection between the strategic potency of mediation and the first format of power knowledge, justification knowledge: thus, as we shall show below, truthfulness is a necessary condition of the justification structure of power in the political system.

249   For a captivating and informative treatment of this topic, see McTague, Tom, Spence, Alex, and Dovere, Edward-Isaac (2016): How Cameron Blew It, in: Politico from 25th June 2016, [online] http://www.politico.eu/article/how-david-cameron-lost-brexit-eu-referendum-prime-minister-campaign-remain-boris-craig-oliver-jim-messina-obama/, retrieved on 21.12.2017.

million in donations from hedge funds, banks and insurance companies in 2015,[250] attempted to build on the capitalism-critical narrative of her in-party opponent Bernie Sanders. She called for a storm on Wall Street. As a result of this all-too-obvious divergence between discourse and practice, Clinton lost both left-leaning young voters and pro-business voters – and ultimately the election.

Political cynics might argue that truthfulness is only a crucial factor in mediating ability if power actors are unable to adequately disguise the discrepancy between their statements and actions. This objection should be taken seriously. There are two things to say about this. *Firstly,* of course, concealment and secrecy are part of any political strategy. This fact is already evident in the initial intrinsic connection between knowledge and power. An advantage in power knowledge brings a clear advantage in power, and this in turn significantly increases strategic chances of success. Therefore, withholding information from rivals, critics and potential adversaries, leaving them unaware of one's own abilities and goals, is a strategic imperative. *Secondly,* however, the capacity for concealment has practical limits, no matter how much a power actor has perfected it: the greater the discrepancy between discourse and practice, the easier it is to identify and the harder to disguise. In addition, caution is needed for another reason: the global, digitally networked communication spaces of our day offer greater investigative potential than ever before in world history. This is not changed by the current debates about fake news. Due to the exponential increase in the risk of being exposed as erratic or bigoted, in short, not truthful, such a concealment tactic may well be unsuccessful, at least in the long term.

The second factor of mediation, rhetoric, seems to clash with the principle of truthfulness. However, the impression that these two conflict is due to a conceptual narrowing – on the one hand of the concept of mediation, on the other hand of rhetoric. Prominent critics, including intellectual historical figures such as Plato, Goethe and Bismarck, like to characterize rhetoric as a technique of adept persuasion, but not one of convincing, and they decry it as a tool of demagogues and pied pipers. The enlightened Kant even spoke of a "deceitful art"[251]. We see this crushing verdict, however, as a distortion of the great tradition of political rhetoric, which – when used responsibly and well understood – revolves around

---

250 Cf. Rubin, Jennifer (2016): Hillary Clinton, blind to her own greed, makes another blunder, in: Washington Post from 4th February 2016, [online] https://www.washingtonpost.com/blogs/right-turn/wp/2016/02/04/hillary-clinton-blind-to-her-own-greed-makes-another-blunder/?utm_term=.2605df8f25ad, retrieved on 22.01.2018.
251 Kant, Immanuel ([1790] 2002): *Critique of the Power of Judgment,* London: Cambridge University Press, p. 205.

three major guiding principles: logos, pathos and ethos.[252] True rhetoric addresses the passions of the listeners as well as their reason and judgment, and reflects the speaker's veracity and integrity as discussed above. Behind this triad is an equally simple and plausible anthropological assumption: as a political creature, as zoon politikon, humankind is never merely rational or sentimental, and is not motivated solely by selfish or altruistic reasons. Rather, human beings seem to be creatures traversed by various impulses and motives. Political mediation, if it is to succeed, must address all this.

This assessment also speaks against an exaggerated intellectual and elitist image of political mediation, as we know it from the Frankfurt School, in particular Habermasian discourse ethics.[253] Adherents of this line of thought suggest, concisely put, that the mediation of political content has to be strictly rational and dispassionate because any other procedure is manipulative and detrimental to the truth. Now it is open to debate whether politics should really be seen as analogous to a university seminar or a judicial process and classified as primarily aiming to discover the truth (for more on this, see Chapter 2.4). Considerable doubts seem appropriate. But all that is in the end irrelevant. Habermas' discourse-ethical model of political mediation is unfit for practice and thus at best interesting as a theoretical exercise in thought. Let us remember that the potency of mediation capability is part of a political-strategic complex and thus comes into play in a situation in which strategic actors compete for power. In such a scenario, the renunciation of rhetoric in favor of a strictly rational and dispassionate style of argumentation is an unprecedented competitive disadvantage. In short, because rhetoric is the art of convincing and inspiring listeners alike, and because any power actor who does not use this tool loses political influence, the model of discourse ethics is simply irrational from a power theory perspective.[254] Accordingly, the approach we propose, combining truthfulness and rhetoric, is not only founded in the historically proven tradition of thought leaders such as Aristotle and Cicero, but is also based on pragmatism.

---

252 Cf. Aristotle (1959) *Ars Rhetorica*, W. D. Ross (ed.), Oxford: Oxford University Press.; Cicero, Marcus Tullius (1986): *De oratore*, David Mankin (ed.), New York: Cambridge University Press.

253 Cf. Habermas (1984).

254 Significantly, this finding is also reflected in the more recent deliberative theory of democracy, which has developed a much more open and constructive relationship to political rhetoric, see, e.g. Dryzek (2000); and Mansbridge, Jane et al. (2012): A Systemic Approach to Deliberative Democracy, in: John Parkinson and Jane Mansbridge (eds.), *Deliberative Systems,* Cambridge: Cambridge University Press, pp. 1-26.

Complementary to mediation capability, there is another potency, which is also closely linked to the public: *fame*. Those who are famous enjoy a specific form of public attention that sets them apart from other actors and enables them, by virtue of their reputation, to strategically influence the political power field. Their words have weight, their actions inspire people, their names are on everyone's lips. Now, fame – and political glory in particular – is not synonymous with *sui generis* attention.[255] Social media personalities, YouTubers and pop stars may have millions of followers on digital platforms and enjoy significant economic leverage, for instance through product recommendations. They are, in the diction of marketing, highly effective influencers. Still, this influence cannot be translated into strategic political potency. The reason is that even their followers do not usually attribute political skills to these people, but rather, e.g., artistic brilliance or an outstanding sense of fashion and trends. Here, in our estimation, is the *differentia specifica:* fame consists of the attainment of public attention combined with the attribution of power competence, power knowledge and power itself. Not without reason does one think of the word 'fame' first of all with respect to personalities such as Alexander the Great, Caesar, Napoleon or Winston Churchill. They all gained world-historical prominence while serving as outstanding power strategists.[256] At the same time, this list makes it clear that fame is not necessarily linked to a good reputation or to a sense of mutual esteem. Autocrats such as Vladimir Putin may be far more feared than valued, especially in the Western world. Nevertheless, it does not detract from their fame. Even the greatest critic of the Kremlin would not hesitate for a second to classify the Russian president as an exceptional political figure and as a person whose words and deeds attract the eyes of the world.

Now, it is one thing to define fame as strategic potency, and quite another to determine the foundations on which it is based and how it is obtained. There is no

---

255 See also Franck, Georg (1998): *Ökonomie der Aufmerksamkeit: Ein Entwurf,* München: Hanser. Franck classifies fame as an independent form of attention alongside prestige, prominence and reputation. For a concise English-language summary, see Franck, Georg (undated): The Economy Of Attention, [online] http://www.t0.or.at/franck/gfeconom.htm, retrieved on 21.12.2017.

256 A vivid example of a decision-maker who received great political attention, but who failed to be attributed with political capability, is the former French President Francois Hollande. Thanks to his private escapades, his clumsy political tactics and failed reforms Hollande was in the headlines throughout his tenure, but just as an 'inglorious' example of a statesman. This circumstance was also reflected in Hollande's low power strategic potency.

general guide to fame – too great are the historical, sociological and cultural differences between the political communities and too decisive factors such as personality and esprit that cannot be influenced. Instead of sufficient conditions, therefore, only a series of favorable conditions can be cited: birth, money, achievement and symbolic dexterity.

Those who grow up in a wealthy nation as part of the upper or middle class have far greater prospects of bringing their power competence and power knowledge into the limelight than anyone from the slums of Nairobi or Calcutta. It is a sobering but significant fact that the great majority of the glorious power actors in history have always been recruited from the resource-rich states and classes. Monetary resources, like the correct place of birth, are not a guarantee for fame, but they are crucial in the social struggle for attention. The media scientists Georg Franck and Jörg Bernardy underline the insight that attention – especially in modern media companies – is a highly sought after and extremely scarce commodity, for which more and more players compete with ever greater capital expenditure.[257] Consumers are constantly oscillating between countless publications, news programs, websites, feeds, newsletters etc. Those who want to assert themselves permanently in this fight must invest in their public and media presence; otherwise they suddenly lose the attention of their audience. The aspect of performance in this context is decisive: it feeds the narrative of fame. Only if power actors have actually achieved political merit – whether by winning a war, reforming a state, reviving the national economy or reconciling warring ethnic groups – does their self-staging also have political substance. Undoubtedly, in the course of history, charlatans and braggarts have repeatedly achieved fame. But glory without substance is fragile. In the above-mentioned digitally networked communication space of our present time, the risk of being exposed as a liar is constant. The last and perhaps most important requirement is symbolic dexterity. For attention to become fame, it must be charged with symbolism. The conditions under which the public looks at a person can be controlled by gestures, metaphors and signs. One might think of Willy Brandt's spontaneous kneeling before the memorial for the dead of the Warsaw Ghetto in 1970, or of the handshake between Helmut Kohl and Francois Mitterrand at Verdun in 1984. However, one of the great historical masters of symbolic staging was unquestionably Napoleon Bonaparte. In an attempt to expand his position of power in republican France, the Corsican strategist

---

257 Cf. Franck (1998): S. 49f. and Bernardy, Jörg (2011): Attention as Bounded Resource and Medium in Cultural Memory: A Phenomenological or Economic Approach?, *Empedocles: European Journal for the Philosophy of Communication*, 2 (2), pp. 241-254.

initiated the invasion of Egypt in 1798.[258] From a purely military point of view, the expedition was unsuccessful, but this circumstance played no part whatsoever in public judgment: Napoleon, accompanied by numerous chroniclers throughout, not only founded the Cairo Institute d'Égypt and laid the foundation for modern research into antiquity, he also reformed the Egyptian administration, had the entire country mapped, eradicated the bubonic plague and introduced book printing. In short, Napoleon used the military expedition as a stage to present himself to the local audience and the world as a promoter of the arts and sciences, a reformer, and a nation builder. Upon his return to Paris, he was enthusiastically welcomed by huge crowds. Five years later, he was emperor.

The sixth factor of strategy capability we want to discuss is financial potency. This factor has already been mentioned in discussion of the other powers. Therefore, we can keep our discussion short. Obviously, the ability of power actors to effectively and efficiently implement strategic decisions ultimately also depends on their financial resources. All previous factors – organizational capability, mobilization capability, network capability, mediation capability and even fame – already presuppose the availability of monetary resources. Good and reliable personnel have to be paid, campaigns have to be financed, and of course the same applies to technological and communicative tools as well as the necessary infrastructure.

Financial potency is necessary for strategy capability. Nevertheless, this does not mean that it is sufficient or that every power player needs equivalent resources to pursue his or her strategic goals. The first point is obvious. If an actor has sustained lasting reputational damage this strategic disadvantage can often not be compensated by the most expensive campaigns. A striking example is provided by the global exhaust gas scandal of the German automotive industry in 2016 and 2017, in which automobile companies had obscured the emission values of their diesel vehicles by means of illegal devices. Uncovering this process led to a diesel sector crisis that is still having an effect today and that even multibillion-dollar global companies can no longer control.[259]

The second point requires a certain amount of explanation: actors in the political power field whose strategic goals are seen by widespread public opinion as having a high altruistic quality, such as environmentalists, human rights activists

---

258 Cf. Cole, Juan R. (2008): *Napoleon's Egypt: Invading the Middle East*, New York: Palgrave Macmillan.; and Burleigh, Nina (2007): *Mirage: Napoleon's Scientists and the Unveiling of Egypt*, New York: Harper Collins.

259 Cf. Bowens, Luc (2016): The Ethics of Dieselgate, *Midwest Studies in Philosophy*, 40 (1), pp. 262-283.

or development workers, have a strategic resource that can be termed moral capital – based on Bourdieu (see also Chapter 2.3). Their objectives are compatible with the ethical convictions of broad social classes. Moral capital provides a strategic competitive advantage over actors whose goals are not perceived as being equally altruistic – and, more importantly, compensates to a certain degree for financial capital. It is e.g. easier, and therefore less costly, to attract people to a cause that they either explicitly or implicitly agree with out of ethical conviction, rather than one that they first need to be convinced of. To put it bluntly, human rights sell better than nuclear power. Moreover, for actors whose strategic goals are inextricably linked to a moral narrative, in individual cases substantial financial resources may even prove to be a burden because they may give the impression of superiority or venality. In spite of everything, however, the principle remains that power actors without financial power cannot make use of the other strategic powers, for the reasons mentioned above. So here it is not a question of whether, but a question of how much. Financial power remains the *conditio sine qua non* of strategy capability.

The seventh and final strategic potency is the willingness to make a sacrifice. This term, which may at first sight appear martial, refers simply to the will of power actors and their supporters to accept deprivations in pursuit of the strategic goal and to take risks (also concerning their own well-being). The development, implementation and management of a political strategy is never a risk-free or effortless project. Strategies cost time, money, nerves and above all strength. The imponderables of the power field inevitably bring setbacks. They can go hand in hand with the loss of money, prestige, friendships, and even life and limb in the case of strategies that challenge the established order (such as revolutions or organized civil disobedience against dictatorships). Actors who are not sufficiently motivated to take and also to bear these risks are clearly inferior to actors willing to make sacrifices. To underline this point, we do not need to recall historically exceptional figures such as the Indian statesman Mahatma Ghandi, who was ready to sacrifice the integrity of his own body for his strategy of pacifist rebellion against the British Empire.[260] The long and extremely exhausting day-to-day work

---

260 Incidentally, we deliberately speak of Gandhi's pacifistic strategy and not of a philosophical attitude. The Indian revolutionary used non-violent resistance deliberately as a strategic means against the colonial troops, so as to clearly show the world the 'barbarism' of the occupiers. In the later conflict with Pakistan, Gandhi clearly favored a military option; see Tønnesson, Øyvind (1999): Mahatma Gandhi, the Missing Laureate, [online] https://www.nobelprize.org/nobel_prizes/themes/peace/gandhi/in

of a political leader – especially during election campaigns – suffices as an example to show what willingness to make sacrifices can mean in terms of political strategies.

At this point we want to conclude discussion of strategy capability and turn to the third component of the political strategy: *strategy development*. Successful strategy development is based, as Raschke and Tils put it in an interesting mathematical analogy, on correct calculations.[261] In the broadest sense, such calculations are benefit evaluations. By virtue thereof, actors define their cross-situational goals in the context of available resources or their own power assets, system conditions and the power resources of political opponents, and thus derive a plan of action. In short, actors play through the various causal paths that can lead to their goal, and choose the one that is characterized by the optimal relation between probability of success and expected effort. The ideal objective is to identify a path with maximum effectiveness and efficiency, i.e. the greatest possible chance of success with the smallest possible use of resources. At this point, however, Raschke and Tils' mathematical analogy reaches its limits, for unlike arithmetic operations that are based on universal axioms, strategic calculations are not logical inferences, but probabilistic operations based on empirical knowledge.[262] They have the following general form: from the empirically based assumption that I can mobilize resource r, the political environment follows development path d and the political opponent performs action a, there is a probability of x% that I will reach my goal. Such calculations, because they anticipate future actions and events, are characterized by a risk of unpredictability. This increases with the time horizon of the strategy and the number of variables and constants.

---

dex.html, retrieved on 21.12.2017.; and Freedman, Lawrence (2013): *Strategy: A History*, Oxford/New York: Oxford University Press.; p. 247.
261   Cf. Rasche, Joachim & Tils, Ralf (2011): p. 113.
262   To be precise, mathematical calculations are a priori; they are not based on empirical knowledge, but – if we follow Kant – in pure reason. Strategic calculations are a posteriori, they have their basis and justification in our knowledge of the world.

Figure 8: Strategic Calculations

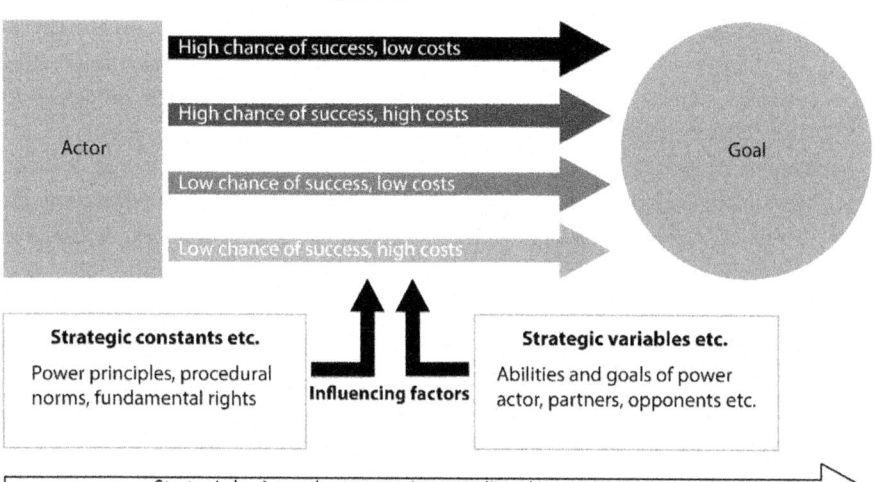

To put it another way, whoever carries out a strategic calculation strikes a balance *(a)* between their strategic goal and their available means of power; predicts *(b)* the future behavior of political opponents and allies as well as the occurrence of policy-relevant events and political developments; *(c)* recalls their past experience of the political power field, its actors, processes and constraints in order to *(d)* identify the ideal causal path towards the goal. This highly condensed recapitulation readily makes it clear that strategy-building is a very complex process.

Although the influencing factors for strategy formation can be extremely numerous and difficult to survey in any particular case, they can still be systematized and thus made manageable by utilizing a few categories. As a first step, we can divide the entire spectrum into two basic categories: *strategic constants* and *strategic variables.*

With *constants,* we refer to all those factors that are extremely difficult to change – either because they are stable, cross-cultural principles or habitual, firmly anchored patterns of action of the respective communities.[263] These include basic economic laws, such as principles, which state, e.g. that a high demand for

---

263 Our concept of strategic constants is inspired by the historiographical core concept of the longue durée, which Ferdinand Braudel, as one of the most important representatives of the Annales School, introduced into historical science. Cf. Lee, Richard E. (2013): *The Longue Duree and World-Systems Analysis,* New York: State University of New York Press.

low supply leads to price increases, but it also encompasses the universal principles of power and anthropological constants, such as humankind's vulnerability.

Furthermore, this category can also encompass the constitutional and procedural norms of the community in which the strategy is to be implemented. This includes, among others, political and civil rights, electoral systems, forms of horizontal and vertical separation of powers, and involvement in supranational institutions such as the EU or the Commonwealth of Nations. These norms describe the formal rules of the game of competition for political power and demarcate the limits of the legal and legitimate use of strategic power resources. A caveat is appropriate, of course, because these rules are not universal but historically contingent and can indeed be changed or abolished by humans. However – and this is crucial – they are protected by extremely demanding procedural hurdles (for example, two-thirds majority clauses in both US Houses of Congress and both German chambers) and deeply rooted elements of their respective political practices. Therefore, strategies rarely target constitutional and procedural norms (or their modification), but operate within the scope of those norms.

This statement is generalizable: constants of strategy formation are influencing factors due to their longevity and minimal variability, and they have to be taken into account in calculations – but they are usually not the object or goal of the strategy. The practical consequence of this statement is, firstly, that power actors must know which constants are relevant to their strategic goal and which ones are not. Secondly, they must be able to assess how the constants affect the ideal causal path and what interactions exist between them. Thirdly, there is virtually no need to observe and evaluate constants during strategy implementation and control. The reason for this is their expected stability. Once you have identified all the constants of your strategy and included them in the goal-means-environment calculation, you can devote yourself to the strategic variables for the remaining time.

The category of strategic *variables* includes all factors that are decidedly changeable – be it through deliberate action, through natural events or as a non-intentional consequence of uncoordinated collective behavior.[264]

Firstly, we can distinguish the strategic variables *directly attributable to the strategy-making actors themselves:* their strategic capability and strategic goal.

---

[264] Classic examples of variables that can be changed by natural events (rain, flood, drought, earthquakes, volcanic eruptions, etc.) are crops or visitor numbers in tourist destinations. Examples of variables that may change as a result of non-coordinated collective behavior are, for example, the flow of traffic or the prices of speculative objects.

Obviously, actors have to take their own powers into account in strategy formation, assessing them realistically and, if necessary, supplementing them. If you have strong network and mediation skills, but neither fame nor great financial power, you are well advised either to seek a suitable ally or to increase these potencies yourself. Classifying the strategic goal itself as a variable, means that actors in strategy formation have to reflect on whether their goals are realistic in terms of their own capabilities and resources, or whether they need to be adapted or even abandoned. Classic questions here are: Can I pursue the goal at all, without giving up my mediation capablity, that is, without making myself untrustworthy? Do I have sufficient organizational skills to realize a complex goal with a long time horizon, or do I need to focus on a simpler, shorter-term goal? Is the pursuit of my goal beneficial or detrimental to maintaining existing alliances? Is my goal x in conflict with my goal y, and if so, which is the priority? The list continues of course, as this short sketch implies.

Secondly, we can summarize all the factors that affect the realm of political allies. These are: number, strategy skills and goals of the partners. Obviously, the strategy-forming actor can influence all these variables only indirectly, but they are directly relevant to one's own goal development and to the corresponding choice of means. As already indicated in our discussion of network capability, the relationship between the quantity and the quality of a political alliance is essential for strategic calculation. Nevertheless, the goals and preferences of partners are also decisive. An example of this is one of the most controversial construction projects in recent German history: the construction of a bridge through the UNESCO-protected Dresden Elbe Valley. The Saxon state government, which strongly advocated and promoted the construction, opposed an alliance of radical environmentalists and moderate citizens' initiatives. Both partners in this alliance agreed on their rejection of the bridge. However, while local representatives of the two environmental groups categorically rejected any form of Elbe crossing, the citizens' initiatives agreed on an Elbe tunnel as an alternative to the construction of the bridge. This internal dissent led to such a massive weakening of the anti-bridge camp that the state government was able to implement its project and gained the support of large parts of the Dresden population.

The *third* class of strategic variables includes the *number, strategic capabilities and goals of political opponents*. All of these variables have a massive impact on strategic calculation, both in terms of goal definition and the choice of strategic and alliance partners. If you have to contend with political opponents whose strategic goals are diametrically opposed to your own, and who have a high level of strategic capability, then in case of doubt you are well advised to modify your goals and transform some of your opponents into allies.

A legendary example of this form of calculation is provided by the French statesman and bishop Charles-Maurice de Talleyrand-Périgord, who played a major part in French politics from 1780 to 1838, spanning five regime changes.[265] He began his career as a general agent of the royalist French church and deputy to the Estates General (clergy, nobility, third estate). During the upheavals of 1789, however, Talleyrand broke away from the monarchist orientation of the clergy, which had no chance of success in view of the decline of the *ancien régime*. Instead, he sought an alliance with moderate revolutionaries like Mirabeau and spoke, following the spirit of the time, in favor of the nationalization of church property. Nevertheless, he remained faithful to the core interests of the liberal clergy, supporting the continuation of the church within the framework of a French civil constitution. Talleyrand's ability to forge strategic alliances and incorporate changes in power into his own calculations was enough to make even Jacobins like Danton his supporters. This ability also led to the statesman serving under the five-member Directory after the end of Jacobin terror, then under the Empire and finally in post-Napoleonic France. Talleyrand's flexibility earned him the reputation of being a wryneck among contemporaries, and Napoleon himself dubbed him a pile of "shit in silk stockings."[266] Nevertheless, this assessment does not change the fact that his work is virtually prototypical of strategy building with maximum efficiency and effectiveness, oriented to the power capacities of political antagonists and fully comprehending strategic goals as a flexible entity.

The *fourth* and final class of variables includes all those changeable factors that form the extended context of *strategy development and implementation,* and thus cannot be assigned to the previous three classes. In the following, we will thus talk about *contextual variables*.[267] This section covers aspects such as public opinion, national and international macroeconomic developments (wars, revolutions, peace agreements), natural phenomena and technical disasters (floods, droughts, nuclear disasters), the aforementioned consequences of uncoordinated collective behavior (real estate collapses, recessions, depressions, mass panic) and technological innovations (printing press, gunpowder, the internet). All of these

---

265　Schell, Eric (2010): *Le bréviaire de Talleyrand*, Paris: Horay.

266　Cf. Scurr, Ruth (2006): He quipped while Napoleon quaked, in: Telegraph from 17th December 2006, [online] https://www.telegraph.co.uk/culture/books/3657043/He-quipped-while-Napoleon-quaked.html, retrieved on 21.12.2017.

267　These variables are also referred to as wild cards by prognostic researchers. Cf. Steinmüller, Angela and Steinmüller, Karlheinz (2004): *Wild Cards. Wenn das Unwahrscheinliche eintritt*, expanded and updated edition of 'Ungezähmte Zukunft', Hamburg: Murmann.

factors can have a positive as well as a negative impact on strategic success, but they are – with the limited exception of public opinion – generally speking hardly predictable and difficult to influence. The meltdown of the reactor of Fukushima in 2011, for instance, proved a strategic turning point for the success of the anti-nuclear movement. Under the impact of this severe accident, the already small proportion of nuclear power supporters in Germany fell from 34% to 26% within a few weeks, while the share of the anti-nuclear force increased from 64% to 72%.[268] The political context had changed in such a way that the strategic goal of a nuclear exit and energy transition could be implemented with the greatest possible public support.

In view of the low predictability of context variables and the difficulty of influencing them, combined with their great level of impact, two strategic principles for calculations can be identified: *exploit* and *arm*. On the one hand, successful calculations must be flexible enough to identify and exploit unforeseen contextual variables (such as the Fukushima meltdown mentioned above) as strategic opportunities. And on the other hand, they must be predictive and robust enough to avert any risk from contextual variables, or at least to mitigate it.

In summary, we can state that power actors must take account of political constants (power principles, economic laws, procedural norms, etc.) as well as four classes of variables (their own goals and potencies, the goals and potencies of allies and opponents, contextual variables, etc.). Given this complexity, it does not come as a surprise that Raschke and Tils classify strategy formation as a "great cognitive and creative challenge."[269] We would do well to clearly distinguish between the two aspects of this challenge, the cognitive and the creative. On the one hand, the development of a goal-oriented and efficient strategy involves immense informational effort, and it also involves the need to systematize the information collected and, in the case of variables, to keep it up-to-date. On the other hand, we have to realize that the use of this information in the form of goal-means-environment calculations is a process that is not just about induction and reflection, but also intuition. In the development of strategies, those who always navigate in accordance with plans of action that have been successful in the past, strictly adhering to them, will wind up being just as shipwrecked in the medium term as those who assume an overly intellectualistic view of the political power field. Successful calculations are always also a question of gut feeling, of power competence, of

---

268 WIN-Gallup International (2011): Impact of Japan Earthquake on Views about Nuclear Energy, [online] http://www.gallup.com.pk/JapanSurvey2011/PressRelease-Japan.pdf, retrieved on 21.12.2017.
269 Raschke & Tils (2008): p. 19.

political *téchne* (see Chapter 2.5.1). Without the much-vaunted ability to dare the "new and risky," fed by an intuitive intimacy with political power, political strategy remains predictable, uninventive and, ultimately, unsuccessful. Thus in a core element of political strategy, *épistéme* and *téchne* may be seen to overlap one another. On the one hand, actors take a conscious step back from the concrete context of action in order to reflect on goals, means and conditions of success on the basis of their power knowledge. On the other hand, the final decision to make a strategic choice must nevertheless be fed by power competence which thus, as a creative impulse, breathes life into strategic thought.

Let us now turn to the fourth and final component of political strategy: strategic steering. As a guiding principle, we can state that strategies are not surefire successes; their realization can only be achieved through targeted practical implementation, which adapts dynamically to the requirements of the respective action contexts.[270] Although strategies are cross-situational constructs, they are necessarily realized through sequences of actions that either proceed as planned or are influenced by unforeseen events or the actions of other protagonists of the political field (allies, opponents, neutral actors).

This circumstance brings with it two implications, Firstly, strategic steering always has a tactical component in so far as it requires a "use-oriented approach to peculiarities of the situation which falls through the – coarser – grid of strategic orientation."[271] In short, because the implementation of a strategy can never be planned down to the last detail, the actor requires not only a strategic understanding of the field, but also a tactical sense of the specific requirements of individual situations and the ability to take them into account in the short term. This tactical sense, too, is ultimately part of the governmentality introduced at the beginning of our strategy discussion. It arises – analogous to the understanding of strategy – from a penetration of the political power field and its principles, and from reflection on its practices, habitus and interpretive horizons.

Second, strategic steering requires a continuous review of the relationship between the strategic plan and the actual situation. Those who implement strategies blindly are not only predictable, they are also unable to adequately respond to new

---

[270] Raschke & Tils (2011: p.190) describe strategic steering as 'dynamic navigation.' This nautical metaphor is quite apt: on the one hand, it establishes the reference to a plan that guides action or a strategic map. On the other hand, it makes clear that the navigator must adapt to the changing, volatile conditions of the terrain and, if necessary, modify the planned route.

[271] Ibid.: p. 191.

strategic challenges, such as a dramatic change in contextual variables, abandonment by a supposedly loyal ally, or a sudden slump in their own power resources.

What characterizes an adequate response depends on the severity of the strategic challenge. Raschke and Tils, for example, find that moderate strategy changes are necessary if the real-world developments differ recognizably from the envisaged plan concept that was developed diverges recognizably from developments in the real political environment; surprising interventions and changed constellations can demand that strategy actors *modify* the strategy without creating a 'new' one.[272] If in the course of implementing the strategy, the strategic variables have changed in such a way that the intended goals can no longer be reached in an efficient and effective manner, then mere modification of the strategy will not suffice. At this point, Raschke and Tils see the need to revise the strategy, i.e. for a "correction of central components of the strategic concept,"[273] including a readjustment of goals and means and a repositioning within the power field. Surprisingly, this list leaves out a third option, which nevertheless is worth discussing: the abandonment of the strategy. If, in the course of practical implementation, a strategy turns out to be fundamentally wrong, either because its conception did not take into account the power resources or goals of political opponents, or because the context of realization changed unpredictably, giving up the strategic project can be a rational option. The reasons are obvious: a lost battle not only depletes the financial power of the power actor unnecessarily, but it also impairs other assets such as fame, mediation capability and networking capability. Those who cling to a doomed strategy against their better judgment lose not only the confidence of their allies, but also their credibility in the future mediation of strategic concerns. Admittedly, acknowledging strategic failure requires that power actors reflect on their own mistakes, and demands considerable courage.[274] However, this then creates an opportunity for a fundamental improvement in one's own strategic skills and in the cultivation of governmentality.

---

272 Ibid.: p. 194, our accentuation.
273 Ibid.
274 From Samuel Beckett's novel Worstward Ho (1984, New York: Grove Press) comes the much-cited sentence: "Ever tried. Ever failed. No matter. Try again. Fail again. Fail better." This quote has become the mantra of a new trend in debates on corporate and political leadership, focusing on the positive side of failure as a catalyst for innovation, growth and strategic change. An excellent introduction is offered by Danner, John and Coopersmith, Mark (2015): *The Other 'F' Word. How Smart Leaders, Teams, and Entrepreneurs Put Failure to Work,* Hoboken: Wiley.

Nonetheless, even if a strategy is successfully implemented without requiring adaptive modifications or fundamental change, a final element of strategic steering remains: the retrospective evaluation of the completed strategy – What has been achieved? With what effort? What worked and what did not work? etc. This serves to underscore the success achieved to allies and one's own interest group. However, above all, it should also strengthen strategic foundations, improve strategy capabilities and provide an opportunity to revise possible deficits and develop advantages, finally perfecting future strategy development. Retrospective evaluation thus sets in motion a cascade of strategic improvements that permeates all aspects of the successful political strategy and initiates a reciprocal optimization of the respective components. By now it should be quite clear that the four components we distinguished – strategy foundations, strategy capabilities, strategy development and strategic steering – cannot be regarded as strictly separate but form dynamic aspects of a holistic overall complex. Understanding political strategy as a central aspect of power knowledge thus also means keeping all components simultaneously in view and considering their interdependence.

Figure 9: Interdependence of the Components of Political Strategy

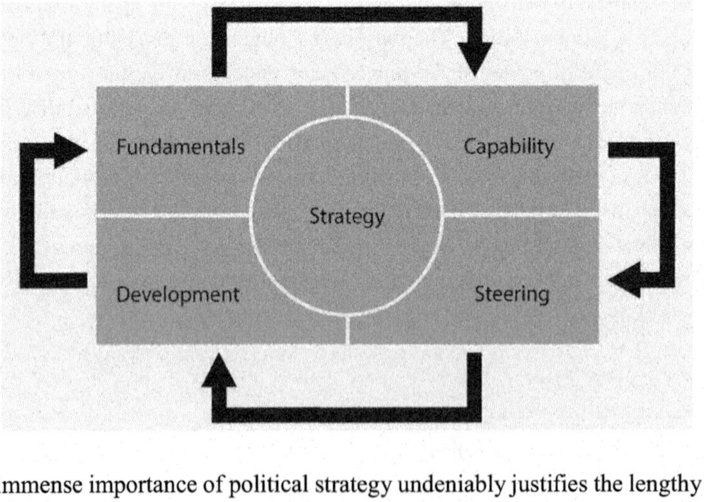

The immense importance of political strategy undeniably justifies the lengthy discussion that we have devoted to this area. At this point, however, we want to draw this topic to a close. Leadership does not exhaust itself in strategic knowledge. If policymakers want to successfully design and implement policies, they must rely on motivated, loyal and competent staff or subordinates within their power structure. Determining motivation and loyalty and, on that basis, distributing positions and competences is difficult enough, but still manageable with experience and common sense. The true crux is, at first glance, substantive expertise. This is a problem that we term the *paradox of experts*.[275] This paradox has two parts. *Firstly,* in forming concrete opinions and decision-making, political leaders rely on recommendations from experts (health, finance, military, infrastructure, education, etc.) because they themselves lack the appropriate expertise or because the acquisition of such knowledge is too time-consuming. *Secondly,* given that the leadership lack the necessary expert knowledge, they are, *eo ipso,* not reliably able to differentiate between true experts and swashbucklers or people with partial knowledge. In short, the lack of substantive expertise makes it necessary to turn to actual experts but one must be an expert oneself to be able to recognize experts.[276] If this paradox were correct, it would amount to a 'catastrophe' of leadership knowledge. So the question is, is there anything like meta-expertise and, if so, what does it consist of? If meta-expertise exists, it is the second pillar of leadership knowledge alongside strategy knowledge.

In his clever, hands-on essay *Experts: Which Ones Should You Trust?* the epistemologist Alvin Goldman takes up the fight against the problem of the paradox of experts.[277] His findings are directly relevant to our discussion. Goldman's thesis is that even laypersons can make a well-informed choice between supposed experts if they consider a number of heuristics and cognitive criteria. The first measure is to identify potential conflict of interest or bias (prejudice and resentment, their own agenda, benefits resulting from certain policy decisions, etc.) among the supposed experts; this applies in particular when a number of persons claim to have expertise and make opposing assessments of a situation. Goldman pragmatically sums up the principle: "If two people give contradictory reports, and exactly

---

275 Cf. Hardwig, John (1985), Epistemic dependence, *Journal of Philosophy*, 88, pp. 693–708.
276 Of course, this paradox is already addressed in Weber ([1921] 1978). Weber insists that the modern administrative state profits above all from the knowledge advantage of its highly specialized civil servants; but he readily admits that their selection is an extremely demanding and error-prone process.
277 Cf. Goldman, Alvin (2001): Experts: Which Ones Should You Trust?, *Philosophy and Phenomenological Research*, 63, pp. 85–111. For an application of Goldman's results to political theory, see Blum, Christian and Zuber, Christina I. (2016): Liquid Democracy: Potentials, problems, and perspectives, *Journal of Political Philosophy*, 24 (2), pp. 162-182.

one of them has a good reason to lie, the relative credibility of the former is seriously compromised."[278] The *second* criterion relates to the track record of the supposed experts. This approach is ultimately an inductive inference: the better the previous findings of the putative expert (whether successful consultations on past policy developments, concise and universally recognized reports or accurate predictions), the greater the likelihood that the person will continue to provide the right advice and guidance. The *third* criterion is perhaps the most obvious. It is based on getting the informed opinion of other experts you trust, either because you have worked with them successfully or because they meet the first two criteria above.

None of these heuristics is guaranteed to succeed, but their compliance ensures that decision-makers can gain meta-expertise without having to become experts themselves. Here, too, another factor is crucial, which is difficult to pinpoint but is best described with the key concept of insight into human nature. Experienced decision-makers who are proficient in the game of political power are often able to reliably recognize bullshitting in the sense of Frankfurt (see Chapter 2.4), because they have experienced it often enough during their long career. To be sure, this ability is not an epistemic but rather an intuitive, habitualized faculty. Accordingly, it falls primarily in the area of the first power vector, that of competence.

The notion of (bureaucratic) expert knowledge has already been mentioned several times in our discussion of meta-expertise. But now we want to turn directly to this central form of power knowledge. The most important author here is an old acquaintance for our readers: Max Weber. It is worthwhile quoting Weber's classic *Economy and Society* here in more detail in order to accentuate the importance of expert knowledge as a factor of power: "Bureaucratic administration means fundamentally domination through knowledge. This is the feature of it that makes it specifically rational. This consists on the one hand in technical knowledge which, by itself, is sufficient to ensure it a position of extraordinary power. But in addition to this, bureaucratic organizations, or the holders of power who make use of them, have the tendency to increase their power still further by the knowledge growing out of experience in the service. For they acquire through the conduct of office a special knowledge of facts and have available a store of documentary material peculiar to themselves. While not peculiar to bureaucratic organizations, the concept of 'official secrets' is certainly typical of them.[...] It is a product of the striving for power."[279]

---

278 Goldman (2001): p. 104.
279 Weber ([1921] 1978): p. 225.

If we want to decompress this dense description, it makes sense to begin with the implicit distinction between leadership and expert knowledge. While leadership as we have discussed in detail is a form of how-to knowledge (*How* do you best achieve a strategic goal? *How* do you best choose people for strategically relevant tasks?), bureaucratic expertise is what-knowledge, that is, "technical knowledge" in Weber's diction. Anyone who has such expertise, as a member of the administrative arm of the power apparatus, knows in detail *what* the content of a legislative amendment on tobacco regulation consists of, *which* specific regulations for railway tunnels by marine waters apply, what the fiscal impact of 5% tax relief for lower income groups is, etc. This is decidedly substantive knowledge with respect to a specific sub-field of the political. As Weber points out, the power potential of this knowledge arises first and foremost from its being "completely indispensable."[280] Governmental rule can only endure (recall here Popitz) if it is institutionalized through a process of political division of labor and specialization (see Chapter 1.2).[281] This means that the establishment of state power brings with it the establishment of a type of political specialist who, in a narrowly tailored field of knowledge, becomes an almost unrivaled expert. Because their expertise is essential for the exercise of political power, and because they are the only people with such expertise, they are indeed indispensable. In other words, the political generalists with leadership knowledge – the 'masters' of the political, in Weber's somewhat antiquated terms – need the political specialists; not just to design and implement strategies, but also to keep the power apparatus itself running.

Do the political specialists also need the generalists? The crux is right here. From a political or macro perspective, leadership and expertise are obviously dependent on one another to shape political rule for the common good. But if political leaders and bureaucratic specialists are understood as potentially competing power and interest formations, each with its own habitus, practices and interpretive horizons, the situation is different. In this case, bureaucratic expertise proves to be a resource of instrumental power (see Chapter 2.1), which the bureaucracy can use in a targeted fashion against the political leadership. Let us remember: instrumental power is the ability to control other people's behavior through credible threats or promises – in this case, by withholding indispensable specialized knowledge. Weber, whose enthusiasm for the efficiency and effectiveness of the

---

280 Ibid.: p. 223.
281 Cf. For an administrative-scientific perspective, see Derlien, Hans-Ulrich, Böhme, Doris, and Heindl, Markus (2011): *Bürokratietheorie. Einführung in eine Theorie der Verwaltung,* Wiesbaden: VS Verlag.; p. 88.

bureaucratic apparatus can be noted in every line, is nevertheless among its sharpest critics. His corollary has been included in the literature as the Independence Thesis. It states in a nutshell that due to the fundamental differences between the roles of the specialized civil servants who have their power base in expertise, and the politicians who have their power base in leadership knowledge, the two drift apart, to the extent of open antagonism and power struggle.[282]

This constellation is exacerbated by the ability of the independent administrative apparatus or bureaucracy (touched upon in the above quote from Weber) to classify essential knowledge as "specialist service knowledge" and, if necessary, to place it under secrecy, i.e. under the concept of "official secrets." In their standard work on bureaucracy theory, Hans-Ulrich Derlien, Doris Böhme and Markus Heindl pinpoint this diagnosis, describing this specialist service knowledge as another possibility for the bureaucracy to withdraw from political control and thereby increase its autonomy.[283] Independent of this protecting of knowledge through secrecy, another method exists to monopolize bureaucratic expertise and secure it as a power resource: the establishment of an *arcane language*. In our section on Power and Symbolism (see Chapter 2.1), we traced the potential power inherent in controlling symbolic forms and modes of communication – through the monopolization of writing by the Catholic church in the Middle Ages or the prohibition of certain written languages to oppress ethnic minorities. Bureaucratic terminology is a variant of this power technique in that it links access to decision-relevant information to the mastery of a highly technical vocabulary and, as in the case of jurisprudence, an idiosyncratic syntax. A mere glance at a memorandum from the tax office or a ministerial bill reveals the exclusionary effect of such nomenclature. Titles of bills like "Outer Continental Shelf Transboundary Hydrocarbon Agreements Authorization Act" are understandable for experts on the topic but laypeople – in this case, not only ordinary citizens but also those in positions of leadership – face difficulties in grasping the content.

Of course, Weber dealt with the question of what measures can be taken to combat the autonomy of the bureaucracy and the destructive antagonism between leadership and administration, naming five concrete approaches.[284] The *first* measure is the introduction of the collegial principle, i.e. decision-making is undertaken by a collegial group and not by monocratic administrative authorities. By distributing power to an entire body of equal members, a system of mutual control is

---

282 Cf. Derlien, Böhme & Heindl (2011): pp. 86-89.
283 Ibid.: p. 92.
284 Cf. Derlien, Böhme & Heindl (2011): pp. 93f.; and Stachura, Mateusz (2010): Politische Führung: Max Weber heute, *Politik und Zeitgeschichte,* 2-3, pp. 22-27.

established in which the actors ideally keep each other in check. The *second* option is administration by non-specialists, who, by definition, have no knowledge advantage over the management elite and thus no corresponding means of power. As a *third* means of control, Weber provides for restrictions on the designation of administrative staff – specifically short terms of office, the possibility of permanent dismissal or appointment by lot.[285] However, these three measures pose a conflict of objectives insofar as they limit power but at the same time increase the risk of a considerable reduction in efficiency – e.g. by blocking the administration or by spreading incompetence. The *fourth* obvious means of control is to establish a strict separation of powers with an independent judiciary, in particular an administrative court that can review and overturn decisions made by the civil service.

Nevertheless, for Weber the fifth and decisive factor is sovereign and responsible political leadership itself. For him, success here consists not only of charisma and the gift of inspiration, but equally of the idea of personal responsibility and the sincere representation of potentially unpopular positions that are perceived as being right. A leadership figure who unites Weber's famous triad of personality traits – "Passion - Responsibility - Judgement" – not only arouses loyalty within the bureaucratic power apparatus, but also wins the respect of potential adversaries and popular support. This, of course, is no longer a question of power knowledge, but of the power competence.[286] At this point, therefore, the mutual dependence of our power vectors is shown once more.

Summing up, it can be stated that expert knowledge is both a decisive power resource and an important form of power knowledge. On the one hand, it is an indispensable basis for stable power in a highly specialized structure of power-reinforced social positions; on the other hand, it plays a role in the competitive struggle between the political leadership and the administration, which must be contained and channeled through control mechanisms and leadership qualities.

2.5.3 Instruments of Power and Organization

Turning now to the *third and final* vector, we address the instruments of power. As we mentioned at the beginning of Chapter 2.5, instruments of power constitute the objective, external side of political power, while power competence and power

---

285 Interestingly enough, in the current debate of political theory lotteries are enjoying renewed interest, cf. Alexander Guerrero's (2014) influential post, Alexander (2014): *The Lottocracy*, [online] https://aeon.co/essays/forget-voting-it-s-time-to-start-choosing-our-leaders-by-lottery, retrieved on 21.12.2017.
286 Cited according to Stachura (2010): p. 26.

knowledge constitute the subjective, internal side. Accordingly, instruments of power are tools for the exercising, expansion and consolidation of power which actors may have at their disposal but which are not intrinsically linked to those actors. However, the quality and scope of these instruments are decisive for how successfully actors can use their expertise and knowledge at all. Based on this definition, two categories of instruments can be distinguished: *artifacts*, i.e. manmade objects, and *social organizations*.[287]

The most basic form of artifacts used to enforce power since the beginning of history are weapons. From Bronze Age spears and chariots, to modern assault rifles, nuclear warheads and malware, weapons have always combined the power of action and instrumental power (see Chapter 2.1). By exponentially increasing the human ability to damage or destroy living beings – be they other humans or livestock – and infrastructure, they also represent a threat to internal and external enemies. The sovereignty of a state exercising a monopoly on violence cannot be enforced without weapons.[288] The notion of a pacifist utopia is rendered unrealistic by, on the one hand, the recognition that not all members of a community are intrinsically motivated to comply with legal norms and, on the other hand, by the insight summarized by Hans Morgenthau that "[i]nternational politics, like all politics, is a struggle for power. Whatever the ultimate aims of international politics, power is always the immediate aim."[289] As long as not all citizens become saints

---

[287] For an overview of the instrumental foundations of political power that overlaps with our approach, see Warren, T. Camber (2014): Not by the Sword Alone: Soft Power, Mass Media, and the Production of State Sovereignty, *International Organization*, 68 (1), pp. 111-141.; pp. 113-117. An alternative but quite readable overview can be found in Worley, D. Robert (2015): *Orchestrating the Instruments of Power: A Critical Examination of the U.S. National Security System,* Lincoln: University of Nebraska Press.; pp. 227-241.

[288] This insight is clearly expressed in the well-known Mao (1938) quote: "Every Communist must grasp this truth: Political power grows out of the barrel of a gun", Mao Tse-Tung (1983): *Selected Works of Mao Tse-tung: Vol. II*, [online] https://www.marxists.org/reference/archive/mao/selected-works/volume-2/, retrieved from Marxist Internet Archive on 16th April 2018.

[289] Morgenthau, Hans ([1948] 1978): *Politics Among Nations: The Struggle for Power and Peace,* New York: Knopf.; p. 29.

and the multipolar world of rival states does not develop into a world republic, weapons will remain a cornerstone of power.[290]

The practical consequence of this principle is that rulers – whether in the form of democratically elected governments, monarchs, or oligarchical governing bodies – must have *de facto* control over the use of the (police and military) weapons of the community.[291] Otherwise, both their internal monopoly of force and their external authority are void. This principle is impressively clear in the recent history of Turkey: a total of four times – in the years 1960, 1971, 1980 and 1997 – the military, sworn to support the founder of the state Kemal Attatürk, has disempowered the democratically elected governments of the Turkish Republic. Each time, the generals declared they were protecting Attatürk's secular ideology, and each time the political Islam-oriented governments were powerless in the face of the armed intervention. That changed in July 2016, when high-ranking officers attempted to overthrow the government again – this time under the AKP-President Erdoğan. In this case, the political leaders succeeded in repelling the coup d'état, and in the following months they decisively weakened the military. The events of 2016 are historically far from over, but there are two lessons to be learned from more than 50 years of Turkish coup history. First, it would be a misjudgment to assume that any democratic government ever held power in Turkey before Erdoğan. Power, in the sense of control over the weapons of the country, had been exercised by the military. Second, the AKP has undertaken the historical achievement of wresting from the military the power instrument of actual control of weap-

---

290 In her essay "Moral Saints", the philosophies of Susan Wolf also propose the provocative but thoroughly readable thesis that a society of moral saints is not only unrealistic, but also undesirable, because it clashes with our central notions of successful life; see. Wolf, Susan (1982): Moral Saints, *The Journal of Philosophy*, 79 (8), pp. 419-439. On the idea of the World Republic see Kant, Immanuel ([1795] 2003): To Perpetual Peace: A Philosophical Sketch, translated by Ted Humphrey, Indianapolis: Hackett Publishing.

291 We are restricting discussion to the control of police and military weapons because many states – such as the USA, Switzerland, Canada and Germany – are apparently in a position to authorize the possession of private weapons and nonetheless to maintain a monopoly of force. The key is to restrict particularly powerful weapons (fully automatic weapons, rockets and grenade launchers, etc.) and weapon systems (tanks, fighter pilots and helicopters, etc.). In Germany, for example, this is i.a. governed by the War Weapons Control Act (Kriegswaffenkontrollgesetz KrWaffKontrG). The US pendant is the Arms Export Control Act (AECA) 22 U.S.C. Chapter 39 § 2751.

ons and thereby established a necessary – though obviously insufficient – condition for representative popular rule.[292] In short, the AKP government not only recognized the indispensable significance of this instrument of power, but it has also successfully seized the opportunity to exploit it.

Now, of course, the question arises whether, beyond the rule of thumb, "If you want to rule, then control the weapons" there is another practical principle for this class of power artifacts. The school of the so-called political realists around Morgenthau (cited above) opts for the simple principle: the more the better. The suggestion is that rulers are always well-advised to arm their services and to continuously advance the innovation of all types of weapon in order to be optimally poised in the global power struggle and – we hasten to add – in the struggle against the internal enemies of their own states as well. This maxim, which had its heyday from the beginning to the middle of the twentieth century, was often criticized in following years, and not without justification.[293] The arming of the state internally and externally does not necessarily create an improved position of power and more security, and it arouses, above all, mutual distrust and thus the risk of violent escalations. In the light of this criticism, the idea of a universal maxim of armament (the more the better!) fails to convince. Instead, the question must always be context-dependent – i.e. with regard to the external and internal level of threat and the other power capacities of the actor concerned (for example, authoritative power and technical power, see Chapter 2.1).

The second power artifact is *means of communication.* The significance of this instrument of power has already been discussed in detail in our section on Power and Symbolism (Chapter 2.2). Therefore, we will be brief and restrict ourselves principally to a recapitulation of what has already been said. Basically, complex political action in cooperation with other people over a considerable period and greater distances requires remote communication and appropriate vehicles for the transmission of commands and information. Otherwise, the exercise of power remains limited in time and space. In addition, the specialized structure of power

---

292 We speak of a necessary, but not sufficient condition of representative popular rule, because additional criteria such as fair political competition and press freedom must supplement civil and political control of weapons. Both requirements are currently not sufficiently fulfilled in Turkey; see Freedom House (2016): Turkey, [online] https://freedomhouse.org/report/freedom-press/2016/turkey, retr. on 21.12.2017.; and Göl, Ayla (2017): The paradoxes of 'new' Turkey: Islam, Illiberal Democracy and Republicanism, *International Affairs*, 93 (4), pp. 957-966.

293 See also March, James G. and Olsen, Johan P. (1989): *Rediscovering Institutions: The Organizational Basis of Politics,* London/New York: The Free Press.

with its complex hierarchy of responsibilities divided between political specialists and generalists requires a continuous flow of communication in order to function at all. Accordingly, since the age of the Sumerians, means of long-distance communication comprise one of the necessary foundations of political power.

These means of communication must meet three central, partially conflicting quality standards: speed, differentiation of content, and security. The requirement of speed is quickly explained. For the coherent and flexible exercising of power within large territories, means of communication between geographically distant broadcasters and recipients must ensure an exchange that is as smooth as possible. Between the legendary run of Pheidippides, who sped by foot from Marathon to Athens to bring the message of the Attic victory over the Persians, and nanosecond messaging via email or instant messaging are two and a half thousand years of technological innovation – and an exponential growth in the importance of communication tools as instruments of power. The second criterion of contentual differentiation means nothing more than that the means of communication can transport the informational content of the intended message as adequately as possible. For instance, smoke and fire signals may have had immense merits in terms of speed and bridging distance prior to the invention of the telegraph – their early perfection was already evident in the construction of the Great Wall in the fifth century BC,[294] but obviously they drastically limited the possible content of the messages. Although the conflict between speed and differentiation of content has been largely defused in the age of digital communication, this innovative thrust has made the third criterion of security dramatically more important and, above all, more challenging. As we have shown in our section on data power (see Chapter 2.3), opportunities to transmit extremely large amounts of data extremely quickly exist as never before in the age of the Internet. However, the technical opportunities and capacities for data extraction by enemy powers are also greater than ever. The resulting security pressure on means of communication creates a practical paradox: the effective protection of vital information, e.g. through blockchains, hermetic intranets or tap-proof 'crypto-phones,' often comes at great expense in terms of speed.[295] The increase in communicative speed provided by digital innovation is directly challenged by these risks. Again, there is no universal maxim in

---

294 Cf. Turnbull, Stephen (2007): *The Great Wall of China. 221 BC–AD 1644*, London: Osprey Publishing.; p. 14.

295 The term 'blockchain' refers to the storage and backup of data over a decentralized peer-to-peer network with countless users. The purpose of this decentralized backup mechanism is to ensure that the data is ideally protected against hacks, tampering and unauthorized copies; see. Kiyaias, Aggelos and Panagiotakos, Giorgos (2016): Speed-

terms of balancing speed and security. The concrete decision remains a question of political judgment and thus falls into the domain of power competence and power knowledge.

Not surprisingly, in light of the preceding discussion, the third power artifact is surveillance technology, understood by us as outwardly and inwardly directed methods and instruments for collecting, systematizing and evaluating power-relevant information about individuals and organizations.[296] In relation to external powers, such as competing states, confederations of states, global companies or international terror groups, these instruments are used to gain insights into strategic goals, power capacities and technologically sensitive information (keyword industry espionage) and serve, among other things, the preparation of risk forecasts and international conflict scenarios. As we discussed in Chapter 2.3, foreign intelligence services increasingly fall back on the possibilities of big data. The foundation of this so-called 'dataveillance' is the storage and algorithm-based analysis of digitized data available worldwide (IP addresses, e-mails, search queries, credit card debits, tweets, etc.). Due to the detailed discussion of the topic elsewhere, we will not go into the technological perspectives of external surveillance here.

In the area of domestic policy, surveillance technology, in the words of the sociologist James B. Rule, acts as a "means of knowing when rules are obeyed, when they are broken and most importantly who is responsible for which [...] A second element of surveillance, also indispensable, is the ability to locate and identify those responsible for misdeeds of some kind."[297] Surveillance technology, however, is not simply a means of verifying and sanctioning violations of the rules, e.g. through speed cameras on highways or security cameras in subways, in order to stabilize the structure of power and its norms. It is also, as Michel Foucault has pointed out in his classic work *Discipline and Punish,* a most effective

---

Security Tradeoffs in Blockchain Protocols, Working Paper, [online] https://eprint.iacr.org/2015/1019.pdf, retrieved on 21.12.2017.

296 It is important to keep an eye on methods – i.e. certain social techniques and patterns of organization – and technological tools. Both together constitute the corresponding instrument of power. See the volume by Mohanan, Torin (ed.) (2006): *Surveillance and Security. Technological Politics and Power in Everyday Life,* New York: Routledge.; Dandeker, Christopher (1990): *Surveillance, Power and Modernity,* Cambridge: Polity Press.; and Rule, James B. (1973): *Private Lives and Public Surveillance,* London: Allen Lane.

297 Rule, James (1973): p. 21f.

means of discipline.[298] Discipline in Foucault's sometimes abstract diction is "the specific technique of a power that regards individuals both as objects and as instruments of its exercise."[299] This means, in concrete terms, that discipline both teaches the members of a community to voluntarily accept a socio-political order and also motivates them to exercise control over one another. However, "The *exercise* of discipline presupposes a mechanism that *coerces by means of observation*; an apparatus in which the techniques that make it possible to see induce effects of power, and in which, conversely, the means of coercion make those on whom they are applied clearly visible. [...] Side by side with the major technology of the telescope, the lens and the light beam, which were an integral part of the new physics and cosmology, there were the minor techniques of multiple and intersecting observations, of eyes that must see without being seen, using techniques of subjection and methods of exploitation."[300] The nexus between discipline and surveillance technology becomes obvious in this way: through the continuous anticipation of surveillance – be it by machines or fellow human beings – on the one hand there arises an individual need to demonstrate that one has nothing to hide and, on the other hand, there is an impulse to report rule-breakers in order to actively demonstrate one's own compliance. Foucault studied these mechanisms using the example of modern prison camps. However, he emphasizes the reflection of this principle "in urban development and in the construction of working-class housing estates, hospitals, asylums, prisons, schools."[301] in short, everywhere in modern society. However, in 1975 – the original year of publication of the French version of *Discipline and Punish* – not even this great theorist of power could have imagined the extent to which "techniques of multiple and intersecting surveillance" would spread. More than 40 years later, mass surveillance is one of the standard repertoires of instruments of power, even in liberal democracies. Britain is at the forefront, with up to 5.9 million surveillance cameras estimated by the British Security Industry Authority in 2013; this would correspond to a ratio of one camera per eleven people.[302] Since the introduction of the Investigatory Power Bill at the end of 2016, this arsenal has been flanked by comprehensive digital

---

298   Cf. Foucault (1995).
299   Ibid.: p. 170.
300   Ibid.: p. 171, our accentuation.
301   Ibid.
302   Cf., Vincent, James (2016): The UK now wields unprecedented surveillance powers – here's what it means, in: The Verge from 29th November 2016, [online] https://www.theverge.com/2016/11/23/13718768/uk-surveillance-laws-explained-investigatory-powers-bill, retrieved on 21.12.2017.

surveillance, which includes the storing of any website visited by a British citizen in a central archive.[303] Despite serious interference with privacy rights, this law has so far encountered little resistance; instead, experts see it as a harbinger of similar developments in other liberal democracies.[304]

The fourth and final artifact we want to talk about is *mass media*.[305] In the coupling of the terms political power and mass media, some readers may make immediate associations with totalitarian regimes and their propaganda machines; the notorious KpdSU, Pravda and the National Socialist Volksempfänger come to mind. But mass media – regardless whether newspapers, radio stations, TV channels or social media – is as central an instrument of power in a liberal constitutional state as in a dictatorship. The reason for this lies in the amalgamation of mass media with an essential form of power, as discussed by Popitz, to which we already referred in Chapter 2.1: authoritative power. A reminder: unlike the power of action or instrumental power, for example, authoritative power is not exercised through violence or by setting positive and negative incentives in the context of the existing preferences of the addressee. It rather works by influencing people's inner attitudes and convictions. Thus from a "deliberate and acquiescent willingness to follow", the authority-bound bow to the desires of the other and 'fixate' on the other as a role model. Authoritative power thus does not arise from coercion or material superiority, but from the strategic potencies of mediaten capability and fame (see Chapter 2.5.2). This is precisely where political communication via mass media plays a key role, as T. Camber Warren writes in his essay *Not By the Sword Alone:* "the legitimacy of appeals to state loyalty must be spoken into existence, on the basis of images, narratives, and other symbols that at least some portion of the population are willing to accept as valid interpretations of their lived realities. It is through this 'alchemy' that political communication produces, maintains, and transforms prevailing visions of the political regime and the political community."[306] Warren's conclusion can be formulated as a syllogism: because

---

303 Ibid.
304 Cf. Bernal, Paul (2016): Data Gathering, Surveillance and Human Rights: Recasting the Debate, *Journal of Cyber Policy*, 1 (2), pp. 243-264.
305 Cf. i.a. Warren (2014); Street, John (2011): *Mass Media, Politics and Democracy*, 2nd edition, Basingstoke: Palgrave Macmillan.; Sarcinelli, Ulrich (2010): *Politische Kommunikation in Deutschland: Medien und Politikvermittlung im demokratischen System,* Wiesbaden: VS Verlag.; and Herman, Edward S. and Chomsky, Noam (2002): *Manufacturing Consent. The Political Economy of the Mass Media*, New York: Pantheon Books.
306 Warren (2014): p. 116f.

authoritative power is central to the maintenance of domination, and because it can only be generated by communication to the largest possible audience in the community, mass media is an indispensable instrument of power.

The political significance of mass media since the invention of the printing press becomes immediately clear through a negative contrast: "[T]he most basic political impact concerns the sheer reproducibility of political messages and symbols. In the absence of mass media infrastructure, political leaders and would-be leaders must physically travel to numerous small-scale venues to disseminate their political messages. In contrast, with thousands of flickering screens dotting the hinterland, or thousands of newspapers dotting city corners, each instance of state authority-making can be instantly and effortlessly reproduced for thousands of citizens."[307] While without media multipliers the ritual and symbolic staging of political power in the form of elections, parades or speeches remains local, it reaches a potentially global audience in the age of the mass media. The symbolic power resource we have already emphasized is exponentially reinforced by media catalysts.

Although the logic of power behind the amalgamation of authoritative power and mass media is universal, liberal constitutional states – which form the focus of our discussion below – are dramatically different from authoritarian regimes and dictatorships in terms of control and the concrete use of these communicative catalysts. With respect to the latter, mass media serve first and foremost as a centrally-directed mouthpiece for the propaganda of their leadership elite;[308] regarding the former, however, they serve as arenas of the competition for public opinion.[309] In his essay *Re-shaping Public Affairs,* which deals with the mediation of interests in the so-called 'mood democracy', Peter Köppl concludes: "In the tough

---

307 Ibid.: p. 119.
308 It is noteworthy that the grand master of totalitarian propaganda and mass influence, Joseph Goebbels, was not a supporter of constant streams of propaganda. In the course of media cooptation in 1933, he complained to the Nazi directors of the "all-too-energetic politicization" of broadcasting and called for "a loosening up of the programs" based on the principle of not being boring or dull and not presenting basic convictions all too obviously (cited from Frei, Norbert and Schmitz, Johannes (1988): *Journalismus im Dritten Reich,* Munich: C.H. Beck.; p. 86). Behind this approach was the insight that totalitarian rule must always combine the elements of indoctrination with those of entertainment.
309 Cf. Peters, Hans P. (1994): Mass Media as an Information Channel and Public Arena, *RISK: Health, Safety & Environment,* 5(3), pp. 241-250.; p. 245.

daily competition for media attention more and more actors are battling one another with ever more elaborate methods."[310] The metaphor of the battle stands for a continuous struggle for the scarce commodities of attention and interest (see also Chapter 2.5.2), which in representative democracies are central resources for the (temporary) attainment of power. In the wake of the digital revolution and with the emergence of new, continually updated forms of media (online news portals, tweets, social networks, etc.), this struggle has not only accelerated, but has also grown more complex. Obtaining attention and effectively placing messages thus becomes more and more demanding, but at the same time more prestigious. Against this background, Frank Marcinkowski's argument is quite convincing: "As public attention becomes a leading social value and a generally applicable resource, the media visibility and journalistic resonance of demands and positions are treated as a valid indicator of their legitimacy."[311] Nevertheless, the equation of media presence with political legitimacy is a fallacy: legitimized influence and political fame, as we noted in our section on power knowledge, do not consist of attaining *sui generis* attention, but rather attention that is coupled with recognition of power competence and power knowledge. Media attention can have a disastorous outcome. In this regard, in Germany, one thinks of the notorious, swimming pool photographs of Rudolf Scharping, the Federal Minister of Defense, that appeared in the tabloid *Bunte* just before Germany's military deployment in Macedonia in 2001. U.S. examples include the poorly ranked tributes to Rosa Parks and Kwanzaa in 2016 during Hilary Clinton's campaign, as pursued on Twitter, or Mitt Romney in the 2012 press conference for the election campaign, as reporters who attempted to interview the Republican presidential candidate were thwarted. Moreover, the Trump Era is providing no shortage of examples in this respect.

Indeed, attention, like the instrument of power of the mass media, is a double-edged sword, and its handling requires symbolic dexterity, power instinct and – of course – media competence.

The classification of mass media as a competitive arena for media attention harbors the risk of a misunderstanding which we want to decisively preclude. The expression could give the impression of a neutral venue for interpretive struggle, but of course that would be far from reality. Newspaper publishers, social media

---

310 Köppl, Peter (2017): *Advanced Power Lobbying. Erfolgreiche Public Affairs in Zeiten der Digitalisierung,* Wien: Linde Verlag.; p. 247.
311 Marcinkowksi, Frank (2015): 'Die Medialisierung' der Politik. Veränderten Bedingungen politischer Interessenvermittlung, in: Rudolf Speth and Anette Zimmer (eds.), *Lobby Work. Interessenvertretung als Politikgestaltung,* Wiesbaden: VS Verlag, pp. 71-95.; p. 89.

portals and TV stations have their own political and economic goals. Accordingly, they affect the political field both through reporting and investigation, and by giving a prominent forum to certain messages, persons and institutions, while denying others access. Ulrich Sarcinelli, the doyen of German communication science, aptly described this reciprocal relationship, noting that politics and the media need each other. Mass media are not a constitutional power (such as executive, legislature and judiciary) in their own right. Rather, they stand in a symbiotic relation towards the political apparatus. Politics needs publicity – it largely lacks its own means of communication and uses the mass media as a platform. For their part, the various media seek proximity to politics because they are interested in exclusive and continuously flowing information.[312] Shaping this symbiotic relationship to serve one's own interests is still one of the most demanding strategic leadership tasks of all. With this interim conclusion we want to conclude the discussion of the power artifacts and turn to the field of social organizations.

It is immediately obvious that, like artifacts, social organizations are central instruments of power and domination. Organizations pool knowledge, skills and resources, create synergies and, above all, facilitate the coordinated actions of thousands – in the case of large armed forces or authorities, hundreds of thousands – of people to pursue political goals. In the hands of skilled power actors, analogous to power artifacts, they can be used as highly effective tools of interest enforcement. Much of what can be said about social organizations as instruments of power is already mirrored in our discussion of the power artifacts. In the following, we focus on a few highlights.[313] An important categorization is, however, required: a differentiation between *formal* and *informal* forms of organization. The former are characterized by an official, codified structure of rules and clear hierarchies of responsibilities with a corresponding distribution of roles and tasks, whereas the latter are constituted by unofficial agreements between the persons involved and implicit norms.[314] Both are equally relevant as instruments of power; we want to start with discussion of formal organizational forms.

Corresponding to the power artifact of weapons discussed above, the focus is first on the two polar types of organization that use force, the *military* and the

---

312 Sarcinelli (2010): p. 302.
313 Sarcinelli (2010): p. 302.
314 We will therefore focus on those social instruments of power that are fundamental to all forms of rule rather than those that are linked to specific political systems.

police.³¹⁵ Although both are characterized by the use of armed action power as an essential feature, their functional distinction is based on the difference between internal and external security. Police authorities, historically far younger than military organizations,³¹⁶ are responsible for law enforcement, internal security and crime prevention in the broadest sense. The military is responsible for deterring enemy aggression and warfare. According to this division of tasks, both organizations differ in terms of potential action and armament: the use of lethal action power is the *ultima ratio* for the police if all other forms of power of action are inadequate; for the military, on the other hand, it is the *sola ratio*, the only means. Of course, power actors have blurred or set asisde this clear distinction between police and military, between internal and external, throughout history. The reasons given for this are usually the (supposed) intermingling of internal and external security interests and an overlapping of areas of responsibility. The corresponding hybrid form of police and military is the *paramilitary*, understood as a highly armed organization, which is trained and used both for warfare and for the fight against crime. Historical examples include the *Cheka,* founded in 1917 by Vladimir Lenin (short for: Extraordinary All-Russian Commission to Combat Counterrevolution, Speculation and Sabotage), and the *Schutzstaffel* (SS) founded by Adolf Hitler in 1925, which acted as an agency of repression and terror within Germany and German-occupied Europe and fought as combat units at the front.

For obvious reasons, the police and military (and paramilitary) are essential instruments of power: they consolidate political power both internally and externally by embodying and realizing the state's monopoly on the use of force. As already mentioned above, organized power of action offers huge potential for abuse, ranging from arbitrary policing to militarily organized genocide. However, due to our descriptive focus on analysis (see introduction), we will not pursue this

---

315 Cf. Geser, Hans (1996): Internationale Polizeiaktionen: Ein neues evolutionäres Entwicklungsstadium militärischer Organisationen, in: Georg-Maria Meyer (ed.), *Friedensengel im Kampfanzug? Zur Theorie und Praktik militärischer UN-Einsätze,* Opladen: Westdeutscher Verlag, pp. 45-74.; p. 45.

316 As we explained in our discussion of power competence (see Chapter 2.5.1), there was no dedicated police force in the Imperium Romanum, nor in the political order of the Middle Ages. Police authorities, as we know them, only emerge in the eighteenth and nineteenth centuries; see e.g. Spencer, Elaine G. (1985): Police-Military Relations in Prussia, 1848-1914, *Journal of Social History*, 19 (2), pp. 305-317.

genuinely ethical issue; the work of peace and conflict research as well as applied military and police ethics offer comprehensive orientation.[317]

From a practical point of view, the organized power of action of the police and military poses a potential dilemma for power actors: on the one hand, it is indispensable for the consolidation of power, and it should therefore be in their interest to strengthen these organizations as comprehensively as possible. On the other hand, history teaches us that strengthening the human and material capacities of armed organizations often encourages their political independence and development into a "state within a state".[318] For the political leadership, therefore, it appears rational not only to strictly and consistently restrict organized action power, but also to keep highly ambitious individuals away from leadership positions – just think of the repeatedly mentioned Napoleon. No matter which horn of the dilemma is chosen, there are negative effects: either the heightened danger of military and police coups or the diminished clout of the respective organizations.[319] Of course, this conflict of objectives does not have to be manifested to the extent described. Pronounced power competence and power knowledge undoubtedly favor the development of lasting loyalty among a country's armed forces, and the same applies to moral codes. Nonetheless, the dilemma described remains a structural political risk and thus a permanent strategic challenge.

Corresponding to the power artifacts of surveillance technologies and communication channels, the second form of organization we discuss is that of foreign and domestic intelligence. The historical roots of these instruments of power are almost as old as those of the military. The early empires of the Near and Middle East – Egypt, Babylonia, Assyria and above all Persia – based their political power

---

317 Cf. The excellent monograph McMahan, Jeff (2011): *Killing in War*, Oxford: Oxford University Press.

318 Cf. Singh, Naunihal (2014): *Seizing Power: The Strategic Logic of Military Coups*, Baltimore: Johns Hopkins University Press.

319 For example, from 1937 on, Stalin's concern over the undisputed power of the Red Army in the USSR led him to subject the ruling elite of the army to a brutal cleansing wave. One of his first victims was the gifted strategist Mikhail Nikolayevich Tukhachevsky, known as the 'red Napoleon.' Stalin's purges proved to be a double-edged sword: on the one hand he was able to contain the military, on the other hand the blood toll significantly reduced the effectiveness of the Red Army in the war against Germany. Cf. Bullock, Alan (1992): *Hitler and Stalin: Parallel Lives*, 1st American edition, New York: Knopf.; and Reese, Roger R. (2000): *The Soviet Military Experience: A History of the Soviet Army 1917-1991*, Warfare and History, London/New York: Routledge.

on intelligence services; specifically on field spies, secret couriers and centrally directed spy networks in conquered provinces.[320] In his monograph on the history of the secret services, the historian Wolfgang Krieger demonstrates that their tasks have remained largely constant since ancient times:[321] obtaining information about opponents (but also about partners and allies); covertly influencing foreign powers and their own population (keyword: fake news, see Chapter 2.3); shielding one's own apparatus of power against secret service attacks; and penetration of opposing intelligence services (i.e. counterintelligence).

As the political scientist Harry H. Ransom notes, the power-strategic relevance of this range of tasks and functions is evident: "control of secret information provides the leverage for political power."[322] Anyone who controls a powerful intelligence apparatus has exclusive access to potent (political, economic, military, but also personal) information about foreign and domestic opponents and thus a strategic advantage over those who are not equally informed. At the same time, they possess a means of power that is "less visible than police and military" due to the covert operations of the secret services.[323] Nevertheless, the use of intelligence services creates a similar dilemma as that found in the context of organized action power: "Intelligence agencies are simultaneously a *resource* and *liability* to nation-states. They provide essential services for the protection of the society and its citizens, but invariably become large, entrenched and secretive state bureaucracies."[324] Because 'secrecy', a lack of transparency and defense against external

---

320 Michael Andregg speaks, with a suggestive wink, of the second oldest profession. Cf. Andregg, Michael (2007): Intelligence Ethics: Laying a Foundation for the Second Oldest Profession, in: Loch K. Johnson (ed.), *Handbook of Intelligence Studies*, New York: Routledge, pp. 52-66.

321 Cf. Krieger, Wolfgang (2009): *Geschichte der Geheimdienste: von den Pharaonen zur CIA*, Munich: C.H. Beck.; pp. 13f. Similarly also: Johnson, Loch K. (1998): *Secret Agencies: US Intelligence in a Hostile World*, New Haven: Yale University Press.; pp. 3f.; Ransom, Harry H. (1980): Being Intelligent about Secret Intelligence, *American Political Science Review*, 74 (1), pp. 141-148.; and Crowdy, Terry (2011): *The Enemy Within – A History of Spies, Spymasters and Espionage*, Oxford: Osprey Publishing.

322 Ransom (1980): p. 147.

323 Krieger (2009): p. 9.

324 Joffe, Alexander H. (1999): Dismantling intelligence agencies, *Crime, Law & Social Change*, 32, pp. 325–346.; p. 325; our emphasis.

influences are part of the day-to-day business of the secret services, controlling and monitoring them becomes a particular problem.[325]

Most democratic constitutional states have established specific supervisory and sanctioning mechanisms for this purpose. These include intelligence inspectorates, which act as an interface between the civilian legislative and judicial organs and the services and monitor whether government decisions are adequately implemented, and also parliamentary institutions with special powers, such as the Parliamentary Control Panel (PKGr) of the German Bundestag or the United States House Permanent Select Committee on Intelligence (HPSCI) of the US House of Representatives.

Totalitarian and authoritarian systems often choose a different path, which can best be described as a system of intelligence checks and balances. It involves the establishment of competing and controlling parallel structures. Under Saddam Hussein, for example, Iraq had a dozen secret services and secret police, who sought the potentate's favor and tried to discredit each other; the situation is similar to this day in Syria or in the Palestinian autonomous regions.

Of course, control has its price – in both cases. The creation of parallel structures and the climate of mutual spying and mistrust that results from them are inefficient; the procedure paralyzes the apparatus. The establishment of civilian political enforcement bodies and the enforcement of (at least selective) transparency create potential security gaps and increase the risk of 'leaks.' In the context of the instruments of power, the primary concern is to be aware of the continuous challenge posed by these conflicting objectives. A universal solution seems implausible given the many strategic variables that may be relevant to the trade-off process.

Another challenge is quoted by Ransom in his entertaining and literally "intelligent" essay *Being Intelligent about Secret Intelligence,* authored in the late phase of the Cold War: "Intelligence systems tend to report what they think the political leadership wants to hear."[326] Other than his decades of experience as a US security expert, the author provides no empirical evidence for this provocative thesis. But

---

325 This is particularly the case in liberal democracies, as Leigh (2007: p. 67) aptly puts it, "the basic problem is easily stated: how to provide for democratic control of a governmental function and institutions which are essential for the survival and flourishing of the state but which must operate to a certain extent in justifiable secrecy". Cf. Leigh, Ian (2007): The Accountability of Security and Intelligence Agencies. in: Loch K. Johnson (ed.), *Handbook of Intelligence Studies,* New York: Routledge, pp. 67-81.; p. 67.

326 Ransom (1980): p. 147.

the blatant inability of Western intelligence agencies to predict the collapse of the Eastern Bloc in the 1980s can at least serve as anecdotal evidence. In any case, the risk highlights the importance of a specific form of leadership knowledge which we discussed in Chapter 2.5.2: meta-expertise. The effective leadership of intelligence instruments of power requires the ability to select and direct personnel who are not only loyal and trustworthy, but who also willing to critically question and challenge established political narratives – in the case of the Cold War, for example, the continuity of a struggle between two stable ideological blocs.

The third form of organization relevant to power is the *bureaucracy*, here understood as a collective term for the state administrative apparatus. We have already discussed this topic in detail under the term bureaucratic expert knowledge (see Chapter 2.5.2). In the context of instruments of power, however, it can be emphasized that the connection between power and administration is already implicit in the etymology of the word 'bureaucracy', which is an idiosyncratic and (originally pejorative) compound from the French *bureau,* standing figuratively for administrative activity, and the Greek verb *kratein,* which can be understood as 'rule' or 'power.' Bureaucracy refers to the exercising of power through the means of administration.

This combination is immediately obvious insofar as the public administration has the core task of organizing the structure of rule and its division of labor and implementing, substantiating and applying the guidelines and objectives authorized by the political leadership (laws, ordinances, budgetary decisions, trade agreements, etc.). Logically, the social scientist Renate Mayntz states that "in all types of rule the administrative body serves to safeguard political rule and to guarantee the enforcement of their objectives."[327] Mayntz, with her reference to the universality of the bureaucracy as an instrument of power, should be taken at her word. The general development of centered territorial rule, referring once again back to Popitz, is inconceivable without financial and tax authorities, trade inspectorates, road construction offices, census records etc. This principle applies at all times, whether in the Roman Republic, in the Ottoman Empire or in a modern nation state.

An impressive example of the significance, but also critical nature, of the administrative apparatus for maintaining and expanding power is provided by the early phase of the Islamic caliphate under the Abbasid dynasty in the eighth and

---

327 Mayntz, Renate (1985): *Soziologie der öffentlichen Verwaltung,* 3rd revised edition, Heidelberg: C.F. Müller.; p. 42.

ninth centuries.³²⁸ After the explosive, military expansion under the Prophet Mohammed and his successors, the Muslim empire extended from North Africa to today's Afghanistan. The undisputed brilliance of the Arab conquerors on the battlefield, however, stood in blatant contrast to their inability to politically control and administer their newly gained empire. However, the pragmatic caliphs knew how to proceed: they delegated all administrative tasks to the Persian bureaucratic elite, who had previously been militarily subjugated and converted and whose leaders have gone down in history as 'viziers.'³²⁹ These viziers implemented a well thought-out, Persian-style administrative system with individual councils (divans) for the army, for finances and taxes, for the post office and for the provinces; the state revenues were precisely regulated and accounted for.³³⁰ In addition, they established a system of communication in the Abbasid Empire. This was supplemented by carrier pigeon post and a system of watch and signal towers, which, as the Orientalist Bertold Spuler notes, also served as the central government's intelligence and surveillance body.³³¹ The dependence of the Arab political leadership on the Persian administrative specialists went so far that the legendary Caliph Harun ar-Rashid felt it necessary to comment desperately: "The Persians have ruled for a millennium, without needing us [the Arabs] for a day, and we now reign for centuries without being able to do without them for an hour."³³² In fact, the recourse to the Persian bureaucrats proved to be a double-edged sword. On the one hand, the Abbasid Empire experienced an unprecedented economic, scientific and cultural heyday that experts classify as the golden age of Islam.³³³ On the other hand, administrators used their political indispensability for the gradual strength-

---

328 Cf. Spuler, Bertold (1959): *Die Chalifenzeit. Entstehung und Zerfall des islamischen Weltreichs,* Leiden: Brill.
329 Cf. Farazmand, Ali (2001): Learning from Ancient Persia: Administration of the Persian Achaemenid Empire, in: Ali Farazmand (ed.), *Handbook of Comparative and Development Public Administration,* New York/Basel: Marcel Dekker, pp. 33-60.
330 Spuler (1959): p. 55.
331 Ibid.
332 Translated from Spuler (1959: p. 55). This account is, from a contemporary perspective, hardly exaggerated, as Ali Farazmand notes: "The fall of the Persian Empire to the Islamic Arabs in 651 A.D. did not result in the demise of Persian administrative excellence. [...] The Persian bureaucracy continued its long tradition with its own language and culture [...]. This happened particularly during the Abbased Caliphate which was totally Persianized and under Persian control.", Farazmand (2001): p. 55.
333 Cf. for example Lombard, Maurice (1975): *The Golden Age of Islam,* New York: American Elsevier.

ening of their position at the court of Baghdad – to the point of a factual takeover after which the caliphs finally acted only as the symbolic leaders of the empire.

The fall of the Abbasid Empire is a historical lesson for the sociologist Max Weber's Thesis of Independence, which we have already discussed. He states in a nutshell that administrative specialists can use their expertise and the corresponding organizational structures as a power resource to decouple the administrative apparatus from the control of the political leadership. This separation need not, as in the case of the caliphate, lead to open usurpation. It can also (just) lead to tension within the power structures between the goal-setting, political power formation and the implementing, administrative power formation – and thus to the immobilization of the political system. The institutional mechanisms for protecting against these tendencies, as outlined in Chapter 2.5.2, do not require repetition here. For Weber and other experts of bureaucracy, the decisive factor remains sovereign and responsible political leadership.

The last formally organized, social instrument of power that we wish to address at this point is also the most obvious one: the party. From the very beginning, the history of the political is also a history of organizations that manifest an open aspiration to power – not just the support of power, as in the case of the military, police, intelligence and administration, but claiming legitimacy and expertise and competing with other organizations.

An early manifestation of this type of organization, which we discussed in Chapter 2.5.1, can be seen in the patrician families of the Roman Republic. Through their organizational structure, which is hierarchically tailored to the *pater familias*, their rigorous training system geared towards the acquisition of power, their political ethos, and their commitment to the *bonum commune*, these dynasties already embody the decisive characteristics of this instrument of power. Their genesis and their success are due to a basic logic of the political field: the open aspiration to legitimized rule can only be achieved in a network of like-minded, loyal, specialized experts – today one speaks of professional politicians. Lone fighters, as well as unorganized masses, will inevitably fail to achieve their goal. We have also dicussed later manifestations of this type: for example, the noble families of the European Middle Ages or the Japanese warrior caste of the *bushi*. They all share the character of a structured and highly professional elite class whose sole purpose is to directly determine the activities of the government in line with their political goals.

The political party according to our understanding, is therefore ultimately only the modern (democratic) incarnation of a historically far older type of organization. Still, it is the focus of our further analysis, because as a tool of power it shapes the political structure and culture of contemporary communities. Historically, the concept of the party emerged only in eighteenth-century England, which was something of a special case among European nations with a constitutional monarchy and an independent parliament.[334] Accordingly, the earliest definitions come from the pen of the English philosopher Edmund Burke: "Party is a body of men united for promoting by their joint endeavours the *national interest* upon some *particular principle* in which they are all agreed."[335] The sociologist Jasmin Siri precisely identifies the internal tension inherent in this still-valid concept, suggesting that the party is an "instrument for enforcing particular interests on the one hand and [...] responsible for the common good on the other".[336] This pinpoints the central challenge for this form of organization. As it fights for temporary rule in a representative democracy – parliamentary majorities – it has to campaign for votes, taking into account both the particular concerns of its own interest formation and the general public. Taking up the etymological root of the word 'party', it must function as *pars pro toto*. In order to meet this challenge, the political parties have gradually developed into highly professional power apparatuses over the past 300 years. Their organization fulfills a number of core functions that are indispensable to the goal of power acquisition: recruiting, indoctrinating, specializing, selecting – ruling. Specifically, this means that parties are constantly recruiting (for example through youth organizations), ideologically consolidating their recruits through training and providing them with knowledge in order to select those whose competence, knowledge, will and willingness to undergo sacrifice renders them suitable as political leaders. Parties must endure a constant tension between loyalty and competition. On the one hand, they can only be powerful candidates for democratically legitimized rule if they can, with one accord, embody a specific set of values, interests and interpretive horizons of the common good and practice coherent, conflict-free politics for the realization of their objectives. On the other hand, they can only survive in the competition over political ideas if they have the best possible leadership personnel; and this can only be achieved through internal competitive pressure and consideration of the principle of merit.

Of course, the political party as an instrument of power is not a unique feature of democratic systems, nor necessarily linked to the decision-making mechanism

---

334 Cf. Siri, Jasmin (2012): *Parteien. Zur Soziologie einer politischen Form*, Wiesbaden: Springer VS.; p. 33.
335 Burke, Edmund ([1770] 2002): Thoughts on the Cause of the Present Discontents, in: Susan E. Scarrow (ed.), *Perspectives on Political Parties*, Basingstoke: Palgrave Macmillan, pp. 37-43.; p. 39; our emphasis added.
336 Siri (2012): p. 33.

of free elections or parliamentarism. For instance, party organizations also played and play a central role in fascist and socialist dictatorships, such as the CPSU in the Soviet Union or the Nazi Party in the Third Reich. Remarkably, even in non-democratic systems, the functional logic of this power instrument is quite analogous to that of democratic parties. This is impressively demonstrated by Lenin's theory of communist parties, which is summarized in his work *What is to be done?*: "I assert: (1) that no revolutionary movement can endure without a stable organisation of leaders maintaining continuity; (2) that the broader the popular mass drawn spontaneously into the struggle, which forms the basis of the movement and participates in it, the more urgent the need for such an organisation, and the more solid this organisation must be (for it is much easier for all sorts of demagogues to side-track the more backward sections of the masses); (3) that such an organisation must consist chiefly of people professionally engaged in revolutionary activity; (4) that in an autocratic state, the more we confine the membership of such an organisation to people who are professionally engaged in revolutionary activity and who have been professionally trained in the art of combating the political police, the more difficult will it be to unearth the organisation; and (5) the greater will be the number of people from the working class and from the other social classes who will be able to join the movement and perform active work in it."[337] It is remarkable with what compactness here the aspects of political professionalization and elitism are combined with the functions of recruitment, training and selection. Behind this is Lenin's insight, which can be transferred to democratic states, that the acquisition and exercise of power in modern territorial states with millions of inhabitants can only be successful if it is carried out by a specialized party apparatus run by professional politicians which reproduces itself through the continuous recruitment of new elites.

In addition to formal organizations such as parties, the police, the military or the administration, *informal networks* constitute the second major pillar of social instruments of power. The notion of informal social networks covers an extremely broad range of personal connections.[338] It ranges from mere acquaintanceships, which are occasionally refreshed, to firm and intimate friendships; and it covers both the smallest groups of people as well as large, unofficial associations. In spite of this heterogeneity, these groups share two qualities that make them relevant as

---

337 Lenin, Vladimir I.: ([1902] 1989): *What is to be Done?*, transcription by Tim Delaney, printable edition produced by Chris Russell for the Marxists Internet Archive, pp. 7-87.; p. 87.
338 Cf. Blum (2015): pp. 76f.

instruments of power, owing to which they are classified by Bourdieu (see Chapter 2.3) as *social capital.*

First, they generate and reproduce so-called *norms of generalized reciprocity.*[339] This means that group members provide services to one another without anticipating that they will immediately receive something in return, but with the legitimate assumption that they can expect equivalent benefits from other members of the network in the future. These flexible conditions of co-operation, which are not exhausted in a simple *quid pro quo* relationship, are indispensable for the exercise, consolidation and expansion of political power, be it in gathering information, implementing unbureaucratic political strategies, creating political majorities before decisive votes, or forming alliances or *ad hoc* afiliations and so on. In other words, the significance of norms of generalized reciprocity arises from the fact that exercising political power would be hopelessly inefficient if all actors were to interact according to a strict 'work-to-rule' principle or if their willingness to cooperate was dependent solely on immediate benefits.

The second relevant feature of informal networks is that they create *social trust,* depending on the intensity of personal connections.[340] Members accordingly make no (or little) effort to monitor or verify the veracity or willingness to cooperate of other members. In this way, concerted actions are greatly simplified and, in the language of economic theory, less costly. Of course, social trust does not have to mean that the members of a network can rely on each other blindly. It suffices if there is a certain degree of assurance about the interests and motives of the others and the certainty that cooperation partners will be true to their word.

Informal networks are thus the 'cement' that holds together the positional fabric of power. Even an efficiently constructed power apparatus equipped with a high degree of leadership knowledge, expertise and justification can falter when there is no social trust among its members and no norms of generalized reciprocity in force. Their cultivation is less a question of *épisteme* and rational strategic planning, but rather one of *téchne,* intuitive authority and political gut feeling. Anyone who wants to expand and use social networks as instruments of power must have developed, as we stated above, a natural inclination for the political, it must flow through their veins as an integral part of their personal habitus.

---

339 Cf. Putnam (1993).
340 Cf. Levi, Margaret (1996): Social and Unsocial Capital: a Review Essay of Robert Putnam's Making Democracy Work, *Politics & Society,* 24 (1), pp. 45-55.

2.5.4 Mastering the Power Vectors: *Homo Consultandus* and *Homo Consultans*

Now, since the last building block of the force vectors is set, they stand complete before us. The bird's-eye view provides two key insights. *Firstly*, the three resources – power competence, power knowledge and instruments of power – are in fact complementary and only together are sufficient foundations for political power. Political *epistémé* and political *techné* complement one another in innumerable areas, from abstract strategy development to the concrete control of the instruments of power, such as the intelligence services or administrations. Only when an intuitive mastery of politics is united with leadership knowledge, expert knowledge and justification knowledge in an architecture of power reified by artifacts and organizations, can interests be purposively realized even against the resistance of others. The much-discussed multiple interdependencies of the three great resources confirm our initial hypothesis that classified them vectors of power.

Secondly, it should have become clear that mastering the power vectors, that is, the targeted development and deployment of the essential resources of power politics and political power, is an *extremely demanding and complex challenge*. Habitualized political competence must be acquired through a time-consuming, hands-on learning process – ideally from early on and under the guidance of savvy all-rounders of power. The *tirocinium fori,* which is described in detail in Chapter 2.5.1 as the policy practice of the young Roman senate elite, may have remained unrivalled since ancient times, but it still represents the premium standard for the acquisition of power competence. In turn, power knowledge, even if we focus only on strategic leadership knowledge for the moment, requires not only an immense amount of information on goal-relevant political constants and variables, but also the ability to creatively synthesize them into a pattern of action. The successful use of social instruments of power, such as the military and police and the corresponding technologies, ultimately requires a strong sense of the balance between organizational clout and political control. Combining the vectors thus seems to be a downright Herculean task.

Of course, the recognition of this threefold challenge is not entirely new. It was already implicitly noted in antiquity, as the philosopher Peter Sloterdijk points out.[341] In the small but extremely competitive Athenian political cosmos of the

---

341 Cf. Sloterdijk, Peter (2017): Konsultanten sind die Künstler der Enthemmung, in: Neue Zürcher Zeitung from 18th February 2017, [online] https://www.nzz.ch/feuille

Periclean age, a clear understanding emerged of the enormous "performance pressure" experienced by power actors – and thus also recognition of their "need for supplementation."[342] Sloterdijk states that this ancient city culture recognized that no urban top performers could operate in their field alone and without advice. "As soon as someone in a differentiated culture steps out of the crowd and engages in a key performance function, they inevitably require someone next to them who supports their activities in an advisory, moderating and motivating manner."[343] In plain English: mastering the power vectors is complex and time-consuming and is recognized in the polis as being dependent upon consultation by specialized service providers. And this step is immediately evident in political structures increasingly characterized by a division of labor. Instead of shouldering the challenges of political power alone, the Attic politicians sought advice and knowledge from actors who had no power *(prima facie)* ambitions of their own – the consultants.

This marks the birth of two historical archetypes, whose reciprocal relationship can henceforth be noted throughout history: the homo consultandus (the person being advised) and the homo consultans (the person doing the advising).[344] In recognizing that the exercising of political power is a challenge, and in accordingly aiming to fill the gaps in knowledge or reduce skill deficits – that is, in recognizing the need for advice – a political actor becomes homo consultandus. This creates, as it were, a niche in the political cosmos, which is occupied by an actor who provides the corresponding know-how as a service, the homo consultans. This function was first assumed in the ancient polis by a professional group which acquired a particularly bad reputation thanks to Plato's dialogues: the *Sophists* (in English: the wise).[345] The Sophists' rivals, the philosophers (in English: the wisdom lovers) pursued the exploration of logos and practice as an academic under-

---

ton/sloterdijk-konsultanten-sind-die-kuenstler-der-enthemmung-ld.146325, retrieved on 21.12.2017.

342 Ibid.
343 Ibid.
344 Sloterdijk (2017) calls this interchange a "bipolarism of performance roles", highlighting the interdependence of both archetypes: homo consultandus needs the consultant's expertise in the vectors of power; the homo consultans requires the power actor as an employer.
345 In order to comprehend how badly the Sophists were vilified in the Occident, one must only think of the words with which Heinrich Faust attacks Mephisto: "You were always a Sophist and a liar." Of course, the quick-witted devil responds, "Indeed, indeed. If we look ahead a little further, to tomorrow, what do we see." Goethe, Johann

taking while, according to Sloterdijk, the Sophists knowingly applied effective and pragmatic reason. In concrete terms, this means that they placed their rhetorical, didactic and logical abilities in the "service of a belligerent urban clientele" struggling for power and influence in the polis. Following the Sophists, there were other historical incarnations of homo consultans, e.g. the great medieval royal advisers, such as Alcuin at the court of Charlemagne, or the Privy Councilors of the modern era. For Sloterdijk, however, the perfect embodiment of the homo consultans is the well-known Machiavelli, whose considerations on the foundations of political power were discussed at the beginning of Chapter 2.5 and are a cornerstone of our own system of power vectors. Noteworthy of Machiavelli's writings is, from Sloterdijk's point of view, the amalgamation of theoretical reflection and applied political advice. Accordingly, he states that the writings of the great Florentine provide an exemplary study of the professionalization of counseling reason."[346]

Since the days of Machiavelli, the professionalization of power consulting has been constantly evolving. Our modern communities are characterized by a consulting cosmos of various service providers who advise actors in the political field – governments, companies, associations, NGOs, political parties, churches, unions, etc. – on how to play the zero-sum game for political power. Nevertheless, the basic principles of consultation, so our thesis, are universal and have remained the same since antiquity. This is so because they start with the great power vectors, which are, as it were, universal and globally uniform. Accordingly, these principles include, *firstly*, the enablement of power competence through training and hands-on apprenticeship; *secondly*, the extraction, systematization and consolidation of relevant information for the development of power knowledge; and *thirdly*, instructions for shaping the political field by means of the various instruments of power. The concretization of this categorical logic must, however, take into account the socio-cultural contexts and laws of the respective communities. Targeted consultation always both draws orientation from the universal guiding principles of political power and is context-sensitive to the specific conditions within which power is being exercised. We will concretely develop these guiding principles in the third and final chapter and thus translate our practical theory of power into an application-oriented guideline.

W. ([1808] 1992): *Faust, A Tragedy, Part I.,* translated by Martin Greenberg, New Haven: Yale University Press.; p. 97.

346 Sloterdijk (2017).

3. The Practice of Power

In the last chapter, we discussed the forms, fields, conditions of legitimacy and resources of power, paying special attention to the domain of the political, which through common norms of action impacts on all other power fields. In this sphere, the resources of power form a triad of interdependent conditions. Therefore, we also speak of the power vectors of the political: power competence, power knowledge and instruments of power. Acquisition and use of these resources is indispensable to protagonists in the political field in order to be competitive in the zero-sum game for power. This is true at all times and for all actors – for top politicians as well as for corporate directors, trade union and association presidents, church leaders and civil society leaders. The challenge, of course, is to master the vectors of political power as well. This task is highly complex, mentally and physically exhausting and demanding. It is almost impossible for a power actor – whether an individual or an organization – to handle alone.

At this point in the assessment of power logic, two archetypes of the political field appear on the scene: the *homo consultandus* and the *homo consultans,* the power-wielder who requires consulting and the power expert who provides it. The homo consultans supports the acquisition and use of power without striving for it directly. He or she is a political consultant, campaigner, communication expert, advocacy officer, chief organizer and confidant. The third and last chapter of our book is dedicated to this figure. We discuss and describe how policy advice works in practice, both in terms of the universal laws of power outlined in the previous chapters, and in terms of the concrete, sociocultural and political characteristics of each community. Good consulting combines *universality* and *contingency.* It is based on insights into the structural-global unity of its object, and is sensitive to the client's specific interests and political environment.

Consequently, this inquiry is more concrete and hands-on than the previous chapters. Because we focus on the practice of consulting in the daily struggle for political power, we consider not only the concrete issues of day-to-day politics, but also look at the numerous subfields of the political (financial, domestic, infrastructure policy etc.) with their specific internal logics as well as the various groups of relevant actors (parties, media, trade unions, associations, companies, NGOs, etc.). At the same time, this higher level of substantiation is accompanied by a narrower focus: we focus solely on the *representative democracy of the twenty-first century*. There are two main reasons for this focus on one type of system in one particular era. First, of course, a political consultancy approach could be developed for one-party states or modern theocracies, but these regimes are distant not only in terms of our cultural milieu and sociocultural starting point, but also regarding our own political ethos and commitment to the democratic common good (see Chapter 2.4). In short, we are neither designated power experts for such systems nor do we share their ethical-political principles. Second, political practitioners throughout the ages have established guidelines for the acquisition, exercise, legitimacy and preservation of political power, such as the Sophist Thrasymachus and the teacher Confucius in antiquity, the royal advisers Alcuin and Ignatius of Loyola in the Middle Ages, and finally the great political doyens of the Renaissance, Nicolo Machiavelli and Thomas More.[1] To penetrate these approaches in political and ideological terms would be a meritorious task. However, in Chapter 3 we are not intent upon offering a historical perspective on the practice of consulting and the development and transformation of the homo consultans, but focus on the political shaping of the here and now. Therefore, as before, we will refer to insights from the history of political thought – but only in terms of their significance for our present.

Our presentation of consulting practice starts from an existential assumption, which we want to call *anthropological-political realism*. To be sure, human beings are *zoon politikon* and technicians, i.e. social and creative creatures who can autonomously shape their political and natural environment – into which they are suddenly thrust – through innovation and cooperation (see Chapters 1.3 and 2.1). But, as the political scientist Joseph Schumpeter maintains, on average they are neither highly politically educated nor endowed with a natural instinct of power

---

[1] The reconstruction of the development and transformation of the homo consultans through the various epochs of world history is unquestionably an extremely attractive and important task, but it is one that we cannot pursue here. To our knowledge, no author has ever tackled this topic. Sloterdijk (2017) offers an inspiring essay on the subject, see also our Chapter 2.5.4. On the assessment that Thrasymachus, mentioned in Plato's Politeia, is the first professional policy advisor in Western history, see Abramson, Jeffrey B. (2009): *The Owl of Minerva,* Cambridge/London: Harvard University Press.; pp. 28f.

or a compass indicating the common good. Let us recall Schumpeter's famous statement, as cited in Chapter 2.4: "Thus the typical citizen drops down to a lower level of mental performance as soon as he enters the political field. [...] He becomes a primitive again. His thinking becomes associative and affective."[2] Schumpeter and other authors, such as the theoretician Jason Brennan, do not blame humans for doing so.[3] We similarly do not wish to judge or admonish, but rather to focus on describing political reality. The notion that all members of the community must devote every spare minute to the cultivation of civic competences and be up-to-date on all political developments, dramatically overestimates the importance of the political for a fullfiled and flourishing life. It also underestimates the value of other life projects and tasks and puts a disproportionate burden on people. Politics is an extremely complex field of power and society that, like other fields, is subject to the principle of division of labor and specialization.

The homo consultans acts as a highly qualified facilitator and mediator in this field, and aims to reduce complexity, to clarify interconnections, to give practical instructions and to make political contents intelligible, especially for laypeople. A central part of the functional spectrum of homo consultans, as we shall see in detail, is therefore to act as a translator between the political field and other power fields. Only if the basic assumption of anthropological realism is reflected in homo consultan's self-image, can he or she do justice to the role of power *consultant*, a service provider oriented towards the requirements and prerequisites of the client.

The program and the objectives of this chapter are thus clear. In the following, we want to outline a *curriculum* of the homo consultans for the representative democracy of the twenty-first century. This curriculum is the result of two decades of political consulting experience and continuous reflection on the basics, strategies and techniques of power, enriched by the reading of classic and contemporary political science literature. It is intended to serve as a practical guide for the budding consultant as well as provide suggestions for the experienced power expert who is already well acquainted with homo consultan's armor. We call this curriculum *power leadership*. It covers the universal principles of power consulting for all areas of democratic policymaking – from governments and state institutions to political parties and civil society advocacy. Of course, the specific focus of advice varies according to whether the homo consultans supports political officials, mandate holders or lobbyists. Accordingly, power leadership includes two specialized disciplines: *political leadership* and *lobbying leadership*. We will often refer to

---

2   Schumpeter ([1942] 2003): p. 416.

3   Cf. Brennan, Jason (2016): *Against Democracy,* Princeton: Princeton University Press.; pp. 3-6.

this distinction in our remarks, but we will not focus on it; we aspire rather to lay the foundations for every field of application of political power consultancy with the following curriculum. Our key question for this chapter is therefore: What constitutes the success of power consultants in the political present – and what are their knowledge foundations, tasks, tools and responsibilities and educational pathways?

We would be wise to take the present challenges facing the power leadership curriculum seriously. In a globalized world characterized by international networking (UN and WTO agreements, investment partnerships, global digital news and information systems, etc.) and supranational legislation and jurisdiction (EU directives, ECJ judgments, etc.), the interests of power actors are no longer confined to a single community. Exercising successful influence increasingly requires the strategic positioning of the actor in a global organizational context characterized by growing regulatory complexity. Therefore, the homo consultans must take into account both the political systems and cultures of different communities and their dependency relationships. The consultant thus moves in a field of tension between capitals cities competing for power on the one hand, and supranational or international institutions, such as the European Commission or the International Monetary Fund, on the other. The ideal of homo consultans is thus the synthesis of a generalist who is familiar with the universal logic of power and the global field of influence, and a specialist who knows the internal logics of specific polities, political subfields, and actor groups.

3.1 THE POWER CHESS MODEL

We want to fill this ideal with life through an analogy. In Chapter 1, we characterized the struggle for (political) power as a zero-sum game, that is, as a competitive game with a constant sum, where every win by one player always involves a loss by another player. We can further concretize this game analogy with a model. In essence, the political contest is *power chess* – and it is the homo consultant's job to lead the client, homo consultandus, skillfully through the game to victory. Like politics, chess is a conflict at the heart of which is dominance achieved through the skillful positioning of actors with varying clout and skill profiles (pawns, castles, knights, etc.), and through anticipation of opposing moves. Like no other game, chess integrates strategic and tactical elements. Victory and defeat are decided by the depth of the calculations made in advance of one's own and one's opponent's moves, and by the exploitation of unforeseen mistakes. The relationship between politics and chess goes so far that even in the Middle Ages the nobility was instructed in the "Game of Kings" in order to hone their power to govern (see Chapter 2.5.1). Since then, chess has become established across different social and cultural spaces as a traditional training tool for power.[4] Because of these parallels, the central prerequisites and challenges for a successful game of chess and politics are analogous,[5] as elucidated in the following.

(1) Understanding the Board

Developing an understanding of the board means, *first*, to internalize the formal rule canon and the mechanisms of the game: goal, starting line-up, movement of the pieces, standard maneuvers (fork, pin, castling). In short, anyone who understands the board knows the spectrum of all possible and impossible actions; they know the terrain and the troops. Thus, the necessary preconditions for even taking part in the game are fulfilled.

With regard to the model of power chess, this understanding of rules and mechanisms firstly includes an overview of the institutional structure of the political arena as well as the distribution of competencies and responsibilities between the institutions. In Germany, for example, this is the federal constitution with bicameralism, the horizontal and vertical separation of powers and multiparty system. Here the negotiation of interests is largely corporatist, i.e. through a concerted exchange of knowledge, positions and problem-solving approaches between authorities, stakeholders and politicians. This corporatist structure is in stark contrast

---

[4] To this day, economists and military personnel as well as psychologists and educators continue to praise chess as an ideal instrument for strengthening planning ability, leadership, sacrifice, stress resistance, empathy and creativity. See Smith, Roger (2010): The Long History of Gaming in Military Training, *Simulation and Gaming*, 41 (1), pp. 6-19.; Dixit, Avinash K. and Nalebuff, Barry J. (1993): *Thinking Strategically. The Competitive Edge in Business, Politics, and Everyday Life*, New York: W. W. Norton & Company.; pp. 41-45; and Hunt, Samuel J. and Cangemi, Joseph (2014): Want to Improve Your Leadership Skills? Play Chess!, *Education*, 134 (3), pp. 359-368.; p. 361. An elucidating inquiry on chess as a tool for strategy learning and its varying interpretations and social functions during history can be found in Clark (2019): pp. 122-130.

[5] Of course, this does not mean that every excellent chess player has the makings of an outstanding political consultant – or vice versa. The structural similarity between power chess and the "game of kings" does not mean a substantive equivalence. It is therefore not our intention to derive the power leadership curriculum from the chess game, but only to provide an appropriate model.

to the US political system, for example, which is characterized by an extremely competitive and pluralistic conflict of interests.

Second, understanding the board involves the internalization of the concrete decision-making rules and processes of the legislative, executive, judiciary and administration at the various levels of the system. A European example is the legislative procedure involving a trilogue between the Commission, the EU Council and the European Parliament, and comitology, that is, the implementation of EU legislation through a fine-tuned system of administrative and expert committees.

The *third* point comprises the specific laws and regulations that define the limits and possibilities for the enforcement of interests and the exercise of power. This outlines a wide range of legal norms, ranging from fundamental principles such as freedom of expression and association, to highly specific rules such as the ID-card scheme for lobbyists in the Bundestag.

The *fourth* and final factor is the political culture and language, both the ethos of the power struggle and the political narrative, and the unwritten rules and vocabulary of discourse. Political language is required to be understandable for all protagonists of the political sphere and to attain the necessary legal, professional legitimacy.

Ideally, these four aspects must become second nature to every player in power chess; they must become part of their power competence. All these factors have in common that they are largely fixed. These are therefore the strategic constants introduced in Chapter 2.5.2. Just like the rules for moving and positioning pieces and for standard maneuvers in the game of kings, they determine which actions in power chess are possible and who can execute them under what conditions. Of course, this says nothing about which moves should be employed by an actor, be it an authority, a company, an association, a civil society association, or – on the other hand – a minister, a CEO, a general manager or the head of an NGO.

(2) Reading the Positions

Chess is a game of positions. Victory and defeat depend solely on whether a king is secured by the pawns, a queen is covered or a pawn is able to make its way unobstructed to the eighth line for promotion. Beginners perceive the mingling of the figures on the board as a confusing jumble; they can provide information about which figure can move where but the strategic and tactical potential of a complex position and the balance of forces on the board are a closed book to them. Professionals, on the other hand, are able to accurately assess the threats or opportunities that arise from any configuration of positions – including strategic statements such as "checkmate in ten moves!"

Analogously, anyone who wants to play power chess successfully must be able to read the positions, i.e. interpret and evaluate political positioning. This not only means knowing which other power actors are relevant to the achievement of one's own policy objectives (regulation of a service sector, amendment of a law, execution of a construction project, etc.), but also what their agendas and motives are, who (potential) opponents and allies are, and – above all – the relationships between these protagonists. This information is required to decipher the balance of power in political issues and to identify directions of development and trends. Accordingly, the ability to read positions requires a comprehensive and highly specialized knowledge spectrum, such as whether a state government maintains close ties to state lotteries and is therefore motivated to maintain public control over sweepstakes at all costs; whether an interior minister is under great pressure from within the party to crack down on illegal immigration, even though this does not correspond to his or her personal values; whether an environmental organization supports a tightening of consumer protection to please their supporters, etc.

These positional factors have in common that they are not fixed; they fall under the category of the strategic variables introduced in Chapter 2.5.2. We are concerned here not with the framework of power chess, but the result of the actions of a specific game. It is possible to speak analogously here of chess compositions, that is, of certain created positions with which the player is confronted and for which a solution must be found. The goal-oriented analysis and evaluation of such positions is a prerequisite for developing a successful strategy.

(3) Taking Control of the Match

Chess is not a game of theoretical contemplation and reflection. It is a game of attack and defense, all about dominating the field. A deep understanding of the game and an excellent positional analysis are therefore useless, if they do not lead to victory match or – at least – to the imposition of a stalemate. Taking control of the match means preempting the opponent's moves, forcing a reaction by attacking, disrupting and destroying the opponent's strategy and tactics. All this is only possible if the player is not only capable of deep calculation and has a good comprehension of the game, but also demonstrates strong nerves, creativity, courage and a willingness to make sacrifices; anyone who hesitates too long loses the initiative and finally the game.

These characteristics are also found in power chess. They are a prerequisite for asserting one's own interests in the struggle for influence against the resistance of other actors, and for exercising interpretive power over the common good. This principle applies to all players, whether political institutions, private sector actors or civil society organizations. In the power chess of the representative democracy, taking control of the match involves using concrete measures to successfully influence the collective decision-making and will-forming process in the long term, for example: organizing majority votes; determining the agenda of a legislative or standing committee; placing an article in a key political medium at the right time; controlling the composition of an influential panel of experts; mobilizing particular groups for a specific topic through targeted campaigning; and forging stable alliances with resource-rich allies. All these instruments, which do not even come close to covering the full spectrum of political influence, are specific features of power chess. Successfully taking control of a game involves not only mastering these tools, but also knowing which instrument is appropriate for which phase of the overall strategy (in chess terminology: opening, midgame or final) and how these instruments need to be coordinated to achieve the game objective. This is the point at which game understanding and position analysis must flow together in a creative process; the point at which power politics is actually made.

The tasks of the political consultant emerge directly from the three challenges of the power-chess model – understanding the board, reading the positions, taking control of the match – which thus provide the three guiding principles and aspects of the power leadership curriculum: empower, condense and influence. First, the homo consultans must empower the client, the homo consultandus, to understand the board of power chess and to internalize its rules and mechanisms as power knowledge. Second, the homo consultans must condense all relevant information about the client's specific game (or games) into a positional analysis in order to lay the foundation for a promising strategy supported by power knowledge. And thirdly, with the client, the homo consultans must actively influence the political space and use suitable political instruments to take control of the game of power chess. This summary of the power leadership approach presents the three main tasks of the consultant and the corresponding challenges of power chess (or the power vectors introduced in Chapter 2.5) as being strictly and unambiguously separate. Of course, in political reality the divisions in everyday consultancy practice are not so sharp. The triad of empowering, condensing and influencing forms – as do their equivalents – a totality: experiences from influencing politics impact on position analyses and on the internalization of the system. Not without reason do we speak of *one* consulting approach with three aspects. This interdependence should be kept in mind when we discuss implementing the three guiding principles of power leadership. In the following, we want to explain concretely what it means to empower, to condense and to influence in the competition for political power.

3.2 EMPOWER MODEL

Empowerment is the cornerstone of competing for political power and enforcing political interests against the opposition of other stakeholders. The focus is on the acquisition and understanding of *political logic, political language* and *political ethos* by the power actor, whereby the term power actor includes both the individual and the organization (see Chapter 3.1). For the homo consultans, empowering involves equipping people and institutions for the game of power chess, giving them an understanding of the game that includes the rules but goes beyond merely memorizing formal laws and norms. The ultimate goal of empowerment is to develop a politically strategic way of thinking and a corresponding course of action (see Chapters 2.3 and 2.5.1 as well as our comments on governmentality in Chapter 2.5.2). For these responsible tasks, the consultant not only needs a diverse set of tools and techniques, but must also display true empathy for the client and undertake a realistic assessment of the latter's abilities. In the following, we first outline the range of topics and tasks associated with the key concept of empowering and then take a look at the concrete tools and techniques associated with it.

3.2.1 Political Logic

The notion "political logic" might seem abstract and dry to some readers, evoking associations of mathematical deduction, formal modeling or syllogisms. However, as before, we use the expression logic in its original, broad meaning as a collective term for the fundamental mechanisms, laws and functions of a specific subject area, here: politics in the representative democracy of the twenty-first century. Political logic is divided into four building blocks: system logic, decision logic, organization logic and communication logic.

System logic provides the answer to a simple and fundamental question: *how does the political system of a state or a community of states really work?* Accordingly, it includes, *firstly*, constitutional or international treaties such as the German Basic Law, the American Constitution or the EU Treaty of Lisbon; institutional orders (governments, parliaments, courts, administrations, etc.) at national, supranational, regional and local levels; the distribution of responsibilities; and the inter-institutional interconnectedness of powers. These are the major points at which the power relations between the executive, legislative, judiciary and administration are adjusted. They determine whether the political system has the character of a parliamentary or presidential democracy, whether political decisions are controlled by a powerful interventionist constitutional court or not, whether the regional units of a state enjoy much or little autonomy, whether the population is immediately involved in legislation through direct democratic instruments or whether legislation lies exclusively in the hands of elected representatives, etc. In short, the institutional framework of the political system determines *who* decides *what*, and to *whom* the decision-maker is accountable. We are thus concerned here with the positional fabric of power after Popitz, as introduced in Chapter 1.2.

Secondly, system logic includes the formal and informal procedures within this institutional order, such as the development of a law from its first draft through the passages and readings in the appropriate chambers to its execution and promulgation or the quorum and conditions for a referendum. Here it is worthwhile to distinguish between the nominal procedure and the *de facto* procedure. For instance, the German Federal Parliament (Bundestag) decides on the passing of laws by parliamentary majority and is thus nominally the legislator of the Federal Republic of Germany, but *de facto* only a very small number of legislative drafts originates from the parliamentarians. It is rather the case that the majority of such drafts are developed by specialist departments in the ministries (often with the involvement of state-level bureaucrats to ensure the smooth passage of the law through the German Federal Council – Bundesrat). They are then submitted to the Cabinet and only presented to Parliament for discussion in plenary session after an internal consensus has been formed.[6] Things are quite different in the United States, for example, where every elected member of the House of Representatives and every member of the Senate serves as his or her own political entrepreneur with a large staff, with whose help he or she takes legislative initiatives and prepares for the detailed work in the committees. Such central differences, which are depicted in Winfried Steffani's classic typology of parliaments (debating parliaments, working parliaments, debating working parliaments),[7] cannot be inferred from the formal constitutional system alone. They are part of lived and traditional political practice, and just as important as the formal institutional order.

The *third* aspect of system logic is best described as the system goal. It stands for the fundamental, historically conditioned guiding principle behind the respective institutional and procedural order. The system goal gives the answer to the why-question of the political system, i.e. explaining why it is structured as it is and not differently. In Germany, for example, the political system is structured in accordance with lessons learnt from National Socialism and from the failure of the Weimar constitution. Hence political power is not be concentrated in the hands of

---

6   Cf. Meier, Dominik (2017b): Germany, in: Alberto Bitonti and Phil Harris (eds.), *Lobbying in Europe,* London: Palgrave MacMillan, pp. 159-170.

7   Cf. Steffani, Winfried (1979): *Parlamentarische und präsidentielle Demokratie. Strukturelle Aspekte westlicher Demokratien,* Opladen: Westdeutscher Verlag.

one public official nor fragmented to the extent of incapacity. This double specification is the key to understanding the basic structure of the Federal Republic of Germany and the functioning of its institutional and procedural rules. In comparison thereto, the US system goal is to restrict as much as possible the exercising of power by the state institutions and to protect the population from excessive government intervention and ostensibly ideological policies – even at the cost of paralyzing the apparatus along party lines. The blockade potential is intentional, for it is purposely and purposefully built into the institutional and procedural order. A noteworthy device in this regard is constituted by the filibuster, a powerful legislative measure dating back to ancient Rome, as the senator Cato the Younger typically obstructed the passage of legislation by delivering long-winded speeches. In modern times, the technique is just as (in)famously employed in the US Senate, as the senatorial rules permit senators to speak for as long as they wish and on any topic they desire, unless "three-fifths of the Senators duly chosen and sworn" (normally 60 out of 100 senators) close the debate by invoking cloture in accordance with US Senate Rule XXII.[8]

A deep understanding of system logic is indispensable to power chess. The logic of the system determines how power is distributed in the political system and how it is exercised, and it thus establishes *starting points* and *channels* for the enforcement of interests. The rules of each variant of power chess are based on the logic of the systems concerned. For example, for a presidential, central-state democracy such as the Fifth Republic of France, where the powers of the National Assembly are extremely limited in relation to those of the head of state, there are different rules for starting line-ups and moves than in a parliamentary, federalist democracy, such as the Austrian one. While in the Fifth Republic the decisive political struggles take place in Paris – more precisely in the Élysée Palace – and the power formations are formed in concentric circles around the president, the Austrian field is decentralized and characterized by competition between the federal government and the states. Anyone who does not know about these differences between the system logics of the communities has no chance to participate in power chess; understanding such features is a prerequisite for being able to make any meaningful moves and bring about decisions.

The second building block of political logic, closely linked to system logic, is decision logic. It answers the follow-up question: *According to which principles are decisions made in the power field of representative democracy?* The focus here, however, is not knowledge of the majority rule in parliamentary votes or the

---

8   Cf. Arenberg, Richard A. and Dove, Robert B.: (2012): *Defending the Filibuster: The Soul of the Senate,* Bloomington: Indiana University Press.

supermajority rule in the Council of the EU (both of which are elements of system logic) but the rationale and justification structures of political decision-making.

We can best illustrate this building block by comparing economics and politics. For example, in a business enterprise, the decisions of CEOs are aimed directly at improving production efficiency, opening up new customer groups and markets or optimizing business collaboration – but the fundamental, unifying purpose is always to increase profits or, for stock companies, to increase stock market prices.[9] Profit is the ultimate goal of the private sector – a goal from which all other goals are derived. Political decisions in democracies, on the other hand, are always geared towards the ultimate goal of the common good, more precisely, the protection and promotion of the common good (see Chapter 2.4). The various measures taken by political decision-makers (laws, regulations, directives, international agreements, institutional reforms, etc.) appear to be heterogeneous in their functions, insofar as they relate to, for example, combating unemployment, increasing internal security, protecting the environment or improving the level of education – but the underlying justification principle is the same: the well-being of the community as a whole. All decisions must be justified by demonstrating that their immediate goals are effectively and efficiently linked to this ultimate goal.[10]

This results in two major consequences for political decision logic. *Firstly*, political decisions should not give the impression that they only serve the wishes of a particular interest group or even a single actor. Anyone in democratic power chess who is (justifiably) suspected of practicing clientele politics or nepotism, generally has no chance of success. Therefore, it is not surprising that, first, all interest formations of the political power field always and with great pathos take

---

[9] Incidentally, this also applies to most entrepreneurial measures in the area of Corporate Social Responsibility (CSR). Numerous studies have shown that the effective public implementation of social or ecological projects by companies leads in the medium term to an increase in profits and, not least because of this, is increasingly becoming part of the corporate philosophy of large corporations; see the much-cited essay by Orlitzky, Marc, Schmidt, Frank L. and Reynes, Sara (2003): Corporate Social and Financial Performance: A Meta-Analysis, *Organization Studies*, 24 (3), pp. 402-441.

[10] On the function of the common good as a unifying principle of political justification, see Blum (2015): p. 26.

up the cause of the common good;[11] and second, that in public debates regular attempts are made to attribute opponents with the pursuit of certain particular interests. This principle does not apply only to parties. It also applies to companies, for example, if they act as political power actors and influence politics. Business lobbying without a credible public interest is hardly possible today. The conclusion to be drawn from this specificity of political decision logic is therefore not to appeal to the common good *sui generis,* but to make a *convincing* appeal – a credible orientation towards the interests of the general public and not (only) the preferences of a particular social formation. This fact – the recognition of the need to aggregate interests in politics and connect them across societal divisions – explains why, for example, actual committee work in the US Congress or in parliamentary legislative bodies is conducted on the basis of bipartisan consensus, even though elections and votes are generally validated in accordance with the principle of majority rule. Here, too, the principle of the common good is applied, which we discuss in more depth in Chapter 3.2.3 as a component of political ethos.

The *second* consequence is that decisions cannot be made permanently against public opinion. The principle of democratic popular sovereignty gives citizens a high degree of freedom in determining the common good. In representative systems, although political decision-making authority is delegated to elected representatives, these representatives act as political trustees and are nevertheless responsible to the sovereign people. It is therefore necessary for political decision logic to take citizens' fears and concerns seriously and to do justice to them either through better policy mediation or substantial course corrections. Politics that does not take this requirement of decision logic seriously is technocratic. It is inspired by an elitist self-image and the belief that the public interest is fundamentally better understood by politicians than by the common citizen; which often leads to political disenchantment and a loss of confidence. A particularly drastic example of technocratic policy is provided by the gradual increase in power of the European Central Bank (ECB) in the course of the euro crisis from 2010, as well as the establishment of the influential European Stability Mechanism (ESM), which is largely independent of democratic control. To prevent a collapse in currency, both institutions are authorized to intervene in the budgetary policies of the member states (via bond purchases and loans tied to austerity regulations), undermining the budgetary rights of national parliaments. The effect is, as the political scientist

---

11   Cf. Neidhardt, Friedhelm (2002): Öffentlichkeit und Gemeinwohl. Gemeinwohlrhetorik in Pressekommentaren, in: Herfried Münkler and Harald Bluhm (eds.), *Gemeinwohl und Gemeinsinn,* Vol. II: Rhetoriken und Perspektiven sozial-moralischer Orientierung, Berlin: Akademie Verlag, pp. 157–177.; and Blum (2015): pp. 7ff.

Wolfgang Merkel described with a touch of disillusionment, "a humiliating disempowerment of democratic self-determination."[12] This applies in particular to the financially dependent debtor countries: "formal institutions of democracy such as elections, parliaments or governments are degraded in the debtor countries to mere facades, politics is being decided outside of the affected countries."[13] This style of policy is likely to be responsible for the fact that the proportion of citizens who trust the EU has been below the 50% threshold for years.[14]

The third building block, *organization logic,* is closely linked to system and decision logic. The thematic spectrum of organization logic can be condensed into a question, as before: *How are political organizations actually structured?* While system logic describes the relationship of the institutions to one another and specifies decision logic, defining the justification principles according to which these two act together, organization logic describes the internal perspective of the actors. On the one hand, this includes the formal, hierarchical structure of the bodies and positions and the corresponding responsibilities, as well as the rules of conduct of the members and the rules governing the workflow. On the other hand, it involves the informal mechanisms of decision-making, programmatic orientation and the allocation of resources and offices. Both aspects define the action spectrum of the organizations. They determine which internal processes they have to go through in order to perform specific maneuvers in power chess and which strategic powers they can mobilize. Accordingly, a knowledge of organization logic is necessary in order to develop an understanding of the rules governing the moves made by the actors – and thus of their strategic and tactical options.

The formal aspects of organization logic are reflected in the basic texts of the organizations. This includes the rules of procedure of Congress as well as the charters of the respective political parties and the statutes of the associations and trade unions. All of these regulations establish, with a meticulousness that may surprise a layperson, how meetings are convened, decisions are made and minutes are

---

12   Merkel, Wolfgang (2013): Ein technokratisches Europa ist nicht überlebensfähig, in: Cicero online from 08th April 2013, [online] https://www.cicero.de/innenpolitik/demokratieverlust-postdemokratie-so-ist-es-europa-nicht-mehr-wert/54106, retrieved on 21.12.2017. See also, although less critical, Selmayr, Martin (2015): Europäische Zentralbank, in: Werner Weidenfeld and Wolfgang Wessels (eds.), *Jahrbuch der europäischen Integration 2015*, Baden-Baden: Nomos.; pp. 113-126.
13   Cf. Selmayr (2015)
14   Cf. In this regard, Standard Eurobarometer, [online] http://ec.europa.eu/commfrontoffice/publicopinion/index.cfm/Survey/getSurveyDetail/instruments/STANDARD/surveyKy/2142, retrieved on 21.12.2017.

taken, and how people are elected to or removed from office. The penetration of formal organization logic is a challenging task that requires, not least, detailed knowledge of organizational charts and structure plans, such as the hierarchy of decision-making in a federal administrative authority from the minister to the secretaries of state to the individual head of unit. In comparison, the informal aspects of organization logic are much harder to pin down because they are not on paper, but are constituted by unofficial discussions, shared values or implicit understandings in the organizations. They can only be understood through years of first-person experience and through interaction.

The *last* building block of political logic is communication logic. Here, the question of the conveyance of contents and positions is in the foreground: *What is communicated how in the power field of politics?* Understanding and penetrating the logic of communication means understanding both the range of communicative channels and knowing what mechanisms these channels obey and what their opportunities and risks are. This knowledge is central to power chess, because in representative democracy the exercise of power is always linked to a communicative *ex ante* duty to provide reasons or to *ex post* accountability. All democratic systems – whether presidential or parliamentary, centralist or federalist – differ from dictatorships in that rule is carried out in a space of public discourse. In this space citizens are recognized as fully fledged communication partners, i.e. as the recipients and providers of reasons. The concomitant obligation to communicate extends not only to governments, parties and representatives of the judiciary and administration. It affects all actors of the political cosmos, i.e. private global players, church representatives and chief activists of environmental organizations. Those who cannot or do not want to communicate their actions are subject to the suspicion that their interests cannot withstand public scrutiny and are incompatible with the common good. Therefore, the crucial point is not whether power actors should act communicatively to enforce their interests, but only at what time and with what means and arguments they need to do so. At this point, there is a major overlap with the second key issue of empowerment: political language. As we discuss this in more detail below, we limit ourselves here to the basic structure of communication logic, its channels and paradigm shifts.

As a result of the ongoing digital revolution, political communication has already undergone far-reaching and profound transformation processes (see our remarks on data power and the mass media in Chapters 2.3.2 and 2.5.3). Therefore, this topic is one of the most discussed aspects of political logic in the current debate.[15] The communication logic of the democracies of the twenty-first century is characterized by a significant dichotomy: analogue versus digital. Until the 1990s, political communication and analogue communication were equivalent: anyone who wanted to convey content (electoral programs, trade union demands relating to industrial policy, boycott calls, appeals for refugees) distributed flyers, printed placards, broadcast radio spots, placed articles in newspapers, scheduled TV interviews or held press conferences. Political communication took place in a media cosmos with clearly defined news cycles, a numerically limited and professionally trained group of journalistic gatekeepers and relatively little interaction between addressees and broadcasters.

These parameters are obsolete in the age of social media, such as Twitter, Facebook, Reddit, WeChat or Instagram, the globally networking 24/7 messaging platforms, and of course, the digital communication technology of instant messaging and e-mail correspondence. This does not mean that, e.g., newspapers, magazines, radio and classical television have lost all importance; however, they have lost their gatekeeper function. So far, it is only certain that the times of a purely analogue political communication culture are irretrievably over. However, the new communicative cosmos is fluid and characterized by continuous technological disruptions. Reliable forecasts are proving extremely difficult in light of increasingly rapid innovation cycles. Peter Köppl, in discussing the digital paradigm shift in communication culture, aptly points out that society and politics, media and communication are subject to constant change. He thereby cites the exploding user rates of social media services, the penetration of smartphones and tablets among the population and the omnipresence of an online existence. By virtue of the active use of social and digital media, today every normal company is basically a media company. Power and communication monopolies are thus being successively eroded.[16]

The effects of digitization on political communication culture can be summarized in three points. *First,* the number of communicators has increased exponentially. Due to the low technical and logistical hurdles, every citizen and every interest group – no matter how small – can participate in the digital discourse and potentially reach not only an audience of millions but also influential decision-makers by simply setting up a Twitter account, a Facebook profile or clicking on the comment columns of news sites such as *Spiegel Online* or *NewYork-Times.Com*. The forerunners of this development were the Latin American democ

---

15　For an excellent overview of the challenges and opportunities of digitization for political communication, see Köppl (2017).

16　Köppl (2017): p. 1.

racies (such as Argentina and Ecuador), where heads of state were the first to engage in regular verbal and political debate via, for instance, Twitter; something that is now becoming a general phenomenon.[17] Secondly, the pace of political communication has accelerated dramatically. In times when the majority of the population are connected to the Internet via smartphones at any time, and only a fraction of a second is needed to post or comment, political power players are under pressure to steadily increase the pace of their messages, arguments and responses, for they loathe having to go on the defensive or – even worse – sink into communicative insignificance. Closely related to this is the third effect: a dramatic increase in the total volume of communicative content. However, this quantitative increase is not accompanied by a corresponding qualitative increase. The combination of a higher cycle rate and an ever-increasing number of channels harbors the very real danger of an increasing lack of substance on the one hand and the dissemination of unproven claims, so-called fake news, on the other. Added to this is the element of ever-increasing volatility of opinion. Many political social media trends, such as the movement #OccupyWallStreet of 2011, often receive national and international attention and approval for a very short time, only to disappear through the cracks in the pavement just as quickly and with no lasting effect. Hashtags do not guarantee lasting success. Nevertheless, some more recent trends are exhibiting the potential to be more longstanding and effective, notably the "MeTooDebate". This actually dates back to the work of the Afro-American social activist Tarana Burke, who started the movement in 2006 to battle against the sexual harassment of women. With the Harvey Weinstein affair, which rocked Hollywood in October of 2017, the hashtag #MeToo was initiated with incandescent force by the Italo-American actress Alyssa Milano, and it began illuminating the problem on various levels, and with varying substantive depths, around the world.

At this juncture, the great challenge of political communication logic in the twenty-first century democracy can be summed up. It is important to broadcast your own messages to the targeted audience rather than being obliterated by the mass of news alerts and pop-ups, but it is also necessary to efficiently filter through all the opinions and information what is relevant to your own interests. A basic rule of political power chess here is not to succumb to the temptation of empty content or fabricated truths. In the digital as in the traditional, analogous communication cosmos, there has always been a principle – to which we return in our discussion of political language and political detail – lies have short legs. As we discuss in our section on the strategic potency of mediation in Chapter 2.5.2,

---

17   Cf. Gimlet Media (2015): *Favor Attendar* [Podcast], [online] https://gimlet media.com/episode/25-favor-atender/, retrieved on 20.1.2017.

in politics it is arguments and clear language that convince. Anyone who continually relies on falsehoods and bullshit (see Chapter 2.4) will sooner or later be unmasked and no longer taken seriously in the political discourse space. These insights must also be reflected in the political language of power chess players.

3.2.2 Political Language

The language of politics has as bad a reputation with many people as the game of power chess of which it is a part. Even policymakers repeatedly flirt with this *cliché*. Among them, the former Prime Minister of the Soviet Union, Nikita Khrushchev, to whom the following statement is attributed: "Politicians are the same everywhere. They even promise to build a bridge when there is no river."[18] With all due respect for Khrushchev's self-irony, his statement remains a caricature. When political language – not just the language of politicians, but of all of the protagonists of the political power field – relies only on breezy promises, vague assertions, lies or empty phrases, then any political system runs the risk of imploding. This is all the more true for democracy. Democratic legitimacy and stability are based on the actors directly or indirectly involved in decision-making – whether public institutions, political parties, economic and civil society interest groups, scientific institutions, etc. – publicly presenting their positions and interpretations of the common good in a clear, verifiable and consistent manner. If this normative and functional requirement remained consistently unfulfilled, the result would be such a massive loss of confidence in the system and the elites that the collectively authorized norms would no longer be worth the paper on which they are written. Reality is therefore more complex, and it is a central political task to make this reality understandable and manageable. We therefore outline below the key language requirements in the democratic contest of interests.

Political language, similar to jurisprudential language, business language, the various scientific languages and even the language of football, is a linguistic field with its own *vocabulary* and *laws*.[19] Translating political statements into another language, and vice versa, is not only essential to establish a communicative ex

---

18   As quoted in New York Herald Tribune (22th August 1963).
19   We could speak here of a 'language game', following the language philosopher and logician Ludwig Wittgenstein ; see. Wittgenstein, Ludwig ([1953] 2001): *Philosophical Investigations*, translated by G.E.M. Anscombe, Hoboken: Blackwell. The Wittgenstein metaphor of a game that combines the specialized use of language with a practical aim (in politics, for example, the exercise and legitimization of power) fits in well with our analogy of politics as strategic-tactical power chess.

change between the various power fields of the community – such as economics, religion, science and culture (see Chapter 2.3) –, it is also often extremely demanding. Those who do not master the special vocabulary and the rule canon of the political language will either not be understood in the political discourse or, sometimes worse, will be misunderstood.

Political vocabulary can be subdivided into three categories: firstly, institutional vocabulary (e.g. Congress, President, draft, bill and hearing); secondly, interaction vocabulary, which designates political interactions or linguistic acts (e.g. scandal, resolution, compromise, demand, agree, discuss) and, finally, departmental vocabulary which comprises the jargon of the respective subject areas.20 The latter includes, for instance, the terms of digital and economic policies, such as Industry 4.0 and Open Access, or fiscal terminology, such as liquidity management or fiscal stimulus. Mastering this vocabulary involves knowing its *denotation and connotation* – knowing what the expressions refer to and what associations are linked with them. It also means understanding the many abbreviations used by day-to-day decision-makers to save time and exclude non-insiders from discourse (see our discussion on bureaucratic terminology as a power technique in Chapter 2.5.2). Anyone who cannot decipher the various abbreviations and acronyms will have difficulty reading political documents in the first place.

The corresponding rules of political language can be determined by three main aspects or levels: *content, mediation and formalization ability*. In democratic competition, it is not always those who have the best ideas and justifications on their side who prevail; but it is certainly the case that those with no valid arguments will lose sooner or later. The success of political charlatans is always fragile and short-term and does not detract from the veracity of this principle. This indicates the central feature of political language: arguments. The importance of arguments for political language becomes clear when we recall the function of this language form: it should not only inspire and mobilize, but also convince. It should therefore satisfy basic human strivings for meaning and justification, for orientation and rationale, as discussed in Chapter 1.3. This gap can be filled only by arguments, because only they can challenge human beings and take them seriously as rational political subjects – as the providers and recipients of reasons. Arguments are constantly being demanded, questioned, rejected and reformulated in the political discourse, by opponents, allies, the media and the public alike. If leaders from politics, business or civil society have no arguments, then they have virtually nothing to say.

---

20 Bazil, Vazrik (2010): Politische Sprache: Zeichen und Zunge der Macht, *Politik und Zeitgeschichte*, (8), pp. 3-6.; p. 3.

Arguments are necessary for convincing political language. However, they are far from sufficient. Not all arguments are good arguments. Obviously, when discussing the quality criteria of arguments, we must leave out the material, substantive side. The substantive plausibility of a labor market policy or a climate policy argument is a question that falls within the domain of economists or meteorologists. We focus here on the formal side. The corresponding quality criteria were already mentioned in Chapter 2.4, introduced as part of our discussion of the legitimacy criteria of political power. Thus, we can now draw on that discussion. *Firstly,* the arguments must not be knowingly based on misinformation or mislead addressees by omitting relevant facts. *Secondly,* they must not be bullshit in the sense of Harry G. Frankfurt, pretending to communicate meaning in meaningless word cascades, where in truth there is none. *Thirdly,* the individuals or organizations that produce the arguments must scrutinize them to the best of their knowledge and ability for logical consistency, plausibility, falsifiability and transparency.

These three stipulations are not primarily ethical obligations in the context of political language; such obligations are dealt with in Chapter 3.2.3 in terms of the ethos of the political. Instead, this is primarily about the rules of prudence that concern political discourse. Thus if a politician presents untenable economic forecasts, the CEO of a chemical company ignores better knowledge and classifies a pesticide as environmentally friendly, or the representative of an association insists against all medical evidence that tobacco products do not damage people's health, then they are disregarding their due diligence obligations and will lose their credibility – and not only in the short term. In the worst case, the resulting reputational damage and the loss of trust can, as in the case of the cigarette industry, continue in the long term and provoke the most devastating counter-reactions. The same is true of the commandments: Thou shalt not lie, do not bullshit. Both forms of pseudo-arguments are associated with such a high risk of detection that their use is not a valid move in power chess.

However, the high priority given to arguments by no means implies that political language should not *emotionalize.* On the contrary, persuasive rhetoric addresses the passions of the listeners as well as their reason and judgment (see also our discussion of rhetoric and mediation in Chapter 2.5.2). It polarizes and provokes, it shakes up and carries its audience along, but it also soothes and pacifies. Without an emotional component that either enters into or actively challenges the state of mind of the addressees, political language (and thus its argumentative side) becomes technocratic and boring. The challenge in this context is threefold: to support one's own position with formal and substantively plausible arguments; to connect with the passions of addressees through targeted and appropriate emotionalization; and finally, to connect both elements – logos and pathos – in the content of political language.

The second level, mediation, concerns the way in which the arguments must be communicated to the addressee in order to fully communicate their persuasive power, i.e. to establish rational insight as well as empathic understanding. Firstly, any form of linguistic communication is either *oral* (speech, interview, public debate, informal conversation, etc.) or *written* (textbook, newspaper article, position paper, dossier, e-mail, instant message, etc.).[21] Both basic forms and their specific formats have certain advantages and disadvantages. Complex arguments cannot be adequately summed up in a tweet. Although point-blank position papers are compact and concise, they rarely produce emotional storms of enthusiasm. Interviews pose the danger of questions being posed that the power player did not want to address. And so on.[22] Secondly, the vocabulary of linguistic mediation moves on a continuum between *specialist expert discourse* (complex sentences, technical terms) and *lay discourse* (simple sentences, no technical terms). It is obvious that the use of vocabulary and the balance between professional and everyday language are crucial. If in the course of a civil society dialogue about an infrastructure project a developer bombards the audience with technical terms on planning approval procedures and spatial planning, for example, this will not lead to understanding and approval but to confusion and alienation. On the other hand, someone who is a political expert in a judicial committee hearing on the subject of crime prevention is well advised to use the department-specific vocabulary (repeated delinquency, predictive validity, false positives and negatives, etc.) in order to do justice to the complexity of the subject discourse and the methodological prerequisites of the interlocutors. In short: optimal positioning on both axes is crucial for the ability to mediate political language.

This depends on four factors. The first is the status of the *sender or communicator*. What position does he or she have? What position is he or she occupying in political space? Which linguistic conventions and rules are linked to his or her

---

21 It is an interesting question whether facial expressions and gestures, for example the raised index finger, the salute or demonstrative eye rolling and frowning, but also Winston Churchill's Victory V and Angela Merkel's Rhombus, are linguistic forms of expression in a broader sense. We do not want to deepen this topic here. In any case, it is clear that these comprise an essential part of power symbolism and therefore often accompany political speech acts in a deliberate staging. See Chapter 2.2.

22 A good introduction in this regard is provided by Girnth, Heiko (2002): *Sprache und Sprachverwendung in der Politik,* Hamburg: De Gruyter.; pp. 83ff.

function? A certain political vocabulary is incompatible with the official status and political position of certain offices. Thus an active Chief Justice of the US Supreme Court, for example, is not normally heard utilizing street talk. On the other hand, this canon of communications does not apply at all to candidates for the office of US President. Moreover, in the Trump Era, it is quite evident that, even subsequent to winning a verbally venomous campaign, the victor can feel free to extend his raw, even rude rhetoric or to appropriately modulate his dog-whistle politics.

Incidentally, the term *dog-whistle politics* refers to an already well-established form of political messaging which utilizes coded language.[23] The code words are aimed at receiving resonance from a specifically targeted, desired and often very loyal subgroup. Actually, the term is of a pejorative nature given the perceived deceptive intent on the part of the speaker who is allegedly employing such techniques, for example, to surreptitiously stir up racial or ethnic sentiments. Indeed, the analogy is clearly being made to a dog whistle, a simple device whose high-frequency tone is heard by canines, while being inaudible to humans. Of course, in the modern political realm, the whistle is received and amplified by the media and political opponents as well. Thus, the rallying cry made to one's own base can thus run the risk of inciting the 'other side' and, for example, fueling a movement such as '#NeverTrump.'

The second factor is the *status and role of the addressee(s):* are they knowledgeable participants in a political discourse or laypersons? Is the addressed group big or small, heterogeneous or homogeneous? Addresses given by heads of state and government to all their citizens often feature pictorial comparisons, short sentences, repetitions, memorable slogans and the renunciation of foreign words. This form of communication not only ensures that the messages are comprehensible to the maximum number of people without political education. It also overcomes the problem of low attention spans through redundancy and conciseness.

The third factor is the *complexity of the content*. Are the arguments logically sophisticated or simple? Do they require specialist knowledge or are they comprehensible without such knowledge? In Germany, for example, the Council of Economic Experts, an advisory council focusing on macroeconomic development, and somewhat informally referred to as the "Five Economic Wise Men" *(Die fünf Wirtschaftsweisen),* faces the challenge of preparing highly complex economic policy topics for both the public and experts. It overcomes this problem by subdividing its reports into a generally comprehensible shortened version accented by

---

23   For the origin and meaning of the term cf. Safire, William (2008): *Safire's political dictionary*, revised edition, New York: Oxford University Press.; p. 190.

keywords ("Strong Upturn in 2017", "Increasing Risks in the Financial System", "Stability for the Euro Area", etc.), and a specialist supplement.[24]

Finally, the fourth and last factor is the *relationship between the sender and the addressee* in the concrete situation. Is the relationship formal or informal? Are they in a hierarchical or equal relationship? Are they allies or opponents? For example, the mediation between an association representative and a group of members of parliament who have known each other for years follows categorically different rules to the mediation between a newly appointed government spokesperson and a host of critical journalists.

The correct mediation strategy is – to use a mathematical analogy – a function of the four factors: sender and recipient status, complexity of content and relationship. The balancing of these four factors against each other, however, cannot be solved schematically by a formula. This is rather a question of political competence, which is acquired through continuous practice as well as through training and coaching (see Chapters 2.5.1 and 3.2.3). This too is part of political empowering.

Figure 10: Factors of Political Mediation

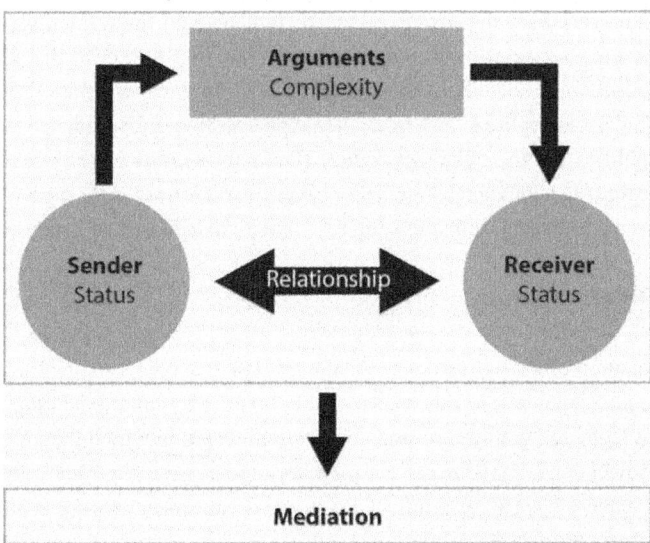

---

24 Cf. Sachverständigenrat zur Begutachtung der gesamtwirtschaftlichen Entwicklung (2017): Für eine zukunftsorientierte Wirtschaftspolitik. Jahresgutachten, [online] https://www.sachverstaendigenrat-wirtschaft.de/fileadmin/dateiablage/gutachten/jg201718/JG2017-18_gesamt_Website.pdf, retrieved on 21.12.2017.

The third main aspect of political language is formalization ability. In this, political language differs greatly from a range of other forms of language, also those from other significant power fields such as the language of religion or culture. It must be possible to translate or condense political linguistic acts – both spoken and written – into the formal diction of the law and administration. However, the emphasis here is on formalization *ability*. Not every political sentence must be couched in legalistic or administrative language. Indeed, that would impact extremely negatively on its general understandability and communicability. But the meaning of its content and the corresponding arguments must be compatible with the appropriate specialist language. There is a decisive reason for this: the principle of the political is the authorization and enforcement of collectively binding standards of behavior and the establishment of standards of legitimacy (see Chapter 2.3.3). Political actors set the rules of social interaction and thus intervene, at times significantly, in the lives of citizens and organizations – ranging from global software companies to local associations of beekeepers. It must therefore be possible to verify the legality and check the legitimacy of political action, even to the extent of an abstract and concrete judicial review in the constitutional courts.

In terms of mastering the political language, the criterion of formalization ability first and foremost implies an adequate fundamental understanding of legal terms and their relationship to policymaking. This does not mean that either the power consultant or the clients must undergo legal training, nor does it mean that they should assess politics only from a legal perspective. Jurisprudence is there to support politics, not the other way round. The focus is rather on the practical consequence that the legal dimension must always be considered in political language, viewed as a possible complication and risk, and included in consultancy activities.

3.2.3 Political Ethos

The acquisition of the political ethos is the third task of empowerment. It deepens the basic understanding of power chess (the 'board') by complementing political logic and language with the responsibilities and duties to which the power actor and the power consultant – *homo consultandus* and *homo consultans* – are equally subject. When we speak of political ethos, we do not mean mere law-abiding or political correctness. The former goes without saying. Compliance with the laws of the liberal constitutional state is essential for participation in democratic power chess and needs no further elucidation at this point. The latter, moreover, has nothing to do with ethics for us. Political correctness is a linguistic power technique with which interest formations influence the accepted vocabulary of the political language and claim sovereignty over the common good. There is much to say about the effects of political correctness and its prohibitions and bans on public discourse. However, we want to leave said subject at this point.[25] By political ethics, we mean instead the unwritten but always implicitly presupposed values and norms of action to which all actors of democratic power chess – both persons and organizations – are committed. They form the counterpart to the legitimacy conditions of the institutions that we described in Chapter 2.4.

Thus understood, the political ethos is based on three fundamental values or virtues: *truthfulness, trustworthiness* and *common-good orientation*. These values do not comprise an (exclusive) purpose in themselves. They are a prerequisite for power actors to be able to credibly communicate their political positions, to forge lasting alliances and to mobilize various groups of people to assert their strategic interests. They are therefore the normative prerequisites of a fair and efficient democratic contest, on which the constitutional state depends but which – to return once more to Ernst-Wolfgang Böckenförde – it cannot guarantee.[26] This guarantee must be assumed by the protagonists of the political power field itself. It is an integral part of lived democratic culture, and it can only be sustained through continuous practice, tradition, reflection and, not least, through voluntary self-control.

The first core value, *truthfulness,* does not require power actors and power consultants to be beyond any doubt. To err is human. If errors are reflected upon rationally, and not just reactionally, they even offer an important opportunity for assessing and improving one's own strategic ability (see our discussion of strategic failure in Chapter 2.5.2). Being truthful rather means that the political statements and actions of individuals and organizations must coincide. The principle of truthfulness is the convergence of discourse and practice in power chess. The relevance of this value becomes particularly apparent when it is trampled upon: in bigotry. An impressively notorious example from the recent past is the devastation of Hamburg's Schanzenviertel by left-wing radicals in July 2017. Thousands of activists invaded the district on the occasion of the G20 summit in Hamburg, carrying as a matter of course slogans like 'peace' and 'justice' on their banners. The divergence between the activists' claim to moral superiority over the summit participants and their actual actions led to a massive loss of solidarity among leftists, and not only in Hamburg. The conclusion is simple: you cannot plausibly support pacifism with a Molotov cocktail in your hand, you cannot genuinely preach global solidarity and plunder shops and businesses. Of course, this lack of truthfulness is not a political rarity, and it is certainly not specific to the leftist scene either. Its

---

25 See also e.g. Braun, Johann (2015): Die offene Gesellschaft und ihre Grenzen, *Rechtstheorie*, 46 (2), pp. 151-177.

26 Böckenförde (1967): p. 93; see also Chapter 2.4.

effects, however, are devastating: political disenchantment, cynicism and apathy. Anyone who assumes that political actors always say one thing and then do something else ultimately turns away from politics. Truthfulness, on the other hand, creates credibility and the assurance of expectations: addressees of political communication can rely on the fact that decision-makers' deeds will actually correspond with their words.

The significance of truthfulness also extends to the closely related principle of sincerity. This is of immense importance for consultancy and policy design alike. For example, when a consultant realizes that a client is facing a serious strategic mistake but conceals that insight (for example, to avoid the displeasure of the client), the consultant is failing to live up to his or her responsibilities and ethos. The principle of sincerity – expressing one's well-founded opinion even at the risk of criticism and resistance – does not mean that homo consultans should patronize homo consultandus or relieve clients of decisions. Homo consultans always remains only the consultant and service provider of *homo consultandus,* he or she is an actor with their own goals and interests. This dual and potentially conflictual task is best described as a tightrope walk between rebellion and humility. This tightrope walk must also be achieved by deputies or parliamentarians and the representatives of associations. Both groups of actors have a mandate to shape politics on behalf of their constituents and members. In doing so, they have a duty not only to disclose unpleasant truths to their political clients, but even – at least temporarily – to act contrary to their clients' current opinions, if a long-term policy goal so requires. At the same time, they remain accountable to their clients. If they continually fail to take their concerns, wishes and beliefs seriously, then they are no longer actually representing them.

The second basic principle, *trustworthiness*, is fulfilled when an actor's positions and actions are coherent and stable over time. To put it bluntly and polemically, anyone who today campaigns as an environmentalist for emission reduction and climate protection, tomorrow enters into consultancy for a coal company, and finally the day after tomorrow works for a solar power producer, is untrustworthy. If you politically support such actors, you always do so at the risk of them suddenly changing their point of view at any time.

It is important in this context to bear in mind the difference between truthfulness and trustworthiness. Those who are not truthful can nonetheless consistently represent the same position over a longer period of time – however they never or rarely put this position into practice. Those who are not trustworthy may always do what they say, the problem is that they always change their position. In short: non-truthful persons are bigoted, untrustworthy persons are unprincipled. This does not mean, however, that actors should never change their position in the course of their political biographies. Nobody could plausibly accuse the German Ex-Minister of the Interior Otto Schily, who gradually transformed himself from a radical left-wing RAF (Red Army Faction, a far left terrorist group founded in 1970) sympathizer to a Law and Order politician, of undermining his trustworthiness. Schily's change of heart is the result of a gradual development process for which there are convincing reasons. The situation is similar with respect to retired four-star General Colin Powell, former Chairman of the Joint Chiefs of Staff, US National Security Adviser and Secretary of State. Powell entered the world stage as a staunch interventionist and member of the neo-conservative Bush administration and – after the experience of the Iraq war and the so-called "War on Terror" – left it as an enemy of war and supporter of the Democrats. Upon hearing that President George W. Bush was "sleeping like a baby" on the eve of war with Iraq, Powell countered: "I'm sleeping like a baby, too. Every two hours, I wake up, screaming."[27] A lack of trustworthiness exists precisely if there are no convincing content-related reasons for such fundamental changes in political positions and if these changes of position do not occur gradually but suddenly.

Trustworthiness is as crucial for political success and for the integrity of the entire democratic contest as truthfulness. Those who lack credibility cannot forge stable and sustainable alliances, mobilize citizens to their ends on a lasting basis, convey credible messages or develop and implement long-term political strategies. Only trustworthiness creates constancy and predictability in political power chess.

The third and final principle of the political ethos is the *common-good orientation*. In determining this basic value, we can refer to the findings of Chapter 2.4 where we discussed the key concept of the common good in detail. A common-good orientation is not a commitment to a – supposedly – objective moral good that exists independently of the factual interests of the population or in relation to a list of universal policy goals (for example, full employment, integration of foreigners, social equality). Such so-called substantialist or material concepts, which determine the content of the common good ex ante, are incompatible with the pluralistic interests of liberal societies and with the open-endedness of democratic decision-making. What constitutes the well-being of a community can only be established ex post – that is, in view of the always provisional result of the democratic contest of ideas, which is contained and limited by the procedural norms, the political culture and the interpretive horizons of the formations of interests.

---

27   Kaplan, Fred (2004): The Tragedy of Colin Powell: How the Bush Presidency destroyed him, in: Slate from 19th February 2004, [online] https://slate.com/news-and-politics/2004/02/the-tragedy-of-colin-powell.html, retrieved on 21.12.2017.

However, if the common good is not an objective, content-wise predetermined quantity, then from what should the power actor and the power consultant draw orientation? What is the fixed point of the common-good orientation? The answer to this difficult and rarely-discussed question has two complementary parts. *First*, the common-good orientation requires unconditional respect for and defense of written and unwritten democratic procedural norms and principles. Because the common good does not precede the democratic decision but emerges from it, only democratic policymaking can serve the common good. In addition to a series of obvious commandments and prohibitions (recognition of election results, no bribery of elected officials, no intimidation of the opposition, respect for press freedom, etc.), this also includes the protection of democratic order. Anyone who denies citizens political rights on the basis of skin color, origin or religion, for example, is not a democratic opponent that must be recognized as a competitor in the competition of ideas, but is an enemy of democracy. You do not owe it to enemies to enter into discussions and argumentative debates; they must be combated by all means of the rule of law. This is the principle of defensive democracy.

The *second* part of the answer refers to the adjective 'common' as part of the compound "common good." The common good is the well-being of the community as a whole, not the well-being of a single and politically victorious formation of interests.[28] The inclusive character of this guiding principle must be taken into account by all power actors and interest groups when articulating their concerns. Here, the homo consultans has a duty to make clear to clients the immense importance of the common good for the representation of interests. To be oriented towards the common good means considering the legitimate and potentially conflicting interests of other social groups in the development of political goals and revising one's own position should there be good reason to do so. The opposite of the common-good orientation is selfish particularism. Selfish policymaking, the ruthless pursuit of particular interests at the expense of others, is incompatible with the common good.

---

28 See Claus Offe's (2001) essay "Wessen Wohl ist das Gemeinwohl? " ("Whose good is the common good?") The insight that the common good concerns the good of the community as a whole, rather than merely that of a subgroup, is basically just the starting signal for a series of other problems: Is this community identical to the totality of all its members? If so, are only Pareto-optimal decisions of benefit to the common good? (See the position of Neidhardt (2002).) If not – and that seems the more likely answer – how should the community be determined? These questions are still awaiting their answer through political theory. However, we cannot go deeper into the subject here.

This unwritten basic norm of our democracy is regularly expressed in the statesmanship of newly elected heads of government. For example, Angela Merkel declared after her election victory in September 2009 that she wanted to be "the Chancellor of all Germans" – not just of the CDU voters. The same gesture is also found in statements made by civil society and economic interest groups on politically contested topics. Environmental lobbyists, such as Greenpeace or WWF, insist, for instance, that the gradual transition of electricity supplies to renewable sources not only protects the environment but is also good for the economy, creating jobs and strengthening Germany's market leadership in future technologies.[29] Drug and medical device manufacturers, in turn, always seek to ensure that their economic interests in gaining the authorization of certain products and the objective of improving public health coincide. In all these and similar cases, the challenge, of course, is not to represent such statements as mere lip service, but as sincere declarations of intent. The accompanying question concerning how much compromise the common-good orientation requires and how willing one must be to critically question and modify one's own interests, has always been a bone of contention for democratic practice and theory.[30] We also do not claim to provide a final answer, but are content to outline the nature of the problem.

In any case, the importance of the common-good orientation for successfully controlling the match in power chess should have become clear. Power chess is indeed a game that revolves around the enforcement of political interests through skillful positioning and strategy building – but these interests must firstly comply with the democratic rules of the game and, secondly, be compatible with other interests (i.e., not purely selfish). If not, the power actor may be excluded from the game or face the devastating accusation of clientism and pursuing a politics of vested interests (see Chapter 3.2.1). As with the other core values of the political ethos, truthfulness and trustworthiness, the common-good orientation is not only a commandment of ethics, but also of political reason.

3.2.4 Tools and Techniques of Empowering

With the political logic, the political language and the political ethos, the central tasks of empowering are outlined. If actors have internalized these three elements of power chess, they have understood the 'board'. They master the mechanisms and rules of the political game. However, this raises the question of which tools

---

29 Cf. https://www.greenpeace.de/themen/energiewende/energiewende-mit-plan and http://www.wwf.de/themen-projekte/klima-energie/energiepolitik/energiewende/.

30 An excellent introduction into this subject is offered by Fung et al. (2012).

and techniques the homo consultans can use to provide their client, the homo consultandus, with such a scheme of thinking and the corresponding competencies. We now want to explain this essential component of the power leadership curriculum.

The skills of empowerment have three aspects: training and coaching, organizational consulting and navigation.

The terms *training* and *coaching* are often thrown together in our everyday language. The reason for this is that both tasks (whether in sports, in business or in politics) are mostly carried out by one and the same person. Nevertheless, a clear distinction is worthwhile. To illustrate this, let's take a look at soccer. Here, training sessions are those intervals between the individual games in which soccer players work on their fitness, practice standards and moves, review game records for mistakes and opportunities, and so forth – all under the guidance of their trainer. Coaching, however, takes place *during* the game from the well-known coaching zone on the sidelines; here, the soccer manager (to avoid the confusing terms of trainer or coach) gives instructions in real time, provides feedback and criticism to individual players, makes tactical changes, substitutes players and cheers on the team.

The situation in political power consultancy is very similar. During training, the power consultant prepares the client for involvement in the political arena. First, he or she provides a fundamental understanding of the political logic of the community (system logic, decision logic, organization logic and communication logic), its institutions and mechanisms. Since the focus here is on the acquisition of practical competence and not theoretical knowledge, this mediation usually has an interactive (and not a lecturing) format. In workshops or in planning games, consultants and clients discuss the detailed structure of legislative processes, the implementation of EU directives or the procedures of a ministerial conference. Second, training includes the acquisition of communication skills, the command of political language in speech and writing. This aspect of empowerment covers a wide range of topics and methods. It ranges from the internalization of principal abbreviations to the different types of salutations for persons of certain high offices ('the Honorable' or 'His / Her Excellency' etc.) to the construction of political texts of various types (dossiers, agreements, laws, regulations, etc.) to rhetorical training in front of cameras. And it also includes, as addressed in Chapter 3.2.2, the process of translation between policy language and the language of business or science, for example. The third aspect of the training is to create an understanding of the political ethos, as well as of the narrative of the community and its value. The latter poses crucial challenges for homo consultans with regard to international clients, such as global conglomerates or foreign trade organizations.

These power actors operate in dozens of states without necessarily being familiar with their cultural specifics (for example, the relevance of data protection to German politics or the importance of personal ties for political and economic relations in China). Thus in addition to translating, homo consultans must act as a cultural mediator.

Coaching then takes place while accompanying the homo consultandus throughout his or her politically relevant activities, both *internally* and *externally*. The former includes, for example, strategy meetings with the supervisory board of the company or the management level of the association concerned, but also, e.g., the internal professionalization and reorganization activities of an NGO. The latter covers a wide range of external communications – from public statements to appearances at specialist conferences to individual discussions with decision-makers. The power consultant is always on hand to provide the client with feedback on position papers, correspondence or speeches. He or she is present at key talks – not to whisper suggestions from the sidelines, but to assess the capabilities of the client *in actu* and to align further training to the client's perfrmance and mediation skills. Last but not least, homo consultans also has the task of familiarizing clients with political events (parliamentary evenings, specialist conferences, party congresses, festivals, etc.), with the relevant actors and their goals, interests, power resources and special features. The power consultant acts as a mentor and pilot for the political field.

While training and coaching aim to make individual persons (or smaller groups) fit for power chess, *organizational consulting* focuses on optimizing institutional structures. Of course, the structure and focus of organizational consulting will vary according to which goal of power leadership – political leadership or lobbying leadership – is the focus. For ministries, departments and other agencies, this includes, e.g., the development and implementation of time- and resource-saving hierarchies or processes to enable increased responsiveness to challenges and crises. For parties, political organizational consulting may aim to establish a campaign center (a so-called 'war room') to prepare for the next election campaign and communicate messages successfully and sustainably to voters. In the case of private sector actors, the focus is on establishing or optimizing interest representation structures to assess the impact of projected changes in regulation on business development, to appoint contact persons for decision-makers and to take on board criticism from the political sphere. Despite these different emphases, political organizational consulting always has the same basic objective: the formation of teams, the creation of decision-making and communication and cooperation structures, and the establishment of working rhythms for effective and efficient action both internally and externally, allowing the development and implementation of political strategies in a purposeful manner.

Successful organizational consulting requires the homo consultans to have a clear analytical view of the *actual state* of the organization on paper (organizational charts, flowcharts of work and information processes, etc.) and their strategic powers (organizational capability, mobilization capability, network capability, mediation capability, fame, financial potency and willingness to make a sacrifice, see Chapter 2.5.2). However, sensitivity to internal power relations, rivalries, mutual sympathies and animosities, and the dominant mood is also required. The most sophisticated restructuring plan is worthless if it fails because of the insulted vanity of a longtime member of the board, because of the self-image of the membership base of an NGO or because of the reluctance of a bureaucratic staff to abandon proven working methods. Homo consultans cannot deal with these challenges through political know-how and substantive expertise; what is required here is empathy and knowledge of human nature, that is, people skills, and not least a realistic assessment of his or her own limitations. Here we encounter, as highlighted in Chapter 3.2.3, the balancing act between rebellion and humility. The power consultant has a duty to keep the client's deficits in mind (always with a sense of proportion and respect) and to suggest solutions; but he or she cannot relieve power actors of the responsibility to recognize their deficits and accept the solutions.

The third aspect, *navigation,* was already mentioned in our comparison of the power consultant with a political pilot. Pilots are so well acquainted with a body of water that they can show the captain a safe course or, better yet, several alternative courses to the destination port – past shoals, stormy areas and treacherous currents. Analogous to this, the challenge of navigation for the homo consultans involves, *first,* elucidating the structural risks and opportunities of the political system with regard to the client's goals; and *second,* indicating which paths through this system can lead to these goals and the challenges connected to these various paths. Providing this orientation concerning the strategic constants of power chess is particularly (but not only) relevant to international clients, who are sometimes far removed from the system logic and day-to-day politics of the community and understand their political positioning as part of a global, transnational strategy. This area of responsibility thus includes the concrete, application-oriented clarification of central questions concerning the political system logic, such as: What decision-making power do regional and national governments have in relation to a policy field that is significant for the actor? What is the relationship between the EU decision-making level and the governments of the Member States – and what steps need to be taken at national level to gain influence in the EU?

Which institutional stages does a relevant law go through from its conception to proclamation – and what channels of influence exist at these stages? Above all, what are the effects of these structural specifics on the interests of the actor? The relationship with the aforementioned training is obvious. While the latter is aimed at developing a political mindset on the part of the client, navigation is about using this mindset for orientation in the power field. Safe navigation builds upon successful training.

Navigation as a consulting task is not to be confused with strategy development. The latter is the identification of the ideal causal path (maximum chance of success, minimum costs) to a specific and clearly defined strategic goal, taking into account the strategic environment, i.e.: time horizon, variables and constants (see Chapter 2.5.2); it falls within the scope of condensing (see Chapter 3.3). Navigation is thus the prerequisite for successful strategy development as well as for organization and coordination. By defining the political terrain and its institutional, procedural paths, it lays the foundations for power consultants and power actors to develop and implement a political strategy. Still, another component is indispensable for this: the collection and analysis of information on political, legal and societal developments and topics, and on actors who are relevant to the interests of the client. This core element will be described in more detail in the following section under the second major concept of power leadership – condensing.

3.3 CONDENSING

In the previous section, we outlined the key concept of empowering and the conditions that exist for an understanding of the board in power chess. The focus there was on the internalization of the strategic constants of the overall political field: political logic, political language and political ethos. Now we turn to the concept of condensing the position analysis of power chess. In order to develop game strategies and take control of the game, the power actor must be able to understand specific constellations on the board and to evaluate them in terms of their goals. Such constellations can be assigned to one political subarea or several subareas – we also speak of an *arena* – of the entire field (e.g. transport and infrastructure policy, health policy and digital policy).[31] These arenas consist of four main elements: *firstly,* political actors or stakeholders, their interests and the balance of

---

31 A short note on the terminology. The term *arena* denotes the concrete political action space in which a power actor moves. Within this action space, numerous policy fields or political subdivisions (consumer policy, tax policy, youth protection policy, health

power between them; *secondly,* political issues and points of contention between actors; *thirdly,* specific laws, regulations, standards, etc. of the political arena; and *fourthly,* reform projects, developments and trends in the political arena.

These four elements make up the *strategic variables* of power chess, those factors that, unlike the basic rules, can always change in the course of a game. The goal of condensing is thus to provide continuously updated, compact knowledge of the respective political arena, which enables the power player to assess his or her own situation and form strategies. This means that the homo consultans needs to inform clients about all relevant political and social developments in a quick, compact and understandable way. However, the mere acquisition and mediation of information only forms the first component or the first phase of condensing. Without successive filtering, classification and (probabilistic) assessment, political information has little strategic value. Below we outline our four-phase model of political position analysis. This model cumulates in the development of a policy action plan. It thus forms the hinge between the two guiding principles of political empowering and political influencing.

3.3.1 The Four-Phase Model

The four-phase model presents the various steps of the positional analysis. Each phase involves the analytical enrichment of political data – commencing with the "raw mass" of the pure information, and culmination with the strategic assessment and recommended action.

Phase (1) Monitoring and Intelligence

The first phase of the political position analysis pursues the central question: What do you need to know? This question is by no means banal in relation to the political arena of the actor, especially in the context of the exponential growth in data due to digitization (see Chapters 2.3.2 and 3.2.2). In the days of 24-hour news cycles, there are thousands of agency reports, press releases, news items, commentaries,

---

policy, etc.) can overlap. The more diverse the goals of the power actor and the larger his or her range of action, the larger the number of relevant policy areas usually is. For a digital technology group, not only the field of economic policy is relevant, but also infrastructure policy (for example, in terms of broadband deployment) and research policy (for example, in terms of the cooperative development of artificial intelligence). Positioning yourself successfully in your arena thus means using all relevant policy areas strategically and tactically.

tweets, social media postings, newsletters, and videos of potential political relevance on the web every minute. In addition there is parliamentary printed matter, court judgments, reports from authorities, foundations and NGOs, scientific publications and, of course, verbal communication in personal (technical) conversations, discussions and lectures. In short, for every policy segment – whether consumer protection, finance or agriculture – there is a tremendous amount of information, both apparent facts and evaluations.

The homo consultan's first task is to continuously gather information from the informational political cosmos that is relevant to his or her client's specific arena. This form of selective information gathering is political *monitoring*. The technical implementation of monitoring is discussed in the following section (see Chapter 3.2.2) where we talk about the tools and techniques of compression; here we focus on the core functions of obtaining information. Target-oriented monitoring focuses on the four main elements of political constellations (actors, topics, regulations, developments) and follows a series of key questions: Which activities, statements and controversies characterize the previously selected political arena – and from whom do they originate? What are the dates and deadlines of significant events (for example, elections, committee hearings, technical meetings, parliamentary votes, etc.) – and who will be there? What are the latest statistics and surveys in the arena, for example, as they relate to unemployment, the level of broadband availability, the approval of the European Union, the Brexit issue, sentiments regarding US immigration policies such as DACA (Deferred Action for Childhood Arrivals) or adolescent adiposity? What concrete legislative proposals exist – and what is their status? And so on.

Figure 11: Political Monitoring as a Selection Process

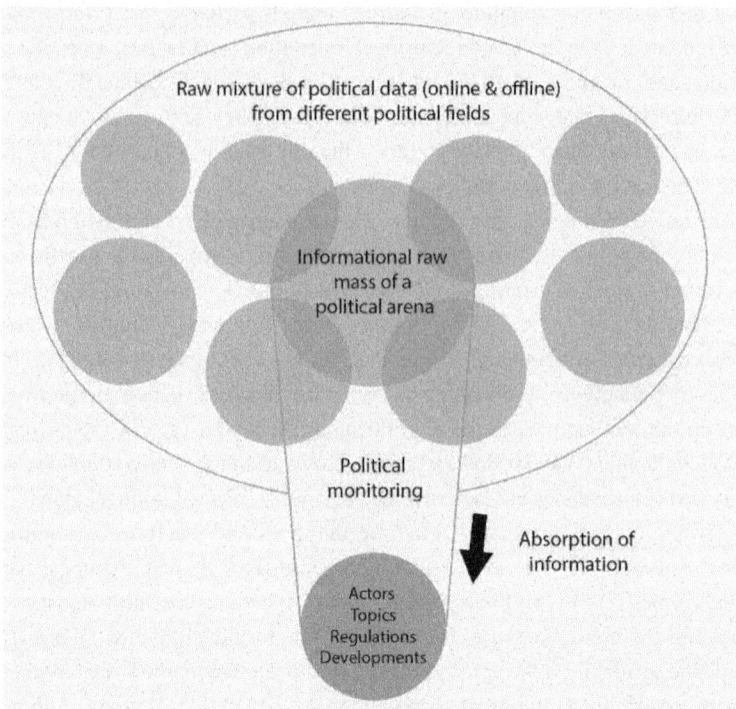

This comprehensive form of data and information gathering from public sources, professional databases and personal contacts is essential for the homo consultans to gain the most detailed picture possible of the arena and to ensure that no potentially significant or explosive information is overlooked. However, this informational raw mass only provides strategic added value for the client as a result of the first stage of analysis: *intelligence*.

The keyword intelligence refers to the combination of filtering and prioritization of the collected information with regard to its relevance for the homo consultandus.

The relevance of information is, *firstly*, a question of its validity: mere rumors (e.g. about reform projects, dismissal of public officials, scandals, etc.) that are anonymously distributed via social media channels are of much lower importance in the compilation of intelligence than facts that are confirmed by more than one reliable source.

Secondly, relevance depends on the power status of the actors. For example, the opinion of a local community chairman of a town in central Hessen as to the alleged risks of GM corn is of far less relevance for a producer of transgenic cereals than a corresponding communiqué from the national Minister of Agriculture. Similarly the comments of the local chapter of the Democratic Party in a yet smaller town in Texas on the alleged risk of global warming to local agriculture would have less impact than a statement by the United States Secretary of Agriculture.

The *third* relevance factor is the impact of the information content on the interests of the power actor: does the issue only affect the power actor's objectives peripherally or does it have such fundamental effects that targets may need to be revised? An example of the latter case is the announcement by New York Governor Andrew Cuomo that from the autumn of 2017, the use of e-cigarettes in restaurants and bars should be banned just as consequentially as that of conventional cigarettes.[32] This regulatory information is of immense significance for tobacco companies that are currently diversifying their product range and need to plan their long-term business development, especially in view of the signal it gives to other US cities.

The definition of relevance criteria is followed by their prioritization. The relevance criteria selected here demonstrate a logical order of priority – validity of information, power status of the actors, and impact of the information on the interests of the power actor. For example, information is of little value if it mentions powerful actors and may have potential implications for the power actor, but the source of the information is unreliable. Information that is not of solid quality can thus be filtered out by the first relevance criterion.

---

32 Cf. Maslin Nir, Sarah (2017), New York State Bans Vaping Anywhere Cigarettes Are Prohibited, in: New York Times from 23th October 2017, [online] https://www.nytimes.com/2017/10/23/nyregion/new-york-bans-vaping-ecigs-bars-restaurants.html, retrieved on 30.1.2018. One also thinks of the Sugary Drinks Portion Cap Rule, the Soda Ban, as proposed by New York City Mayor Michael Bloomberg and his successor Bill de Blasio, aimed at limiting the size of sweetened soft drinks in New York City; it was subsequently repealed in 2015. Cf. Goldberg, Dan (2017): De Blasio sours on tackling sugar, [online] https://www.politico.com/states/new-york/city-hall/story/2017/05/03/de-blasio-sours-on-tackling-sugar-111726, retrieved on 22.05.2018.

Figure 12: Filtering as the First Stage of Intelligence Analysis

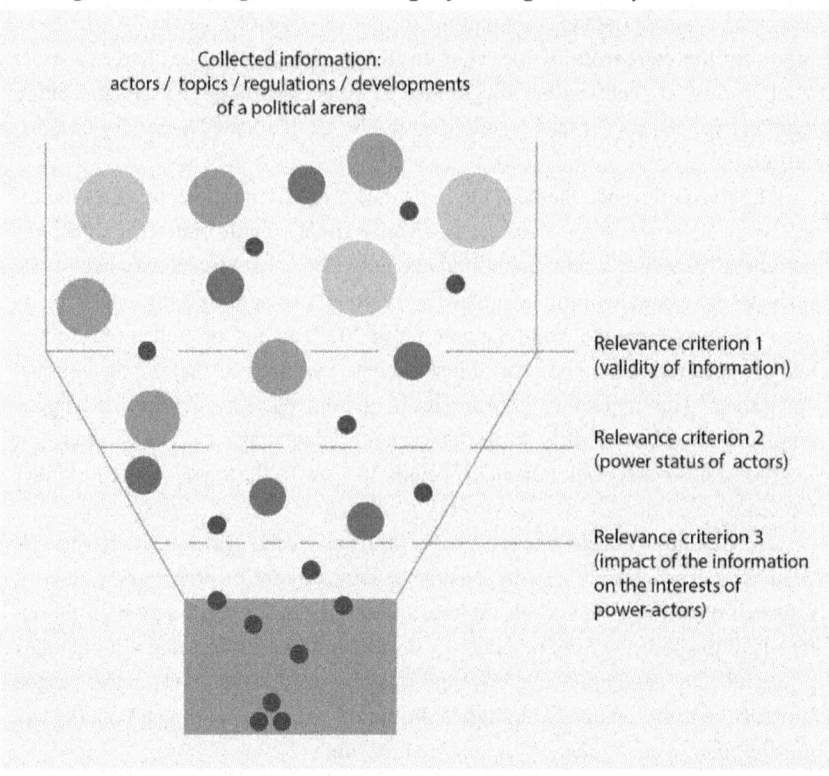

On the basis of these relevance criteria, filtering – as the first stage of intelligence processing – results in the identification of a comparatively small amount of relevant information. In short, filtering focuses on a specific set of information that then becomes the subject of deeper systemization and evaluation. This process requires the power consultant to be practiced in processing large amounts of data quickly, and also to be able to analyze data precisely and client-specifically according to the relevance criteria.

This separation of the proverbial wheat from the chaff is followed by prioritization as the second stage of intelligence processing. Based on the so-called Eisenhower matrix, this method not only structures the data, but can also serve as the basis for subsequent consultancy. Here all the filtered information is evaluated in terms of urgency and importance. The urgency of information is measured by how quickly the consultant has to respond, that is, the timely evaluation and classification of the information. The importance of information assesses the content of the information or its political impact.

The evaluation and sorting of the filtered information results in a four-part categorization, which identifies a small amount of priority information followed by a large amount of subordinate or less urgent information.

Figure 13: Prioritization as the Second Stage of Intelligence Analysis

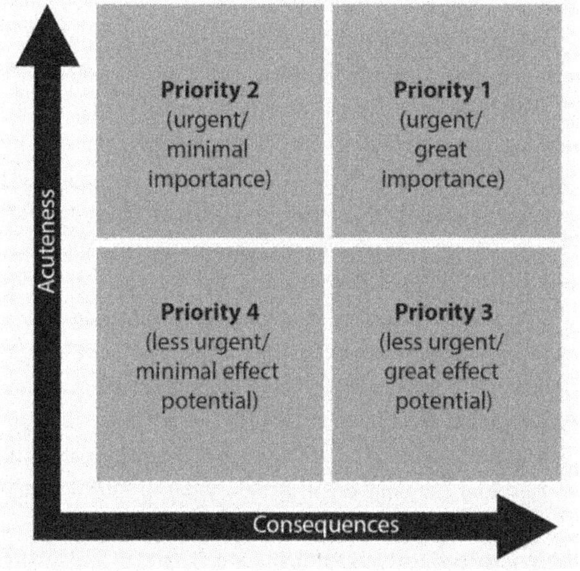

	Acuteness →	
	Priority 2 (urgent/ minimal importance)	**Priority 1** (urgent/ great importance)
	Priority 4 (less urgent/ minimal effect potential)	**Priority 3** (less urgent/ great effect potential)

Consequences →

On the one hand, this continuously updated and hierarchically organized information is vital to ensuring that the power consultant and client are constantly up-to-date with the arena and are able to respond tactically to short-term challenges. This monitoring and intelligence is often referred to as an early warning system. On the other hand, the information is also indispensable for long-term political positioning and strategy building. Thus, unlike the classic Eisenhower matrix, the information categorized in Quadrant 4 is not completely ignored in the consultant's work agenda, but is rather part of the long-term and ongoing policy monitoring of a particular political arena. Specifically, they form the basis or starting point for the second phase of the political position analysis.

Phase (2) Arena Analysis, Stakeholder Identification and Topic Identification

The second phase addresses the key question: Where do you stand? Here the focus is on the precise mapping of the political field of action in which the power actor moves – with regard to legislative and administrative framework conditions; actors or stakeholders from politics, administration, business and civil society who influence the media debate and politics; and discursive topics and issues. In this phase, the previously filtered and prioritized information is condensed into a three-dimensional, political picture of the situation in which the client's position can be pinpointed. The three core functions of this phase – arena analysis, stakeholder identification and topic identification – are not separate processes but are interdependent aspects that supplement one another.

The term "arena analysis" is often used to describe a wide variety of investigations of the socio-political actor environment.[33] We use the concept in a narrower, more concrete sense. *First*, it describes the legally binding rules (laws, regulations governing implementation, directives) and procedural orders at the national and supranational levels which define the scope for action of the actors in the respective policy area or policy areas. *Second*, it includes the relevant international treaties, conventions and protocols – for example the United Nations Framework Convention on Climate Change or the tobacco smuggling protocol of the WHO. *Third*, it describes voluntary standards and conventions, for example, the IT standards of the European Committee for Standardization (CEN) or the German Industry Standards (DIN) or the IBR (incorporated by reference) standards of the American National Standards Institute ANSI). These three categories determine the parameters of the formal system of rules and decision-making for a specific arena; this is therefore the equivalent of the overall political system logic (see Chapter 3.2.1) but as applied to a specific political field.

Accordingly, an arena analysis applied, for example, to broadly focused nature and environmental protection organizations like the National Wildlife Federation (NWF) or NatureServe would describe the most important regulatory areas of federal nature conservation (from the provisions on agriculture and forestry to criteria for planning approval procedures), regulations concerning renewable energy sources, and also the provisions of the chemicals legislation, pollution control and waste management. This is then supplemented by information on the respective legislative responsibilities and decision-making rules for amendments and reforms. A powerful arena analysis thus covers the client's entire range of interests and activities by condensing the rules, norms, standards, etc. of all relevant policy fields (in this case environmental, agricultural, energy and infrastructure policy) into one overall picture or one political map.

Stakeholder identification is not undertaken subsequent to the arena analysis – unlike the relationship between intelligence (filtering and prioritization) and monitoring – but takes place in parallel. Essentially, it involves listing all relevant actors (i.e. organizations and individuals) who are connected with concrete inter

---

33   For an overview, see Köppl (2017): pp. 46ff.

ests to the arena of the client and who can influence politics in that arena directly or indirectly. In the language of the power-chess model, it includes all the figures that make up the concrete play constellation in their positioning relative to one another. Knowledge about these actors is as crucial for the positional analysis as knowledge about the arena's rules and decision-making system: they make up the aggregate of factual or potential allies and opponents, as well as neutral decision-makers. These are the organizations and individuals that the power actor must convince with a powerful communication strategy or from whom it is necessary to be differentiated thanks to unique selling points. However, the mere identification of stakeholders is not yet an evaluation of their strategic potential and goals; that is the subject of the third phase: stakeholder mapping.

Stakeholder identification is divided into the following categories: state actors (government members, MPs, federal agencies, etc.), associations and other bodies governed by public law (e.g. professional self-governments, churches, trade unions), NGOs and non-profit associations and foundations, and finally companies. The extent to which these categories are filled depends largely on the arena of the power actor and his or her goals. Thus, e.g., the political positioning of a producer of alcoholic spirits wanting to improve their position in relation to advertising bans or increased excise taxes will involve numerous stakeholders from the fields of addiction and health policy as well as the main professional associations and financially strong competitors. At the US governmental level, for example, the federal food and drug administration and the Bureau of Alcohol, Tobacco, Firearms and Explosives as well as congressional committees will be relevant. At the association and corporate level, medical associations and health insurances, but also e.g. the brewery associations are pertinent. In the category of non-profit entities, organizations concerned with addiction issues, and at the level of private sector players, global players in the beer and spirits sector come to the fore.

Topic identification is the final element of the second analysis phase. It aims to identify those topics and corresponding theses and arguments that dominate the political discourse of the arena or have the potential to shape it in the future. This class of topics of discussion and disputes is also referred to as *policy issues* in political science and political power consulting. Policy issues can act as a catalyst for fundamental legal reforms or trigger protracted struggles and blockades between different groups, or they can stir up public opinion for or against power actors. Above all, they comprise a set of political content that requires every protagonist in the arena to take a position if they want to participate successfully in shaping politics. These policy issues are highly specific to each policy area. With regard to the important field of digital policy, such key topics are e.g. cyber security and data protection, e-government and e-learning.

Knowing the policy issues of an arena is necessary for the homo consultans for three reasons. First, they determine the scope of content with which they can assert their own interests. If their goals cannot be linked to dominant key issues, or if they cannot be formulated as solutions or answers to related problems, the actor runs the risk of reaching neither decision-makers nor the public. Secondly, because of their potential for mobilization and attention, policy issues are key opportunity and risk factors in the arena. Thus everyday topics of the food discourse, such as sustainability or fair trade, have – since their rapid growth in importance in the 2000s – proved to be major strategic challenges for global food companies such as Nestlé or General Mills. Third, topic identification forms the basis for the power actor to define his or her *unique selling point* (USP). For example, the political USP of a power actor may be the ability to provide an innovative and plausible solution to a policy issue, or a reputation as a credible organization that – unlike its competitors – has been reliably supporting certain core issues for years (see also Section 3.2.3). The USP of Germany's Social Democrats under Gerhard Schröder consisted of the fact that they were the only party in the early 2000s with a credible reform concept for the challenges of the German social system and the labor market – the Agenda 2010. The USP of Bernie Sanders, a serious contender for the office of President of the United States in 2015, was his being "in need of some money." This made him stand out from the mainstream of Democrats and Republicans, parties which support the often very high tuition fees at American universities. The unique feature of the Catholic Church as a power actor, however, is its unrivaled organizational stability and constancy of values and beliefs with regard to moral-political issues. Ultimately, the definition of the USP depends on both the central themes of the political arena and the specific strategic powers or strengths and weaknesses of the power actor. Only if both aspects are synthesized in the positional analysis can a convincing unique selling point be derived.

The core elements of the second phase of political consolidation – arena analysis, stakeholder identification, topic identification – together ensure the classification and systematization of all relevant information in the form of a map of the political arena. This forms the basis for a strategic-probabilistic assessment of the position of the power actor, thus entering the third phase.

Phase (3) Stakeholder Mapping, Network Analysis, Risk Assessment, Scenario Analysis

The third phase focuses on the key question: What can help you, and what can hurt you? Both aspects are aligned. The goal is to determine the opportunities and risks of the strategic environment outlined above for homo consultandus and his or her goals, with regard to three core aspects: strengths and weaknesses of (potential) allies and opponents, strategic potentials and deficits and possible development scenarios of the entire political arena. Once we talk about strengths, weaknesses, opportunities, threats, etc., we abandon the descriptive analysis – which was characteristic of the previous phases – and move into the field of forecasting and probabilities. Thus, the final precursor to strategy formation is achieved through a probability-based goal-means-environment calculation (for the significance of probabilistics for political strategy and the exercise of power see Chapters 1.1 and 2.5.2). The third phase evaluates all previously collected and systematized information in relation to the moves and countermoves the player has to expect in his or her power chess game, assessing the maneuvers that represent a particular risk and the maneuvers from which an advantage can be accrued.

The keyword *stakeholder mapping* covers two blocks of tasks. The *first* includes the ordinal scaling of the other actors in terms of their influence in the arena (from very significant to very insignificant) and their attitude towards homo consultandus or his or her interests (from very positive to very negative).

Figure 14: Scaling of Actors

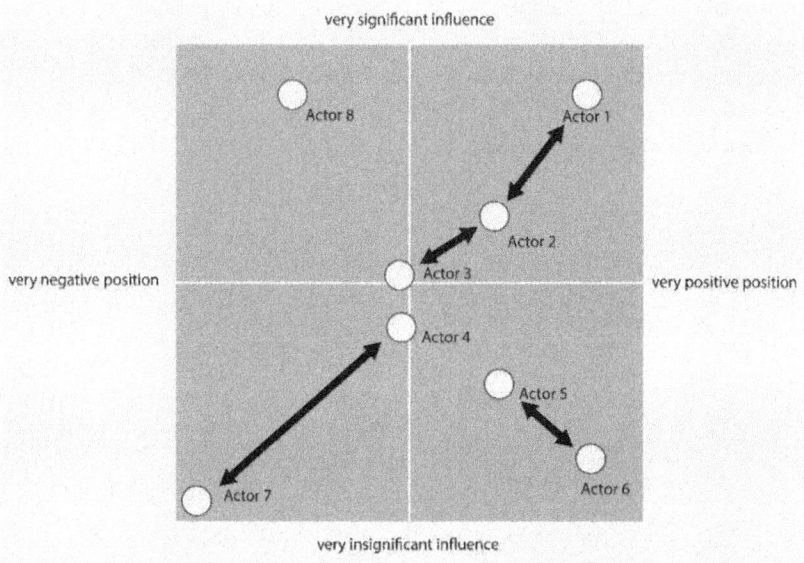

Depending on the specific constellation, this analysis yields up to six classes: strong and weak (potential) allies, strong and weak (potential) opponents, strong and weak neutral players. This two-dimensional scaling is important for strategic positioning as it allows statements about who is useful to homo consultandus in the realization of goals and who may become dangerous, and also determines crucial steps of the policy action plan. Thus it is usually hardly worthwhile to develop a counter-strategy for an organization whose goals are diametrically opposed to one's own but which has little strategic power to enforce their interests against resistance. Powerful neutral actors are strategically relevant in that both sides – opponents and allies – have an interest in attracting them to their side or, at least, not triggering their opposition. For particularly strong opponents, the question arises whether they are best met offensively or defensively or whether the homo consultandus is well advised to avoid the confrontation as completely as possible.

Although this scaling maps the objective power relations it does not depict the interdependencies of the stakeholders. However, these are obviously also strategically relevant: if e.g. the managing director of a – in itself – resource-weak industrial association maintains close links to the senior staff of a powerful administrative institution, they suddenly become important as a political ally. The second task block of stakeholder mapping is therefore the network analysis. It traces cross-links between and within the relevant organizations and reveals the importance of interfaces and multipliers, which are necessarily not captured by two-dimensional scaling. Such connections include formal and informal institutional interconnections (for example, the loose but still tangible political alliance between the NRA and parts of the Republican Party) and also personal ties and friendships, which can sometimes even run counter to political loyalties.

Figure 15: Network Analysis

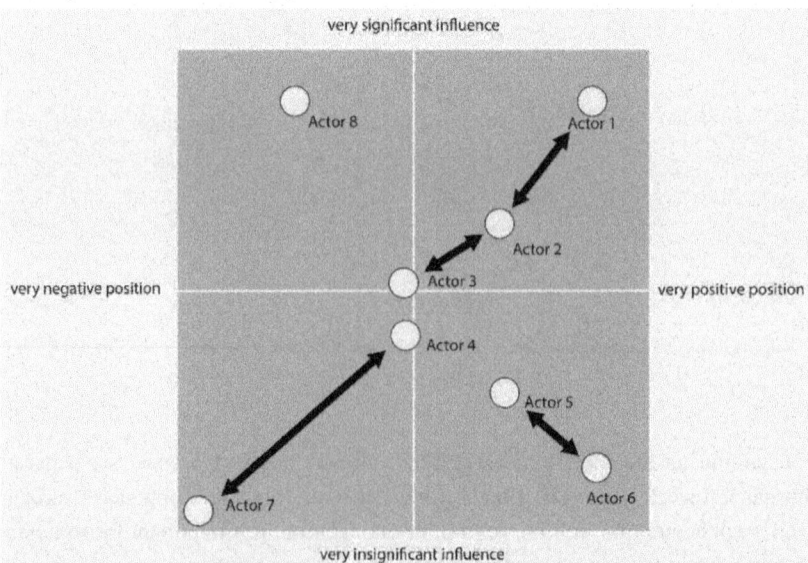

Networks of this type are not only relevant as independent strategic variables. Insofar as the power actor can create and intensify political connections in the course of strategy development and implementation – not only with other actors, but also between them – network building becomes a possible strategic means of establishing one's interests. Decisive for this aspect of stakeholder mapping is thus not only the question of what forms of connections exist between which actors, but also where there are as yet no networks and for what reason. Depending on the nature and extent of the arena and the number of actors, different network analyses may differ greatly in terms of level of detail and density of description, and go far beyond the schematic representation in Figure 15. However, the benchmark remains the reduction of complexity and the establishment of strategic orientation in terms of opportunities and risks. Here the homo consultans has the duty not to overwhelm clients with graphically appealing but confusing diagrams – or to lead them astray with deceptive simplifications.

There are also two core functions associated with the catchword *risk assessment:* on the one hand, the determination of the internal strengths and weaknesses of homo consultandus, i.e. his or her strategic potencies and deficits; on the other hand, the evaluation of external opportunities and threats by means of a probability analysis of political scenarios (for example, legislative processes, public discourse, elections) that positively or negatively affect goals. For example, changes in regulatory conditions have a massive impact on the corporate development of companies. Exemplary for this is the decline of the German solar industry after the drastic curtailment of the photovoltaic subsidy from 2012 and the refusal of the federal government to enter into a competition with China. The two aspects of risk assessment are by no means strictly separate. The external analysis relies decisively on a prior penetration of the internal actor perspective.

The *internal* risk assessment combines the process of condensing and positional analysis with a central element of empowering: organizational consulting (see Chapter 3.2.4). To clarify how well or poorly established the homo consultandus is in his or her arena homo consultans must be very familiar with the organizational structure, the work processes and, in particular, the strategic potential of the client. The client's strengths and weaknesses can be determined using the categories of strategic potencies described in Chapter 2.5.2. Here the rule of thumb is that every potency greater than the average of the other players in the political arena is a strength and any below-average potency is a weakness.[34]

---

34 The comparison with the average values of the potencies of strategic actors in an arena is crucial. Strengths and weaknesses are relational categories, i.e. an actor is always

We distinguish among seven different types of strategic powers (and corresponding strengths and weaknesses):

1. *Organizational capability*: the capability to set clear strategic goals and make corresponding decisions.
2. *Mobilization capability*: the capability to activate different groups of people (voters, members, clients, believers, patients, etc.) to enforce strategic interests.
3. *Network capability*: the ability to forge alliances with other actors to increase the reach of one's own concerns and/or to increase credibility.
4. *Mediation capability:* the capability to communicate those concerns that are relevant to one's own goals in a targeted and convincing manner to individuals and organizations.
5. *Fame:* public attention combined with acknowledgment of proven power competence, power knowledge and power itself.
6. *Financial potency:* monetary resources for staff, infrastructure, campaigns, etc.
7. *Willingness to make a sacrifice:* the motivation to accept deprivation and take risks in pursuit of strategic goals.

The challenge for the power consultant is not only to identify the strengths and weaknesses of the client in relation to these seven categories, but above all to relate them to their strategic environment. External opportunities and threats – that which helps homo consultandus and that which can hurt him or her – are not purely exogenous factors that simply occur. They arise from the meeting of the strengths and weaknesses of the power actor with the elements (topics, actors, trends, etc.) of his or her field of action. Thus, e.g. a discourse characterized by highly moralized policy issues (such as drug or gambling policies) is a strategic threat, especially if homo consultandus has little ability to mediate or is incapable of substantiating a position with credible arguments. The severity of other risk factors, such as a broad alliance of well-connected and financially strong opponents, in turn, strongly depends on whether the networking ability and the financial power of homo consultandus are above average or not. And in some strategic contexts, even perceived weaknesses may turn out to be opportunities and vice versa. For example, the less than glorious (according to our taxonomy – that is, politically inexperienced and previously without major achievements) Austrian politician Sebastian

---

strong or weak relative to a variable set of other actors. He or she is never strong or weak in any absolute or non-relative sense.

Kurz of the Austrian People's Party (ÖVP) was successful in the Austrian elections of 2017, beating his rival, Christian Kern of the Social Democratic Party of Austria (SPÖ), because he was perceived as a 'newcomer' and 'blank slate' in a climate characterized by skepticism of elites.

In short, the assessment of player-specific opportunities and threats requires the power consultant to, first, know the client and his or her interests, strengths and weaknesses; second, to locate the client in the context of the relevant political arena, rule system and policy issues; and third, to assess the client in terms of his or her power-strategic relationships with other players and networks.

This knowledge is also the prerequisite for a precise *scenario analysis.* A scenario analysis is basically a prognostic statement about political and/or economic, media and cultural developments in an arena and their expected impact on the interests of the homo consultandus and those of the other actors. It comprises three elements: an inventory of the status quo; at least two alternative and mutually exclusive scenarios, including probability of occurrence and probable effects; and a time frame for the forecast. Each scenario analysis makes three predictions: first, the probability of a particular scenario occurring; second, the likelihood that the scenario will have – if it happens – effects of a particular type; third, that if the scenario occurs it will do so within a specified time frame. This analysis can be applied to a wide range of issues, from parliamentary elections and their implications for politics, business and civil society, to sectoral development in terms of the concentration or diffusion of market power, to individual legislative reform projects.

Figure 16: Scenario Analysis, Schematic Presentation

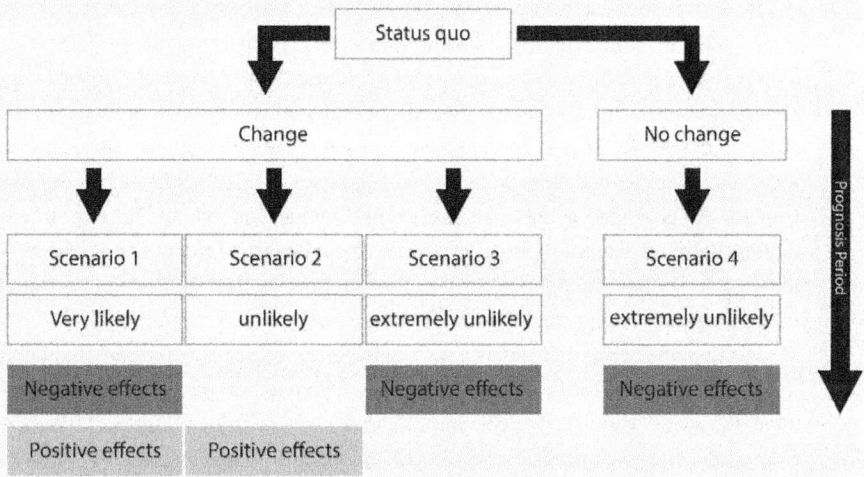

The relevance of scenario analysis for strategic positioning has a *passive* and an *active* dimension. The passive dimension involves the homo consultandus being enabled to organize protection against impairments to his or her interests (coalition negotiations with difficult partners, intensification of competition in a competitive market segment, higher taxes on certain services, etc.) or to make the most of opportunities (a new, more business-friendly government, the emergence of new markets, increased public attention for the concerns of NGOs etc.). In short, once the client is able to gauge what is likely to happen within a clearly demarcated timeframe – and what is not – he or she can better assess how to *react* to it.

The active dimension, on the other hand, involves, firstly, the client being able to exercise a more targeted influence on developments in the arena and shape them in his or her interests. A strategic risk is not simply given. Once identified, the homo consultandus can assess whether – and if so, how – the risk can be reduced, i.e. how he or she has to act. The scenario analysis thus influences the active steps of the political strategy (discussions with decision-makers and stakeholders, development and control of topics, etc.). Secondly, the active dimension derives from insights into how homo consultandus can use resources more efficiently by identifying achievable and unattainable goals. If the analysis shows that one of two scenarios is extremely unlikely, the power actor can spend most resources on influencing the more likely scenario or adapting to its effects. If, for instance, an EU regulation would entail a high logistical adjustment for a particular industry but is already massively supported by the majority of EU states, it is perhaps no longer a rational option for the industry association to lobby directly against the regulation. Instead, it may be better to focus energy on the resource-efficient implementation of the new standards and to anticipate further regulatory tightening.

However, scenario analyses only develop these benefits if they are *valid*, i.e. if they stand on a methodologically and substantively sound foundation. This does not mean that they have to produce exact percentages or even deterministic statements (if event x occurs, necessarily also event y must occur) – in any case the political power field is too complex and characterized by too many unpredictable imponderables, so-called 'wild cards' (see Chapter 2.5.2) for this to be possible. Instead, the goal is to achieve a significantly higher than average hit rate in predicting political scenarios. In other words, the analysis of the political expert is only worth something if it is clearly superior to the level of interested lay people in the long term and is supported by reliable evidence.

For this, the homo consultans has to consider a number of conditions and quality criteria. *First*, before concrete probability forecasts can be set up for development scenarios, it must be clear that the analysis covers all plausible scenarios. One of the biggest jokes of geopolitical forecasting is the inability of Western power consultants, political scientists, military strategists and intelligence officials to predict the collapse of the USSR in the 1980s.[35] The problem was not that they considered the collapse of the giant empire unlikely – they did not even have the event 'on their radar' and therefore did not assign it a probability value. Constructing plausible scenarios is thus a creative act that requires the power consultant not only to have detailed knowledge of the arena and its actors, but also so-called 'out of the box thinking' – i.e. the ability to question habitual thought patterns, predictions, stereotypes, etc. and to assess the client's strategic environment in an unbiased manner.

Second, homo consultans not only needs to know the actual state of the political arena, but also its history. For example, anyone who remembers the power-political marginalization of the FPD in the Merkel II cabinet from 2009 to 2013 and the accompanying grievances and loss of trust, was likely to be less surprised by the failure of the so-called Jamaica coalition talks between Christian Democrats, Liberals and Greens after the 2017 federal elections in Germany. Familiarity with the previous development of the arena is also indispensable because it allows the establishment of parallels or the derivation of laws. Contrary to Mark Twain's statement that history does not repeat itself, most of political and/or economic scenarios are by no means unique, but are merely variations of certain basic types with which homo consultans has to become familiar.

Third, the power consultant must not only know the relevant strategic constants (political logic, procedural rules, etc.) and variables (strategic powers, interests, policy issues, etc.), but also be able to evaluate them probabilistically. The homo consultans must, e.g., be able to assess whether the threat of a Minister-President not to ratify a joint treaty of the German states if his or her demands concerning the content of the contract remain unfulfilled, is credible or just a bluff. This ability depends on political experience, human understanding and a deeper understanding of the economics of threats and promises (see our discussion of instrumental power in Chapter 2.1).

Finally, the *fourth* point is that the homo consultans must take into account the temporal dimension of predictions. Basically, the longer the period for which scenario forecasts are set up, the higher the probability of errors. The statistician and election researcher Nate Silver calls this critical time factor "scenario uncertainty."[36] This uncertainty is also compounded by an increasing number of actors and controversial policy issues. Especially in arenas located at the intersection of

---

35   Cf. Silver, Nate (2012): *The Signal and the Noise: Why Most Predictions Fail – but Some Don't*, New York: Penguin Books.
36   Cf. Silver (2012): p. 392.

numerous, heterogeneous policy fields and used by various protagonists, extremely long-term forecasts (for example, over a period of more than 15 years) often turn out to be a gamble. Especially global players with tens of thousands or even hundreds of thousands of employees and billions of dollars have a particular interest in long-term forecasts because their sheer size makes fast tactical action and reaction difficult; here the homo consultans must master the tightrope walk between rebellion and humility (see Chapter 3.2.3) and highlight not only the potentials of political scenario analyses but also their limitations.

Phase (4) Strategy Building

The development of a political strategy forms the conclusion of the four-phase model and the accumulation point of the previous phases of the position analysis. Here all filtered, systematized and probabilistically evaluated information are condensed into a concrete action plan.

Figure 17: The Four-Phase Model

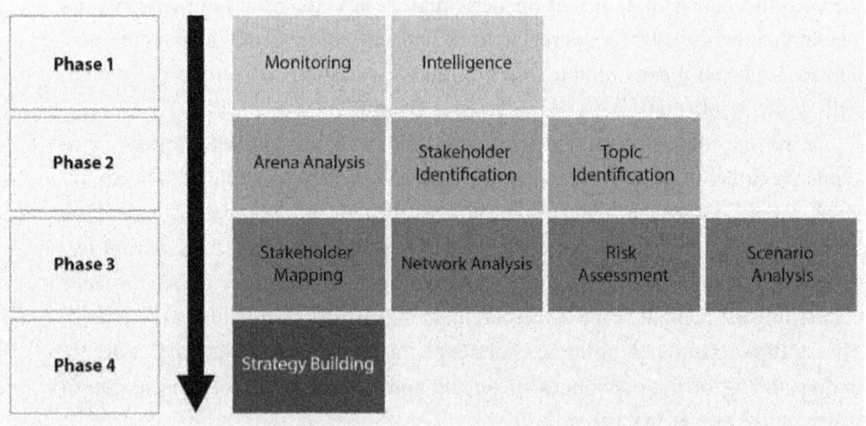

Phase 1	Monitoring	Intelligence		
Phase 2	Arena Analysis	Stakeholder Identification	Topic Identification	
Phase 3	Stakeholder Mapping	Network Analysis	Risk Assessment	Scenario Analysis
Phase 4	Strategy Building			

The focus of the fourth phase is on the concrete recommendation for action by homo consultans. It can thus be summarized in one practical key question: What should you do? Of course, this does not involve (primarily) the recommendation of one individual and situative – that is to say tactical – action, but is rather a situation-independent action calculus. This calculus defines a medium to long-term political goal (for example re-election as Chancellor, reform of federal-state competences, introduction of new, coordinated primary care for patients, legalization of marijuana). It takes into account current monitoring and intelligence results, information and probabilistic evaluations concerning the political arena (as well as the client's powers, stakeholders, topics and scenarios), and determines a cost and benefit-optimized causal path to the goal. The determination of the goal and the path together make up the strategy. At this point, the previously acquired political knowledge is implemented through well-planned, effective and efficient policy design.

In Chapter 2.5, we comprehensively discussed our strategy concept from strategy foundations and capabilities to strategy development and strategic steering. The key challenge is to define a goal that is realistic in terms of the client's potencies in relation to those of others in the arena, and to set a precise timetable with specific but adaptable stages and a clear and efficient decision-making hierarchy. Every political strategy is a planned exercise of power – it determines who is supposed to achieve what when, by what means against which resistance, and how to deal with imponderables in the achievement of goals. In order to not repeat ourselves (see rather Chapter 2.5), we intend to keep our general discussion of strategy as a power technique short. Instead, we focus on the essential components of political strategy: alliance building, thematic governance, and dialogue. These basic elements form the DNA of each action plan. The differences between individual plans exist solely in their combinatorics and concrete execution.

Anyone who wants to achieve a goal in the political arena must always rely on allies to compensate for strategic deficits (e.g. lack of financial power, mobilization or organizational capability) and to increase the reach of their concerns by tapping into additional groups of addressees or networks. Moreover, those who do not actively seek allies run the risk of being isolated in their political arena, both in terms of information gathering and policymaking. Therefore, *alliance building* is a core element of any policy action plan, regardless of the concrete goal or power of homo consultandus. The successive formation of ad hoc alliances (which are limited to the concrete achievement of particular goals) or of long-term networks often represents a starting point for strategy development. Here, overlaps with the interests of other people and organizations are considered, synergies and know-how and expertise are identified, and risks from the strategic deficiencies of potential partners (such as a problematic reputation, numerous opponents in the arena, a lack of trustworthiness) are assessed and evaluated. On the basis of this, contacts will be intensified, cooperation structures established and joint control mechanisms for the alliances implemented. All these steps therefore require a precise arena and network analysis as well as stakeholder mapping. Crucial to strategy development in this context is the insight that political alliances are not self-perpetuating: personal relationships, the cornerstone of any stable alliance, must be nurtured. The values and interests of the cooperation partners must be continuously reviewed and maintained. Otherwise, however well-planned the strategy may be, it will fail due to conflicting objectives between the actors.

While alliance building aims to optimize the actor's position in the arena relative to other actors, *thematic governance* is about positioning oneself in relation to dominant policy issues or future challenges, developing targeted messages and putting key issues on the political agenda and anchoring them in the media discourse. The targeted placement of new topics and the associated generation of attention are often referred to in this context as *agenda setting*, while addressing topics that are already influencing the discourse and using them to pursue one's own communication goals is termed *agenda surfing*. Whereas agenda setting requires a longer-term planning process, not least involving an assessment of the responsiveness of the target audience to different potential messages (e.g. through quantitative or qualitative studies or focus groups), successful agenda surfing requires a good sense for the right time to seize upon a topic and the tactical flexibility to react quickly before the proverbial 'wave of public attention" subsides.

The strategic relevance of thematic governance arises from the fact that the exercise of power in democracies is linked to an obligation for argumentative justification (see Chapter 2.4 and Chapter 3.2.2). Those who cannot provide plausible justification for their political goals and who are unable to establish a connection between their own preferences and the common good will not gain public acceptance or support from other actors for their strategy. Thematic governance does not mean, however, developing messages that are invariably acceptable to all the protagonists of the power field. Such a requirement would be completely unrealistic in our pluralistic societies.

Instead, plausible messages must *firstly* be credible, i.e. convincingly match the profile of homo consultandus, their values, beliefs and history. A medium-sized cigar and cigarillo producer can, for example, credibly portray themselves as representing a worthy manufacturing tradition and sophisticated culture in their political positioning strategy. But such a portrayal would be impossible for a global cigarette manufacturer.

Secondly, the messages must link the client's USP to the arena's prevailing policy issues. Strategic thematic governance is sensitive to the concerns, hopes, fears and expectations of community members in the various policy fields, and is based on a clear awareness of the strengths and weaknesses of homo consultandus. A negative example is the strategic communication planning of the SPD Bundestag election campaign of 2017. A unique selling point of the Social Democrat chancellor candidate, Martin Schulz, was his European political expertise as a long-time President of the European Parliament. Instead of capitalizing on this USP and deducing the European policy relevance of issues such as migration and internal security, Schulz's EU past was ignored in favor of his position as 'Mayor of Würselen' a smallish town in the westernmost part of Germany. Thus, the Social Democrats failed to emphasise an important characteristic that would have provided differentiation from the CDU.

Another example is provided by Jeb Bush, one-time governor of Florida, USA, and his failed campaign for the Republican nomination for the 2016 presidential election. Key term in this regard was the concept of detaching Jeb from his brother's policies, most prominently the 2003 Iraq War. His campaign had the opportunity to emphasize its achievements in educational policy and crisis management for natural disasters, for example. Unlike many governors, Bush was very focused on education reform throughout his tenure. He set up Florida's first state-wide voucher program, expanded charter schools and established standardized testing. In other words, his campaign had the chance to capitalize on grievances that were relevant to Trump voters, but they were only relevant to small parts of the Republican electorate.

The *third* criterion is that the message must be appropriate to the addressee. As we discussed in Chapter 3.2.2, the communicated political positions must not only correspond with the interests of the addressee but, above all, with their language and professional knowledge. For example, the authorization of pain medications necessarily involves a complex evaluation and administration process for drug companies. The integration of patient associations and self-help groups in these central processes requires immense simplification and a focus on the core issues.

In addition to these three substantive aspects thematic governance has an important formal side – namely the question of through which channels and in which formats messages should be communicated to their addressees. In our section on communication logic in Chapter 3.2.1 we discussed in detail the requirements of political mediation and the dichotomy of analogue and digital channels; accordingly, we can be brief at this point. We have noted that in the course of digitization, the communicative cosmos has become more plural, faster, more volatile and increasingly empty of content. These trends make topic-setting and mediation more challenging and strategy-building more complex. The challenge is not only to generate attention and interest in one's own policy issues but also to retain it. There is no strategic recipe for this. However, we can say that digital and analogue media are not exclusive to one another but are complementary tools in this task. In particular, broad-based communication strategies, which are aimed not at a narrow target audience but at a variety of stakeholders, must be both online and offline. A one-sided digital or analogue focus not only fails to address certain generational cohorts but can make the fatal impression that the homo consultandus is deliberately ignoring these groups.

The choice and design of communicative formats are equally important decisions within thematic governance. The timely launch and intuitive ease of use of a campaign website can determine the success or failure of a strategy, as can the graphic design of a brochure or the argumentative plausibility and research quality of a position paper. Strategy development here thus involves combining messages, channels and formats appropriate to the addressees, policy issues and USP of the homo consultandus to create a coherent overall design.

The third basic element of strategy development, *dialogue*, consists of the purposeful planning of talks and discussions with the relevant players in the arena. As with alliance building and thematic goovernance, it is a universal building block of the strategy. Political design lives not only from powerful alliances and appropriately addressed topics, but also from personal exchanges – be it at parliamentary evenings, podium discussions, citizen forums or one-on-one meetings. Through this exchange, confidence and empathy can be built; dialogue promotes the mutual understanding of others' interests and goals more than any other form of communication. Thus, dialogue serves to personally persuade others of the value of one's own goals and to convey information, but also to reflect on the legitimate interests of the interlocutor and to include them in one's own strategy formation.

The type and number of interlocutors and the design of the dialogues differ significantly depending on the strategic goal. If, for example, a medium-sized business alliance is working towards the construction of a tram stop in its commercial park, dialogue planning primarily includes discussions with local actors: from citizens' initiatives wishing to upgrade an adjacent residential area, to district mayors and members of district councils, to the responsible transport companies. Ideally, these dialogues will gradually consolidate in the form of regular round tables or coordination days, which in turn can influence higher political decision-making levels. Compared to this, global corporations, because of their economic status and their influence, already enter into dialogue at a higher level of decision-making. Regardless of questions of power and status, however, all forms of dialogue are valid: the more comprehensively homo consultandus is informed about his or her interlocutors (and their responsibilities, interests, beliefs, abilities and scheduling), the greater the chance of successfully understanding strategically relevant positions. This statement may seem rather obvious, but it underlines the immense importance of intelligence gathering for the strategy; without a reliable informational foundation, dialogue is blind. Since as part of strategy development, the power consultant must plan in advance who has to talk to whom at what time, he or she must know both relevant topics and dates as well as the characteristics of the interlocutors.

As mentioned earlier, alliance building, thematic governance and dialogue are the universal DNA of any political strategy. The key question of strategy building – What should you do? – is always answered in terms of these three elements. In this context, the power consultant faces the threefold challenge of *concretization*, *timing* and *coordination*. The consultant must plan: (a) when and with which specific actors alliances must be forged and for what purpose, (b) which thematic-argumentative emphases are set in the arena and when they are transmitted via which channels, (c) which dialogues are held with which interlocutor when; and must also (d) coordinate these building blocks of overall political strategy.

In view of this range of tasks, it is worthwhile revisiting Raschke & Tils' assessment mentioned in Chapter 2.5.2: "Forming a strategy is a great cognitive and creative challenge if you do not rely solely on your gut feeling."[37] Precisely because the development of a political strategy is a creative act, it is not possible to provide a schematic guide to tackle this challenge. Each strategy is based on the same elements, but each remains unique. Their development requires experience and competence, power knowledge and an in-depth familiarity with the instruments of political influence – that is, a mastery of the three great vectors of power which we described in Chapter 2. It should be clear from the sketch of the four-phase model that a profound level of information and knowledge about actors, topics, arenas, etc. is also indispensable for the planned exercising of political power. If the three questions –- What do you need to know? Where do you stand? What can help you and what can happen to you? – are answered plausibly, then decisive prerequisites are fulfilled for providing a convincing answer to the practical question of strategy – What should you do?

3.3.2 Tools and Techniques of Condensing

As we have seen, condensing as a guiding principle of the power leadership curriculum covers three thematic priorities: information, analysis and strategy. The methods used to address these focal points are as different as the priorities themselves. Most of them have already been explicitly or implicitly discussed in our description of the four-phase model. Here we want to briefly summarize and systematize the resources of the power consultant again.

Collecting information was for a long time one of the most time-consuming and burdensome challenges for the political power consultant. Until the 2000s, this task involved the daily manual scanning of hundreds of news items, press

---

37   Cf. Raschke & Tils (2008): p. 19.

releases, draft bills and court rulings. Only in recent years has the digital revolution brought forth web crawlers, which scour the internet via text mining, social media mining and other specialized search forms, leading to a paradigm shift (see also our discussion of data power in Chapter 2.3.2). Effectively deployed monitoring software and intelligent bots can filter through the bulk of arena-relevant information from news sites, institution and company homepages, online editions of trade journals, etc., in seconds, generating output for which a power consultant would need hours. However, policy-oriented crawlers need to have over 98% probability of indexing relevant websites to ensure that the homo consultans is actually up-to-date with the arena in question. In addition, linguistic problems have to be solved, especially with regard to monitoring services that extend to various nations. Thus, e.g. German does not correspond to English in terms of syntax and grammar, not to mention the potential pitfalls provided by more distant languages such as Chinese or Arabic.

The use of this indispensable digital tool of compression, which is usually combined with professional databases on political institutions and actors, requires a completely new skill profile from the homo consultans. Instead of diligent work in obtaining information, there is an increasing need for digital know-how and a deep understanding of political language and semantics. The best software agent is only as powerful as the search terms (including synonyms, slang words and hints) and the search strings with which it is programmed and fed.

Despite this rapid informational paradigm shift, it is not yet possible to outsource the actual intelligence and analysis tasks to computerized algorithms. Here, the power consultant has the key function of prioritizing and classifying the collected policy information for homo consultandus, e.g. in the form of policy alerts on daily topics, daily updates or weekly and monthly reports. The quality of these intelligence services depends not least on the judgment with which the power consultant can assess the relevance and validity of information and how well he or she is able to structure and condense it in a manner that is comprehensible for the client. Ideally, homo consultandus receives compressed information that, firstly, refreshes his or her political background knowledge, secondly, can trigger concrete activities, and thirdly, represents the basis for a (re)alignment of strategic positioning in the arena and with respect to people and content.

In comparison, the central tools of policy analysis – from the arena and its stakeholders to complete scenarios – are borrowed from the methods of project management. Insofar as the core issue is always determining the position of homo consultandus in relation to the strategic environment, numerous instruments borrowed from management literature, such as the SWOT table, the stakeholder issue interaction diagram and other management tools are relevant.[38] We focus here on two highlights. The classic SWOT analysis can be used to determine the current state of the client's political positioning. It depicts internal strengths and weaknesses and external threats and opportunities (SWOT stands for: Strengths, Weaknesses, Opportunities, Threats) in the political arena, including possible legislative changes and regulatory initiatives as well as the product or service range of a group.

Figure 18: SWOT Matrix

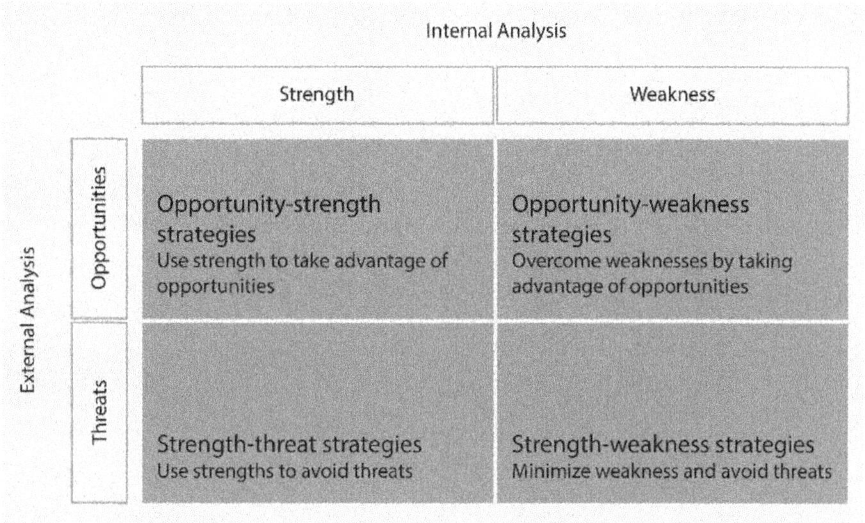

		Internal Analysis	
		Strength	Weakness
External Analysis	Opportunities	**Opportunity-strength strategies** Use strength to take advantage of opportunities	**Opportunity-weakness strategies** Overcome weaknesses by taking advantage of opportunities
	Threats	**Strength-threat strategies** Use strengths to avoid threats	**Strength-weakness strategies** Minimize weakness and avoid threats

In contrast thereto, a *stakeholder issue interrelationship* diagram reconstructs the attitudes of other influential actors to the topics that dominate discourse in the arena. It is therefore an analysis tool that combines the elements of stakeholder mapping with those of topic identification and condenses them to create a clear, strategic picture of the situation. In this way, it illustrates, on the one hand, the relative importance of policy issues and, on the other hand, the connections, potential synergies and conflict potentials between the protagonists of the power field. The diagram provides the homo consultans with orientation as to which content he or she must relate to and how the political arena is structured beyond the mere power relations and networks of the actors.

---

38 For a more in-depth analysis, see i.a. Bryson, John M. (2004): What To Do When Stakeholders Matter. Stakeholder Identification and Analysis Techniques, *Public Management Review*, 6 (1), pp. 21-53.

Figure 19: Stakeholder Issue Interrelation Diagram

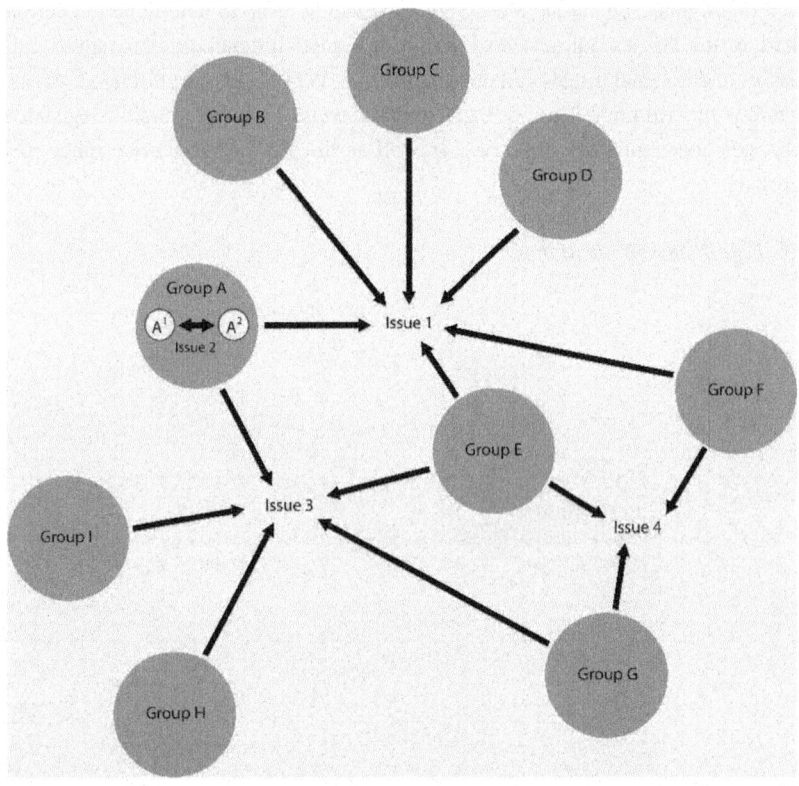

Source: Bryant (2003): p. 196

These and similar analysis tools are key to creating the foundations for policy development. While the homo consultans often conducts political analyses and evaluations as 'preparatory work' and only communicates the essential results and assessments to the homo consultandus, the development of the actual strategy is always a collaborative activity undertaken by the power actor and the power consultant. The consulting tool of choice here is the *strategy workshop*. The interactive and usually multi-hour workshop or dialogue format is indispensable for a number of reasons. First, because it allows both sides to agree on strategic goals; second, because it offers the opportunity to compare inside and outside perspectives on the potentials and deficiencies of the power actor; and third, because it creates the conditions for an action plan that is mutually endorsed by homo consultandus and homo consultans. A key challenge for the power consultant is the much-discussed tightrope walk between rebellion and humility. Strategies that look perfect on homo consultans's drawing board but to which the client only responds with a frown of disbelief – perhaps because they do not reflect his or her political self-image, represent a radical break with important traditions or are simply too complex and technically challenging – are ultimately not practicable. The same applies to approaches that may reflect all the preferences of homo consultandus and fit exactly with his or her political ideology or corporate philosophy, but are not covered by a sound risk assessment or a realistic arena analysis. Here the power consultant is called upon to establish a strategic agreement through professionalism and empathy.

Strategy development is the bridge between the consolidation of political information and knowledge on the one hand and concrete policymaking on the other. Only when the strategy is implemented by tactical savvy, motivated and efficient people and organizations, can the homo consultandus can take control of the game of power chess. The great German soccer coach Alfred Preißler very strikingly paraphrased an old Faust quotation: "All theory is grey – what matters is what's on the field."[39] In the following section, we therefore go directly to the political playing field and clarify the guiding principle of political influence and the organizational practice of exercising power.

3.4 INFLUENCING

Political influence, the concrete exercise of power in the field of politics through interaction with organizations and persons, is the litmus test for the previous empowering and condensing. Only if the first two elements of the power leadership approach have been implemented effectively can homo consultandus and homo consultans jointly take control of the game of power chess. This applies equally to both forms of the approach – political leadership and lobbying leadership. What it means to successfully influence politics depends entirely on the goals of the power actor: re-election to a post, organizing a voting majority, revising a directive, averting regulatory restrictions, legalizing a product, subsidizing an industrial sector, or implementing a new business development calculus. Planned policy influencing always involves transforming a power strategy into an actual event by the purposeful use of power leadership tools.

---

39 Cf. The original quote by Preißler – "Grau is' alle Theorie – entscheidend is'auf'm Platz", in: Westdeutsche Allgemeine Zeitung from 7th April 2015.

This reveals the dominant focus of this section. Political influencing is 'only' about the practical implementation of a strategy and the organizing and coordinating of the relevant action steps, thus in this section we briefly describe the guiding principle of influencing with its instruments, methods and techniques. The essential tools used for influencing have already been detailed in Chapters 3.2 and 3.3. Their scope is ultimately slim and minimalistic. For the sake of clarity, it can be summarized in tabular form:

Figure 20: Tools of Political Influencing

Team Composition	Coordination
Task distribution and definition of a decision hierarchy within the strategic project team	Creation of a timetable for the strategic project and management of the relevant schedules
Political Talks and Formats	**Stakeholder Dialogues**
Contacting decision makers and organizing discussion formats (Roundtables, Panel Discussions, One-on-Ones, Parliamentary Evenings, Breakfast Debates, etc.)	Contact relevant stakeholders and organize exchanges on positions, interests and perspectives
Alliance Building	**Campaigning and Mobilizing**
Active formation of partnerships in the pre-political and political area (ad-hoc alliance, permanent alliance, founding of an association, etc.)	Target-oriented development and steering of political key messages via relevant communication channels (online, offline)

It is already clear from this set of tools that the power consultant performs numerous management functions in parallel during the design phase, acting as a project manager, event manager, communications manager and customer manager. Each of these roles has its own tasks and responsibilities. Exercising all these functions requires sensitivity for power relations, discretion and, not least, a social instinct, for instance in deciding how to address a particular conversation partner.

Setting up a team and coordinating between homo consultandus and homo consultans involves the classical tasks of project and customer management. Here the power consultant requires the ability to manage personnel and to define solid, stable and clear work packages, as well as conscientious time management. In the daily work process, regular telephone or video conferencing with the client (and, where applicable, the client's partners) must be organized in order to discuss the implementation status of the strategy and acute, tactical and organizational requirements. The power consultant or project team prepares and adjusts the agendas, moderates the conferences, and then summarizes the results. In addition, internal meetings and workshops must also be planned and prepared. Professionalism and sensitivity are required not only with regard to content here, but also as concerns the organizational side: from the daily agenda to route descriptions to the provision of technical infrastructure (beamer, laser pointer, WiFi connection, etc.) to catering.

There are numerous operational challenges in this area that call for strong nerves and routine: problems getting hold of interlocutors, scheduling overlaps and shifts, short-term changes to plans or trivial technical problems, such as the failure of conferencing software. These challenges are more pronounced and serious, since the individuals involved are usually active on a high hierarchical level in their organizations and have little time. Accordingly, the homo consultans is subject to double pressure in the performance of the coordinative tasks: the precious time of both his or her own team and that of the client must be used to maximum efficiency.

The role of an event manager in the political field, on the other hand, comes with the planning and implementation of political discussion formats – with state decision-makers as well as with stakeholders from business, civil society, science and culture. Organizing such an event (for example, a parliamentary breakfast, a charity event or a multi-session conference) is a highly political act: Who is invited? Who should sit where? In what order are the guests presented? What background information should be provided in advance? What content is presented how? These practical questions need to be clarified in light of the results of intelligence processing, stakeholder mapping, network analysis and other condensing tools (see Chapter 3.3.1). Only when condensing and influencing are seamlessly interlinked can an event be a success.

Political event management is not exhausted in ensuring the right composition of guests and interlocutors and maintaining and updating the corresponding mailing lists. Even the choice of appointment can sometimes prove challenging. On the one hand, it is necessary to plan in accordance with the rhythms of political business (session weeks, committee meetings of Congress, parliaments, EU Council meetings, etc.) and major political events (elections, coalition negotiations, referendums, G20 summit, etc.). On the other hand, the extreme density of events during these high phases of business operation must be taken into account. For example, during the weeks when the German Bundestag sits there are around 700 evening events of political relevance every day. Accordingly, homo consultans usually has to be prepared for and able to deal with very high no-show rates at events. In addition short-term cancellations by keynote speakers, celebrity guests or subject matter experts are not uncommon. To compensate for such no-shows – for example, by subsequently inviting new participants or by persuading the undecided – hundreds of phone calls are often required. Those who are unable to remain both conciliatory and determined under time pressure are unsuited to the tasks of the power consultant.

Both alliance building and campaign leadership demand that the power consultant use the talents of a communication manager and communicator. In both cases, the focus is on communicating content and topics, and on creating trust and credibility and attracting attention. The initiation of political alliances calls for communicative empathy and the ability to use present knowledge about the contact person to build common ground; this can be found in the shared awareness of certain pressing political issues, but also in personal connections, such as an enthusiasm for craft beer or literature. When building alliances, the definition of the initiators is of paramount importance, as well as the decision as to whether it is an open or closed initiative. The success or failure of political alliances depends to more than 80% on their structure and the clarification of such issues.

Political campaign mobilization, in turn, requires a high degree of sensitivity to ongoing changes in the communications environment. Precisely because campaigns cannot be linearly planned and implemented, the power consultant must be able to keep a finger on the pulse of the discourse during the influencing phase and react creatively and spontaneously to new parameters.

There are also numerous practical challenges associated with the communicative focus of activity. So, it is one thing, for example, to draw up political messages in the context of strategy development *in abstracto;* but it is quite another to fill them with life through concrete formulations (in letters, e-mails, brochures, position papers, newspaper articles, social media postings, speech manuscripts, etc.). Here, all the lessons of the field of political language (see Chapter 3.2.2) must be applied, sometimes within a few minutes in cases of crisis communication or in extremely short-notice policy decisions. It is necessary to consider: Is the message suitable for the addressee, and does it strike the right tone? Is it understandable? Does it articulate any important point? Does it distinguish itself from the countless other messages communicated within the arena by a unique selling point?

Even if all the requirements are met, it must be borne in mind that communication in the direction of politics and administration suffers from a massive bottleneck problem. Around 40% of all documents addressed to central decision-makers are lost on the way or do not reach the addressees. E-mails fall victim to screening by employees, postal items go unread to the wastepaper basket, documents are incorrectly sorted or filed, etc. And even if messages reach the intended addressee processing times are extremely long, especially in state institutions and authorities. As a result of rigid line organization and complex filing systems, a single file within a ministry sometimes passes through 100 hands; and at each stage, there is a real risk that it will be permanently put to one side. In this context, perseverance and a high tolerance for frustration are necessary.

The bottleneck problem on the addressee side corresponds to the problem of a communicative oversupply on the sender side. The sheer number of think tanks, foundations, agencies, law firms, political consultancies etc. in national capitals leads to a massive and highly accelerated competition for attention, which has to be faced on a daily basis (see also our discussion of the struggle for communicative recognition in Chapters 2.5.2 and 3.2.1.). According to current estimates, between 23,000 and 40,000 professional lobbyists are romping about in Washington.[40] In his study of 2017, Andreas Schieder determines, by means of comparison, that over 10,000 persons are employed in the political services sector in Berlin alone (agencies, consulting firms, individual consultants, law firms and 'other service providers').[41] This figure does not include the non-profit sector, associations or similar protagonists of corporatist interest intermediation. This competitive situation reinforces the relevance of the thematic content of the USP, as discussed in Chapter 3.3.1, a matter which the homo consultans and the homo consultandus have to work out and communicate together. If this fails, influencing will fail simply by virtue of the law of large numbers.

Nevertheless, political influencing not only involves the technical and organizational implementation of empowerment and condensing. As we discussed in Chapter 2.5.2, practical experience (response to an event, successful mobilization or the failure of a campaign, the regulatory influence of a position paper, the sustainability of internal restructuring, etc.) must be continuously reflected upon and evaluated: What has been achieved and when? With what effort? What worked and what did not work? And so on. Answering these questions not only serves to ensure success for homo consultandus and his or her allies. Above all, it has the function of further improving the understanding of the board in power chess,

---

40 Cf. Herschel, Thomas F. and LaPira, Timothy M. (2017): How Many Lobbyists Are in Washington? Shadow Lobbying and the Gray Market for Policy Advocacy, *Interest Groups & Advocacy*, 6 (3), pp. 199-214.

41 Cf. Schieder, Andreas (2017): *Kommerzielles Lobbying und Public Affairs-Management*, Wiesbaden: Springer VS.; p. 514.

strengthening the political position analysis, honing strategic powers, eliminating deficits and finally optimizing future strategy development.

Influencing is therefore always a learning process, the results of which flow into perfecting the first two guiding principles. Accordingly, the principles of the power leadership curriculum – empowering, condensing and influencing – do not form a chronological order but a complex of interdependent factors. The evaluation of success, which links practical influencing back to preliminary questions on coaching, training, monitoring, intelligence, stakeholder mapping, etc., does not have the character of a quantitative study. Political influence can hardly be captured in exact and replicable data. Therefore, quantitative surveys on strategy implementation (number of quarterly policy formats, meetings with stakeholders, feedback on letters, etc.) are at best inconclusive and, at worst, misleading. For these reasons, the focus is on the qualitative measuring of results. Thus the power consultant does not recount the number of conversations he or she has held with parliamentarians, but rather explains how the content of the discussions has affected the overall strategy of advocacy. At this point, sometimes the working methods of consultant and client collide – especially with companies that are accustomed to measuring progress through key performance indicators (i.e., metrics such as spending, revenue, leads or click rates). Again, the power consultant has no alternative but to tackle the tightrope walk between rebellion and humility. On the one hand, the client's criteria of success must be reflected in the consultant's work, but on the other hand the peculiarities of the political field – in particular the impossibility of quantifying influence – must be made clear. Only if this mediation succeeds can the experiences won from influencing be used to sustainably optimize the common power strategy of homo consultandus and homo consultans.

3.5 GLOBAL GOVERNMENTAL RELATIONS

Now that the three guiding principles – empower, condense and influence – have been expanded upon, let us return to a core topic already discussed at the beginning of Chapter 3 that has since accompanied us implicitly: the challenge that globalization creates for the power leader curriculum. The twenty-first century is an era of international networking – both political and economic, informational and technological – and supranational legislation, such as in the EU. On such a playing field, the political and economic interests of the homo consultandus are often no longer limited to a single community. Mutual transnational interdependencies mean that domestic events (changes of government, coalition negotiations, reform projects, referendums, etc.) often have immediate effects on the strategic, political and economic room for maneuver in other states.

These effects are not always as dramatic as the Brexit decision in June 2016, when a national plebiscite massively influenced budgeting, domestic and foreign policy and, most importantly, the economic developments of 27 other nation states. But the British people's vote to leave the EU and the cascading influence this has on all policy fields is paradigmatic for an environment that is more and more akin to the pick-up-sticks game of Mikado: it is, literally speaking, almost impossible to move a stick without also moving dozens of others.

This has two crucial consequences for the power consultant and the client. First, if both of them want to influence policymaking in a single community A in order to reach a goal p, they must consider or predict the impact of their actions on policies in the other communities B, C, D and/or in the community supranational institution E. This problem is particularly relevant for global companies, which produce goods, offer services or maintain branches in dozens of states, and pursue corresponding strategic goals there. Second, if the homo consultandus and the homo consultans want to influence politics in a community A, then – thanks to the ubiquitous networks – there is the possibility to do so indirectly via the communities B, C, D and/or the supranational institution E. Globalization thus offers both risks and opportunities for power actors: risks because one single act of influence in the national context of one single state can have unintended negative consequences on other states; opportunities because international connections and supranational institutionalizations can open up new forms of indirect influence if the power player can develop an adequate strategy to take advantage of this.

All these tasks fall into one area of the power leadership curriculum, the area which we call *Global Governmental Relations (GGR)*. GGR refers to the development, implementation and continuous coordination of a political strategy that is specifically oriented towards the challenges and opportunities of a global field of action and strives for the optimal positioning of homo consultandus in an inter- and supranationally networked arena. GGR strategies are characterized by three core features:

1. A strategic policy objective that is not limited to a single state but relates to several, relevantly networked states (e.g. EU members, ASEAN members, G20 nations, states with main branches of an international corporation)
2. A network of national and/or regional teams implementing the strategy locally and in contact with local decision-makers and stakeholders
3. A central strategic control center, which coordinates the work of the teams, controls the implementation of the strategy or orders subsequent adjustments,

is in constant contact with the homo consultandus and continuously ensures a cultural balance between the actors

The coordinated political strategy that is associated with the term GGR is more than the mere sum of the individual national strategies of various local power consultants. Rather, it is an individually designed, single-source strategy that realizes the client's political interests across countries but through specific measures adapted to national or regional needs, taking into account the interdependencies between state actors. Such an approach offers a number of *advantages*. Firstly, GGR strategies are the only option for resolving global challenges or problems arising from inter- and supranational policy interconnections (e.g. the economic management of Brexit, the design of multinational trade relations, the restructuring of a global enterprise at different locations, the fight against climate change and the alleviation of the humanitarian causes of refugee movements).

Secondly, this approach conserves the power resources of homo consultandus by releasing synergies. A mediation strategy accompanying the international rollout of digital security technology benefits, for instance, from clarifying possibilities for cooperation and compatibility between national security apparatuses in the target countries, thus pointing out opportunities for increasing efficiency. A globally active charitable organization, in turn, profits from a GGR approach, for instance, through transferring national best practices (e.g. in lobbying for political support or fundraising) to other states.

Thirdly, a GGR approach prevents misunderstandings within the global organization of a power actor and restricts antagonisms between national branches. This aspect is e.g. highly relevant for all companies that produce different product components at locations with different regulatory frameworks and are absolutely dependent on smooth coordination.

And last but not least, the GGR approach is indispensable for mastering the problem complex of fake news (see Chapters 2.3.2, 2.4 and 3.2.1 for detailed discussion). This poses a double challenge. Firstly, homo consultandus is faced with the question of how to respond to disinformation and slander campaigns by political or economic opponents via international social media, news sites or social bots. Secondly, he or she must be able to deal with fake news allegations of critics in the field of politics who as a matter of course claim to have a monopoly on the truth. The second point in particular is often ignored or considered from the naive perspective that in the political sphere – in the field of values, norms and conventions – there are only objective, bare facts (see our critical discussion of an objective concept of the common good in Chapter 2.4). Each actor inevitably faces these two challenges in the global space of digital communications. More than almost any other term, fake news thus stands for cross-border struggles over power and interpretation and the involvement of multinational protagonists and technologies.

For the homo consultans, the GGR approach has a number of central *preconditions*. The first and most important is recognition of the findings discussed at length in Chapters 1 and 2, according to which the general logic of power and politics is the same everywhere. This applies to the fundamental principles of power (the omnipresence of power, its purposive production, the natural pursuit of power, etc.) as well as to the characterization of the power struggle as a zero-sum game, the political resources (knowledge, competence, instruments), the basic building blocks of strategy (fundamentals, capabilities, education, influence), the relevance of the common good as a universal principle of legitimacy and the essential techniques of influencing. There is no political arena that cannot be grasped using these basic concepts.

What differs from community to community and from culture to culture, however, is the way in which this globally uniform basic logic must be adapted and contextualized; that is, the specific political system logics of the communities, their organization logic, their political ethics and narratives etc. These differences are not limited to the institutional design of the legislative, executive, judiciary and administration (see Chapter 3.2.1). They also include e.g. fundamental differences in understandings of political or economic responsibility, in the definition of offenses such as corruption and undue advantage, or in the work-life balance. In her monograph *The Culture Map: Breaking Through the Invisible Boundaries of Global Business* from 2014, the management expert Erin Meyer compares the working and organizational cultures of 30 states.[42] On the basis of a few key questions, she draws a highly differentiated picture of transnational similarities and differences: Does the trust between people rely on personal acquaintance or on working successfully together? Is feedback for success and failure communicated directly or indirectly and discreetly? Are collective decisions made consensually or hierarchically? Is scheduling handled flexibly or strictly? And so on.

---

42 Cf. Meyer, Erin (2014): *The Culture Map: Breaking Through the Invisible Boundaries of Global Business,* New York: PublicAffairs.

Figure 21: Organizational and Working Cultures in Comparison

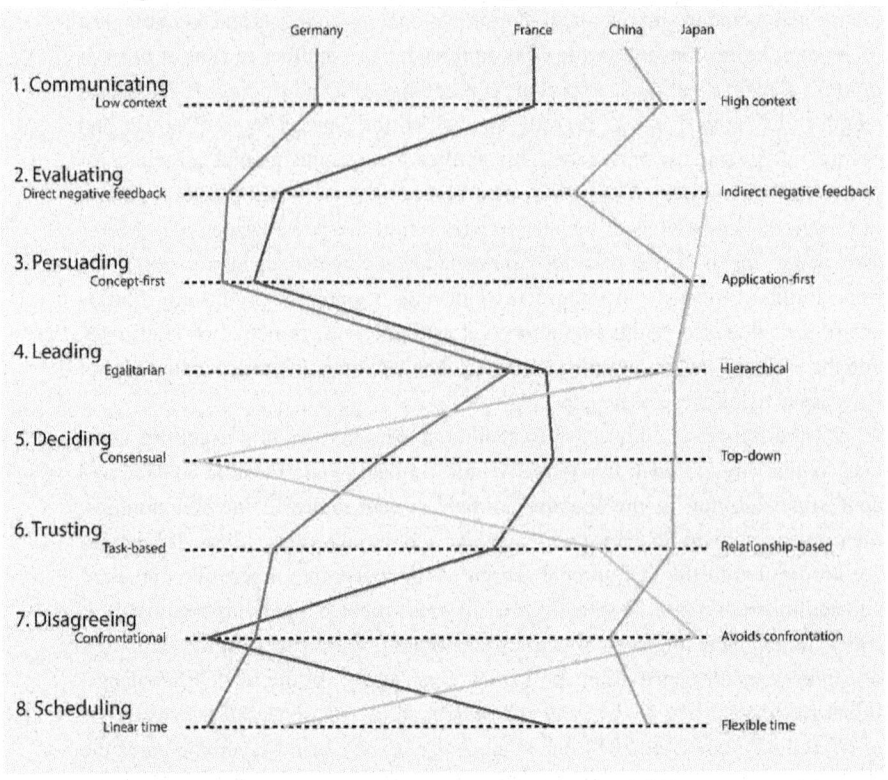

Source: Meyer, Erin (2016)[43]

Such knowledge is essential for power consultants who want to implement a global strategy. Those who do not know the German and Swiss appreciation of punctuality, the great respect for old age in countries like Kenya and Namibia, or the importance of small talk in the Anglo-Saxon cultural area, will soon be shipwrecked with GGR projects. At the beginning of Chapter 3 we stated that good consultancy always combines universality and contingency. This principle applies in particular to this aspect of the power leadership curriculum. The power consultant is faced with the challenge of neither blindly implementing an abstract scheme of action in all national contexts nor of submitting exclusively to the local internal logics of its various fields of application.

---

43 Meyer, Erin (2016): Mapping out Cultural Differences on Teams, [online] http://erinmeyer.com/2016/01/mapping-out-cultural-differences-on-teams/, retrieved on 21.12.2017.

Another requirement that arises in this context is the area of *compliance* with national and international laws, and voluntary codes of ethics and behavioral standards by companies, associations, NGOs, institutions and other actors in the political field. Self-imposed rules for companies and their service providers, for instance, specify behavioral requirements to ensure data protection, combat sexism and racism or prevent corruption and conflicts of interest. For the homo consultans, as a consultant to homo consultandus bound to such compliance standards (often covering hundreds of pages), practical conflicts with the political culture of certain communities may arise. While the cultural norms of one particular country may mean that the political elite exchange gifts or favors as a matter of course, this may be classified as bribery by the rules of many large corporations. This situation is complicated by the fact that compliance standards not only demand strict regulatory compliance from the power consultant, but also make him or her liable for the behavior of subcontractors (for example, national teams or employees commissioned by homo consultans). For the power consultant, this means that they must be as familiar with the regulatory conditions and practices of their national operations as they are with their client's voluntary conduct policies and the ethos and work practices of the various teams.

The *implementation* of GGR reflects the challenges of an action environment rendered increasingly complex by inter- and supranational networks. The basis for success is the aforementioned division of labor between national and/or regional teams on the one hand and a strategic control center on the other hand. The need to deploy specialized teams stems from the fact that effective and efficient policy-making requires immense familiarity with the written and unwritten rules, conventions and values of the relevant communities. This familiarity usually results only from national affiliation. To put it more clearly, only a French power consultant can successfully assist a client in France to enforce his or her interests, only a Russian power consultant in Russia, and so on. In contrast, the strategic control center fulfills the essential task of coordinating and controlling the activities of the teams and of providing homo consultandus with a permanent, direct contact; it acts as a point of articulation and mutual mediation between the client and the individual teams. Its members need to have an adequate overview of the challenges and power resources in all the countries relevant to the GGR strategy (which, of course, cannot and need not achieve the level of detail of the specialized teams). And they must also master the project management and leadership skills discussed in Chapter 3.4 and be able to work efficiently and effectively in multiple time zones.

However, the specific requirements for GGR implementation concern not only the organizational structure of the working group of homo consultans. In addition, they are reflected in the coaching and training for homo consultandus and in the navigation. In order to enable clients to achieve successful positioning in a globalized field of action, it is not only necessary to familiarize them with the system logics of the relevant nations and supranational institutions, but also to guide them through the power relations, competitive field and interdependencies of the actors. With regard to the political field of the EU, this includes, for instance, comprehensive knowledge of the power blocs (German-French tandem, Visegrád states, NORDEFCO etc.), the various sectors of the European public, the rivalries between the capitals and between the Member States and Brussels, and not least the European language policies at national and sub-national levels.

The condensing (or prioritization, systematization and evaluation) of information as well as thematic governance and strategy development must be adapted to the requirements of GGR. The fact that a disproportionately large amount of information and analysis is required at the global level for the implementation of the four-phase model (see Chapter 3.3.1) is immediately apparent. In this context, simply combining the monitoring and insights from different languages is a great challenge. The same applies to scenario analyses.

At this point, however, we do not intend to become entangled in the details of technological implementation. Instead, we highlight the substantive requirement of GGR strategy-building and implementation: unified messaging. A coherent and consistent GGR strategy can only be used if the various national activities of the homo consultans and the associated teams are held together by a substantive focus. This can consist of a simple, universal message based on the USP of homo consultandus which is suitable for use in all the political discourses of the relevant communities, such as the client's individual innovative power in a technological sector, trustworthiness in interacting with stakeholders, ethical role model, credible commitment to improving the quality of life of customers, or the comprehensive guarantee of security in the execution of financial transactions. Or it can underscore that all states involved in the GGR strategy make important and complementary contributions to a major overall project that unites them. This approach has immense potential, for example, with corporations such as the Airbus Group, Boeing or BAE Systems, which manufacture the components of their aircraft and spacecraft (cabs, turbines, wings, navigation software, etc.) at different locations in various countries, and thus already use the principle of an international division of labor and cooperation as the basis of their business model. It is hardly surprising that a mission statement from Airbus has the title "European Unity."[44]

---

44   See also Karabell, Shellie (2016): Why Airbus Is A Model For European Unity, in: Forbes from 27th February 2016, [online] https://www.forbes.com/sites/shelliekara

The GGR approach can only come to fruition and exhibit its merits – managing global and/or inter- and supranational challenges, developing synergies and preventing antagonisms – if it is perceived as *one* strategy in the relevant countries and if its key themes and issues are *shared* by decision-makers and the public at large across national borders,. As we discussed in Chapters 2.4 and 3.2.3, the political position of the power actor can only be mediated if there is a link between his or her goals and interests on the one hand and the common good of the state on the other. The essential challenge here is to transfer this universally valid principle to the inter- and supranational arena as part of a GGR strategy and implement it there in organizational terms. There is no magic recipe for this highly demanding goal, but the last few chapters should have made clear the essential preconditions and guiding principles – and also the pitfalls.

Without a doubt, global power consulting is one of the most important areas of work of homo consultans and is characterized by the greatest performance and innovation pressure. It does not require clairvoyant skills or sophisticated predictions to envision the future. This is a field that will continue to challenge seasoned veterans as well as industry novices worldwide.

3.6 CONCLUDING REMARKS

With this outlook on the inter- and supranational field of activity for homo consultans, our book has reached its final point. Of course, that does not mean that there is nothing left to say about this continuously compelling and challenging topic. On the contrary, *Power and its Logic* is only one voice in a polyphonic, interdisciplinary discourse on the exercise and legitimation of power in our globalized present. This vital and constantly advancing debate lives on by virtue of the sustained exchange between consultants, academics, lawyers, economists, entrepreneurs and political decision-makers, as well as between nations, states and cultures. In light of its diversity and changeability, the phenomenon of power can never be completely illuminated once and for all, however thorough the investigation might be. Each inquiry – including this one – thus remains a snapshot. In three consecutive chapters on the nature of power, the concretions of power and the practice of power, we have traversed and charted a wide range of topics: from the general definition of power and its universal anthropological principles to its

---

bell/2016/02/27/why-airbus-is-a-model-for-european-unity/#347b0a2b5838, retr. on 21.12.2017.

concrete forms, fields and resources and finally to a power leadership curriculum for the representative democracy of the twenty-first century.

Two principles have guided us from the first to the last page – they are the unique selling point of our work. The *first* principle is to address practitioners and theorists of power equally, overcoming their antogonism. Anyone who consistently thinks through the fundamental concepts of power and decision-making necessarily arrives at the everyday world of political practice; anything else would be an arbitrary termination of the analysis. However, this practice can only be understood and shaped by those who have internalized the specific techniques of power and influence, hence the elements of empower, condense and influence. Conversely, anyone who wants to systematize and master the resources of the power consultant must tackle the logic of power and its universal laws, otherwise the curriculum remains a mere hodgepodge without a methodological foundation. Of course, all of this does not mean that every power theorist must become a practitioner and every power practitioner a theoretician. Nevertheless, *Power and its Logic* demonstrates that both sides complement each other optimally: they can only benefit from a deeper dialogue.

Secondly, our monograph is a plea for an honest, unvarnished and ruthlessly frank look at power itself. The phenomenon of power is steeped in unprecedented myth-making. For some, it is the root of our society, others view it as an indeterminable, uncontrollable force that eludes any rational access. The dream of a rule-free society in which no one has power over anyone has always accompanied our social discourses – not infrequently as the utopian background noise of a fundamental political critique. We have tried to clean up with these legends and misunderstandings. Power is not obscure, but clearly definable and identifiable. It is neither *sui generis* bad nor good, but gains its ethical valence solely from its relationship to the common good. It is not an uncontrollable force of nature, but can be targeted, acquired and expanded through the resources, strategies and techniques of power. And finally, it is not a social phenomenon that may be turned on and off at will. The zero-sum game for power is a *conditio humana*. As long as there are people, they will compete for influence in the fields of politics, economics or religion – out of the urge for freedom, necessity, idealism, thrills or the joy of playing. Whoever wants to leave this game and depart from the chess board of established rules, does so at the high price of the dissolution of social bonds, the renunciation of the world, and a turn to mysticism. Everyone else is well advised to learn to live with and to handle power. We wrote this book for you.

What our readers ultimately do with these considerations, methods and tools of power – if they do anything at all – is something we should and indeed must leave to them. *Power and its Logic* is not a guide to the ethics of power, but a treatise dealing with the practical and theoretical understanding of its subject. We have made no secret of our own position, firmly rooted in the democratic constitutional state. Our desired audiences are not supporters of the authoritarian state, of populism or technocracy, but are those pragmatic idealists who hold to the principle of popular sovereignty against all defeatism. Our democracies deserve responsible decision-makers, consultants and stakeholders.

4 Literature

4.1 SPECIALIST LITERATURE

Abramson, Jeffrey B. (2009): *The Owl of Minerva,* Cambridge/London: Harvard University Press.

Agamben, Giorgio (1998): *Homo Sacer: Sovereign Power and Bare Life,* Werner Hamacher and David E. Wellbery (eds.), translated by Daniel Heller-Roazen, Meridian: Crossing Aesthetics, Stanford: Stanford University Press.

Al-Baghdadi, Ahmad M. (1981): The political thought of Abu Al-Hassan Al-Mawardi, Thesis Presented for the Degree of Doctor of Philosophy, University of Edinburgh, [online] https://www.era.lib.ed.ac.uk/handle/1842/7414, retrieved on 21.12.2017.

Allen, Amy (1999): *The Power of Feminist Theory: Domination, Resistance, Solidarity,* Boulder, CO: Westview Press.

Allen, Amy (2016): Feminist Perspectives on Power, in: Edward N. Zalta (ed.), *Stanford Encyclopedia of Philosophy.* [online] https://plato.stanford.edu/archives/fall2016/entries/feminist-power/, retrieved on 21.12.2017.

Al-Mawardi, Abu al-Hasan (1996): *Al-Ahkam as-Sultaniyya. The Ordinances of Government,* translated by Wafaa H. Wahba (ed.), Reading: Garnet.

Alvarez, Maria (2016): Reasons for Action: Justification, Motivation, Explanation, in: Edward N. Zalta (ed.), *Stanford Encyclopedia of Philosophy*, [online] https://plato.stanford.edu/entries/reasons-just-vs-expl/, retr. on 21.12.2017

Anderheiden, Michael (2006): *Gemeinwohl in Republik und Union,* Tübingen: Mohr Siebeck.

Anderson, Benedict (1994): *Imagined Communities. Reflections on the Origins and Spread of Nationalism*, London / New York: Verso.

Andregg, Michael (2007): Intelligence Ethics: Laying a Foundation for the Second Oldest Profession, in: Loch K. Johnson (ed.), *Handbook of Intelligence Studies,* New York: Routledge, pp. 52-66.

Arenberg, Richard A. and Dove, Robert B.: (2012): *Defending the Filibuster: The Soul of the Senate,* Bloomington: Indiana University Press.
Arendt, Hannah (1961): *Between Past and Future,* New York: Penguin.
Arendt, Hannah (1969): *On Violence.* New York: Harcourt, Brace and World.
Aristotle (1959) *Ars Rhetorica,* W. D. Ross (ed.), Oxford: Oxford University Press.
Aristotle (2002): *Metaphysics,* translated by Joe Sachs (ed.), 2nd edition, Santa Fe: Green Lion.
Aristotle (2017): *The Politics,* translated by Sir Ernest Barker, Oxford: Oxford University Press.
Ashrati, Mustafa (2008): *Islamic Banking. Wertvorstellungen, Finanzprodukte, Potenziale,* Frankfurt am Main: Frankfurt School Verlag.
Assmann, Aleida (2007): *Geschichte im Gedächtnis. Von der individuellen Erfahrung zur öffentlichen Inszenierung,* Munich: C.H. Beck.
Bacon, Francis ([1620] 1902): *Novum Organonon,* New York: P.F. Collier.
Bando, Shojun (1973): Jesus Christus und Amida. Zu Karl Barths Verständnis des Buddhismus vom Reinen Land, in: Yagi Seiichi and Ulrich Luz (eds.), *Gott in Japan: Anstöße zum Gespräch mit japanischen Philosophen, Theologen, Schriftstellern.* Munich: Kaiser, pp. 72-93.
Barry, Brian (1989): *Democracy and Power,* Oxford: Clarendon Press.
Bauer, Matthias (2016): The Political Power of Evoking Fear: The Shining Example of Germany's Anti-TTIP Campaign Movement, *European View,* 15 (2), pp. 193–212.
Bazil, Vazrik (2010): Politische Sprache: Zeichen und Zunge der Macht, *Politik und Zeitgeschichte,* (8), pp. 3-6.
Beamish, Thomas D. and Luebbers, Amy J. (2009): Alliance-Building Across Social Movements: Bridging Difference in a Peace and Justice Coalition, *Social Problems,* 56 (4), pp. 647-676.
Benhabib, Seyla (1996): Toward a deliberative model of democratic legitimacy, in: Seyla Benhabib (ed.), *Democracy and difference: Contesting the boundaries of the political,* Princeton: Princeton University Press, pp. 67-94.
Berlin, Isaiah (1969): *Four Essays on Liberty,* Oxford University Press.
Bernal, Paul (2016): Data Gathering, Surveillance and Human Rights: Recasting the Debate, *Journal of Cyber Policy,* 1 (2), pp. 243-264.
Bernardy, Jörg (2011): Attention as Bounded Resource and Medium in Cultural Memory: A Phenomenological or Economic Approach?, *Empedocles: European Journal for the Philosophy of Communication,* 2 (2), pp. 241-254.
Blau, Robert (1965): *Exchange and Power in Social Life,* New York: Wiley.

Blum, Christian and Zuber, Christina I. (2016): Liquid Democracy: Potentials, problems, and perspectives, *Journal of Political Philosophy*, 24 (2), pp. 162-182.

Blum, Christian (2010): Dilemmas Between the General and Particular Will – a Hegelian Analysis, in: Ignacia Falgueras, Juan A. García, and Juan J. Padidal (eds.), *Yo y tiempo: la antropología filosófica de G.W.F. Hegel*, Malaga: Contrastes, pp. 231-239.

Blum, Christian (2014): Why the Epistemic Justification of Deliberative Democracy Fails, in: Andre S. Campos and José G. André (eds.), *Challenges to Democratic Participation: Antipolitics, Deliberative Democracy, and Pluralism*, Lanham: Lexington Books, pp. 47-65.

Blum, Christian (2015): *Die Bestimmung des Gemeinwohls*, Berlin: De Gruyter.

Böckenförde, Ernst-Wolfgang (1967): Die Entstehung des Staates als Vorgang der Säkularisation. Säkularisation und Utopie, Ebracher Studien, Ernst Forsthoff zum 65. Geburtstag, Stuttgart / Berlin / Cologne / Mainz, pp. 75-94.

Bohlken, Eike (2011): *Die Verantwortung der Eliten: Eine Theorie der Gemeinwohlpflichten*, Frankfurt/New York: Campus.

Böhm von Bawerk, Eugen (1914): Macht oder ökonomisches Gesetz?, *Zeitschrift für Volkswirtschaft, Sozialpolitik und Verwaltung*, 23, pp. 205-271.

Bourdieu, Pierre (1987): *Die feinen Unterschiede. Kritik der gesellschaftlichen Urteilskraft*, translated by Bernd Schwibs and Achim Russer, Frankfurt a.M.: Suhrkamp.

Bourdieu, Pierre (1993): *Sozialer Sinn. Kritik der theoretischen Vernunft*, Frankfurt am Main: Suhrkamp.

Bourdieu, Pierre (2002a): *Outline of a Theory of Practice*, Ernest Gellner, Jack Goody, Stephen Gudeman, Michael Herzfeld, and Jonathan Parry (eds.), translated by Richard Nice, 16th edition, Cambridge: Cambridge University Press.

Bourdieu, Pierre (2002b): *Habitus. Habitus a Sense of Place*, Jean Hillier and Emma Rooksby (eds.), Aldershot: Ashgate.

Bourdieu, Pierre (2005): The Political Field, the Social Science Field, and Journalistic Field, in: R. Benson and E. Neveu (eds.), *Bourdieu and the Journalistic Field*, Cambridge: UK: Polity Press, pp. 29-47.

Bowens, Luc (2016): The Ethics of Dieselgate, *Midwest Studies in Philosophy*, 40 (1), pp. 262-283.

Bowering, Gerhard (2015): Introduction, in: Gerhard Bowering (ed.), *Islamic Political Thought. An Introduction*, Princeton/Oxford: Princeton University Press, pp. 1-23.

Bracher, Karl-Dietrich (1991): *Betrachtungen zum Problem der Macht*, Opladen: Westdeutscher Verlag.

Braun, Johann (2015): Die offene Gesellschaft und ihre Grenzen, *Rechtstheorie*, 46 (2), pp. 151-177.

Brennan, Jason (2016): *Against Democracy,* Princeton: Princeton University Press.

Brockers, Wolfgang (2014): *Karate – Essays,* Norderstedt: BOD.

Brown, Donald E. (2004): Human Universals, Human Nature, Human Culture, *Daedalus,* 133 (4), pp. 47-54.

Bryson, John M. (2004): What To Do When Stakeholders Matter. Stakeholder Identification and Analysis Techniques, *Public Management Review*, 6 (1), pp. 21-53.

Bullock, Alan (1992): *Hitler and Stalin: Parallel Lives,* 1st American edition, New York: Knopf.

Burke, Edmund ([1770] 2002): Thoughts on the Cause of the Present Discontents, in: Susan E. Scarrow (ed.), *Perspectives on Political Parties*, Basingstoke: Palgrave Macmillan, pp. 37-43.

Burleigh, Nina (2007): *Mirage: Napoleon's Scientists and the Unveiling of Egypt,* New York: Harper Collins.

Burton, John (1994): *An Introduction to the Hadith,* Edinburgh: Edinburgh University Press.

Caplan, Bryan (2007): *The Myth of the Rational Voter: Why Democracies Choose Bad Policies,* Princeton: Princeton University Press.

Carter, Ian (2008): How are Power and Unfreedom Related?, in: Cécile Laborde and John W. Maynor (eds.), *Republicanism and Political Theory,* Malden/Oxford: Blackwell Publishing, pp. 59-82.

Cassirer, Ernst ([1910] 2010): *Substanzbegriff und Funktionsbegriff,* Werkausgabe Vol. 6, Hamburg: Felix Meiner.

Cassirer, Ernst (1955): *The Philosophy of Symbolic Forms,* translated by Ralph Menheim, introduced by Charles W. Hendel, New Haven/London: Yale University Press.

Christiano, Thomas (2004): The Authority of Democracy, *The Journal of Political Philosophy*, 12 (3), pp. 266–290.; p. 269.

Cicero, Marcus Tullius (1986): *De oratore,* David Mankin (ed.), New York: Cambridge University Press.

Cicero, Marcus Tullius (1998): *The Republic. The Laws,* translated by Niall Rudd, Oxford/New York: Oxford University Press.

Cicero, Quintus Tullius (2009): *Commentariolum petitionis,* translated by Günter Laser (ed.), Darmstadt: Wissenschaftliche Buchgesellschaft.

Clark, Christopher (2019): *Time and Power Visions of History in German Politics, from the Thirty Years' War to the Third Reich,* Princeton/Oxford: Princeton University Press.

Clausen, Jens (2006): Die Natur des Menschen: Geworden und gemacht. Anthropologische Überlegungen zum Enhancement, *Zeitschrift für medizinische Ethik,* 52, pp. 391-401.

Clausen, Jens (2009): Man, Machine and in between, *Nature,* 457 (7233), pp. 1080-1081.

Clegg, Stuart (1989): *Frameworks of Power,* London: Sage Publications.

Clinton, Hilary (2003): *Living History,* New York: Simon & Schuster.

Confucius (2005): *Lun Yu,* translated by Chichung Huang (ed.) as 'The Analects of Confucius (Lun yu)', New York: Oxford University Press.

Cole, Juan R. (2008): *Napoleon's Egypt: Invading the Middle East,* New York: Palgrave Macmillan.

Condorcet, Marie J. (2011): Ausgewählte Schriften zu Wahlen und Abstimmungen, translated by Joachim Behnke, Carolin Stange and Reinhard Zintl (eds.), Tübingen: Mohr Siebeck.

Conolly, William E. (1993): *The Terms of Political Discourse,* Princeton: Princeton University Press.

Crisp, Roger (2013): Well-Being, in: Edward N. Zalta (ed.), *Stanford Encyclopedia of Philosophy,* [online] http://plato.stanford.edu/entries/well-being/, retrieved on 21.12.2017.

Crowdy, Terry (2011): *The Enemy Within – A History of Spies, Spymasters and Espionage,* Oxford: Osprey Publishing.

Culoma, Michael (2010): *La religion civile de Rousseau à Robespierre,* Paris: L'Harmattan.

D'Ancona, Cristina (2013): Greek Sources in Arabic and Islamic Philosophy, in: Edward N. Zalta (ed.), *Stanford Encyclopedia of Philosophy,* [online] https://plato.stanford.edu/archives/win2017/entries/arabic-islamic-greek/, retrieved on 21.12.2017.

Dahl, Robert (1957): The Concept of Power, *Behavioral Science,* 2, pp. 201-215.

Dahl, Robert ([1968] 2002): Power, in: Mark Haugaard (ed.), *Power. A Reader,* Manchester: Manchester University Press, pp. 5-25.

Dal Bó, Ernesto, Dal Bó, Pedro and Snyder, Jason (2009): Political Dynasties, *Review of Economic Studies,* 76 (1), pp. 115-142.

Dandeker, Christopher (1990): *Surveillance, Power and Modernity,* Cambridge: Polity Press.

Danner, John and Coopersmith, Mark (2015): *The Other 'F' Word. How Smart Leaders, Teams, and Entrepreneurs Put Failure to Work,* Hoboken: Wiley.

Derlien, Hans-Ulrich, Böhme, Doris, and Heindl, Markus (2011): *Bürokratietheorie. Einführung in eine Theorie der Verwaltung,* Wiesbaden: VS Verlag.
Derrida, Jacques (2004): *Die Différance. Ausgewählte Texte,* Stuttgart: Reclam.
Diakonoff, Igor. M. (1976): Ancient Writing and Ancient Written Language: Pitfalls and Peculiarities in the Study of Sumerian, *Assyriological Studies,* Vol. 20, Sumerological Studies in Honor of Thorkild Jakobsen, pp. 99–121.
Dixit, Avinash K. and Nalebuff, Barry J. (1993): *Thinking Strategically. The Competitive Edge in Business, Politics, and Everyday Life,* New York: W. W. Norton & Company.
Dorsey, Dale (2012): Subjectivism without Desire, *Philosophical Review,* 121 (3), pp. 407-442.
Dowding, Keith M. (1996): *Power.* Minneapolis: University of Minnesota Press.
Dryzek, John (2000): *Deliberative Democracy and Beyond: Liberals, Critics, Contestation,* Oxford/New York: Oxford University Press.
Durkheim, Émile ([1912] 1915): *The Elementary Forms of the Religious Life,* translated by Joseph Ward Swain, London: George Allen & Unwin.
Dworkin, Ronald (1977): *Taking Rights Seriously,* Cambridge: Harvard University Press.
Eales, Richard (2002): *Chess: the History of a Game,* London: Hardinge Simpole.
El-Gamal, Mahmoud A. (2006): *Islamic Finance: Law, Economics, and Practice,* Cambridge: Cambridge University Press.
Elias, Norbert (1983): *Die höfische Gesellschaft. Untersuchung zur Soziologie des Königtums und der höfischen Aristokratie,* Frankfurt a.M.: Suhrkamp.
Estlund, David (2008*): Democratic Authority: a Philosophical Framework,* Princeton: Princeton University Press.
Eßbach, Wolfgang (2014): *Religionssoziologie I,* Paderborn: Wilhelm Fink.
Fantl, Jeremy (2012): Knowledge How, in: Edward N. Zalta (ed.), *Stanford Encyclopedia of Philosophy,* [online] https://plato.stanford.edu/entries/knowledge-how/, retrieved on 21.12.2017.
Farazmand, Ali (2001): Learning from Ancient Persia: Administration of the Persian Achaemenid Empire, in: Ali Farazmand (ed.), *Handbook of Comparative and Development Public Administration,* New York/Basel: Marcel Dekker, pp. 33-60.
Farwell, James P. and Rohozinski, Rafal (2011): Stuxnet and the Future of Cyber War, *Survival,* 53 (1), pp. 23-40.
Fink-Eitel, Hinrich (1992): Dialektik der Macht, in: Emil Angehrn, Hinrich Fink-Eitel, Christian Iber, and Georg Lohmann (eds.), *Dialektischer Negativismus. Michael Theunissen zum 60. Geburtstag.* Frankfurt/M: Suhrkamp, pp. 35-56.

Fiva, John H. and Smith, Daniel M. (2016): Political Dynasties and the Incumbency Advantage in Party-Centered Environment, *CESifo Working Paper Series,* 5757, pp. 1-46.

Flaig, Egon (1998): War die römische Volksversammlung ein Entscheidungsorgan? Institution und soziale Praktik, in: Rainhard Blänker and Bernd Jussen (eds.), *Institution und Ereignis. Über historische Praktiken und Vorstellungen gesellschaftlichen Handelns.* Göttingen: Vandenhoeck & Ruprecht, pp. 49-73.

Flaig, Egon (2013): *Die Mehrheitsentscheidung: Entstehung und kulturelle Dynamik,* Paderborn: Ferdinand Schöningh.

Flaig, Egon (2017): *Die Niederlage der politischen Vernunft. Wie wir die Errungenschaften der Aufklärung verspielen,* Springe: zu Klampen.

Forsthoff, Ernst (1984): *Der Staat der Industriegesellschaft. Dargestellt am Beispiel der Bundesrepublik Deutschland,* Munich: C.H. Beck.

Foucault, Michel. (1980): *Power / Knowledge: Selected Interviews and Other Writings, 1972 – 1977,* in: Colin Gordon (ed.) Translated by Colin Gordon, Leo Marshall, John Mepham and Kate Soper. Brighton: Harvester.

Foucault, Michel (1984 [1990]): *The Use of Pleasure*, The History of Sexuality, Vol. 2, translated by Robert Hurley (ed.), New York: Random House.

Foucault, Michel (1988): The Care of the Self, The History of Sexuality, Vol. 3, translated by Roberet Hurley (ed.), New York: Random House.

Foucault, Michel ([1984] 1990): The History of Sexuality: The Will to Knowledge, An Introduction, Vol. I, translated by Robert Hurley (ed.), New York: Random House.

Foucault, Michel (1995): *Discipline and Punish: The Birth of the Prison,* 2nd edition, translated by Alan Sheridan, New York: Random House.

Fort, Sylvain (2002): *Les Lumières francaises en Allemagne. Le cas Schiller,* Paris: Presses Universitaires de France.

Fraenkel, Ernst (1991): *Deutschland und die westlichen Demokratien,* Frankfurt am Main: Suhrkamp.

Franck, Georg (1998): *Ökonomie der Aufmerksamkeit: Ein Entwurf,* München: Hanser.

Frankfurt, Harry G. (2005): *On Bullshit,* Princeton: Princeton University Press.

Franks, Benjamin and Wilson, Matthew (eds.) (2010): *Anarchism and Moral Philosophy,* Basingstoke: Palgrave.

Freedman, Lawrence (2013): *Strategy: A History,* Oxford/New York: Oxford University Press.

Frei, Norbert and Schmitz, Johannes (1988): *Journalismus im Dritten Reich,* Munich: C.H. Beck.

Freud, Sigmund ([1923] 1989): *The Ego and the Id. The Complete Psychological Works of Sigmund Freud,* James Strachey (ed.), introduced by Peter Gay, New York: W.W. Norton & Co.

Furniss, Richard and Snyder, Edgar (1955): *An Introduction to American Foreign Policy,* New York: Rhinehart.

Gallopín, Gilberto C. (2006): Linkages Between Vulnerability, Resilience, and Adaptive Capacities, *Global Environmental Change,* 16 (3), pp. 293-303.

Geary, Patrick J. (2013): *Language and Power in the Early Middle Ages,* authored in the course of the Menahem Stern Jerusalem Lectures. Waltham: Brandeis University Press.

Gehlen, Arnold ([1940] 1988): *Man, his Nature and Place in the World,* translated by Clare McMillan and Karl Pillemer (eds.), New York: Columbia University Press.

Geser, Hans (1996): Internationale Polizeiaktionen: Ein neues evolutionäres Entwicklungsstadium militärischer Organisationen, in: Georg-Maria Meyer (ed.), *Friedensengel im Kampfanzug? Zur Theorie und Praktik militärischer UN-Einsätze,* Opladen: Westdeutscher Verlag, pp. 45-74.

Giddens, Anthony (1984): *The Constitution of Society. Outline of the Theory of Structuration,* Berkeley: University of California Press.

Gierer, Alfred (2001): Ibn Khaldun on Solidarity ("Asabiyah") – Modern Science on Cooperativeness and Empathy: a Comparison, *Philosophia Naturalis,* 38 (1), pp. 91-104.

Girnth, Heiko (2002): *Sprache und Sprachverwendung in der Politik,* Hamburg: De Gruyter.

Goethe, Johann W. ([1808] 1992): *Faust, A Tragedy, Part I.,* translated by Martin Greenberg, New Haven: Yale University Press.

Göl, Ayla (2017): The paradoxes of 'new' Turkey: Islam, Illiberal Democracy and Republicanism, *International Affairs,* 93 (4), pp. 957-966.

Goldman, Alvin (2001): Experts: Which Ones Should You Trust?, *Philosophy and Phenomenological Research,* 63, pp. 85–111.

Griffin, James (1986): *Well-Being, its Meaning, Measurement, and Moral Importance,* Oxford/New York: Oxford University Press.

Guerrero, Alexander (2014): *The Lottocracy,* [online] https://aeon.co/essays/forget-voting-it-s-time-to-start-choosing-our-leaders-by-lottery, retrieved on 21.12.2017.

Gumbrecht, Hans Ulrich (2004): *Production of Presence: What Meaning Cannot Convey,* Stanford: Stanford University Press.

Gutman, Amy and Thompson, Dennis (2004): *Why Deliberative Democracy?,* Princeton/Oxford: Princeton University Press.

Habermas, Jürgen (1984): *Theory of Communicative Action*, Vol. 1, translated by A. McCarthy, Boston: Beacon Press.

Hackett, Jeremiah M. (2013): *A Companion to Meister Eckhart.* Leiden: Brill.

Hamilton, Peter (2015): *Knowledge and Social Structure,* London/New York: Routledge.

Han, Byung-Chul (2005): *Was ist Macht?,* Ditzingen: Reclam.

Hardwig, John (1985), Epistemic dependence, *Journal of Philosophy*, 88, pp. 693–708.

Hartmann, Bernd J. (2012): Self-Interest and the Common Good in Elections and Referenda, *German Law Journal*, 13 (3), pp. 259-286.

Haugaard, Mark (2010): Power: A 'Family Resemblance' Concept, *European Journal of Cultural Studies,* 13 (4), pp. 419-438.

Hayek, Friedrich A. (1939): *Freedom and the Economic System*, Chicago: Chicago University Press.

Hegel, Georg W. F. ([1821] 2003): *Elements of the Philosophy of Right: Or Natural Law and Political Science in Outline,* Allen W. Wood (ed.), translated by H.B, Nisbet. 8th edition, Camebridge: Cambridge University Press.

Hegelich, Simon and Janetzko, Dietmar (2016): *Are social Bots on Twitter Political Actors? Empirical Evidence from a Ukrainian Social Botnet*, Proceedings of the 10th International AAAI Conference on Web and Social Media, [online] https://www.aaai.org/ocs/index.php/ICWSM/ICWSM16/paper/view/13015/12793, retrieved on 21.12.2017.

Hegelich, Simon (2016): Invasion der Meinungsroboter, *Analysen und Argumente,* 221, pp. 1-9.

Herschel, Thomas F. and LaPira, Timothy M. (2017): How Many Lobbyists Are in Washington? Shadow Lobbying and the Gray Market for Policy Advocacy, *Interest Groups & Advocacy*, 6 (3), pp. 199-214.

Heidegger, Martin (1953): *The Question Concerning Technology and Other Essays X,* translated and with an Introduction by William Lovitt, New York: Garland Publishing.

Herman, Edward S. and Chomsky, Noam (2002): *Manufacturing Consent. The Political Economy of the Mass Media*, New York: Pantheon Books.

Herodotus (1997): *Histories,* translated by Robin Waterfield (ed.), introduction and notes by Carolyn Dewald, Oxford: Oxford World Classics.

Hess, Stephen (2016): *America's Political Dynasties: From Adams to Clinton,* Washington: Brookings Institution Press.

Hesselbach, Walter (1971): *Public Trade Union and Cooperative Enterprises in Germany,* London: Frank Cass.

Hillebrandt, Frank (1999): Die Habitus-Feld-Theorie als Beitrag zur Mikro-Makro-Problematik in der Soziologie – aus der Sicht des Feldbegriffs, Working Papers zur Modellierung sozialer Organisationsformen in der Sozionik, [online] https://www.tuhh.de/tbg/Deutsch/Projekte/Sozionik2/WP2.pdf, retrieved on 21.12.2017.

Hinde, John R. (2000): *Jacob Burckhardt and the Crisis of Modernity*, Montreal: McGill-Queen's University Press.

Hiriyanna, Mysore ([1949] 2005): *The Essentials of Indian Philosophy*, New Delhi: Shri Jainendra Press.

Hobbes, Thomas ([1651] 1997): *Leviathan. Or the Matter, Forme, and Power of a Common-Wealth Ecclesiasticall and Civill*, Michael Oakeshott (ed.), New York: Touchstone/Simon & Schuster.

Hochschild, Jennifer L. (1996): *Facing up to the American Dream. Race, Class, and the Soul of the Nation*, Princeton: Princeton University Press.

Holler, Manfred J. (2009): Niccolò Machiavelli on Power, *Rationality, Markets, and Morals*, 0 (1), pp. 335-354.

Hu, Margaret (2014): Small Data Surveillance vs. Big Data Cybersurveillance. *Pepperdine Law Review*, 42 (4), pp. 773-844.

Hunt, Samuel J. and Cangemi, Joseph (2014): Want to Improve Your Leadership Skills? Play Chess!, *Education*, 134 (3), pp. 359-368.

Imbusch, Peter (2007): Macht: Dimensionen und Perspektiven eines Phänomens, in: Klaus-Dieter Altmeppen, Thomas Hanitzsch, and Carsten Schlüter (eds.), *Journalismustheorie: Next Generation. Soziologische Grundlegung und theoretische Innovation*, Wiesbaden: Springer, pp. 395-419.

Janks, Hilary (2010): *Literacy and Power*, London/New York: Routledge.

Jansen, Marius (ed.) (2008): *Warrior Rule in Japan*, Cambridge: Cambridge University Press.

Joffe, Alexander H. (1999): Dismantling intelligence agencies, *Crime, Law & Social Change*, 32, pp. 325–346.

Johnson, Loch K. (1998): *Secret Agencies: US Intelligence in a Hostile World*, New Haven: Yale University Press.

Joos, Klemens (2016): *Convincing Political Stakeholders: Successful lobbying through process competence in the complex decision-making system of the European Union*, Weinheim: Wiley.

Kahn, Charles H. (2008): *Art and Thought of Heraclitus*, Cambridge: Cambridge University Press.

Kant, Immanuel ([1790] 2002): *Critique of the Power of Judgment*, London: Cambridge University Press.

Kant, Immanuel ([1795] 2003): To Perpetual Peace: A Philosophical Sketch, translated by Ted Humphrey, Indianapolis: Hackett Publishing.

Karabell, Zachary (2003): *Parting the Desert. The Creation of the Suez Canal*, New York/Toronto: Knopf.

Karlberg, Michael (2005): Power of Discourse and the Discourse of Power: Pursuing Peace Through Discourse Intervention, *International Journal of Peace Studies*, 10 (1), pp. 1-23.

Kasten, Brigitte (1997): *Königssöhne und Königsherrschaft. Untersuchungen zur Teilhabe am Reich in der Merowinger- und Karolingerzeit*, Hannover: Hahnsche Buchhandlung.

Kaufman, Whitley (2007): Karma, Rebirth, and the Problem of Evil: a Reply to Critics, *Philosophy East and West*, 57 (4), pp. 559-560.

Keller, Johannes (2004): Römische Interessengeschichte. Eine Studie zu Interessenvertretung, Interessenkonflikten und Konfliktlösung in der römischen Republik des 2. Jahrhunderts v. Chr., Inaugural-Dissertation zur Erlangung des Grades eines Doktors der Philosophie, [online] https://edoc.ub.uni-muenchen.de/5172/1/keller_johannes.pdf, retrieved on 21.12.2017.

Khagram, Sanjeev (2009): *Dams and Development. Transnational Struggles for Water and Power*. Ithaca/London: Cornell University Press.

Khaldun, Ibn (2011): *Die Muqaddima: Betrachtungen zur Weltgeschichte*, translated by Alma Giese, München: C.H. Beck.

King, Winston L. (1993): *Zen and the Way of the Sword: Arming the Samurai Psyche*, New York: Oxford University Press.

Kiyaias, Aggelos and Panagiotakos, Giorgos (2016): Speed-Security Tradeoffs in Blockchain Protocols, Working Paper, [online] https://eprint.iacr.org/2015/1019.pdf, retrieved on 21.12.2017

Köppl, Peter (2017): *Advanced Power Lobbying. Erfolgreiche Public Affairs in Zeiten der Digitalisierung*, Wien: Linde Verlag.

Koselleck, Reinhart (2004): *Futures Past: On the Semantics of Historical Time. Series: Studies in Contemporary German Social Thought*, translated and with an introduction by Keith Tribe, New York: Columbia University Press.

Korpi, Walter (1983): *The Democratic Class Struggle*, Boston: Routledge & Kegan.

Krieger, Wolfgang (2009): *Geschichte der Geheimdienste: von den Pharaonen zur CIA*, Munich: C.H. Beck.

Krugman, Paul and Wells, Robin (2015): *Economics*, 4th edition, New York: Worth Publishers.

Lao Tzu (2009): *Tao-Te-Ching*, translated by John H. McDonald (ed.), New York: Chartwell Books.

Lee, Richard E. (2013): *The Longue Duree and World-Systems Analysis,* New York: State University of New York Press.

Leigh, Ian (2007): The Accountability of Security and Intelligence Agencies. in: Loch K. Johnson (ed.), *Handbook of Intelligence Studies,* New York: Routledge, pp. 67-81.

Lemke, Thomas (2001): The birth of bio-politics: Michael Foucault's lectures at the College de France on neo-liberal governmentality, *Economy and Society,* 30 (2), pp. 190-207.

Lenin, Vladimir I.: ([1902] 1989): *What is to be Done?*, transcription by Tim Delaney, printable edition produced by Chris Russell for the Marxists Internet Archive, pp. 7-87.

Leo XIII. (1891): Circular issued by our Most Holy Father Leo XIII, by Divine Providence Pope, on the Labor Question. Rerum Novarum, Munich: Herder.

Levi, Margaret (1996): Social and Unsocial Capital: a Review Essay of Robert Putnam's Making Democracy Work, *Politics & Society,* 24 (1), pp. 45-55.

Libicki, Martin C. (2009): *Cyberdeterrence and Cyberwar,* Santa Monica: Rand.

List, Christian and Goodin, Robert (2001): Epistemic Democracy: Generalizing the Condorcet Jury Theorem, *Journal of Political Philosophy,* 9 (3), pp. 277-306.

Locke, John ([1689] 1988): *Two Treatises of Government,* Peter Laslett (ed.), Cambridge: Cambridge University Press

Lombard, Maurice (1975): *The Golden Age of Islam,* New York: American Elsevier.

Luhmann, Niklas ([1975] 2003): *Macht,* Stuttgart: UTB.

Lukes, Steven (1974): *Power. A Radical View,* London: MacMillan Press.

Luz, Ulrich (2002): *Das Evangelium nach Matthäus,* Neukirchen-Vluyn: Benziger/Neukirchener.

Lyon, David (2016): Snowden, everyday practices and digital futures, in: Tugba Basaran, Didier Bigo, Emmanuel-Pierre Guittet, and R. B. J. Walker (eds.), *International Political Sociology, Transversal lines.* London/New York: Routledge, pp. 254-271.

MacIntyre, Alasdair (1984): *Is Patriotism a Virtue?*, Kansas: University of Kansas Press.

Mackie, Gerry (2003): *Democracy Defended,* Cambridge: Cambridge University Press.

Madison, James, Hamilton, Alexander, and Jay, John (2002): *The Federalist Papers,* Richard Beeman (ed.), New York: Penguin.

Major, John (1993). *Prize Possession: The United States and the Panama Canal, 1903–1979,* Cambridge: Cambridge University Press.

Mann, Michael (1986): *The Sources of Social Power*, Vol. 1: A History of Power from the Beginning to A.D. 1760, Cambridge: Cambridge University Press.

Mansbridge, Jane et al. (2012): A Systemic Approach to Deliberative Democracy, in: John Parkinson and Jane Mansbridge (eds.), *Deliberative Systems*, Cambridge: Cambridge University Press, pp. 1-26.

March, James G. and Olsen, Johan P. (1989): *Rediscovering Institutions: The Organizational Basis of Politics*, London/New York: The Free Press.

Marcinkowksi, Frank (2015): 'Die Medialisierung' der Politik. Veränderte Bedingungen politischer Interessenvermittlung, in: Rudolf Speth and Anette Zimmer (eds.), *Lobby Work. Interessenvertretung als Politikgestaltung*, Wiesbaden: VS Verlag, pp. 71-95.

Marples, Nicola M., Kelly, David J., and Thomas, Robert J. (2005): Perspective: The Evolution of Warning Colors is Not Paradoxical, *Evolution*, 59 (5), pp. 933-940.

Marshall, Robert (1993): *Storm from the East. From Ghengis Khan to Khubilai Khan*, Berkeley: University of California Press.

Mass, Jeffrey P. (1975): *Warrior Government in Early Mediaeval Japan: Study of the Kamakura Bakufu, Shugo and Jito*, New Haven/London: Yale University Press.

Mayer, Frederick W. (2014): *Narrative Politics: Stories and Collective Action*, Oxford: Oxford University Press.

Mayntz, Renate (1985): *Soziologie der öffentlichen Verwaltung*, 3rd revised edition, Heidelberg: C.F. Müller.

McMahan, Jeff (2011): *Killing in War*, Oxford: Oxford University Press.

Meier, Dominik (2017a): Das Gemeinwohl: Ein Blick aus der politischen Praktik, *INDES Zeitschrift für Politik und Gesellschaft*, 4, pp. 153-159.

Meier, Dominik (2017b): Germany, in: Alberto Bitonti and Phil Harris (eds.), *Lobbying in Europe*, London: Palgrave MacMillan, pp. 159-170.

Meinecke, Friedrich ([1957] 1998): *Machiavellism: The Doctrine of Raison D'État and Its Place in Modern History*, translated by Douglas Scott, introduction by Werner Stark, New Brunswick, N.J.: Transaction Publishers.

Miller, Fred (2011): Aristotle's Political Theory, in: Edward N. Zalta (ed.), *Stanford Encyclopedia of Philosophy*, [online] https://plato.stanford.edu/archives/win2017/entries/aristotle-politics/, retrieved on 21.12.2017.

Mohanan, Torin (ed.) (2006): *Surveillance and Security. Technological Politics and Power in Everyday Life*, New York: Routledge.

Morar, Tulsi (2006): The South African's Educational System's Evolution to Curriculum 2005, in: Jayja Erneast and David Treagust (eds.), *Education Reform in Societies in Transition. International Perspectives,* Rotterdam: Sense Publishers, pp. 245-258.

Morgenthau, Hans ([1948] 1978): *Politics Among Nations: The Struggle for Power and Peace,* New York: Knopf.

Mouffe, Chantal (1993): *The Return of the Political,* London/New York: Verso.

Mulgan, Richard (1974): Aristotle's Doctrine That Man Is a Political Animal, *Hermes,* 102 (3), pp. 438-445.

Müller-Jentsch, Walter (2014): Macht als Ressource von Organisationen, in: Monica Budowski and Michael Nollert (eds.), *Private Macht im Wohlfahrtsstaat: Akteure und Institutionen,* Zürich: Seismo, pp. 14-29.

Münkler, Herfried (2009): *Die Deutschen und ihre Mythen,* Berlin: Rowohlt.

Nagel, Thomas (1987): *What Does It All Mean?,* New York/Oxford: Oxford University Press.

Neidhardt, Friedhelm (2002): Öffentlichkeit und Gemeinwohl. Gemeinwohlrhetorik in Pressekommentaren, in: Herfried Münkler and Harald Bluhm (eds.), *Gemeinwohl und Gemeinsinn,* Vol. II: Rhetoriken und Perspektiven sozialmoralischer Orientierung, Berlin: Akademie Verlag, pp. 157–177.

Newman, Saul (2004): The Place of Power in Political Discourse, *International Political Science Review,* 25 (2), pp. 139-157.

Niehaus, Andreas (2013): "So gibt es nichts schändlicheres als illiterat zu sein" – zur Literalität der Kriegerklasse im frühmodernen Japan, in: Gesine Boesken and Uta Schaffers (eds.), *Lektüren 'bilden': Lesen – Bildung – Vermittlung,* Münster: Lit Verlag, pp. 199-216.

Nietzsche, Friedrich ([1844-1845] 1968): *The Will to Power,* translated by Walter Kaufmann and Reginald J. Hollingdale (eds.), New York: Vintage Books.

Nora, Pierre (1996): *Realms of Memory: Rethinking the French Past,* Lawrence D. Kritzman (ed.), translated by Arthur Goldhammer, New York: Columbia University Press.

Nozick, Robert (1974): *Anarchy, State, Utopia,* New York: Basic Books.

O'Flynn, Ian (2010): Deliberating About the Public Interest, *Res Publica,* 16, pp. 299-315.

Offe, Claus (2001): Wessen Wohl ist das Gemeinwohl?, in: Lutz Wingert and Klaus Günther (eds.), *Die Öffentlichkeit der Vernunft und die Vernunft der Öffentlichkeit. Festschrift für Jürgen Habermas,* Frankfurt am Main: Suhrkamp, pp. 459-488.

Orlitzky, Marc, Schmidt, Frank L. and Reynes, Sara (2003): Corporate Social and Financial Performance: A Meta-Analysis, *Organization Studies,* 24 (3), pp. 402-441.

Ostheim, Tobias and Schmidt, Manfred G. (2007): Die Machtressourcentheorie, in: Manfred G. Schmidt (ed.), *Der Wohlfahrtsstaat: Eine Einführung in den historischen und internationalen Vergleich*. Wiesbaden: VS Verlag, pp. 40-50.

Palumbo, Antonino and Scott, Alan (2018): *Remaking Market Society: A Critique of Social Theory and Political Economy in Political Times*, New York/London: Routledge.

Pansardi, Pamela (2012): Power to and power over: two distinct concepts of power?, *Journal of Political Power*, 5 (1), pp. 73-89.

Papadis, Dimitris (2006): Is Man by Nature a Political and Good Animal, According to Aristotle?, *Phronimon*, 7 (1), pp. 21-33.

Parry, Richard (2014): Episteme and Techne, in: Edward N. Zalta (ed.), *Stanford Encyclopedia of Philosophy*, [online] https://plato.stanford.edu/entries/episteme-techne/, retrieved on 21.12.2017.

Paulus, Nikolaus ([1922] 2000): *Geschichte des Ablasses im Mittelalter. Vom Ursprunge bis zur Mitte des 14. Jahrhunderts*, Darmstadt: Wissenschaftliche Buchgesellschaft.

Paulus, Nikolaus ([1923] 2000): *Geschichte des Ablasses am Ausgang des Mittelalters*, Darmstadt: Wissenschaftliche Buchgesellschaft.

Pecknold, Chad C. (2010): *Christianity and Politics: A Brief Guide to the History*, Eugene: Cascade Books.

Perez, Louis G. (1998): *The History of Japan*, Westport/London: Greenwood Press.

Perroux, François (1950): The Domination Effect and Modern Economic Theory, *Social Research*, 17 (2), pp. 188-206.

Peters, Hans P. (1994): Mass Media as an Information Channel and Public Arena, *RISK: Health, Safety & Environment*, 5(3), pp. 241-250.

Petesch, Donald A. (1989): *A Spy in the Enemy's Country. The Emergence of Modern Black Literature*, Iowa City: University of Iowa Press.

Pitkin, Hanna F. (1972): *Wittgenstein and Justice*. Oxford: Oxford University Press.

Plato (2006): *The Republic*, translated by R.E. Allen (ed.), New Haven: Yale University Press.

Poggi, Gianfranco (1988): Phänomene der Macht: Autorität-Herrschaft-Gewalt-Technik. Review, *Contemporary Sociology*, 17 (4), pp. 664-556.

Poggi, Gianfranco (2001): *Forms of Power*, Cambridge: Polity Press.

Polletta, Francesca (2011): Storytelling in Politics, *Contexts*, 7 (4), pp. 26-31.

Popitz, Heinrich (1992): *Phänomene der Macht*, 2nd edition, Tübingen: Mohr Siebeck.

Popitz, Heinrich (2017): *Phenomena of Power: Authority, Domination, and Violence*, Andreas Göttlich and Jochen Dreher (eds.), translated by Gianfranco Poggi, New York: Columbia University Press.

Popper, Karl R. (1989): Falsifizierbarkeit, zwei Bedeutungen, in: Helmut Seiffert and Gerard Radnitzky (eds.), *Handlexikon zur Wissenschaftstheorie*, München: Ehrenwirth, pp. 82-85.

Preiser, Erich (1971): Power, Property, and the Distribution of Income, in: Kurt W. Rothschild (ed.), *Power in Economics*, Harmondsworth: Penguin, pp. 119-140.

Putnam, Robert D. (1993): *Making Democracy Work: Civic Traditions in Modern Italy*, Princeton: Princeton University Press.

Quante, Michael (2010): After Hegel. The Realization of Philosophy Through Action, in: Dean Moyar (ed.), *Routledge Companion to 19th Century Philosophy*, London: Routledge, pp. 197-237.

Rahner, Karl (1984): *Grundkurs des Glaubens. Einführung in den Begriff des Christentums*, Freiburg: Herder.

Ransom, Harry H. (1980): Being Intelligent about Secret Intelligence, *American Political Science Review*, 74 (1), pp. 141-148.

Rapaczynski, Andrzej (1996): The Roles of the State and the Market in Establishing Property Rights, *The Journal of Economic Perspectives*, 10 (2), pp. 87-103.

Raschke, Joachim and Tils, Ralf (2007): *Politische Strategie. Eine Grundlegung*, Wiesbaden: VS Verlag.

Raschke, Joachim and Tils, Ralf (2008): Politische Strategie, *Forschungsjournal NSB*, 21 (1), pp. 11-24.

Raschke, Joachim and Tils, Ralf (2011): *Politik braucht Strategie – Taktik hat sie genug*, Frankfurt am Main/New York: Campus.

Rawls, John (1971): *A Theory of Justice*, Cambridge: Belknap Press of Harvard University Press.

Reese, Roger R. (2000): *The Soviet Military Experience: A History of the Soviet Army 1917-1991*, Warfare and History, London/New York: Routledge.

Richards, Neill M. and King, Jonathan H. (2014): Big Data Ethics, *Wake Forest Law Review*, pp. 394-422.

Richey, Jeffrey L. (2015): *Daoism in Japan. Chinese traditions and their influence on Japanese religious culture*, Routledge Studies in Taoism, Oxon: Routledge.

Rigby, T. H. (1978): Stalinism and the Mono-Organisational Society, in: Robert Tucker (ed.), *Stalinism: Essays in Sociological Interpretation*, New York: Norton, pp. 53-76.

Ringgren, Helmer (1972): On the Islamic Theory of the State, *Scripta Instituti Donneriani Aboensis,* 6, pp. 103-108.

Roetz, Heiner and Schleichert, Hubert (2009): *Klassische chinesische Philosophie. Eine Einführung,* Frankfurt a. M.: Klostermann.

Röttger, Ulrike (2009): Campaigns (f)or a better world?, in: Ulrike Röttger (ed.), *PR-Kampagnen. Über die Inszenierung von Öffentlichkeit,* 4th revised and expanded edition, Wiesbaden: VS Verlag, pp. 9-26.

Rousseau, Jean Jacques ([1775] 1992). *Discourse on the Origin of Inequality,* translated by Donald A. Cress, Indianapolis/Cambridge: Hackett Publishing.

Rousseau, Jean Jacques ([1762] 2012): *Of the Social Contract and Other Political Writing,* translated by Quintin Hoare, London/New York: Penguin.

Rule, James B. (1973): *Private Lives and Public Surveillance,* London: Allen Lane.

Saar, Martin (2010): Power and Critique. *Journal of Power,* 3 (1), pp. 7-20.

Sandretto, René (2009): François Perroux, a precursor of the current analyses of power, *The Journal of World Economic Review,* 5 (1), pp. 57-68.

Sanger, David A. (2012): *Confront and Conceal: Obama's Secret Wars and Surprising Use of American Power,* New York: Crown Publishers.

Safire, William (2008): *Safire's political dictionary,* revised edition, New York: Oxford University Press.

Sarcinelli, Ulrich (2010): *Politische Kommunikation in Deutschland: Medien und Politikvermittlung im demokratischen System,* Wiesbaden: VS Verlag.

Sartre, Jean-Paul ([1945] 2007): *Existentialism is a Humanism,* John Kulka (ed.), translated by Carol Macomber, New Haven: Yale University Press.

Scheidel, Walter (ed.) (2015): *State Power in Ancient China & Rome,* Oxford/New York: Oxford University Press.

Scheler, Max (1980): *Problems of a Sociology of Knowledge,* translated by Manfred S. Frings, London: Routledge.

Schell, Eric (2010): *Le bréviaire de Talleyrand,* Paris: Horay.

Schieder, Andreas (2017): *Kommerzielles Lobbying und Public Affairs-Management,* Wiesbaden: Springer VS.

Schlinkert, Dirk (1996): *Ordo Senatoris und Nobilitas. Die Konstitution des Senatsadels in der Spätantike,* Stuttgart: Franz Steiner Verlag.

Schmitt, Carl ([1932] 1991): *Der Begriff des Politischen,* Berlin: Duncker & Humblot.

Schmitt, Carl (1934): *Politische Theologie. Vier Kapitel zur Lehre von der Souveränität,* Berlin: Duncker & Humblot.

Schmitt, Carl ([1963] 1992): *Theorie des Partisanen. Zwischenbemerkung zum Begriff des Politischen,* Berlin: Duncker & Humblot.

Schölderle, Thomas (2002): *Das Prinzip der Macht*, Berlin/Cambridge: Galda + Wilch.
Scholz, Peter (2011): *Den Vätern folgen. Sozialisation und Erziehung der republikanischen Senatsaristokratie*, Berlin: Verlag Antike.
Schubert, Glendon (1960): *The Public Interest: a Critique of the Theory of a Political Concept*, Glencoe: Free Press of Glencoe.
Schumpeter, Joseph A. ([1942] 2003): *Capitalism, Socialism and Democracy*, London: Routledge.
Schwab, Klaus (2017): *The Fourth Industrial Revolution*, Köln: World Economic Forum.
Schwentker, Wolfgang (2008): *Die Samurai*, Munich: C.H. Beck.
Scott, John (2001): *Power*, Cambridge: Polity Press.
Selmayr, Martin (2015): Europäische Zentralbank, in: Werner Weidenfeld and Wolfgang Wessels (eds.), *Jahrbuch der europäischen Integration 2015*, Baden-Baden: Nomos.
Silver, Nate (2012): *The Signal and the Noise: Why Most Predictions Fail – but Some Don't*, New York: Penguin Books.
Singh, Naunihal (2014): *Seizing Power: The Strategic Logic of Military Coups*, Baltimore: Johns Hopkins University Press.
Siri, Jasmin (2012): *Parteien. Zur Soziologie einer politischen Form*, Wiesbaden: Springer VS.
Skaperdas, Stergios (2008): Anarchy, in: Donald A. Wittman and Barry R. Weingast (eds.), *The Oxford Handbook of Political Economy*, pp. 881-898.
Smith, Adam ([1776] 2012): *An Inquiry into the Nature and Causes of the Wealth of Nations*, London: W. Strathan.
Smith, Roger (2010): The Long History of Gaming in Military Training, *Simulation and Gaming*, 41 (1), pp. 6-19.
Soeffner, Hans Georg and Tänzer, Dirk (2007): Figurative Politik. Prolegomena zu einer Kultursoziologie politischen Handelns, in: Hans Georg Soeffner and Dirk Tänzer (eds.), *Figurative Politik. Zur Performanz der Macht in der modernen Gesellschaft*, Opladen: Leske und Budrich, pp. 17-33.
Sofsky, Wolfgang and Paris, Rainer (1994): *Figurationen sozialer Macht. Autorität – Stellvertretung – Koalition*, Frankfurt am Main: Suhrkamp.
Spencer, Elaine G. (1985): Police-Military Relations in Prussia, 1848-1914, *Journal of Social History*, 19 (2), pp. 305-317.
Speth, Rudolf (2010): Grassroots Campaigning, in: Olaf Hoffjann and Roland Stahl (eds.), *Handbuch Verbandskommunikation*, Wiesbaden: VS Verlag, pp. 317-332.

Speth, Rudolf (2013): Verbände und Grassroots-Campaigning, in: Rudolf Speth (ed.), *Grassroots-Campaigning*, Wiesbaden: VS Verlag, pp. 43-59.

Spuler, Bertold (1959): *Die Chalifenzeit. Entstehung und Zerfall des islamischen Weltreichs,* Leiden: Brill.

Stachura, Mateusz (2010): Politische Führung: Max Weber heute, *Politik und Zeitgeschichte*, 2-3, pp. 22-27.

Steffani, Winfried (1979): *Parlamentarische und präsidentielle Demokratie. Strukturelle Aspekte westlicher Demokratien,* Opladen: Westdeutscher Verlag.

Steiner, Jürg (2012): *The Foundations of Deliberative Democracy. Empirical Research and Normative Implications*, Cambridge: Cambridge University Press.

Steinmüller, Angela and Steinmüller, Karlheinz (2004): *Wild Cards. Wenn das Unwahrscheinliche eintritt*, expanded and updated edition of 'Ungezähmte Zukunft', Hamburg: Murmann.

Stetter, Stephen (2004): Cross-Pillar Politics: Functional Unity and Institutional Fragmentation of EU Foreign Policies, *Journal of European Public Policy*, 11 (4), pp. 720-739.

Stocker, Michael (1992): *Plural and Conflicting Values,* Oxford: Clarendon Press.

Strachen, Hew (2005): The Lost Meaning of Strategy, *Survival*, 47 (3), pp. 33-54.

Street, John (2011): *Mass Media, Politics and Democracy*, 2nd edition, Basingstoke: Palgrave Macmillan.

Stulberg, Adam N. (2015): Out of Gas? Russia, Ukraine, Europe, and the Changing Geopolitics of Gas, *Problems of Post-Communism,* 62 (2), pp. 112-130.

Sumner, Leonard W. (1996): *Welfare, Happiness and Ethics,* Oxford: Oxford University Press.

Tacitus, Cornelius (1996): *The Annals of Imperial Rome,* translated by Michael Grant (ed.), London: Penguin.

Tajfel, Henri (1981): *Human Groups and Social Categories,* Cambridge: Cambridge University Press.

Taureck, Bernhard (1983): *Die Zukunft der Macht. Ein philosophisch-politischer Essay,* Würzburg: Königshausen & Neumann.

Taylor, Charles (1989): *Sources of the Self: The Making of the Modern Identity,* Cambridge: Cambridge University Press.

Taylor, Mark C. (2007): *After God,* Chicago: University of Chicago Press.

Turnbull, Stephen (2007): *The Great Wall of China. 221 BC–AD 1644*, London: Osprey Publishing.

Uhde, Bernhard (2009): Religionen als Denkmöglichkeiten. Skizzen zur Logik der Weltreligionen, *Zeitschrift für Didiaktik der Philosophie und Ethik,* 1, pp. 7-16.

Urlacher, Brian R. (2016): *International Relations as Negotiations,* New York: Routledge.
Vale, Malcom (2001): *The Princely Court,* Oxford/New York: Oxford University Press.
van Ackeren, Marcel (2006): *Heraklit: Vielfalt und Einheit seiner Philosophie,* Bern: Peter Lang.
Vavova, Katia (2014): Moral Disagreement and Moral Skepticism, *Philosophical Perspectives,* 28 (1), pp. 302-333.
Veyne, Paul (1992): *Bread and Circuses: Historical Sociology and Political Pluralism.* Oswyn Murray (ed.), translated by Brian Pearce. London: Penguin.
Vickers, John (2014): The Problem of Induction, in: Edward N. Zalta (ed.), *The Stanford Encyclopedia of Philosophy,* [online] https://plato.stanford.edu/archives/spr2019/entries/induction-problem/, retrieved on 21.12.2017.
Villa, Paula-Irene (2011): Symbolische Gewalt und ihr Scheitern. Eine Annäherung zwischen Butler und Bourdieu, *Österreichische Zeitschrift für Soziologie,* 36 (4), pp. 51-69.
Volk, Konrad (ed.) (2015): *Erzählungen aus dem Land Sumer,* Wiesbaden: Harrassowitz Verlag.
Wagner, Claudia, Mitter, Silvia, Körner, Christian, and Strohmaier, Markus (2012): When social bots attack: Modeling susceptibility of users in online social networks, Proceedings of the WWW'12 Workshop on Making Sense of Microposts, pp. 41-18.
Walls, Jerry L. (ed.) (2008), *The Oxford Handbook of Eschatology,* Oxford/New York: Oxford University Press.
Walter, Anton J. (1960): Schriftentwicklung unter dem Einfluß von Diktatoren, *Mitteilungen des Instituts für Österreichische Geschichstforschung,* 68, pp. 337-361.
Walworth, Arthur (1946): *Black Ships Off Japan: The Story of Commodore Perry's Expedition,* New York: Knopf.
Warren, T. Camber (2014): Not by the Sword Alone: Soft Power, Mass Media, and the Production of State Sovereignty, *International Organization,* 68 (1), pp. 111-141.
Weber, Max ([1921] 1978). *Economy and Society: An Outline of Interpretive Sociology,* translated by Guenther Roth and Claus Wittich. Berkeley: University of California Press.
Wittgenstein, Ludwig ([1953] 2001): *Philosophical Investigations,* translated by G.E.M. Anscombe, Hoboken: Blackwell.
Wolf, Susan (1982): Moral Saints, *The Journal of Philosophy,* 79 (8), pp. 419-439.

Wong, David (2013): Chinese Ethics, in: Edward N. Zalta (ed.), *Stanford Encyclopedia of Philosophy,* [online] https://plato.stanford.edu/archives/fall 2018/entries/ethics-chinese/, retrieved on 21.12.2017.

Woolley, James C. (2016): Automating Power: Social Bots Interfere in Global Politics. *First Monday,* 21 (4), [online] http://firstmonday.org/ojs/ index.php/fm/article/view/6161/5300, retrieved on 21.12.2017.

Worley, D. Robert (2015): *Orchestrating the Instruments of Power: A Critical Examination of the U.S. National Security System,* Lincoln: University of Nebraska Press.

Young, Iris M. (1990): *Justice and the Politics of Difference,* Princeton: Princeton University Press.

Yu, Jiyuan (2005): Confucius' Relational Self and Aristotle's Political Animal, *History of Philosophy Quarterly,* 22 (4), pp. 281-300.

Zaman, Muhammad Q. (2006): The Ulama of Contemporary Islam and their Conceptions of the Common Good, in: Armando Salvatore and Dale F. Eickelman (eds.), *Public Islam and the Common Good,* Boston/Leiden: Brill, pp. 129–155.

Zhang, Ellen (2010): Community, the Common Good, and Public Healthcare, Confucianism and its Relevance to Contemporary China, *Public Health Ethics,* 3 (3), pp 259-266.

Zunshine, Lisa (2008): *Strange Concepts and the Stories They Make Possible,* Baltimore: The John Hopkins University Press.

4.2 ADDITIONAL SOURCES

Bakir, Daniel (2016): Big Brother Awards 2016: Change.org - eine Weltverbesserer-Plattform als gierige Datenkrake, in: Stern from 22th 2016, [online] http://www.stern.de/wirtschaft/news/big-brother-awards--change-org-als-datenkrake-ausgezeichnet-6807950.html, most recently retrieved on 21.12.2017.

Bild (2015): Schalke feiert Torheld Sané, in: Bild from 27th September 2015, [online] http://www.bild.de/sport/fussball/leroy-sane/schalke-feiert-torheld-sane-42697996.bild.html, retrieved on 26.01.2018.

Casano, Olivia (2016): Why You Should Think Twice Before Signing a Change.org Petition, [online] http://www.konbini.com/en/lifestyle/change-org-data-mining/, retrieved on 06.02.2018.

European External Action Service (2015): Joint Comprehensive Plan of Action, [online] http://www.eeas.europa.eu/statements-eeas/docs/iran_agreement/iran_joint-comprehensive-plan-of-action_en.pdf, retrieved on 21.12.2017.

Figg, Erinn (2014): The legacy of Blue CRUSH, in: High Ground News from 19th March 2014, [online] http://www.highgroundnews.com/features/BlueCrush 031214.aspx, retrieved on 21.12.2017.

Franck, Georg (undated): The Economy Of Attention, [online] http://www.t0.or.at/franck/gfeconom.htm, retrieved on 21.12.2017.

Freedom House (2016): Turkey, [online] https://freedomhouse.org/report/freedom-press/2016/turkey, retrieved on 21.12.2017.

Gimlet Media (2015): *Favor Attendar* [Podcast], [online] https://gimletmedia.com/episode/25-favor-atender/, retrieved on 20.1.2017.

Goldberg, Dan (2017): De Blasio sours on tackling sugar, [online] https://www.politico.com/states/new-york/city-hall/story/2017/05/03/de-blasio-sours-on-tackling-sugar-111726, retrieved on 22.05.2018.

Hill, Kashmir (2012): How Target Figured Out A Teen Girl Was Pregnant Before Her Father Did, in: Forbes Magazin from 16th February 2012, [online] https://www.forbes.com/sites/kashmirhill/2012/02/16/how-target-figured-out-a-teen-girl-was-pregnant-before-her-father-did/#418017cd6668, retrieved on 21.12.2017.

Internet World Stats in June 2016, the number of internet users worldwide amounted to 3,675,824,813 people, [online] http://www.internetworldstats.com/stats.htm, retrieved 21.12.2017.

Kaplan, Fred (2004): The Tragedy of Colin Powell: How the Bush Presidency destroyed him, in: Slate from 19th February 2004, [online] https://slate.com/news-and-politics/2004/02/the-tragedy-of-colin-powell.html retrieved on 21.12.2017.

Karabell, Shellie (2016): Why Airbus Is A Model For European Unity, in: Forbes from 27th February 2016, [online] https://www.forbes.com/sites/shelliekarabell/2016/02/27/why-airbus-is-a-model-for-european-unity/#347b0a2b5838, retrieved on 21.12.2017.

Mao Tse-Tung (1983): *Selected Works of Mao Tse-tung: Vol. II*, [online] https://www.marxists.org/reference/archive/mao/selected-works/volume-2/, retrieved from the Marxist Internet Archive on 16th April 2018.

Maslin Nir, Sarah (2017), New York State Bans Vaping Anywhere Cigarettes Are Prohibited, in: New York Times from 23th October 2017, [online] https://www.nytimes.com/2017/10/23/nyregion/new-york-bans-vaping-ecigs-bars-restaurants.html, retrieved on 30.1.2018.

McTague, Tom, Spence, Alex, and Dovere, Edward-Isaac (2016): How Cameron Blew It, in: Politico from 25th June 2016, [online] http://www.politico.eu/article/how-david-cameron-lost-brexit-eu-referendum-prime-minister-campaign-remain-boris-craig-oliver-jim-messina-obama/, retrieved on 21.12.2017.

Meyer, Erin (2014): *The Culture Map: Breaking Through the Invisible Boundaries of Global Business,* New York: PublicAffairs.

Meyer, Erin (2016): Mapping out Cultural Differences on Teams, [online] http://erinmeyer.com/2016/01/mapping-out-cultural-differences-on-teams/, retrieved on 21.12.2017.

Miller, Zeke (2013): Political Dynasties Return, in: Time from 5th March 2013, [online] http://content.time.com/time/subscriber/article/0,33009,2148168-3,00.html, retrieved on 21.12.2017.

Netzwerk Datenschutzexpertise (2015): Datenschutzrechtliche Bewertung des Internet-Beteiligungsportals Change.org von Dr. Thilo Weichert, [online] http://www.netzwerk-datenschutzexpertise.de/dokument/datenschutzrechtliche-bewertung-des-internet-beteiligungsportals-changeorg, retrieved on 21.12.2017.

Rubin, Jennifer (2016): Hillary Clinton, blind to her own greed, makes another blunder, in: Washington Post from 4th February 2016, [online] https://www.washingtonpost.com/blogs/right-turn/wp/2016/02/04/hillary-clinton-blind-to-her-own-greed-makes-another-blunder/?utm_term=.2605df8f25ad, retrieved on 22.01.2018.

Sachverständigenrat zur Begutachtung der gesamtwirtschaftlichen Entwicklung (2017): Für eine zukunftsorientierte Wirtschaftspolitik,[online] https://www.sachverstaendigenrat-wirtschaft.de/fileadmin/dateiablage/gutachten/jg201718/JG2017-18_gesamt_Website.pdf, retrieved on 21.12.2017.

Scurr, Ruth (2006): He quipped while Napoleon quaked, in: Telegraph from 17th December 2006, [online] https://www.telegraph.co.uk/culture/books/3657043/He-quipped-while-Napoleon-quaked.html, retrieved on 21.12.2017.

Sloterdijk, Peter (2017): Konsultanten sind die Künstler der Enthemmung, in: Neue Züricher Zeitung from 18th February 2017, [online] https://www.nzz.ch/feuilleton/sloterdijk-konsultanten-sind-die-kuenstler-der-enthemmung-ld.146325, retrieved on 21.12.2017.

Standard Eurobarometer, [online] http://ec.europa.eu/commfrontoffice/publicopinion/index.cfm/Survey/getSurveyDetail/instruments/STANDARD/surveyKy/2142, retrieved on 21.12.2017.

Swipe Toolkit, Data Calculator, [online] http://archive.turbulence.org/Works/swipe/calculator.html, most recently retrieved on 21.12.2017.

The Economist (2014): Islamic finance: Big interest, no interest, in: Economist from 13th Sepmtember 2014, [online] http://www.economist.com/news/finance-and-economics/21617014-market-islamic-financial-products-growing-fast-big-interest-no-interest, retrieved on 21.12.2017.

Tønnesson, Øyvind (1999): Mahatma Gandhi, the Missing Laureate, [online] https://www.nobelprize.org/nobel_prizes/themes/peace/gandhi/index.html, retrieved on 21.12.2017.

Transparency International, [online] www.transparency.org.

Vincent, James (2016): The UK now wields unprecedented surveillance powers – here's what it means, in: The Verge from 29th November 2016, [online] https://www.theverge.com/2016/11/23/13718768/uk-surveillance-laws-explained-investigatory-powers-bill, retrieved on 21.12.2017.

Washington Times, 03.07.2017.

WIN-Gallup International (2011): Impact of Japan Earthquake on Views about Nuclear Energy, [online] http://www.gallup.com.pk/JapanSurvey2011/PressReleaseJapan.pdf, retrieved on 21.12.2017.